ECONOMICS, SEXUALITY, AND MALE SEX WORK

Male sex work generates sales in excess of one billion dollars annually in the United States. Recent sex scandals involving prominent leaders and government shutdowns of escort websites have focused attention on this business, but despite the attention that comes when these scandals break, we know very little about how the market works. *Economics, Sexuality, and Male Sex Work* is the first economic analysis of male sex work. Competition, the role of information, pricing strategies, and other economic features of male sex work are analyzed using the most comprehensive data available. Sex work is also social behavior, however, and this book shows how the social aspects of gay sexuality influence the economic properties of the market. Concepts like desire, masculinity, and sexual stereotypes affect how sex workers compete for clients, who practices safer sex, and how sex workers present themselves to clients to differentiate themselves from the competition.

Trevon D. Logan is Hazel C. Youngberg Trustees Distinguished Professor of Economics at the Ohio State University and Research Associate at the National Bureau of Economic Research. He has won the American Sociological Association's Section on Sociology of Sexuality's Best Article Award. He is a member of the Committee on the Status of Minority Groups in the Economics Profession at the American Economic Association and a member of the Executive Board of the North American Association of Sports Economists. He is a former president of the National Economic Association, was a Robert Wood Johnson Foundation Scholar in Health Policy Research at University of Michigan, and former chair of the Economic History Association Committee on Data and Archives.

Economics, Sexuality, and Male Sex Work

TREVON D. LOGAN
The Ohio State University

CAMBRIDGE
UNIVERSITY PRESS

CAMBRIDGE
UNIVERSITY PRESS

Shaftesbury Road, Cambridge CB2 8EA, United Kingdom

One Liberty Plaza, 20th Floor, New York, NY 10006, USA

477 Williamstown Road, Port Melbourne, VIC 3207, Australia

314–321, 3rd Floor, Plot 3, Splendor Forum, Jasola District Centre, New Delhi – 110025, India

103 Penang Road, #05–06/07, Visioncrest Commercial, Singapore 238467

Cambridge University Press is part of Cambridge University Press & Assessment, a department of the University of Cambridge.

We share the University's mission to contribute to society through the pursuit of education, learning and research at the highest international levels of excellence.

www.cambridge.org
Information on this title: www.cambridge.org/9781107569577
10.1017/9781316423899

First published 2017

A catalogue record for this publication is available from the British Library

Library of Congress Cataloging-in-Publication data
Logan, Trevon D. (Trevon D'Marcus), author.
Economics, sexuality, and male sex work / Trevon D. Logan,
The Ohio State University.
New York, NY : Cambridge University Press, 2017. | Includes
bibliographical references and index.
LCCN 2016032381 | ISBN 9781107128736
LCSH: Male prostitutes – United States. | Male prostitution –
United States – Economic aspects.
LCC HQ119.4.U6 L64 2016 | DDC 306.74/3–dc23
LC record available at https://lccn.loc.gov/2016032381

ISBN   978-1-107-12873-6   Hardback
ISBN   978-1-107-56957-7   Paperback

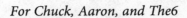

For Chuck, Aaron, and The6

Contents

Figures

ix

Tables

Note to Readers

Throughout this book, the terms "sex work," "prostitution," and "escorting" are used largely interchangeably. In general, "sex work" is used most often, as it references an occupation that involves being hired to provide sexual services. Since this book deals with men who explicitly advertise as being paid for their time, escorting is also used because the sex may or may not be included in the transaction. Prostitution is usually reserved for references to the larger market, which includes those coerced or forced into sex work, and where "worker" would be inappropriate to describe all participants.

Some chapters in this book are revised versions of coauthored work. For editorial consistency, these chapters have been revised to read in the first person and to integrate with the single-authored chapters of the book. These chapters are identified as such in their first endnote, and when cited should include the reference to the coauthored work.

Acknowledgments

Authors accumulate many debts when they write books. I have certainly accumulated more than most. This project owes a special debt to Manisha Shah, who first encouraged me to work on the topic of male sex work when I first approached her about data from the online market. My original plan was that Manisha would work on male sex work on her own, but our collaboration led me to consider the issues in this book. Manisha has always been open and willing to share her expertise and keen criticism, and I am very grateful for her enthusiastic support at times when I was not sure if this project would come to fruition.

I have discussed nearly every idea in this book with Rodney Andrews, and he continues to be one of the most thoughtful and open-minded economists I know. I am also thankful that Rodney continues to push me to reach for the highest levels of empirical scholarship, which included collecting new data and pushing the analysis further than I had thought possible to find information about the demand side of the market. Lisa Cook told me that this project was well worth the professional risks and, as in most things, she was spot-on. Tod Hamilton gave me extremely useful advice in how to integrate the economic and sociological aspects, and in the process forced me to rethink the interpretation of many of the results here.

This project spanned my time at three universities. At Ohio State, I have greatly benefitted from conversations with Randy Olsen, Audrey Light, Rick Steckel, Jim Peck, Bruce Weinberg, Paul Healy, Dan Levin, Joe Kaboski, Howard Marvel, Elizabeth Cooksey, Korie Edwards, Townsand Price-Spratlen, Masanori Hashimoto, John Kagel, Lung-Fei Lee, Lucia Dunn, John Casterline, Steve Cosslett, Reanne Frank, Ruth Peterson, and Patricia Reagan. I thank Deborah Moddelmog and members of the Diversity and Identity Studies Collective for sharing their ideas on the project when it was in its infancy. I have also benefitted from the support of both the Initiative in Population Research (seed grant funding through NIH grant R24-HD058484) and the Criminal Justice Research Center.

I am grateful to Christina Paxson for inviting me to visit the Center for Health and Wellbeing at Princeton just at the time when I was considering expanding the project beyond asymmetric information. While there, I benefitted greatly from conversations with Anne Case, Angus Deaton, and Gustavo Bobonis. The majority of this project took shape while I was a Robert Wood Johnson Foundation Scholar in Health Policy Research at the University of Michigan. I thank Alan Cohen, Paula Lantz, Edward Norton, and Catherine Player for their support. The constant interaction with scholars across the social sciences changed my perspective not only about male sex work, but in all of my projects. I thank Hans Noel, Fabio Rojas, Monique Lyle, Graeme Boushey, Kevin Stange, Seth Freedman, and Megan Andrew for their willingness to share their ideas and challenge my own. I am especially grateful to Brendan Nyhan, Alice Goffman, and Edward Walker for our book club, which kept this project on the front burner. In addition, Martha Bailey, Paul Rhode, Warren Whatley, and Raj Arunachalam provided additional feedback on various ideas developed in Ann Arbor. The results of my time in Michigan would have been impossible without Theresa Ramirez, who did everything that she could to ensure that I could concentrate on my research.

A large number of scholars have provided feedback on various aspects of this work, and it is a much better work for it. Franklin Wilson, Scott Cunningham, Mustafa Emirbayer, Rene Almeling, Bryan Sykes, Evelyn Patterson, Steven Goodreau, Jason Orne, Jennifer Johnson-Hanks, Ken Wachter, Ron Lee, Claudia Goldin, John Wilmoth, Darrick Hamilton, Rashawn Ray, William Darity, Larry Katz, Nzinga Broussard, Olugbenga Ajilore, Victor Minichiello, John Scott, Christopher Carpenter, John Murray, and Mike Hout each gave generously of their time to read and react to ideas presented here. Seminar audiences at Princeton, Wisconsin, Toledo, Berkeley, and Ohio State provided a great environment to develop and extend the project. Bernardo Quieroz and his colleagues at Cedeplar and Universidade Federal de Minas Gerais invited me to visit at a time that allowed me to bring all of the parts together into a cohesive core.

This project allowed me to work with excellent research assistants. Colin Odden and Michael Bommarito helped with data collection. Chih-Sheng Hsieh, Leigh Fine, and Brian Soller each became collaborators on this work, and I learned a great deal from them. Jaromir Kovarik introduced me to the literature on networks and showed me its possibilities and limitations in empirical economics. Glenn Rondo, Jr., Dez Taylor,

Dwayne Zimmerman, Gamal Brown, Rahmundo Imani, Aaron Thomas, Hubert Hill, Anthony Lewis, Gary Dixon, James Mathis, Arnold Smotherman, Ryan Fields, and Richard Clyburn read various chapters and provided a fresh perspective on the broader implications of studying commercial sex.

My work here took me away from other projects. I thank my coauthors for their forbearance when this project delayed our work: Yang Chen, Michael Sinkey, Kyle Kain, Stephen Bergman, Rodney Andrews, Lisa Cook, Shari Eli, Paul Rhode, Jonathan Pritchett, John Parman, Joe Kaboski, Brendan Nyhan, and Stacy Sneeringer. Janet Myers and Michelle Chapman helped to ensure that all administrative matters were handled. I am deeply indebted to Ana Ramirez, whose very dedicated work has allowed me to fulfill my administrative duties while maintaining an active research agenda.

Karen Maloney was excited about this project from the start and her enthusiasm was contagious. I thank her for seeing the potential in this project and guiding me through this process.

Lastly, I thank my family for their support. My parents, brothers, and sisters-in-law – Thomas, Diana, Thomas, Jr., Travis, Pamela, and Camille, respectively – kept me focused on the goal. It is in conversations with them that I realized the ways that commercial sex was not only about commercial sex but about much more fundamental aspects of human interaction. My extended family has been a constant source of humor, fellowship, and encouragement. Throughout, of course, I have had Morgan. I thank him for his patience with my travel schedule and other commitments that kept me away from home, and for caring absolutely nothing about this project. Watching him live the canine lifestyle while I tried to figure out the complexities of male sex work has convinced me that he has the better part of the bargain.

Introduction

Economics, Sexuality, and Male Sex Work

In these days of "new media" it can be difficult to spot an interloper. He had appeared at press conferences regularly for several months on daily press credentials and was not a familiar face in the Washington press corps. But that did not necessarily raise suspicions. Washington's media has its share of transient members. Weak questions to an embattled president, however, have a way of raising eyebrows. The question he asked on January 26, 2005, finally caused members of the press to turn a critical eye on one of their own. Who was this guy? Was he planted by the Administration? As the media began to dig, they found their surface pay dirt: Jeff Gannon, the reporter, was a pseudonym for James Dale Guckert, and the media firm employing him was entirely virtual. Talon News had no actual physical presence and Guckert, the only employee, had no prior professional journalistic experience. That such an inexperienced member of the press was granted access provided fodder for a few days. Further investigation eventually revealed a much more salacious fact: Guckert, in addition to sitting in the White House Press Briefing Room, with its carefully assembled seating chart, was a male sex worker who served an exclusively male clientele. He openly advertised his services online, complete with pictures and descriptions of the services he offered to interested clients. He could be reached by email or phone, both of which he provided on the Internet. Clients praised his work outside of the Press Room. Worth every penny, they said.

Guckert was not the first male sex worker reported by the press to gain access to the halls and people of power. Rep. Barney Frank (D-MA) was reprimanded by the House of Representatives in 1990 when it was revealed that his lover, a reported sex worker, was operating as an escort service out of Frank's Massachusetts home. Lobbyist Craig Spence committed suicide in 1989 after it was revealed that he used political connections to gain unauthorized access to the White House. He was accused of taking male sex workers on unauthorized tours.

In each of these cases the media response was typical. The newsreels spun with titillating pictures of men who sell sexual services to other men. The clandestine encounters. Deception. Money. Power. Sex. Homosexuality. The mix proves intoxicating, equal parts excitement, titillation, ridicule, and amazement. Men selling sex to other men? Who could think of such a thing?

Male sex work is hidden in plain view. In every instance the evidence of male prostitution has been terribly easy to find. Law enforcement, in fact, has an odd relationship with male sex work. Since most male sex work in the United States now takes place through the Internet, it has received little intrusion from legal authorities as it does not bring the same public nuisances as street prostitution. The lack of law enforcement has allowed male sex work to flourish online. In fact, one prominent website for male escorts host an annual awards show, the Hookies. Men compete regionally in hopes of making the national event, which is held in New York City each spring and covered by mainstream media outlets such as the *Village Voice*. There, male sex workers compete in categories including "Best New Escort" or "Best Fetish Escort" and where the top title is "Escort of the Year." It is so popular that the *Manhattan Digest* devoted a column to the 2015 awards, reviewing the nominees and giving editorial picks on who should win in selected categories.[1]

The website that sponsored the awards, Rentboy.com, was reported to have netted $10 million in sales revenue from 2010–15. Rentboy, like most male escort websites, is not an intermediary. Rentboy.com earned revenue from escorts, who paid a fee to host their ads on the website. Rentboy.com did not receive a portion of transaction fees from escorts, as a pimp or madam would. The website was decidedly hands off—they do not arrange appointments and made no guarantees for services. In fact, Rentboy did nothing more (or less) than provide a website where clients can browse through advertisements and directly contact the escorts they would like to meet. Escorts paid them for the service and along with advertisement revenue from gay-oriented media, the website netted roughly $2 million per year.

Rentboy was generous in sharing the spoils from male sex work. In 2015 they announced the Cash4Class Scholarship that would help male sex workers enroll in and complete post-secondary education. Applicants had to provide information on their involvement in sex work and submit evidence of the necessary academic credentials. In addition, the application required a brief essay, which would describe how the scholarship would help the applicant achieve their career goals outside of sex work. The scholarship competition was to be judged by a star of gay pornography, who himself was not a sex worker. All of this announced publicly on YouTube.[2]

Despite these public displays – the fact that prices for services were freely visible, specific sexual services were searchable by potential clients, and direct contact information for escorts was available, this receives little public notice. Until it does. Federal authorities finally moved to close Rentboy.com in August of 2015 – more than 15 years after the website first debuted. Indeed, Rentboy had become the subject of a sting carried out by the Department of Homeland Security because it was believed to be promoting prostitution across state and national borders. If this was the case, it had been involved in that business for well over a decade. In fact, Rentboy made no attempt to hide itself or what its business practice was. They were frequently reported on in the mainstream media, maintained a corporate office in Union Square in New York City, filmed their own channel on YouTube where they featured interviews with male sex workers who spoke about their careers, and in the process became the highest-profile online prostitution service in the last decade.

When word of the federal charges first hit, the news media, again, paid special attention to male sex work. The stories were filled with awe that men posted detailed profiles of themselves for others. Particular attention was paid to explicit pictures, detailed descriptions of sexual behaviors, and the fact that escort attributes could be sorted by clients looking for a man of a particular height, build, or sexual proclivity. The media also noted the ingenious business model, where escorts pay to have the website host their ads (which in 2015 on Rentboy.com ranged from $59.95 to $299.95 depending on how prominently an escort wanted their advertisement displayed), such that the website was not involved in any specific transactions between escorts and clients. The legal disclaimer noted that men could not use the website to exchange sex for money, but federal prosecutors said this stipulation was openly violated by the website owners and employees. The media had to both acknowledge their ignorance of the practice and simultaneously admit its open availability and popularity among men seeking commercial sex with other men.[3] Again, male sex work showed itself to be hidden in plain view.

Even after the demise of the Rentboy.com website, it continued to receive media attention. In late 2016, the gay television network Logo set to debut "Prince Charming," a television show where gay men competed to win the affections of Robert Sepulveda, Jr., an interior designer. Even before the show debuted, however, the media found that Sepulveda, the star of the series, had been an escort, advertising several years earlier on Rentboy.com under the name Vincent Romen. As with Guckert, the media reported on Sepulveda's clients' reviews of his services and posted pictures from his online advertisement. The press also ruminated on why a major television outlet would cast a man with an easy-to-find, online history of prostitution and bill him as one of the most eligible gay bachelors in America.[4]

For the media, such immediate attention and eventual disinterest is par for the course. Once the story stops being news the media must move on to more promising stories. But men are still selling sex to other men. Despite Rentboy's end in operation in August 2015, Rentboy.com is not the only website involved in male sex work, and clients could move to any number of competitors to choose escorts. The escorts who posted advertisements on Rentboy simply migrated elsewhere, if they had not already maintained advertisements on competitor websites. Missing in all of the media accounts of the websites and individual escorts is a basic understanding of male sex work. We know that it is prostitution, but the details of the industry are left to the public's imagination. On the one hand, leaving the public to fill in the blanks adds to the salacious appeal of male prostitution. On the other hand, serious journalists would have precious few sources to turn to give them an accurate account of the industry.

While the media's high-gloss treatment of the inner workings of male sex work may be understandable, the same treatment by social scientists is not. Unlike the media, who place male sex work on the front page for its novelty, scholars have cast male sex work to the lowest realm of academic discourse – obscurity. Less than 10 percent of the scholarship on sex work is concerned with male sex work.[5] In general, male sex work is difficult to classify since' it is presumed that men in the market as sex workers operate in a different manner than female sex workers. One common presumption is that female sex workers are more likely to be exploited in sex work than male sex workers. While male sex workers in the United States are much more likely to be independent owner-operators, this argument neglects the fact that as self-owned firms, male sex workers therefore make indepen-dent, presumably economically informed choices that would be quite amenable to economic analysis.

The obscurity of male sex work as an area of academic interest stems from many sources. First, male sex work does not fit easily into the gendered lines guiding the vast majority of sex work scholarship. Statements claiming prostitution is the commodification of women's bodies or inherently exploitative ring hollow when both buyers and sellers are men. Male sex work lacks the dynamic of explicit control of women by men, either as brokers or as clients. Second, male sex work invites unpleasant discussions of homosexual sex as opposed to sexuality. Even among the enlightened, serious academic discourse on the particulars of homosexual sex is disquieting and therefore discouraged. Also, the work on male sex work is more concerned with the possibility of disease epidemics more common among men who have sex with men as opposed to a full understanding of the market. Third, most scholarship uses male sex work as a means to an end, furthering developments in queer, masculinity, feminist, and other humanistic theories. The idea of male sex work has received far more attention than empirical analysis as a market. We know much less about what male sex work *is* as opposed to what it *represents*. While theoretical work is an indispensable part of our knowledge of the phenomenon, it has not yielded the rich empirical knowledge about male sex work that would move the scholarship to new areas of inquiry.

Male sex work *is* a market. There are buyers, sellers, supply, demand, prices, and transactions. The main contribution of this book is to treat male sex work as the market it is and use that market feature to its fullest advantage. Perhaps the most surprising fact about this market is how well developed it is in the United States. Unlike female sex workers, male sex workers advertise publicly on the Internet. They display pictures of themselves, describe the services they provide, post their contact information, and list the price of their services. For one interested in the market aspects of male sex work, such information is invaluable. Until now, this information has not been exploited by social scientists looking for comprehensive information about this market.

The market for male escort services is large, with estimated annual revenues in excess of $1 billion in the United States, which implies millions of transactions per year.[6] Unlike their female counterparts, the majority of male sex workers work independently and online. There are few intermediaries in the male sex trade in the United States.[7] Male sex workers are independent owner-operators whose fees are not shared with others and who compete with one another for clients. Even the most expensive advertisement fee is recouped with one or two hourly appointments. This is in stark contrast to female sex work, where fees for services are usually set by and shared with pimps or madams. These intermediaries can disrupt the market by rationing services, raising prices, and increasing transaction costs. Despite the interesting market features of male sex work, which make it easier to apply the basic principles of supply and demand, this market is seldom studied by economists.[8]

Our empirical knowledge of the market is remarkably thin, given its size and complexity. There are studies exploring the experiences of small groups of sex workers, including some recent studies of male sex workers who advertise online. These studies shed light on individual motivations to enter the market and the reasons for participating in the industry, but they have not been able to describe the market in general. Many of the most basic questions one would ask about male sex work are inherently about the *market* for male sex work. How many male sex workers are there (*how large is this market*)? Where are they located (*what is the scope of this market*)? What are their ages and races (*what are the characteristics of the supply of male sex workers*)? Who are the clients (*where does the demand come from*)? How much money do male sex workers earn, and do sex workers earn more for some services than others (*what is the profit function*)? Answers to our most basic questions require comprehensive evidence about the market for male sex work.

This book provides an answer to those questions about the basics of the market for male sex work. For the first time, the breadth of the online market is used to answer many of the most pressing questions about what the male sex work market is and how it operates. This book concentrates on the online market, and there are undeniable tradeoffs in focusing on the online market. For example, this book says little about either men with temporary attachments to male sex work or men who participate in survival sex. The focus here is on men involved in sex work as a professional occupation. The disadvantage is that we cannot discuss the most vulnerable men involved in male sex work. The advantages are that we concentrate on those engaged with sex work as a profession and discuss the majority of male sex work in the United States in a rigorous way.

To set the landscape, the first chapter gives a brief history of male sex work, focusing on the class distinctions that have been regularly observed between clients and sex workers. Male sex work has been regulated in a different way than female sex work. This gives rise to several unique features for the practice that remain to this day. For example, male sex workers do not use pimps, madams, or other intermediaries as female sex workers often do. Also, male sex workers are better integrated into gay male society. Some have argued that they are a sexual archetype among gay men. Gay novels, film, and other aspects of gay culture prominently feature male sex workers.

Since men who desire sex with men (the client base) are relatively few in number, male sex workers need to advertise their services more openly than female prostitutes. There are not enough clients to form street markets in most cities. Male sex workers therefore use gay-oriented media to reach their clients. While the information once presented in the gay newspaper classifieds (which included separate sections for callboys) is much more limited than what is provided today, this historical pattern is the paradigm that still guides the market. The market has been national since at least the early 1970s – nationally distributed classified advertisements have been used to solicit clients for more than forty years.

After reviewing the history, I move to a brief description of the data sources used to analyze the market and answer the basic questions we would ask about any market. The data described in the first chapter form the backbone of the analysis that follows through the rest of the book. The newspaper advertisements of the past have given way to the national websites of the present. I detail the various sources that one can use to analyze the market. In general, there are two types of information: online advertisements and client reviews. Both are distinct sources of information, but contain important pieces of overlap that allow us to confirm trends observed in one data source by looking for evidence of those same trends in the other. I describe the sources available for each type of information and show why I concentrate on the specific online sources I use. The advertisement and client reviews I use in this book come from the largest and most popular sources for male sex workers – I show that they represent the market better than other available sources.

The first chapter also gives answers to the most basic economic questions. *How many male sex workers are advertising online?* A few thousand. *What is their age, ethnic, and racial composition?* They are quite diverse. Male sex workers are of every race and ethnic origin and range in advertised age from 18 years old to men in their 60s. The average man advertising is nearly 30 years old – this is not a market of very young men. *What is the average price of sex worker services?* An hour of an escort's time will cost you more than $200.00, on average. (Readers less interested in the history of sex work and the description of the data can skip this chapter.)

The rest of Part I consists of chapters that economically analyze the market for male sex work in the United States. This market, however, is illegal. That poses a very interesting question – given that the market is illegal (irrespective of the taboos regarding male homosexuality), how can it function so well? It is not as if clients can be assured that they will always get what they want. There are no means to ensure services advertised will actually be offered. Even more, this market does not use pimps, madams, or other intermediaries or brokers that would negotiate transactions and could act to regulate and enforce quality standards. Also, unlike female sex work, in male sex work the client is at relatively greater risk of being violated by an escort. A search online will quickly yield news stories documenting how some clients have been assaulted or even murdered when they hired the wrong escort.

As discussed in Chapter 2, the market for male sex work is rife with asymmetric information (the sex worker knows whether he is a thief, but the client does not), and this would appear to be an insurmountable problem (the client has no recourse if he is victimized, and should be disinclined to hire an escort). Yet, the market exists and functions – how does this happen? The problem for male sex work is that there is no formal enforcement of contracts. I show how clients of male sex workers informally police the market in a way that makes signaling, where the escort provides a specific type of information to establish that he is a "good guy," credible. Using the institutional knowledge embedded in client reviews of male escort services, I identify the specific signal male sex workers use to communicate quality to their clients: face pictures. I find that there is a substantial return to the signal in this market. Sex workers who post pictures of their faces earn substantially more than other sex workers, and they earn more because they have provided a credible signal to their clients that they are the "good guys" in the profession. The face picture is like posting a bond, a credit report, or a detailed vehicle history – it makes the client feel better about the transaction about to take place. This market functions remarkably well as a result, despite its illegal and stigmatized status.

Knowledge of some features of the market masks considerable variations at the local level in both the number of sex workers and the price of male escort services. It also obscures a fundamental aspect of any free market – competition. Chapter 3 considers more sophisticated questions about male sex workers. In particular, it looks at location patterns and how travel and location are related to market forces. Male sex workers have always been traveling salesmen, to a degree. They serve a variety of markets and travel at the expense of their clients, but they also travel at their own expense, setting up shop in specific locations for short periods of time to generate new business.

This feature of the market raises a number of questions. Where are male sex workers located? Where do they travel? Are their location and travel patterns related to gay male location patterns or the competition a sex worker faces in his home location? Does the price of male sex work service vary by location, as the prices of other services do? How far do sex workers travel when they travel, and what cities are popular destinations? I find that many of the travel patterns are consistent with basic theories of market competition – male sex worker location and travel are driven by competition between sex workers for clients.

Male sex workers respond to the market incentives to travel. Although the home location of male sex workers is not strongly related to gay location, male sex workers travel to locations with high demand for male sex work services. This affects overall market prices because sex workers who travel charge higher prices than those that do not. These links between cities are not just related to travel, but to prices as well. The links between cities form a network of cities that are key for male sex work. Overall, this shows that the market is quite well developed and mature. Sex workers respond to market forces of demand, and prices in the market are affected by the demand-driven, competition-based travel of male sex workers.

The second section of the book (Part II) moves beyond traditional economic analysis and considers the ways social constructions of gender and sexuality influence how this market functions. This part of the book has a different focus: to see how the application of gender and sexuality theory alters the conclusions we draw from a traditional, neoclassical economic approach to this market. I apply the theoretical work in gender, sexuality, and masculinity, and integrate them into an economic analysis. The result is a hypothesis-driven, scientific approach to male sex work that is informed by economic and social theory.

The mutual exclusivity of the previous work creates a false barrier that inhibits our ability to empirically investigate how market function is mitigated by social, gender, and sexual norms. I do not argue that all analysis of male sex work can proceed in this fashion, but empirical analysis can be enhanced by this integration. In a sex work market, theoretical assertions are transformed into hypotheses about how social processes impact the economic function of the market. While scholars of masculinity and sexuality assert that many of the central tenets of sex work (desire, power, erotic capital, sexual hierarchies, and the like) cannot be measured empirically, they also make explicitly quantitative statements about gendered relations, social constructions, and performance. For example, if some men are more desired than others, we should see that difference reflected in a commercial sex market. Desire would undeniably be related to demand in a sexual market. Are these theoretical predictions consistent with the way the market operates?

The application of social theory involves assumptions about relationships between variables, hypotheses about the size and direction of effects, and descriptions of potential mechanisms that are not orthogonal to economic analysis. If the evidence does not support the hypotheses, then the theories should be reformulated or, perhaps, rejected. If the goal of theory is to enhance our understanding of underlying social, economic, and historical processes relating to the construction and function of gender and sexuality in human societies, formal testing of the predictions of these models in male sex work serves a useful purpose. This integrated approach helps to resolve a tension in the theoretical approach to gender and sexuality. In this section of the book I adopt an explicit quantitative approach to the issues, a novel advance in a literature that usually relies on qualitative empirical evidence.

In applying this social-economic integrated approach, I make two specific theoretical advances in the study of masculinity and sexuality. First, I combine the relational, performance, and intersectional approaches to masculinity and sexuality. While each has been used on its own to describe gendered relations in sex work, they are rarely used in concert. In the market for sex work that I study, they are inherently linked – masculinity is not only in the interactions that men have with each other in this market, it is also performed due to the fact that the interactions are based upon sex work, the construction of erotic personas, and cultural cues about sex and masculinity among gay men. The audience (clients) conditions the ways that gender and sexuality are performed and presented by sex workers, which itself can influence who interacts with whom and why. Furthermore, each type of relation and performance is distinct, yielding specific predictions about who performs what, and when. By using these theories in concert, we can gain a more comprehensive understanding not only about sex work, but also and more generally, how these theoretical concepts can and do interact.

The thrust of this integrated approach is that men in this market rely on relations through class, race, and *within-gender* gendered relations to help them achieve their desired masculinity. Masculinity in this market is not about men and women but about men and other men. When sexuality is added to the mix there is an additional wrinkle: The classed, raced, and within-gendered relations also *define* the masculinity that is desired. The market and social theory interact – desire (which may be socially constructed) is demand, and performance (the social interpretation of types) is supply.

The traditional tools of economic analysis are not useful here because socially constructed desire is beyond neoclassical economic theory. To the economist, such preferences reflect "primitive" demand that we need not account for. To the social theorist, however, it is exactly this construction that is the most interesting, as it reflects the ways in which culturally constructed social archetypes influence impersonal market processes. With social theory we can identify where this demand comes from and what it represents. Economically, I argue that this demand should manifest itself in the prices that men who embody specific types of masculinity charge in the market.

The second theoretical innovation is the extension of sexual field theory to the study of male sex work. The theory has been developed for and applies to the most prominent aspects of collective sexual life, which is noncommercial. Social theorists have developed sexual field theory to derive predictions about collective sexual life – who will mate with whom and why, and what is considered desirable and attractive, for example. Economists have consistently shown, however, that market forces operate on what has been described as nonmarket behavior. I extend that approach to male sex work. For example, the desirability of certain men over other men would apply to *both* commercial and noncommercial sexual fields. This is not to say that the demand is isomorphic between the two, but the essentials of desirability would likely hold for both commercial and noncommercial sexual desire. Similarly, the profit motives of a sex worker should respond to the collective insofar as this is the customer base of the sex worker – the nonmarket collective is, in a sense, a proxy for the demand side of the market. I argue that the sexual field is not divorced from the commercial sexual market, but rather intimately related to its function.

To be clear, there is an unmistakable trade-off between sociological nuance and economic analysis as done here. The goal is not to develop an approach that speaks to the specific social world governing each individual sex worker's experience. Rather, it is to accept that sex workers must consider the economic and social market when making choices about how to sell their services. The social market contains the very clients sex workers are trying to reach for economic gain. As with any marketing strategy, sex workers must use cues from the broader social world about what is desired and how best to package themselves to the broadest audience possible. The question here is to see if those cues, which are derived from noncommercial sexual behavior among gay men, inform the way that male sex work is commercialized, commodified, and compensated.

Chapter 4 begins this section by considering the value of the sexual services men offer in this market. I use hedonic pricing techniques standard in the economic analysis to estimate the value of male sex worker services and personal characteristics in this market. Reaching past simple notions of supply and demand, I derive hypotheses of value from theories of gender and sexuality. In particular, scholars have asserted that in hegemonically masculine environments behaviors that are traditionally "masculine" will be highly prized. Consistent with the theory of hegemonic masculinity, I find that male sex workers who advertise behavior that is characterized as more masculine charge higher prices for their services, while sex workers who advertise less-masculine behavior charge significantly less, a price differential on the order of 17 percent.

Even more, I test implications of *intersectionality*. Intersectionality theory asserts that the hegemonic masculine ideal is highly variable by its relationship to other characteristics. In other words, depending on other characteristics of a male sex worker, such as race, height, weight, muscularity, and the like, certain behaviors will be read as more hegemonically masculine than others. Results show that race and sexual behavior interactions exert a strong influence on the prices charged by male sex workers. The differential between masculine and non-masculine behaviors varies substantially by race in a manner consistent with American racial-sexual stereotypes. Not only are all men not equal in this market, but certain men are more able to meet the expectations of the masculine ideal than are others, and they are rewarded for it.

In Chapter 5 I consider the photographs posted in sex worker advertisements in a manner that departs from asymmetric information covered in Part I. Rather than investigating signaling, a social approach to the photos in advertisements allows us to analyze *how* escorts present themselves to potential clients. As in any other business, firm advertisements tell us about expectations of consumer demand in the market. This analysis provides empirical support for the concept of presentation of self, feminist scholars' ideas of the body as a site of performance, hegemonic masculinity, intersection theory, and the theory of erotic capital. Because male sex workers can be assumed to present a persona that is likely to lead to the largest financial gain – the attraction of a large number of clients – they will be very sensitive to the norms and values that dictate how they should present themselves. They will highlight the features of their product that will command higher prices in the market. I find that sex workers of different advertised types use very different pictures to advertise their services. The bodies of sex workers are presented in distinct ways along racial, sexual, and racial-sexual lines. Male sex workers display for their clients the physical selves believed to be most germane to their sexual personas. And, unlike the face pictures described earlier, these pictures are *not* related to prices but do have a statistically significant relationship to the persona advertised on the Internet.

These social distinctions have implications for sex worker and population health. Chapter 6 analyzes advertised safer sex practices among male sex workers. There are two related questions about sexual practices and male sex work, one related to the supply of safer sex and the other to the demand for it. The first question is whether there are differences among escorts in their propensity to advertise condom or condomless sex to clients. The second is whether there are market incentives to participate in condomless sex or to provide condom sex in the market. This chapter answers both questions.

I find that some sex workers are more likely to advertise condom ("safe") sex than others. Consistent with gay male sexual field theory, I find that sexually dominant (penetrative) sex workers, Asian ethnicity, established reputations, and age are strong positive predictors of the likelihood of advertising condom sex. I also find that advertised condom sex comes with a substantial price premium in the market – sex workers who advertise condom sex earn 5 percent more than those who do not, a finding that is both statistically and substantively significant. This finding runs counter to estimates for female sex workers. Further, I find that the returns to safer sex vary by race and sexual behaviors in ways that are consistent with social theories about sexual desire but inconsistent with the economic theory of compensating differentials, where sex workers would earn more for engaging in riskier behavior. Using transaction-specific data I find that it is the client who demands condomed sex with a male sex worker. What is most intriguing about these results is that although they are inconsistent with neoclassical economic theory, they are consistent with social theories of masculinity, desire, and risk. This analysis shows the pitfalls of attempting to analyze a market without consideration of its social context and the stratification therein. The results suggest that sexual dynamics and racial-sexual stereotypes among gay men may exacerbate and contribute to health inequalities among gay men.

Another innovation from this integrated approach, which features prominently in Part II, is an explicitly *nuanced* approach to race in gay sexual interactions. Recent scholarship has called attention to the ways that gay men exclude members of certain races from their social and/or sexual activity. In online forums and in other spaces, gay men have set clear criteria for the desired races of their partners. This has been identified as "sexual racism" in the literature, as the exclusion of men based upon race is presumably based upon racialized assumptions of sexuality and desirability. What scholars have failed to note, however, is that the *inclusion* of non-White men into gay sexual spaces primarily occurs on terms dictated by the racial hierarchy as well. Rather than focusing on exclusion, the analysis of male sex work allows us to investigate the mechanisms behind inclusion in sexual spaces. Black men who conform to racial-sexual stereotypes are the ones welcomed into gay sexual spaces, while black men who defy those stereotypes are not. The notion that gay interracial sexual intimacy fosters improved race relations is cast in doubt as the racial stereotypes that underlie inclusion are shown to be based on racial stereotypes of Black sexual performance and Black hypermasculinity.

In the Conclusion, I show that male sex work is a mirror of larger gay society. I do so by way of quantitative analysis of the newest forms of gay sexual organization. Online and social media are now used for noncommercial sexual relationships as well. In recent years, gay men have created a number of websites and smartphone applications to better facilitate noncommercial sexual encounters with other men. The Conclusion features a rigorous analysis of the way gay men use the same social cues for their noncommercial sexual encounters.

There are differences between the ways noncommercial sex web resources are organized, but one unique feature of the modern technology is that it is very similar to the advertisements that are used by male sex workers – the men in noncommercial web resources list their physical descriptions (age, height, weight, race, relationship status, desired connections, etc.), a picture of themselves, and a brief description. I provide a comparison of the two markets. Analysis of these profiles shows that men in the noncommercial market are quite similar to those in the commercial market in terms of age and physical features. One interesting exception is that men in the noncommercial market are less racially diverse, which may explain the premiums attached to certain men in the commercial sexual market, as they may be under represented in the noncommercial market.

Analysis of the texts that accompany the profiles reveals that the men show a strong desire to connect with men who show a picture of their face in their profile. Men explicitly mention that they will not engage with men who do not show their faces in their profile – some men who do not show their own faces make this stipulation. Also, a sizable portion of the men in the noncommercial market place a high premium on masculinity. Not only do they stress their own masculinity, but they are also explicit about their exclusive desire for sexual connections with other masculine men. The "masculinity requirement" is endemic, and some profiles even mock the preponderance of "masculinity" in other profiles. This analysis is suggestive evidence that the commercial and noncommercial markets display a high degree of similarity. Masculinity is the (sexual) ideal in the commercial and noncommercial sexual market, and the men in the noncommercial sexual market want to know who they are encountering just as much as men in the commercial market do. I also find that the racial-sexual stereotypes that featured prominently in the commercial sex market also feature prominently in the noncommercial market. If anything, the racial-sexual stereotyping is far more severe in the noncommercial market.

Far from being an obscure and unimportant part of prostitution, this book shows that male sex work is important. By itself, male sex work presents us with a market that is inherently different from its female counterpart, and those differences reveal themselves in novel ways. This market functions very differently from the one for female sex work, and for good reason. When men are both the supply and demand of sexual services, the market is inherently different. Moreover, the reasons for those differences are not only economic but also social. To analyze the market in one form without the other denies the interplay between the two.

The analysis of male sex work carries over to gay sexual organization in general. The male sex work market draws its social cues from the ways that gay men have organized their sexual spaces. Male sex work is a place where traditional masculine norms are celebrated, where racial-sexual stereotypes run amok, and where different men have substantially different power in their ability to negotiate over sex. For the sex worker, this becomes a part of the market they must master if they are to be successful in the trade, and the evidence shows that they do take these social considerations into account. The same dynamics are true, as best as we can tell, for gay men in general. The image that results is counter to the popular conceptions of the gay community as a place where gender binaries are relatively muted and where racial, sexual, and gender diversity are celebrated. Indeed, the norms are rigidly enforced and influence the way men present themselves and interact with other men in sexual spaces. In the end, we find that male sex work is not only a window, but also a mirror to contemporary social organization in gay communities.

PART I

THE HISTORY AND ECONOMICS OF MALE SEX WORK

1

Male Sex Work: Antiquity to Online

Male sex work as an occupation is as old as its female counterpart. There is little evidence from the historical record that male sex work was not present in any society where female sex work operated. Then and now, the primary buyers and sellers of male sexual services have been men. As such, male sex work has always carried the added stigma of homosexuality, causing male sex to be socially distinct from the more widely practiced female sex work. In ancient Greek culture male prostitution went by the name *porneia*. The term distinguished male sex work both from the accepted *paederastia*, relationships that existed between old and young men, *porne* (female prostitution), and *hetaera*, female mistresses.[1] This distinction was more than linguistic. There were social restrictions on what a male sex worker could do and be even if he were no longer active in the profession, which did not apply to those in *paederastia*.[2] Greek law forbade those who had been involved in *porneia* from addressing the Athenian assembly. Even in a culture with relatively lax attitudes towards homosexual sex, men providing sexual services to other men commercially were not granted the full privileges of citizenship.[3] Whether or not *porneia* was a crime was beside the point, the very involvement in the market as a man who sold sexual services to another man was enough to render one socially cut off from political power.

Scholars have claimed that male sex work in ancient Greece operated to exacerbate existing class inequalities. Young men of the upper classes could avail themselves to a sexual and social mentor via *paederastia,* while young men from less advantaged backgrounds participated in *porneia* and faced the lifelong consequences of those choices. The actual practices between the two differed primarily through the social expectations of the relationship. While young men in *paederastia* could expect to be mentored by their older patrons and exposed to the arts, politics, and social norms of the upper classes, young men in *porneia* could not. The explicit commercial exchange inherent in *porneia* relegated it to an undesirable social exchange.

In the Roman Empire, men could legally engage in sexual acts with other men in exchange for money as long as their participation was voluntary and their services were not offered as servants.[4] Male sex work could be secured by anyone – unlike other services in the Roman Empire, one need not be a citizen to be a buyer. Given the social class hierarchy, Roman citizens were discouraged from offering a sexual service to slaves, foreigners, or others of lower social standing. These social restrictions on male sex work made the practice particularly unappealing for Roman citizens. This meant that male sex workers largely came from the slave or foreigner classes. By the fourth century BCE political acts which restricted the number of slaves and foreigners reduced the supply of sex workers and led to increasing prices for male sex work. Polybius noted that male sex workers were regularly secured for a talent (more than several months of wages for the average worker) and Cato complained that sex workers were priced higher than farmland.[5] With little in ways of counts of male sex workers, however, it is difficult to know how much of the price increases were driven by increased demand from Roman gentry as opposed to the supply restrictions.

The large-scale acknowledgment of the practice in the Roman Empire also comes from public policy. Beginning with Caligula (37 CE) and lasting approximately until 500 CE, the Roman Empire taxed the earnings of all sex workers and formal registration of the occupation was common. Historians now believe that while these policies legitimized male sex work, they also brought the profession to light and therefore discouraged many men from entry. The private practice could be tolerated, but public disclosure of the occupation was not. Archeological work has found evidence of male brothels, however, suggesting that public meeting places for male sex workers and their clients occurred with some regularity. The brothels have been identified through markings and depiction of homosexual sex in the building. The presence of male brothels in the Roman Empire has been used as evidence of the relatively open attitudes towards male homosexuality.[6] In ancient Greece, young men would grow their hair out and wait at male establishments such as barbershops for clients.[7]

As with Greek language, different terms were applied to male sex workers in the Roman Empire. Male sex workers were referred to as *exoleti,* while younger sex workers were known as *pueri delicate* and *catamati.* Unlike its earlier Grecian form, male mentorship by elders did not include sexual interaction. The lack of sex in mentoring relationships may be related to the professionalization of sex work. Another factor would be the growing Christianization of the Roman Empire, which led to decreasing social acceptance of male sex work and homosexuality in general.[8] By the end of the sixth century a growing distinction related to homosexuality caused even starker social distinctions between male and female sex work. As early as 390, penalties were harsher for selling a male into prostitution, and by 533 all homosexual acts, commercial, consensual, and coerced, were punishable by death.[9]

The history of male sex work is not confined to the West, although there are fewer historical sources specifically referencing the practice. In Japan, for example, kabuki was a place for commercial sex between men. While monks and Samurai warriors engaged in pederasty in a manner similar to the practice in Greece, kabuki commercial sex was largely practiced between social classes. This practice continued until the seventeenth century, when sexual conduct between men of different social classes was outlawed by the Tokugawa government.[10]

The existing literature on the history of male sex work does lead to some general assumptions on the way the practice existed in historical settings. The ancient practice of male sex work was socially and legally distinct from older/younger sexual relations and from female sex work. A key distinction in historical male sex work was the class difference or similarity between buyers and sellers. Class differences were grounds to label the practice as sex work, and this meant that the historical practice of sex work was, in general, something that took place between classes. Male sex work was a service procured by those of high social status and supplied by those of low social status. Within the same social class, however, the practice was generally taboo and discouraged. From the historical scholarship, we find that the commercial aspects of the market were embedded in social ideas about who could (and should) supply and demand sexual services between men.

Male sex work has always had to contend with changing attitudes toward homosexuality. In periods and places where homosexuality was socially accepted, male prostitution was more likely to be professionalized along with its female counterpart.[11] When and where homosexuality became taboo, male sex work and all homosexual practices were commonly grouped together and sanctioned. Even in ancient times, the social acceptability of homosexuality had direct effects on the social acceptability of male sex work. This is not to say that male sex work disappeared, but the social recognition of male sex work appears to be related to the social recognition of homosexuality. This is in stark contrast to female sex work, which was commonplace, and was always separated socially and legally from heterosexual social relations such as marriage.

In medieval Europe, social sanctions on male homosexuality continued the practice of the late Roman era, which grouped male sex work and homosexuality together. In many instances, both were punishable by death. Indeed, in order to be allowed entry the priesthood, a man could not be discovered to have been involved sexually with another man.[12] Despite these legal and social sanctions, male sex work continued to be practiced. Historical records now point to a renewed linguistic distinction between homosexuality in general and male prostitution in particular in the Renaissance, where the term *bardassa* came into use to describe men engaged in sex work.[13]

By the end of the seventeenth century male prostitution was institutionalized in almost every major European city. This institutionalization included public knowledge (for those desiring such information) of the places where male sex work could be purchased and a language that facilitated the commercial activity. In Victorian London, for example, the Piccadilly Circus was well known as a place where one could purchase male sex work services. Men would adopt styles that would advertise their occupation, such as playing with one's lapel or wearing distinctively colored clothing. There is also some evidence that the urban male sex work of this time had changed from passive young men seeking to sell their services to dominant older men, to one where passive older men sought the sexual services of dominant young men.[14] Without comprehensive information, however, it is difficult to draw general conclusions. While still a criminal act, the prosecution of such crimes was relatively lax. When punishment was meted out, it was rarely as draconian as in earlier periods, owning to the relatively liberal attitudes toward homosexuality in European urban centers.

American male sex work predates the founding of the United States. Although the colonies prosecuted men for sodomy, and in more than ten cases executed men for the crime, some of these cases are known to have involved elements of solicitation. In May of 1677, Nicholas Sension was tried for the crime of sodomy. A deeper reading of the historical record reveals that the crime was not simply one of homosexuality, but of solicitation. In the court documents it was revealed that Sension had a long history of propositioning young men in the surrounding community for sex. Sension had been privately reprimanded for his activity at least twice over more than 20 years of known attempts to have sex with other men in return for compensation. In his sodomy trial it was revealed that he had, in at least two instances, offered payment in exchange for sexual services. Samuel Barboe testified that Sension offered him a bushel of corn if he would disrobe for him, and Peter Buoll testified that Sension offered him gunpowder in exchange for "one bloo at my breech." Sension was convicted of sodomy, but his sentence did not meet with any jail time.[15]

Historians note that this trial, and its instances of sex for payment, reflects the class distinctions in male sex work that were present in ancient times. Sension was a prosperous landowner in Connecticut and most of the men who accused him were of lower social class. Sension was first privately sanctioned to stop propositioning young men, and was only publicly tried when he attempted to sue his indentured servant for slander because that servant, Daniel Saxton, wished to be released from service due to Sension's numerous sexual advances. Only after Sension took legal action against his servant was he investigated and brought to colonial justice. As Saxton defended himself against slander, he showed that Sension had a history of sexual advances toward young men that involved payment. Given the private investigations and warnings that had been issued in the past, it is likely that Sension's acts would have gone uninterrupted had he not sought to silence Saxton.

In the nineteenth century, male sex work on both sides of the Atlantic was institutionalized in large industrial cities. Part of this was due to ever-increasing urban population and the greater personal freedom allowed in urban areas, but there were also legal developments in Europe. In the early nineteenth century, the Napoleonic Code ended legal sanctions against sodomy. Given the fact that the First French Empire ruled a significant portion of the continent, the decriminalization allowed the male sex trade to flourish from Paris to Berlin. Male sex also flourished in American cities. For example, in 1899 the New York City Vigilance League found that the Bowery district contained more than five places where male prostitution was well known. Reports at the time suggested that there were more than 100 male sex workers in New York City. Given the size of the city and the generally hostile attitudes toward expressions of same-sex desire, this number of male sex workers speaks to the prominence of male sex work in urban areas at the time.[16]

This modern form of male sex work operated under different norms than earlier variants. While it was still the case that clients were older than providers, on average, the sexual roles assumed by each took on a different routinized pattern. The class distinctions of the earlier era married to a new form of industrial masculinity, which conferred upon young working-class men an authentic masculinity that they traded for money. The higher-class clients were more likely to assume a passive sexual role and the male sex workers were prized for their masculine appearance and sexual conduct.

Men in the military were particularly popular as sex workers if they acted as "trade," presumably heterosexual men who were temporarily engaging in homosexual sex for compensation. Weeks (1989b) notes that military members were also thought to be more trustworthy and ethical in their dealings with clients.

Modern sex work was more intimately tied to increasing recognition of sexuality and masculinity. While cities openly noted that the fairy – effeminate man – was a commonly encountered urban inhabitant, male sex work in urban centers was not focused on effeminate men. There were cross-dressers and transgender sex workers, who sold either the illusion of femininity or transgender sex work to male clients, but male sex workers were primarily prized for their masculinity.[17] The sexual identity of male sex workers was less important than their ability to provide an authentic masculinity to clients who desired the new industrial masculinity that was developed during this time. With the primacy on masculinity, the earlier notion of the young sex worker gave way to an older sex worker would could more reasonably convey adult masculinity. Sex work moved from being about youth to being about adult men engaged in a commercial exchange for sex.

The dawn of the twentieth century presented a modern form of sex work that bore striking similarities and differences with regard to ancient and medieval practices.[18] First, sex work then and now constituted an average age difference between client and sex worker. Older men, who were more likely to be able to afford such services, made up the largest proportion of the client base. Young men, some of whom were in fragile economic circumstances, were likely to be service providers. Second, there were significant class differences between sex workers and their clients. As Friedman (2014) notes, this was different from the earlier class distinctions in male sex work, in that the new class distinction was predicated on the authentic masculinity afforded to working men in the modern era. Third, the change in the relationship to one that was transaction-specific was due to the fact that the circumstances surrounding sex work had changed. No longer was sex work part of the mentored relationship between men that also included some monetary and perhaps non-pecuniary compensation. Sex work by the end of the nineteenth century was an occupation.

By the beginning of the Gay Rights movement in the twentieth century, male sex workers had carved out a key niche in urban gay spaces. They had become an archetype in gay culture and they played a key role in public representations of gay people. Importantly, sex work became embedded into gay communities in a different way than it was for heterosexuals. Part of this is because the history of male sex work sought clear distinctions between commercial and noncommercial relationships between men. Without the sanctions of marriage and other traditional recognitions for family forms, the sexual relationships between men have been placed in a different sphere, putting them into closer social contact with male sex work and male sex workers.[19] For example, in the early and mid-twentieth century United States, many gay establishments would be frequented by male sex workers and men who desired noncommercial sexual encounters. This is not necessarily because the two groups desired to be in close contact, but because the limited number of social spaces safe for male homosexuals left little room to demarcate spaces for subcultures.

This close social relationship has allowed male sex workers a prominent position in social representations of male homosexuality. When anti-gay political commentators made note of the alleged perversity of gay men, they most commonly cited the cases of young men who entered into prostitution relationships with older men as a rhetorical technique to label gay men as pedophiles and gay relationships as inherent power imbalances between old and young men. Young men became natural embodiments of "innocents" who were "victimized" by older men who could entice them into sexual exchanges that provided money that the young men needed to survive. Ironically, these charges were coming at a time when young men as a fraction of the male sex worker population were on the decline given the changing nature of male sex work. Still, the age distinction between clients and sex workers and the ingratiation of male sex work into urban gay spaces proved to be problematic as gay men sought social acceptance for homosexuality, while at the same time maintaining close contact with an arrangement considered as vice even in its heterosexual form.

At the other end of the spectrum, gay men themselves had begun to develop an archetype of the gay male hustler, a presumably heterosexual man (but clearly an adult) who provided sexual services to other men. The development of a unique gay masculinity in urban spaces borrowed from the archetype of masculinity offered by male sex workers. Although the growing acceptance of homosexuality in urban communities led some gay-identified men to provide commercial sex services, the archetype of the male hustler (and the industrial masculinity he offered) did not fit into the anti-gay narrative, but rather molded into contemporary constructions of urban gay masculinity.[20] The male hustler was a man's man – a masculine man with few (if any) observable traits that would label him a homosexual. In the scholarship on male prostitution in the 1950s, 1960s, and 1970s, this modern male hustler archetype featured prominently.[21] This type of male sex worker was a "hoodlum" or "thug" who sought to use prostitution for wage income, rejecting the formal labor market. The fact that these men were presumably heterosexual added to their allure in a gay subculture that socially celebrated nontraditional representations of masculinity, but still held traditional male masculinity as a sexual ideal. In fact, the development of modern male physique and bodybuilding industries has direct links to male sex work. Men in the earliest era of bodybuilding would seek male sponsors, an arrangement that would allow them to concentrate on weight training. The early history of physique modeling is replete with men who used their masculine and muscular appearance in exchange for remuneration that freed them from the formal labor market.

The fusion of modern conceptions of masculinity, which imbued working-class and lower-class presentations of aggressive men as inherently masculine, did have effects on the ways that male sex work operated in modern urban environments. Some male sex workers who adopted gay identities found that clients demanded "trade" – men who did not identify as gay but who participated in homosexual sex. Gay identified male sex workers would be inclined to describe and present themselves as "trade" for their clients. In a market where desire and demand are closely intertwined, male sex work began to take on more performance elements than before. This also meant, however, that the range of sexual practices expanded and could not be presumed on the basis of one's position as client or sex worker.

In the most popular depictions of male sex work in mass media, male (homosexual) sex work has been depicted as a last resort for heterosexual men. Although the films *Sunset Boulevard* (1950), *Sweet Bird of Youth* (1962), *Midnight Cowboy* (1969), *American Gigolo* (1980), and *Deuce Bigalow: Male Gigolo* (1999) as well as the television series *Hung* (2009) and *Gigolos* (2011–) are the most popular media images of male sex workers, they actually present the least-typical part of the market. Women are very rarely the clients of male sex workers. In fact, the (heterosexual) male escort agent featured on the reality television series *Gigolos* noted that the escorts he employs cannot support themselves through work with female clients. Indeed, the program, despite being billed as authentic, has had to remunerate female participants, and some have never been clients of the featured escort service. The popular image of a male sex worker as a gigolo stands in contrast to the limited evidence that women have ever made up anything more than a negligible fraction of the client base for male sex workers.

Gay films and art films of the same era depict male sex in a manner closer to the most common experience, which is to say they depict male sex work as homosexual activity. *My Hustler* (1965) contains two half-hour vignettes of male sex workers. Both of the scenes are explicit in noting that male sex work is the buying and selling of sexual services by and for men. The documentary style of the film and its explicit homoerotic content were some of the first homosexual representations of male sex work. In *The Boys in the Band* (1972), a male sex worker is hired as a birthday gift, and the price of his services is discussed in the production. As public and academic discussion of homosexuality and prostitution moved to the mainstream, so did the concept of the homosexual male sex worker. The later representations of male sex work in film also reflected a new gay sensibility about gay life in the United States. For example, both *My Own Private Idaho* (1991) and *The Living End* (1992) feature the reality of HIV/AIDS as part of the lives of male sex workers. Later works focused on the professional lives of male sex workers and their personal selves. *Boy Culture* (2006) featured an openly gay male escort who was seeking to form a long-term, monogamous relationship despite his involvement in the commercial sex industry.

These gay films better reflect the reality of modern male sex workers. While the most popular representations suggest that gigolos are common, they have never been a substantial fraction of the male sex worker market. In historical times and at present, male sex work, in the vast majority of cases, is a homosexual activity. Sex workers and clients are male and are selling and purchasing homosexual sex. Earlier scholarship has always noted this, but has tended to concentrate on sex work as a form of deviance (not necessarily for its homosexual orientation but due to its taboo nature and illegal status), or as a means to study psychological factors related to entry into sex work. With the advent of HIV/AIDS in the 1980s, research concentrated on male sex work as a vector of transmission of sexually transmitted infections, where sex workers could spread disease.

While all of these scholarly goals are admirable, the reality of sex work as a market has been obscured. Neither in the past nor now is male sex work primarily about these factors. It is about the supply and demand for sexual services from a man by another man. That fact is reflected in the ways in which male sex work takes place – that is, how male sex workers secure clients and how clients choose between sex workers. Given that the gay male population is relatively small, sex work is better aided by technology than female sex work, as cities would have relatively small "street tracks" where male sex workers would congregate. Male sex workers needed to reach their client base (homosexually identified men), and as of the mid-twentieth century were using gay media to reach clients. Magazines and newspapers of the time regularly featured the advertisements of male sex workers in the back pages. There are examples of escort advertisements in the pages of the *Bay Area Reporter,* the San Francisco Bay Area's local gay newspaper. The use of gay media was common in early sex work advertisements. It created the largest local market possible for male sex work services while also keeping the activity relatively discreet – clients would phone sex workers and arrange appointments. The earliest forms of communication provided coarse information for clients. Escorts typically listed a form of contact and a brief physical description, and, in many cases, the sexual services they offered to clients.[22] There was one national magazine devoted to male sex worker advertisements, and it ceased publication only when male sex workers had cheaper options to secure clients.

The Internet changed the dynamics of male sex work entirely, in a manner similar to the transformation of gay society in general. While not fully supplanting the advertisements in local gay newspapers, the Internet allowed for easier entry and exit from the market, and the "feedback" features of the Internet allowed sex workers to establish reputations. The Internet has become the primary medium through which male sex workers secure clients. As the Internet has flourished, escorts have been able to distinguish themselves by creating online personas that were not possible in earlier modes of communication.[23]

The medium provided by the Internet allows the analysis of male sex work, for the first time, to fully embrace its economic underpinnings. Male sex work is not charity – it is a service provided by a seller to a buyer. For most of its history, however, we had little information about what was actually being provided and at what price the services were being sold. This is in contrast to female prostitution, where prices from a variety of sources have been known for some time.[24] For historical periods, we have few sources for pricing of male sex work. Even in contemporary settings, the best estimates of the market price come from individual responses in work devoted to the experiences of a small number of sex workers.

For economic analysis this poses several problems. First, price variation in a market like male sex work could come from a variety of sources. Smaller samples of sex workers are usually confined to small geographic areas. Differences between sex workers, local market prices, and the substitutability of sex workers in markets can all play a role in the prices observed. Economic analysis of a market requires extensive information about the market. For nearly all economic analysis, this implies quantitative data. Measures of prices, quantities, product quality, firm size, and consumer characteristics are standard. Throughout this work, quantitative data will be emphasized, and the sources of that data are described below.

Second, sex workers themselves may be more or less willing to divulge their prices to surveyors. That is, the price information we have from surveys may be driven by selection, where only certain sex workers provide their prices. If this is related to other attributes (say, only sex workers who are successful and popular are willing to divulge their prices), we will be unable to describe the market in any detail. In other words, we would like the same price information that a consumer of male sex services would see. This would ensure that the analysis of the market is working from the same base of information that clients use.

This book exploits two primary sources of data to empirically analyze male sex work and its social and economic underpinnings. The first source of data is advertisement data for male sex workers. This is drawn from the largest and most comprehensive data on male sex workers in the United States. The advertisement data has been the key source for analysis of the market to-date. Since escorts post their prices publicly, the advertisement data gives a direct measure of prices, which differs from the usual approach of surveying or inferring prices.[25] Inferring prices runs the risk of spurious correlation – prices may or may not be related to the factors that are assumed to be sources of price variation. The data used here comes from the universe of male sex workers advertising on the chosen website in the United States at the time of data collection. As such, these data represent the entire population.

Relative to other data sources, online advertisement data has several advantages. First, this data allows one to collect information on escorts' attributes, prices, and information without regard to some of the selection problems that one would encounter in a survey of escorts. For example, escorts who charge very high (or very low) prices may not respond with accurate prices in a survey. Another concern would be that escorts in general would not report their typical price but, instead, the highest price they had ever charged. This would result in an average price that would be far above the prices actually charged. Second, escorts have one account on the website and may list themselves in multiple cities that they serve. Third, the escort characteristics are entered by escorts from dropdown menus; this is particularly advantageous for features one would like to control for in pricing models, such as body type or hair color, whereas free-form responses may be difficult to evaluate consistently or may be missing altogether. There are other sources that allow for free-form escort responses; these sources are not as comprehensive as the one used here. Fourth, the website is free for viewing by all: there is no charge or account required to view any advertisements, photos, or reviews of escorts.

| Example Escort | ★★★★ |

Services Provided

Escort	
Erotic Massage	
Non-Erotic Massage	
Registered Massage Therapist	Yes
Modeling	
Stripping/Dancer	
In Calls $200.00/hr	Yes
Out Calls $250.00/hr	Yes
US Travel:	Yes
Int'l Travel:	Yes

Contact Info

Cellular: (NNN) NNN-NNNN

PREFERS PHONE CONTACT

"PRIVATE CALLER"
PHONE CALLS
MAY NOT BE ACCEPTED

Email Him

Location

CA - San Francisco / Oakland
CA - San Diego
CA - San Jose
CA - Vallejo / Fairfield / Napa

Example Escort
Text of escort advertisement
CA - San Francisco / Oakland

| Email Him | Review Him | His Reviews | Stud |

Age:	NN	Race:	XX	Body Type:	XX
Height:	NN	Hair Color:	XX	Body Hair:	XX
Weight:	NN	Eye Color:	XX		

Availability

	S	M	T	W	T	F	S
7am-11am	✓	✓	✓	✓	✓	✓	✓
11am-3pm	✓	✓	✓	✓	✓	✓	✓
3pm-7pm	✓	✓	✓	✓	✓	✓	✓
7pm-11pm	✓	✓	✓	✓	✓	✓	✓
11pm-3am	✓	✓	✓	✓	✓	✓	✓
3am-7am	✓	✓	✓	✓	✓	✓	✓

Read text reviews on Example Escort

Figure 1.1 Diagram of online escort advertisement

In particular, the advertisement data is a set of nearly 2,000 men from the largest and most comprehensive website for male sex workers in the United States. Beyond its geographic coverage, there is a rich amount of information that can be exploited to uncover more about male sex workers than before. Figure 1.1 shows a diagram of an escort advertisement. Escorts list their age, height, weight, race, hair color, eye color, body type, and body hair type. They give clients contact information and also their preferred mode of contact (phone or e-mail), their availability to travel, and their prices and availability for in-calls and out-calls. In-calls occur when a client travels to the escort; out-calls when an escort travels to the client. Escorts also provide clients with the range of services they offer in addition to escort work such as modeling, erotic massage, and stripping. Escorts have a simple table they can use to let clients know their weekly availability.

There is also the actual text of the advertisement itself, which allows escorts to write about their services and quality. The largest piece of the advertisement is made up of the escort's pictures, which are uploaded by the escort. These pictures may be of any feature of the escort that he chooses, and may be clothed or nude.[26]

One unique feature of the advertisement data source is that it provides two types of reputation measures that come from clients. These are proxies for escort quality, which is an important component in any service such as male sex work. These are survey reviews (similar to feedback on eBay.com) and detailed reviews of escorts. The survey reviews ask the reviewer five questions about the escort (four of which are "Yes/No") and a rating on a four-star scale.[27] The detailed reviews, "text reviews," are the detailed, free-form client reviews described earlier. In addition to providing a review of escort services, clients also give the date of their encounter with the escort, the type of appointment made (in-call, out-call, or an extended appointment such as an evening or weekend), and the price paid, which I term the "spot price," as it reflects the price paid in a specific transaction.[28] As noted earlier, a key advantage of these reputation measures is that escorts have no control over their reviews – all reviews of both types are retained if the escort allows reviews, not a selected sample that is posted or chosen by the escort. However, a key disadvantage to note is that anyone can post a review, including an escort, though this sort of thing is likely to make up only a small percentage of the reviews.

Table 1.1 shows the summary statistics for the escorts in the advertisement data. First, the data contains nearly 2,000 male sex workers who advertise online. This is a large number of sex workers, and at a minimum, it establishes that the number of participants in the market is substantial. Second, male sex work is well compensated. On average, escorts charge more than $200 an hour. This is consistent with other estimates of escort services, which are close to the $200-an-hour range.[29] Escorts are reasonably fit – on average a male sex worker is 5 feet 10 inches tall and weigh around 165 pounds. According to the National Center for Health Statistics, the average man aged 20–74 in the United States is 5 feet 9.5 inches tall and weighs 190 pounds, which implies that escorts are slightly taller and thinner than the average adult male in the United States.

The average male sex worker is 28 years old. While 28 is certainly young, it is a far departure from the young men described in historical accounts of male sex work. The median age of male sex workers in the data is 26.[30] Escorts are also racially diverse: while more than half of all escorts are White, more than a fifth are Black and more than a tenth are Hispanic.

Table 1.1 Summary statistics for the escort advertisement data sample

Variable	Observations	Mean	Std. dev.	Physical trait	Observations	Mean	Std. dev.	Behavior	Observations	Mean	Std. dev.
Price	1,476	216.88	64.46	Hair color				Top	1,932	0.16	0.37
Log of price	1,476	5.34	0.29	Black	1,932	0.37	0.48	Bottom	1,932	0.06	0.24
Weight	1,932	167.11	24.54	Blonde	1,932	0.13	0.34	Versatile	1,932	0.21	0.40
Height	1,932	70.43	2.69	Brown	1,932	0.46	0.50	Safer	1,932	0.19	0.39
BMI	1,932	23.64	2.89	Gray	1,932	0.02	0.13				
Age	1,932	28.20	6.93	Auburn/red	1,932	0.01	0.11				
Asian	1,932	0.01	0.12	Other	1,932	0.01	0.10				
Black	1,932	0.22	0.41	Eye color							
Hispanic	1,932	0.14	0.35	Black	1,932	0.02	0.14				
Multiracial	1,932	0.08	0.28	Blue	1,932	0.18	0.39				
Other	1,932	0.01	0.10	Brown	1,932	0.55	0.50				
White	1,932	0.54	0.50	Green	1,932	0.11	0.31				
				Hazel	1,932	0.14	0.35				
				Body hair							
				Hairy	1,932	0.04	0.20				
				Moderately hairy	1,932	0.30	0.46				
				Shaved	1,932	0.17	0.38				
				Smooth	1,932	0.49	0.50				
				Body build							

(continued)

Athletic/swimmer's build	1,932	0.48	0.50
Average	1,932	0.13	0.34
A few extra pounds	1,932	0.01	0.08
Muscular	1,932	0.30	0.46
Thin/lean	1,932	0.08	0.27

Price is the out-call price posted by an escort in his advertisement. See the data appendix for variable definitions.

Escorts in the data are racially diverse – 54 percent are White, 22 percent are Black, 14 percent are Hispanic, 8 percent are multiracial, and 1 percent are Asian.

For physical traits, escorts are likely to have black (36 percent) or brown (46 percent) hair (fewer than 15 percent are blond). More than half of all escorts have brown eyes (55 percent), although significant fractions have blue (18 percent) and hazel (14 percent) eyes. Nearly half of all escorts are smooth (49 percent), and 17 percent shave their body hair, but more than a third are hairy or moderately hairy (34 percent). Very few escorts are overweight (1 percent), and relatively few are thin (8 percent); the majority of escorts claim to have athletic (48 percent) or muscular (30 percent) builds. For sexual behaviors, 16 percent of escorts offer penetration to clients (this is known as being a "top"), while 6 percent offer to be penetrated (and are known as "bottoms"), and 21 percent of escorts list themselves as "versatile."[31] In addition, 19 percent of escorts advertise that they exclusively practice safer sex. Overall, the summary statistics for the men in the data are similar to the descriptive statistics noted by Cameron et al. (1999) for male escorts in British newspapers in the 1990s and Pruitt's (2005) more recent sample of male escorts who advertise on the Internet.

Overall, this diversity points to there really being no "typical" male sex worker. They come in a variety of ages, races, physical appearances, and sexual behaviors. At one level, this is what we would expect from sex work. Clients could have demand for a variety of men, and this demand should lead a variety of men to supply sex work. At another level, this diversity reflects the fact that earlier descriptions of male sex work that make appeals to a monolithic experience are somewhat outdated to the extent that this diversity in male sex worker supply requires a more careful description of the men involved in sex work. Lastly, the compensation offered to male sex workers shows it to be a lucrative profession. At $200 per hour, a male sex worker who sees one client per day Monday to Friday would earn more than $50,000 per year. This is more than the median household income in the United States, and matches the median earnings of male college graduates in the United States.

The second data source comes from transaction-specific data from client reviews of escort services. The data come from the online reviews hosted by *Daddy's Reviews* (www.daddysreviews.com), the oldest and most popular client-based forum for reviews and discussions of male sex workers. This website has been in existence since 1998 and provides a rich structure for clients to review male sex worker services. The website contains both a forum (message board) for clients to discuss male sex workers and a review feature where clients provide detailed reviews of their specific encounters with male sex workers. The individual reviews of male sex workers are the data used here. A key for this data is that all reviews of male sex workers are held in a holding tank and individually verified by the website administrator before they are posted. Male sex workers cannot remove reviews, and reviews are flagged if they are suspicious (for example, entered by a competing male sex worker or by the sex worker himself). As described by Logan (2016), Logan and Shah (2013) and discussed earlier, this website acts to police male sex workers, allowing clients to inform each other about the quality of male sex workers – and this function minimizes the opportunity for male sex workers to exploit clients. Logan and Shah (2013) also note that it is extremely difficult for a male sex worker to create new identities for himself, as clients track them over time using this source. When a male sex worker changes his location, over time all of his previous reviews are retained and linked to him, and the same is true if the male sex worker changes his professional name. Male sex workers who have retired are not removed from the website, but are listed as "retired." Male sex workers do have the ability to post comments on reviews. Male sex worker reviews can be searched by individual male sex worker name or geographically.

For each male sex worker's review page, the male sex worker's contact information is listed as well as all reviews, which are listed in reverse chronological order (newest to oldest). Figure 1.2 shows an example of a client review on the website. (Because client free-form reviews are sexually explicit, that field is obscured in Figure 1.2.) Reviews were collected using a script that pulled the information from the website into a database organized by the fields in the advertisement. As the figure shows, reviews detail the date and location of the transaction, the length of the appointment, the price paid, the client's perception of features of the escort (height, weight, age, etc.), and the sexual behaviors that took place in the given transaction.

The reviews also allow for clients to enter free-form text that describes their encounter in more detail. This field is read manually and coded for sexual behaviors not categorized in the reviews. In addition, clients rate the experience. At the end of the review, clients identify themselves with a unique "handle" username. The total sample contains 6,269 transactions for 1,418 male sex workers in the United States over a 6-year period. Table 1.2 shows the summary statistics for the data. The majority of transactions (60 percent) are hourly appointments, and another 25 percent are less than 3 hours. Slightly more than a tenth of the appointments are of long duration (more than 4 hours).

```
Review #NN, MM/DD/YYYY

Name:
Location:
Email:
Phone:
Website:

Ethnicity:              Age:
Height:                 Weight:         Build:
Eyes:                   Hair:
Cock:
Smoking:                Drinking:       Tattoos:

Orientation:            Calls:
Roles:
Masturbation:           Anal:           Oral:           Kink:
Rates for time only (US$):

Date: MM/YYYY           Type:           Where:          Rate:
Rating:                 Hire Again?
Where Found?            Which:
Reviewed Before?        Match Description?  Lived up?

Experience:



Handle:
Submissions:

You:
```

Figure 1.2 Example of escort review

For the transactions, I find that the average price of an hourly session is $227, consistent with other estimates of male sex worker services from escort advertisements and the advertisement data. As a check against the advertisement data, the basic features are quite comparable. In terms of escort characteristics, the largest proportion of male sex workers in the transaction data are White (49 percent), while a significant share are another race

Table 1.2 *Summary statistics for the client reviewed transactions data sample*

Variable	Observations	Mean	Std. dev.
Transaction measures			
Hourly rate*	5,452	227.07	299.23
1-hour appt.	6,269	0.59	0.48
90-min. appt.	6,269	0.06	0.23
2-hour appt.	6,269	0.15	0.36
3-hour appt.	6,269	0.04	0.19
4-hour appt.	6,269	0.02	0.15
> 4-hour appt.	6,269	0.13	0.34
Variable	**Observations**	**Mean**	**Std. dev.**
Escort characteristics			
Asian	1,418	0.01	0.09
Black	1,418	0.12	0.15
White	1,418	0.49	0.50
Other race	1,418	0.30	0.49
Latino	1,418	0.09	0.28
Endowment (in.)	1,418	8.00	1.04
Circumcised	1,418	0.76	0.43
Age 20s	1,418	0.38	0.49
Age 30s	1,418	0.26	0.44
Age 40s	1,418	0.05	0.22
Age 50s	1,418	0.31	0.46
BMI	1,418	24.79	2.71
(BMI)^2	1,418	621.87	140.82
Height (cm)	1,418	179.81	6.58
Weight (kg)	1,418	80.35	10.74
Variable	**Observations**	**Mean**	**Std. dev.**
Sexual behaviors			
Versatile	6,269	0.40	0.46
Top	6,269	0.37	0.44
Bottom	6,269	0.17	0.25
No anal sex	6,269	0.03	0.17
Kissing	6,269	0.62	0.49
Masturbation, mutual	6,269	0.49	0.50
Masturbation, receives	6,269	0.03	0.18
Masturbation, provides	6,269	0.02	0.15
No masturbation	6,269	0.43	0.07
No condom	6,269	0.20	0.29

Note: Sexual behaviors are defined from the perspective of the escort.
*Hourly rate is defined for appointments lasting less than 4 hours.
"No condom" requires that the client noted penetration in the transaction.

(30 percent). For age, nearly 40 percent of escorts are noted by clients to be in their twenties, and more than a quarter in their thirties (26 percent).

The transaction data establishes that male sex work does involve sex. In terms of sexual behaviors, 37 percent of transactions involved male sex workers penetrating clients, 17 percent involved clients penetrating sex workers, and 40 percent involved both client and male sex worker penetration. Only a small fraction of transactions, fewer than 5 percent, involved no penetration.

Other sexual details show that male sex work involves more than just sexual services, but extends to other intimate behavior. More than half (62 percent) of transactions involved kissing and more than half (54 percent) involved masturbation. In addition, 80 percent of transactions involved sex with condoms, which suggests that male sex work is nearly as likely to involve condoms as noncommercial gay sex.[32] Overall, the summary statistics for the male subjects (age, race, height, weight, etc.) are similar to the descriptive statistics noted by Cameron et al. (1999), Pruitt (2005), Logan (2010), and Logan (2016) in analysis of male sex worker advertisements. The behaviors described in the transactions are also consistent with the patterns seen in small-sample surveys of clients, such as those in Grov et al. (2013).

These two data sources give us information on both the supply and demand for male sex work services. The advertisements give us a rich set of information akin to that used in most market studies. From all comparisons, the data appears to be consistent with data from smaller samples, but is more diverse than the smaller samples in that it is national in scope and contains a more diverse range of men – racially, physically, and sexually. In addition, the availability of price information is particularly important as these two data sources are the largest available sources of information on the prices of male sex work in the United States. Since both data sources also contain additional personal and geographic measures, there are a number of additional items in advertisements and transactions that allow us to test whether there are significant price differentials that are driven by economic or social phenomena. Obtaining prices and detailed information for such a large illegal market is rare, and the recent criminal prosecution of male sex worker websites decreases the likelihood that this sort of analysis can be consistently performed into the future. Nevertheless, the remaining chapters of this book will investigate the present (and, perhaps, future) status of male sex work in the United States.

2

Face Value: How Male Sex Workers Overcome the Problem of Asymmetric Information

Male sex work presents a number of challenges for traditional market analysis. Despite its appearing online in a manner similar to that of other products in the age of the Internet, an economic approach to male sex work must begin with by considering several preliminaries that we usually neglect in economic analysis because we can safely assume them away. For example, in a traditional market we are not usually worried about whether prices in the market accurately reflect equilibrium prices – the point where producer supply and consumer demand intersect. When we observe a price in an online marketplace we take that to mean that the firm is choosing the price to maximize profit, and implicitly assume that the maximization takes into account consumer demand for the good.

If the prices in the market do not reflect underlying economic principles, it is difficult to know how this market operates, or if it operates at all. A traditional supply-and-demand approach would be inappropriate if observed prices had little relationship to economic primitives. The illicit nature of the transactions in male sex work make it difficult to argue that the market "gets prices right" simply because they are publically posted online. After all, in what other illegal market are the prices of goods and services openly displayed? The basic tenets of market analysis require that we first confirm that the prices in the market reflect underlying fundamentals about consumer and producer behavior. The first question to answer is the most basic: Does this market work? (And if so, how does it work?)

To answer this question, we must step back and think more abstractly about what a sex worker transaction is. At its most basic level, sex work is a contract. Whether purchasing gasoline, a candy bar, or a home, transactions are contracts. A good or service is sold at a specific price offered by a seller to a buyer at a specific place and time. The contract does not have to

39

be formal or written, and the law acknowledges that most contracts are informal ones whose terms are implied by the context of the transaction itself. Payment terms are stipulated and our legal system enforces these contracts if they are disputed. This helps both buyers and sellers – if the good or service is not delivered as advertised, or if payment is not received, either party can turn to the courts to have the contract enforced.

If a consumer were purchasing shoes from an online retailer, for example, the customer would be confident that the product he or she ordered would be the product they would receive. If this turned out not to be the case, they could resort to a payment service, the vendor, or even the courts if they were duped and either sold a different product or received nothing. In other words, they would buy with confidence – if not confidence in the seller, than certainly confidence in a system that would enforce or void their contract, depending on the situation. The same applies for the seller. For that reason, analysis of the market would proceed with an understanding that both buyers and sellers are acting with full faith that their transactions will be completed. The analysis of markets usually presumes that contracts will be enforced.

In an illegal market such as male sex work this presumption does not hold. Courts will not aid those seeking to enforce contracts for illegal acts. This poses a problem for market analysis of male sex work because we cannot assume that buyers and sellers are acting with any confidence that their transactions will be enforced. We therefore lose confidence that what we observe from the illegal market is what actually occurs. In other words, we need to first check that the prices we observe from these online sources are plausibly related to actual transactions.

In addition to formal enforcement, information is also critically important in markets. Economists have long recognized that information exchanged between buyers and sellers helps to ensure that more transactions will take place. Even with contract enforcement, it is still possible that information will improve market function, lead to more transactions, and increase consumer welfare. In the classic example, if a seller offers a used car for a certain price, any reasonable buyer would have to fear that the car may be worth (much) less than the advertised price. Unless the seller can provide additional information about the car's quality or offer a guarantee, it is unlikely that a buyer will be found at the price advertised. In this case, the seller has more information than the buyer, and a smart buyer will realize this and naturally fear that he or she can be duped by the seller. This case of asymmetric information can stop transactions before they start. In the most extreme case, no buyer will be found.[1]

Even when there is contract enforcement, buyers and sellers would rather not use them. Contract enforcement is costly in both time and money, and buyers will rightly be wary of sellers whom they do not trust. The seller must therefore provide a great deal of information to the buyer in order for the transaction to take place. As such, information helps to make transactions possible because they build trust between a buyer and seller. The market can and does take information into account, and the more objective the information the better. One reason this information can be taken into account is because it, too, is an implicit part of the transaction.

Male sex work does not necessarily have this market structure. While the information structure of the online market is quite rich, the transactions themselves are completely illegal. This is the reason the Department of Homeland Security moved to close Rentboy.com in 2015 – the federal government argued that the website was facilitating prostitution through the website, even though the website did not profit from transactions. Every transaction that takes place within male sex work is done with full knowledge that any agreements between sex worker and client cannot be enforced. For economic analysis, this creates a serious problem. Formal enforcement is often seen as the cornerstone of contracts. While information can overcome the problems of asymmetric information, this assumes that the information provided is credible and verifiable, which is made more likely when contracts can be enforced.[2] At a minimum, if the information were false economists assume that there would be a means of redress for fraud. While the use of formal institutions such as courts is rare relative to the volume of transactions, the standard argument is that the *presence* of formal institutions gives contracts their authority and information its credibility. In Schelling's classic terminology, "the power to sue and be sued" gives parties the ability to make credible exchanges of information and enforceable commitments, a prerequisite to most transactions.[3]

Without any means of redress, the information that buyers and sellers share would have little value. Since there would be no punishment for misrepresentation, a reasonable consumer would heavily discount all promises made by sellers. With no recourse for fraud, gross misrepresentation, or failure to provide the service, the market might not exist at all – no buyer would trust any of the information provided by a seller, and honest sellers would not be able to distinguish themselves from fraudulent ones. This implies that what we see online is an illusion with little connection to the actual practice of male sex work.

This is not to say that economists are naïve and always assume that formal enforcement is necessary or available. There are many transactions that take place without formal enforcement, and some that do not require the presence of formal enforcement. Numerous studies have documented how informal networks, long-term relationships, and reputations over-come problems of asymmetric information. Indeed, researchers have developed large literatures that look at limited contractibility and situa-tions where formal enforcement is costly, as a way to consider the addi-tional mechanisms that must be in place if existing institutions are lacking or unable to settle disputes.[4] The literature has not developed an empirical answer to whether the value of information without formal enforcement approaches its value when formal enforcement is present, however.

This question matters a great deal for the study of the market for male sex work. Without an answer to this question it is not clear that this market behaves in a way that can be described by traditional economic theory. There is information transmitted in the market, but the question is whether (and how) it is valued. In most illegal markets this is not a problem because the good exchanged (say, narcotics) is done in a face-to-face process. Reputations, networks, and relationships are key in most illegal markets, and prices are private and negotiated directly between buyer and seller. In the modern world for male sex work, however, this is not so. Male escorts are not hired off of the street. Rather, they are selected online in a highly impersonal process. There are few escort agencies that could act to vouch for a sex worker – the websites simply host advertisements. Reputations established online could be entirely false. Men enter the market regularly, and new entrants need to be able to establish themselves in the industry like any other service provider, but there are few ways to do this in an illegal market. Most important, every client knows this to be the case.

The question, "Does this market work?" is therefore actually two related questions: Are formal enforcement mechanisms *necessary* in order for the information that male sex workers and clients share to have value? And if not, what is the value of information in this environment without formal enforcement? These questions are refinements of the basic question asked before, and get to the heart of the issue – in order to study the market for male sex work in a traditional way, we first need to know whether the market functions like a traditional market. In traditional markets, infor-mation has value, and if the information in this market has no value, then it is unlikely that the prices and quantities correspond to what we would assume in traditional supply and demand analysis.

The problem is most illegal markets have coarse information environ-ments. Take the example of illegal narcotics. It is rare that someone looking to purchase drugs can choose between several sellers the way that someone shopping for a book would. Most illegal markets are also highly secretive and heavily dependent on personal connections. Unlike regulated businesses, illegal markets work by word of mouth and knowledge of the goods and services being provided is not usually in plain view. In these markets, reputations and networks operate to ensure that transactions take place. Given the types of networks, it is challenging to obtain information on prices, quantities, and consumer and producer behavior, making empirical answers to these questions especially difficult. The online market for male sex work must overcome the problems posed by asymmetric information but in an impersonal manner for an illegal service, a very tall order.

So, then, how *does* this market work? Does it get prices right? In this chapter, I show how the male sex work market leverages high technology and a rich information structure to make this market work. I begin by documenting the ways in which the clients of male sex workers informally police the market: by informing other clients of deceptive sex workers and by reviewing sex workers on independent, client-owned websites. The informal policing in the market is critically important and allows this market to function. In economic terms, the policing raises the cost of misrepresentation for would-be fraudulent escorts and simultaneously rewards the truthful self-disclosure of honest escorts. This acts to encourage credible escorts to enter or remain in the market and to prevent fraudulent escorts from entering or persisting in the market. In an illegal market such as male sex work this policing works as one of the only means of enforcement, and it is entirely informal.

I exploit this institutional knowledge further to identify the specific information clients treat as a signal of escort quality. Both clients and escorts explicitly mention face pictures in discussions of escort credibility and misrepresentation. Using narrative evidence from qualitative studies, news reports, and online forums, I show that clients look for face pictures in an escort's advertisement as a sign that the escort is trustworthy. Being mentioned as the signal of escort trustworthiness is one thing, though, and whether the market values that information is another. If this market is well functioning, the signal of quality should have value.

The market values face pictures, and escorts who post face pictures are able to earn 11 percent more than escorts who do not, on average. In dollar terms, this would be in excess of an additional $10,000 per year in earnings. Spot prices – specific transaction prices recorded by clients – independently confirm the estimates from advertised prices. This is important because spot prices are prices we know that clients actually paid, which could be different from the prices that have been advertised. Consistent with the institutional analysis, I find that escorts who post pictures of their faces receive a sizable price premium: twice the premium to that on pictures in general. Indeed, the premium that accrues to pictures is actually completely attributable to face pictures.

This finding is robust with regard to a number of considerations. First, it holds when looking at escorts who have no reputation measures in their advertisements. This implies that new entrants to the market understand the value of face pictures, and price their services accordingly. Second, the premium holds when looking at spot prices only. This means that the premium is not an artifact of escorts with face pictures simply posting higher prices than others – clients actually do pay more for the services of escorts who post their face pictures. Third, I find that the premium is not driven by beauty. It could certainly be the case that only attractive escorts show pictures of their faces, and this would mean that the value of face pictures is not about information in an abstract sense but about the physical features revealed in face pictures. I find that the premium remains even when controlling for the physical beauty of the male escort.

Male sex workers and their clients successfully overcome the problem of asymmetric information in an illegal market. I show how this market functions without formal enforcement, describing how clients police the market and identify the specific information consumers take as the signal of quality in this market. Interestingly, the per-picture price premium I estimate, 1.7 percent, is similar to the per-picture premium observed for used automobiles on eBay.com.[5] Irrespective of the reputational concerns of escorts, I document how client policing can increase the costs of doing business for low-quality escorts. Increasing their cost is one of the primary ways of minimizing their numbers. While previous empirical work looks at how information technology improves market function, I provide the first evidence that an illegal online market is quite responsive to information, even when it cannot be verified or where misrepresentations cannot be punished.[6]

The market for male sex work provides a case where the richness of the information environment overcomes some of the problems of asymmetric information. The illegality of the market and the near-impossibility of guaranteeing truthful disclosure imply that the market should disappear or be a market where information has dubious value. However, I find that clients informally police the market, successfully punishing misrepresentation and rewarding credible escorts. This enables male escorts to signal their quality and allows prices in the market to respond accordingly.

Despite its being an illegal market, male sex work exploits high technology to ensure that the market functions well. The answer to the question, "Does this market work?" is, despite obstacles generally presented by illegal markets, "Yes."

THE ONLINE MARKET FOR MALE ESCORT SERVICES

The male sex work market now largely takes place online.[7] Although female sex work has recently begun to appear online in Internet forums such as Craigslist.com, male escorts have had access to large and profitable websites devoted to the male sex trade for well over 15 years.[8] Unlike escort agencies and other online, two-party transactions such as eBay.com purchases, the websites themselves do not derive any profits from the transactions escorts conduct with clients; they simply allow escorts to post their advertisements and contact information. The websites charge a set fee to escorts for hosting an advertisement and act as a clearinghouse where escorts advertise their services and clients choose between escorts. Consequently, these sites do not screen clients for escorts or vice versa, make no claims or guarantees about the quality of the escorts, and offer no recourse to clients in cases of poor escort performance or fraud.

The large number of male escorts and their ability to price directly without intermediaries create a market setting similar to others that are compatible with competitive market assumptions.[9] Competitive markets generally rest on relatively simple criteria: many buyers and sellers, free entry and exit of sellers, the same good or service is sold by all sellers, and buyers and sellers have the same information. Under these conditions we expect markets to function well. Since this market is an illegal market, however, there is a potential for escorts to mislead clients and engage in fraud. In particular, an escort's ability to post unreliable information and to misrepresent himself should lead to adverse selection in the market. The adverse selection here would be one where fraudulent male escorts would be the predominant actors in the market.

While escort claims are verifiable *ex post,* there are no formal institutional penalties for *ex ante* misrepresentation. Similarly, it is unclear how much weight a reputation in an illegal online market carries, and whether any client would respond to claims of high-quality service. Without formal enforcement and with the stakes particularly high (especially for men who are married or not generally assumed to partake in homosexual behavior), it is unclear whether a rich information environment alone can prevent the adverse selection described above. Previous research based on newspaper advertisements for male escorts found no differences in pricing due to information.[10] Since the market has moved online, however, there are more service providers and more likely clients than before. The open question is whether the rich information environment offered by the Internet increases opportunities for escorts to disclose information about themselves, which could signal their trustworthiness, and whether the pricing of male escort services is related to this information.

The market for escort services is one of the few instances where illegal behavior is openly advertised. While this is extremely rare for illegal markets, there are reasons why escorts publicly announce their prices for services. First, and somewhat counterintuitively, is that it minimizes the legal risks of sex work. In most police stings for solicitation, the sex worker and the client must agree to both a price and sexual conduct. In order to be prosecuted for prostitution the illegal contract must specify, verbally or otherwise, the terms of the transaction. By posting prices and sexual behaviors online, clients and escorts obviate the need to discuss payment, prices, and sexual behaviors at the same time. In fact, escorts are wary of clients who discuss prices, as this is taken as evidence that they could be police officers.[11] In fact, how-to guides for clients and escorts advise both to keep contractual discussions to a minimum:

Understand, though, that they might not be able to fully describe over the phone what they do because they don't want to get busted . . . Most escorts will not discuss specific sexual acts for sale. Such is illegal and their services are for time and companionship only. Money is exchanged for time only, the decision to have sex would be a mutual and consensual decision two adults make. Upon meeting the escort, you may be asked certain questions about any possible affiliation with law enforcement.[12]

Second, escorts compete with one another on these websites. While clients calling a traditional escort agency can be steered to a particular sex worker, clients of male escorts can freely choose between hundreds of options. This is close to the assumption of a market with many sellers. In such a market, clients may be unwilling to engage escorts who do not post their prices or who appear to be less forthcoming about the services they offer, especially if their competitors are forthcoming. Some qualitative interviews with escorts have revealed that escorts post prices as a way to ensure that clients who contact them can afford their services.[13]

Third, by setting their prices publicly, escorts avoid the time otherwise spent haggling with clients over prices, a staple of street prostitution.[14] Escorts assume that any client contacting them knows their price and will pay the posted rate for services, just as any other business owner would expect customers to pay the advertised rate. While the online advertisement sites are clear that money is not exchanged for sex and is only compensation for an escort's time, the value of that time is not subject to negotiation, either. Despite this publicly posted information about illegal activity, police raids of online male escorts are surprisingly rare.

There are several sources that describe the generic male escort encounter.[15] Clients contact escorts directly and arrange for appointments either at the home of the escort (an "incall") or at the home or hotel of the client (an "outcall"). In the most basic form of an outcall, a client will search escort advertisements and choose an escort. If an appointment is immediately desired, such as the same day, the client will usually phone the escort. Appointments for future dates may be arranged by e-mail, although some escorts prefer to make all appointments by phone. Escorts generally encourage clients to describe the length of the desired appointment and to note any circumstances of which the escort should be aware (e.g., manner of dress required by client and clients who may be disabled). Escort and client then discuss the time and location of the appointment. Once the escort arrives at the location, he meets the client and the two may have a brief discussion to reaffirm the earlier phone conversation. Payment is almost never discussed face-to-face. Money is usually exchanged after the appointment ends, but clients are encouraged to place the money in plain view, such as on a dresser or desk, either before the escort arrives or at the beginning of the appointment.

Interestingly, one reason the street market may be preferred to the online market, from a client perspective, is that misrepresentation would be rare. On the street, a client can see the available sex workers and choose one after negotiation. The problem is that the client can only choose from the escorts available at the time he is looking – he cannot schedule a future meeting nor can he see all of the available sex workers. Itiel (1998) notes that male escorts and clients have less leeway to informally penalize misrepresentation than street sex workers and their clients. While street sex workers and clients can freely disengage from a transaction for whatever reason by simply walking away, the clandestine nature of an "incall" or "outcall" makes it difficult for either party to escape penalty free if there has been any misrepresentation. For example, once the escort has arrived at the hotel door or home of a client, it may be difficult to induce him to leave without payment of some sort. Also, once the misrepresentation is revealed, the client (and potentially the escort) is already exposed: the escort knows the client's location, almost certainly some form of contact information, and the client may be open to blackmail and harassment depending on his circumstances. Moreover, clients cannot appeal to an intermediary's reputation to minimize their exposure. There is no pimp, madam, or escort agency acting as a guarantor. The very nature of the male sex market alters the usual interpretation of the risks involved in sex work. While male escorts are seen as a "safer bet" than male street sex workers, the overall structure in the market is one in which the client is at risk of harm.[16]

Unlike female sex workers, who are at greater risk of being violated by clients, male sex workers are more prone to violate their clients. Clients are at risk in a number of ways, and the harm from hiring an unsavory escort can have serious consequences. First, escorts may simply rob clients; a traditional scam is to request payment up front and then feign an excuse to leave, never to return. Another common ploy is to steal the client's wallet in the course of an appointment. In online forums, by far the most frequent complaint from clients is that escorts take payment but do not deliver services.

Second, an escort may blackmail a client or expose his client's sexual behaviors. As noted earlier, clients and escorts usually communicate by way of telephone or e-mail before the appointment. Most escorts refuse calls from clients who have a "blocked" phone number, and this exposes clients to a risk of blackmail because escorts can trace the client's phone number. Escorts could threaten to "out" a client, to inform his family of his sexual practices, to contact his employer, or even to contact legal authorities, since the client has solicited prostitution. The case of Ted Haggard (the former president of the National Association of Evangelicals, who became embroiled in a sex scandal involving a male escort in 2006) is one in which the escort kept voicemail messages from the client and later released them to the press. The additional social stigma attached to being exposed as a homosexual, particularly for men who hold positions of power in conservative religious or political organizations, can be career ending.

Several prominent political careers have been damaged by allegations of involvement with male sex workers.[17] In addition to the well-publicized national cases, local politicians have also been exposed. In 2003, Utah State Representative Brent Parker (R) resigned when accused of soliciting an undercover police officer. In 2006, Tom Malin lost a Democratic primary bid for the Texas State Legislature when it was revealed that he had formerly been an escort.

Finally, since escorts are relatively young and virile men, physical violence is not uncommon. While escorts usually have someone they will keep abreast of the location and contact information for every appointment in case of an emergency, clients are less likely to let others know of their whereabouts, leaving themselves particularly vulnerable.[18] In online forums, clients themselves mention instances in which escorts either attacked them or threatened them with bodily harm. Clients describe being punched, kicked, threatened or attacked with knives, guns, and other deadly weapons. For example, one client noted "The time an escort grabbed me by the throat and slammed me up against wall rifling my pockets for my wallet. Then punched me a couple of times for not bringing my ATM and credit card."[19] Moreover, these crimes are likely to be unreported, since the client would be forced to reveal how he came to know the escort in question.

Unlike the markets for other services, where clients may not choose to pursue legal redress for small matters, clients of male escorts do not have the option of seeking redress for any grievance, regardless of size. While one may be compensated in-kind for poor service at a restaurant, for example, there is no evidence of similar arrangements in the male escort market, even for relatively petty grievances. Escorts are not known to offer compensation or in kind services to dissatisfied clients.

The dangers that clients face increase their incentive to police the market. Without some form of policing, the market would be difficult for clients to navigate. Even with policing by clients, there are limits to how effectively an illegal market can be policed. Even in well-functioning online markets there are fraudulent sellers, and online services spend a great deal of time screening sellers. In the next section, I show exactly how clients informally police the market to minimize the probability that they will hire an unscrupulous escort.

EVIDENCE FROM THE DEMAND SIDE OF THE MALE ESCORT MARKET

Informal Enforcement in the Male Escort Market

Why would clients be driven to police the market for male escort services? While policing helps the market to function, it comes at a cost to individual clients that benefits not only themselves but also clients who do not police the market. The precise motivations behind client policing are difficult to ascertain. The clients active in policing are providing a service to the market that enhances its ability to operate. It may be due to egalitarian feelings, a desire to protect others, or knowledge that their activities are critical to a market they are eager to be active in.

When a firm discloses information it is inherently making a promise to the consumer. Theoretically, in order for the signals that escorts send to be informative, there must be a reasonable basis for the client to trust the accuracy of the signal.[20] Most economic models of signaling assume that signaling is truthful and that misrepresentation does not exist. In these types of models, when an escort signals, his sending a signal acts as a commitment device.[21]

The key issue when misrepresentation is forbidden is whether to disclose information at all, since the information must be truthful. This issue is pertinent for firms that would expose themselves to significant liability if they were to knowingly mislead consumers. In an illegal market, however, such guarantees cannot be made and informal policing may be the only option. Clients may police the market because they have little choice if they would like to minimize the probability of dealing with a deceptive escort. Since the websites that host advertisements for male escorts derive no income from clients and maximize profits by hosting the largest number of advertisements, they pay little attention to clients' complaints about deceptive escorts who advertise on the websites. Interestingly, one client framed the situation in the classic used-car reference familiar to most economists:

That site is an advertising site, not an agency. If the used car you buy turns out to be a lemon, do you take it up with the paper that ran the classified ad for it? Could you imagine what managing that he said/he said would be like?

Just as the purchaser of a car advertised in the newspaper does not hold the newspaper responsible for the car being a lemon, clients of escorts cannot hold the website responsible for hosting advertisements of escorts who turn out to be fraudulent, dangerous, or deceptive.[22]

In this market, clients police escorts in two ways: through posts to independent, client-owned forums and through detailed reviews of escort services on the escort websites, which are linked to the respective escort's advertisement. The primary functions of client-based forums are information gathering by potential clients and posting of detailed reviews of escort services. In the forums, clients ask other clients for leads to good escorts in an area with which they are not familiar and clients post unsolicited information about escorts.[23] This information is available to all interested users. The following exchange is typical. "CLIENT #1: I've been drooling over an ad in Chicago who had been listed on XXX as "XXX." Anybody know more? CLIENT#2 (Response): I can add some information on this guy. I actually can't remember the name he used, but I do remember the photos. He quoted me $300 and listed himself as a dominant top. He showed up at my hotel on time and when I opened the door I didn't think his face looked the same as the face pic on the ad. I don't think the other pics on his current ad are him though. So in a nutshell, buyer beware."

These forums can be used to highlight a number of dangers regarding escorts. Escorts can create deceptive advertisements on escort websites, use multiple aliases, and even steal from their clients. The forum acts to ensure that these rogue escorts are exposed to clients. The following is an example of such a warning. "[Link to escort advertisement] I hope this link works and I want to let everyone to know to STAY AWAY!!!! He stole $500 from my house and is in partnership with John, Johnny, Joe . . . [he] also goes by Jake, Michael and many other names . . . ."

The reviews on the website offer a different type of assessment. The reviews of these escorts act as public goods, much more so than the forums. The reviews describe a specific transaction with an escort. The reviews contain a great deal of information that is free form. The reviews are searchable by city or escort, allowing any client to obtain information about an escort without having to ask.

Additionally, clients can also write reviews of escort services on escort websites. These reviews allow for free form opinions of the escort's services and are directly linked to, and a product of, the advertisement website. They usually contain a great deal of information about the escort and his behavior during a particular appointment – clients give information on how the appointment was made, specific information regarding the escort during the appointment, such as escort hygiene, physical appearance, conversational ability, the escort's manner of dress, sexual activities provided, and the price charged. While the escort websites do give escorts the option of allowing themselves to be reviewed by clients (nearly 95 percent in the data allow it), escorts have no control over the reviews and all reviews are posted if the escort allows reviews. This all-or-nothing nature of reviews is a key advantage of these reputation measures, in that escorts have no control over their reviews: all reviews for the escort are retained on the website, not a selected sample posted or chosen by the escort.

The market policing by clients allows for the stock of information to be large: clients who would never meet exchange information about escorts, and clients who never review escorts can access a large amount of information about escorts. While the cost per client to share information is relatively high, given the amount of time it would take to write a detailed review, the returns to the accumulated knowledge are also high. These policing measures also allow disclosure to be credible. Theoretically, the policing and reviews raise the cost of deception for the untrustworthy escort, creating a wedge where the honest escort can credibly signal and receive a premium for doing so. A deceptive escort would need to create a totally new advertisement with new pictures and new contact information to continue to operate in the market once he had been discovered as being deceptive. These new identities are not without cost. This means the cost of being a deceptive escort is greater than that of being a truthful escort. This cost differential is a necessary condition for signaling to be informative – and the cost differential could only exist if clients police the market.

Identifying the Signal

Due to the inherent dangers in male sex work and the unique situation where male sex workers have to provide information to their clients with regard to their honesty and safety, the information flow is from escorts to clients. Clients choose escorts from many available options, and clients reveal that they choose escorts based on both physical characteristics and cues as to who will not pose a threat to their security and privacy. High-quality escorts will show up on time, match their advertised description, provide the agreed upon services at the advertised price, be discreet, and generally act in a manner respectful of the client's privacy and safety.

What information do clients consider when they hire a male escort? What type of information is more likely to be observed, given a particular type? Using the same client-based forums that serve as policing, I identify the types of information that escorts and clients take as important in male escort advertisements. Clients reveal that they pay particular attention to the presence of face pictures (ideally multiple face pictures) in an escort's advertisement as a signal of truthfulness. Clients explicitly and implicitly note that face pictures are more likely to be observed when the escort is high quality.

I've been tempted [to hire an escort with no face pictures] but have always ended up feeling let down by anyone without a face-shot so I've stayed away.

As far as pics that are probably not real, same deal, do not hire. No one has just a professional modeling pic or two and no other pics. They need to have more than one face pic in their ads.

Even in their advertisements, escorts note that face pictures are what clients take into account. Escorts agree that face pictures transmit information about quality in their advertisements to clients and in their advice to other escorts.

Don't get fooled by escorts using headless picture, they are often fake! Choose the certified one! A real man!

Indeed, escorts who do not have face pictures in their advertisements apologize for the lack of them.

Good looking all-American . . . clean-cut type . . . Sorry no face pic but you won't
be disappointed!!

The qualitative evidence suggests that escorts and clients treat face pictures
as particularly valuable information and a signal that the escort is unlikely
to misrepresent himself.

There are several reasons why face pictures would be a signal of quality.
Face pictures give a key measure of immediate representativeness: upon
meeting the escort, the client would know whether the escort was "as
advertised." This would allow a client to minimize any potential losses,
since misrepresentation would be obvious. Escorts who do show their face
convey that they have less to hide. They are willing to be publicly identified,
making it less likely they will violate the client or expose him to blackmail
or harassment, since they could be readily recognized by third parties.
Posting a face picture is similar to posting a bond – it decreases the
probability that an escort would misrepresent himself, and therefore act
as advertisements for quality.[24] Showing face pictures not only acts as
a signal of quality, but could also be interpreted by clients as commitment
device (a special case of disclosure). A deceptive escort, once discovered,
cannot costlessly reinvent himself. Also, clients can use face pictures as
a search characteristic when looking for male escort services. Escorts who
do not show their faces may not want to be identified because of their
occupation and/or because they are not high quality. Not signaling is one
way of ensuring anonymity, which makes it easier to deceive clients.

CONCEPTUAL AND EMPIRICAL FRAMEWORK

The key issue is whether or not there is a response by the clients to the
signal. There are two possibilities: either the market responds to the signal
offered by escorts or it does not. Theoretically, this would be a separating or
pooled equilibrium. In the pooled equilibrium, the signal does not lead to
wage differences – all escorts would be paid the same, whether they signal
or not. In the separating equilibrium, there is separation between types,
where the signalers receive a higher wage than non-signalers. In this case
the signal is informative as it leads clients to believe that the escort is more
likely to be a high-quality escort.

In an illegal market such as male sex work, it is difficult to specify which
equilibrium would hold. Most signaling models implicitly assume that
some type of formal enforcement or institution guarantees truthful disclosure. For example, in the simplest version of the classic signaling model in

Spence (1973), workers obtain otherwise useless education to signal their ability to employers. If schools could not certify that an agent had actually obtained the years of schooling she claimed (for example, by printing fraudulent degrees or transcripts), anyone could act as if they had the highest level of education possible. Such fraud would obviously decrease the value of the signal and, in the extreme, the signal would have no value.

There are several reasons we might expect a pooled equilibrium for male sex work. First, the degree of uncertainty could be large, which can cause clients to react to signals weakly, if at all. The information being provided comes from websites advertising sex work services, after all. Second, the cost differential for signaling by type may be particularly small in this market. Although clients act to police the market, this may not result in a substantial cost differential between those that would signal and those that would not. If deceptive escorts could easily produce fake face pictures, clients would have no ability to discern quality from the signal itself. Any client without direct experience with a given escort would be fundamentally uninformed (or less than fully informed) as to the escort's true quality, since deception is a distinct possibility. Since the cost of signaling against type for the deceptive escort may not be much higher than that of the genuinely high-quality escort, it is difficult to argue on theoretical grounds that clients would trust the veracity of the signal.[25] By the same token, it is not clear that reputation would solve the problem, since those describing the reputation of the escort may have ulterior motives. For example, positive reviews may be left by the escort or his associates, and negative reviews by competitors.

I therefore test for whether information – in particular, the signal of face pictures – leads to wage difference (separation) in this market. If there is separation, then the market partially overcomes the problem of asymmetric information. Most important, it would do so without formal enforcement.[26] While, theoretically, the question is whether or not the signal has value, an additional empirical question looks at how much value the signal has relative to the value of a signal in a market where formal enforcement is present – whether legal and illegal markets value information to the same degree.

The key empirical question is the value of the signal. The task is to test whether the expected value (average price, w) of male sex workers who use face pictures, the signal (s) identified earlier, is greater than the average price of those who do not, holding other escort characteristics (x) constant

$$E(w|x, s > 0) > E(w|x, s = 0) \qquad (1)$$

Following empirical studies of information in markets, I use a regression of the escort's price (which is also the wage he earns for his services) on the information he provides in his advertisement. I take the usual interpretation that the coefficients reflect a consumer's willingness to pay for each characteristic, and therefore reflect the characteristic's value. While there have been criticisms of this interpretation due to restrictive assumptions, Bajari and Benkard (2005) show that the interpretation holds and that the price function is identified under very general conditions that apply to this case.[27] If the market separates based on the signal identified, then face pictures will have value in terms of escort prices. I therefore regress the escort's hourly price on the signal in the advertisements (*Signal*), reputation and reviews (*R*), personal characteristics (*Z*), and identifiers for location/market (*X*).[28]

$$\ln(P_i) = \phi + \gamma Signal_i + \varphi R_i + \delta Z_i + \lambda X_i + \varepsilon_i \qquad (2)$$

In contrast to other studies that analyze the total amount of information in the market, I disaggregate the information in order to estimate the value of particular types of information. While pictures may have value, pictures were not the signal that clients looked for from escorts. I therefore estimate the value of pictures in general and specific types of pictures, namely face pictures. Based on the institutional analysis presented earlier, I hypothesize that face pictures are the key type of information that leads to separation in the market for male sex work, which is a clue to see whether this market functions well by overcoming the problems of asymmetric information. If the market takes face pictures as a signal of escort quality, we would expect γ to be positive. If not, then participants do not respond to the signal either because it is not believed or because it is a noisy signal of quality to which market prices do not respond.

DATA FROM THE ONLINE MALE ESCORT MARKET

Since the issue is type of picture listed, I recorded not only the number of pictures, but also the type of pictures in each advertisement. In particular, I look at three categories of pictures – pictures that show an escort's face in a distinguishable way (which may or may not include nudity), pictures that show a nude body only (either from the front or the back, but with no face shown), and pictures that show neither nudity nor an escort's face (pictures of torsos, biceps, legs, feet, etc.). While nudity is allowed, escorts may not post pictures that display sex acts and may not

Table 2.1 *Summary statistics for the escort sample*

Variable	Whole sample		No face pictures		Face pictures	
	Mean	Std. dev.	Mean	Std. dev.	Mean	Std. dev.
Price	216.88	64.46	187.09	64.54	231.59	59.15
Log of price	5.34	0.29	5.18	0.31	5.41	0.25
Spot price	217.86	64.49	188.52	64.52	232.30	59.40
Number of pictures	6.14	2.84	5.17	2.81	6.61	2.73
Body-only pictures	2.08	2.07	3.16	2.39	1.55	1.66
Face pictures	2.90	2.96	0.00	0.00	4.32	2.63
Survey reviews	3.18	6.72	3.25	7.43	3.15	6.34
Text reviews	0.35	1.03	0.36	1.16	0.35	0.96
Fraction Good Survey	0.88	0.27	0.86	0.31	0.89	0.25
Fraction Good Text	0.88	0.30	0.89	0.29	0.87	0.31

Notes:
Fraction Good Survey and Fraction Good Text are defined over escorts with survey or text reviews, respectively.
Price is the outcall price posted by an escort in his advertisement.
If an escort has both a spot price and a posted price, or no posted price and a spot price, the spot price replaces the posted price.

display pictures that include persons other than the escort. Uploaded pictures are placed in an online holding tank until cleared by the website's management. Every advertisement must be accompanied by at least one picture.

Table 2.1 shows the summary statistics for the escorts in the data. In terms of information, escorts post an average of six pictures in their advertisements and have three survey reviews, and one escort in three has a text review. Two-thirds of escorts post at least one face picture and, on average, escorts post three pictures containing their face and two containing their nude body with no face shown. There are some differences when looking at the summary statistics for escorts sorted by whether they post face pictures. For example, the average escort who shows pictures of his face posts nearly seven pictures, four of which are of his face. The average escort who does not show pictures of his face posts five pictures, three of which are of his nude body. Escorts who post face pictures charge approximately $230 an hour, while escorts who do not post face picture charge approximately $190 an hour. Below, I check to see if these differences in prices hold after controlling for various individual, reputation, and geographic differences that have the potential to explain the price difference between sex workers who post face pictures and those who do not.

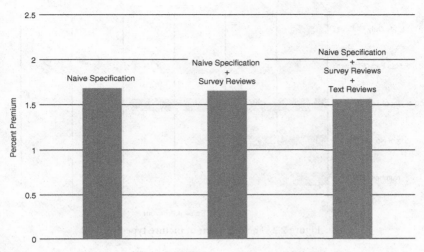

Figure 2.1 The value of pictures in escort advertisements

FACE VALUE

Figure 2.1 reports the results from various ordinary least squares (OLS) regression specifications, where I regress the escort's log hourly price on the number of pictures and a large number of controls such as escort characteristics and location.[29] This is a naïve specification, since it treats all pictures equally and considers only the quantity of pictures. The first estimate shows that the number of pictures in an escort's advertisement is strongly related to the escort's price, controlling for individual characteristics and market location. Each additional picture increases an escort's price by 1.7 percent. The magnitude of the premium for pictures is close to the premium noted by Lewis (2009) for used cars on eBay.com (which is between 1.66 and 1.82 percent), one of the few estimates for the value of information in legal markets. I find that information has value in this illegal market just as it does in legal markets where enforcement is formal.[30]

The second estimate is the value of pictures when I add the more coarse measure of reputation: survey reviews. By themselves, survey reviews do not exert a significant effect on prices, but the effect of pictures on prices remains the same even when this measure of quality is included. Recall that these reviews were just star ratings of escorts and asked a simple set of questions about performance. They did not reference a specific transaction nor do they allow clients to offer further details. For the third estimate, I add the more detailed and informative measure of reputation: free form text reviews. Text

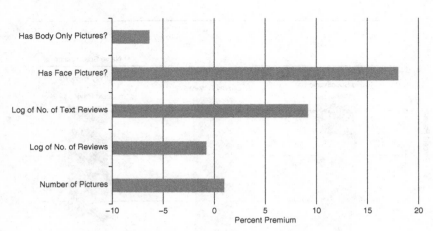

Figure 2.2 The premium of picture types

reviews are strongly and positively related to prices, but the effect is quite small, less than one-half of one percent. Consistent with other results in the literature, reputation affects prices in the male escort market.[31]

Figure 2.2 shows a set of results for a different specification, where the number of pictures is included as well as a dichotomous measure for the presence of face pictures in an advertisement. The institutional evidence presented earlier suggests that face pictures are the key measure of truthfulness in the market, and we therefore expect their presence to be positively related to escort prices if they are a signal of quality. The effect of face pictures on prices is quite large. Escorts who post pictures of their faces have prices that are more than 20 percent higher than those that do not, even after controlling for both measures of reputation and a host of individual escort and market characteristics.[32] Additionally, including a measure of whether face pictures are present significantly reduces the relationship between total pictures and the escort's price – the coefficient on number of pictures is reduced by more than 50 percent once the indicator for face pictures is included (see Figure 2.1). I also include a dichotomous measure of having a nude body picture with no face shown. The effect of having nude, headless photos actually *reduces* the price by more than 5 percent. If an escort sees an average of twenty clients per month, the difference would amount to roughly $10,000 per year in additional earnings for the escorts who post face pictures.

While Figure 2.2 examines the role of information at the extensive margin, Figure 2.3 presents the results from the preferred specifications, in which I use the number of face and body pictures in the specification.

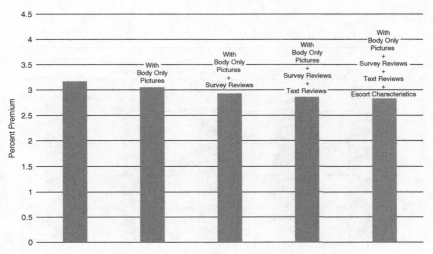

Figure 2.3 The premium of face pictures

I investigate the premium to each additional face picture and body picture to see how much of the total premium to pictures in Figure 2.1 can be attributed to each type of picture an escort will display.

In Figure 2.3 I use the number of face and body-only pictures as the measures of information. This specification is similar to the naïve specification for all pictures, where now I can estimate, directly, the value of face pictures. The first estimate shows that the premium to each face picture is large – each additional face picture increases the price charged by an escort by roughly 3 percent, nearly twice the premium of total pictures reported earlier. Put another way, one standard deviation in the number of face pictures increases escort prices by 0.3 of standard deviations, a large effect on prices for sex workers. In the second estimate I add body-only pictures and find that they are not significantly related to prices. For the third and fourth estimates I add the two measures of reputation and find that they behave similarly to the results in Figure 2.1, where survey reviews are not related to prices and where text reviews are strongly related to escort prices. Finally, I control for a host of escort- and market-specific characteristics and the result holds – the premium to face pictures is much larger than the premium to pictures overall, and body-only pictures are not significantly related to prices.

In Figure 2.3 the results come from a specification where I allow picture types to enter directly, but this can be problematic since escorts who convey different information may also use different numbers of pictures. As the summary results (Table 2.1) showed, escorts who post face pictures also post

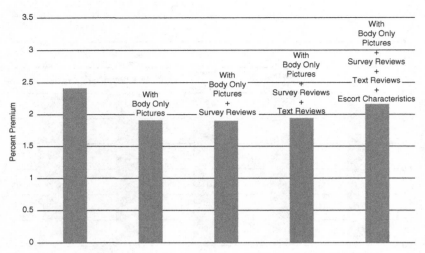

Figure 2.4 The premium for the fraction of pictures that are face pictures

more pictures overall. To see if this drives the relationship between prices and face pictures, in Figure 2.4 I report the results where I use a specification that controls for the total number of pictures in an advertisement to focus on the *composition* of the information, the fraction of pictures that are face pictures, rather than the quantity of information. To ease interpretation, the results are presented in terms of the premium for a 10 percent increase in the fraction of face pictures in an escort's advertisement, such as having three of ten pictures being face pictures as opposed to two of ten pictures being face pictures. For the first estimate I include only the number of pictures and the share of pictures that are face pictures. Consistent with the results in Figure 2.3, the fraction of face pictures is strongly related to escort prices. One standard deviation in the fraction of face pictures increases escort prices by 0.12 of a standard deviation. I then add the fraction of pictures that are body-only pictures and find that they are negatively related to prices, but their effect on prices (in absolute value) is much smaller than the effect of face pictures. As earlier, I then add measures of reputation, and the effect of a larger fraction of pictures being face pictures is still positive and of similar size to the most basic results.[33] (The inclusion of the additional reputation measures does lessen the magnitude of the effect of body-only pictures, and they cease to be statistically significant.[34]) The effect of face pictures is robust to the inclusion of reputational measures, which suggests that face pictures are a different signal of quality and not a direct substitute for the information contained in reviews.

Taken together, Figures 2.1–2.4 establish that information and reputation are important in the market for male sex work and that each is priced in a different manner. While the amount of information matters (each picture increases prices by roughly 1.5 percent), the quality of the information matters more (each face picture increases prices by 3 percent). In fact, the entire premium to information in the market is driven by face pictures.[35] Also, reputation matters in the market, but only in the form of free form text reviews, which contain more information about an escort's quality and behavior than do survey reviews. This implies that the information regarding reputation also varies depending upon how it is delivered.

What, exactly, do face pictures and the text reviews signal? While they both appear to signal quality, it is likely that they each signal a different component of quality. The first and most important would be "basic quality." Basic quality includes the escort's truthfulness and the client's safety, and is the most fundamental aspect of quality. Escorts who are high in basic quality will show up on time, match their advertised description, provide the agreed upon services at the advertised price, be discreet, and generally act in a manner respectful of the client's privacy and safety. This is the type of quality likely signaled with face pictures. A second aspect of quality is something I define as skill at providing services, or "service quality." Service quality refers to how well the escort performs services relative to others. Given that the two types of quality are different and serve different functions, it is not surprising that they have similar (but empirically distinct) effects on prices.

The results support the idea that the information environment afforded by the Internet allows male sex workers to signal their type successfully via face pictures and receive a premium for doing so. It also supports the hypothesis that face pictures are a specific signal of quality in this market. The results also support the idea that reputations are best established with evidence of the type of experience clients could expect from an escort. More importantly, the results suggest that the value of information conveyed in an illegal market is similar to the value of information provided in a legal market.

RULING OUT ALTERNATIVE EXPLANATIONS FOR THE VALUE OF FACE PICTURES

The previous section presented evidence in support the interpretation of face pictures as a signal of basic quality. However, that interpretation is subject to several criticisms, given the cross-sectional nature of the data.

First, though the price responds positively to the presence of face pictures, the value of face pictures should be finite – if every face picture increased prices that would be implausible. Below I show that the marginal value of face pictures decreases as a function of the number of face pictures. This is what we would expect – while showing the first few face pictures is a signal of basic quality, sending several would not increase the signal itself. Second, it is possible that clients respond to empty signals of quality. In other words, price differences do not reflect signaling as much as a client's wishful belief that face pictures convey credibility. I explore this possibility below and find it to be inconsistent with the evidence. Third, the results could be driven by a beauty premium as opposed to a signal of quality. Naturally, physical attractiveness would be related to prices and would be displayed via face pictures. I provide suggestive evidence that beauty is not the driving force behind the face picture premium. Lastly, I construct a counterfactual and show that where client policing is stymied, the value of the signal decreases substantially. This is confirmatory evidence that information only has value when the signal is rendered credible by client policing.

Marginal Face Value

Since the interpretation of the price effect of face pictures hinges on face pictures being a signal of quality, it is critical to estimate the marginal value of face pictures. The marginal value of face pictures should be a decreasing function of the number of face pictures. Once a threshold of credibility is attained, additional pictures should not convey additional quality. If this were not so, escorts could be rewarded for infinite numbers of face pictures. This would imply that the signal had infinitely positive value, and that would certainly be difficult to justify if the signal is one of basic quality. In the review of client forums, clients note that they look for multiple pictures of an escort's face, but there should be a limit to their value after some reasonable number of pictures establishes that the escort in question is not deceptive.

To estimate the marginal value of face pictures, I estimate a polynomial function of the value of face pictures.[36] I plot the marginal value as a function of the number of face pictures in Figure 2.5. As the figure shows, the marginal value of face pictures decreases sharply, approaching zero at the seventh picture. These marginal values are consistent with the interpretation of the results for face pictures being a signal of basic quality. The average value of face pictures is large, but the marginal value of the eighth

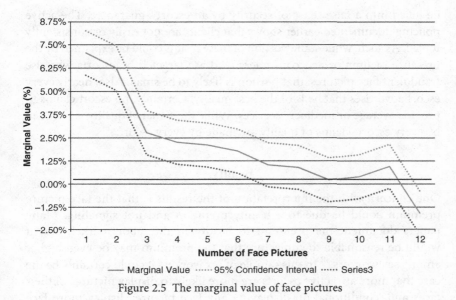

Figure 2.5 The marginal value of face pictures

additional face picture is indistinguishable from zero. While the signal has value, excessive signaling is not rewarded in this market.[37]

True Quality

It could be that clients are responding to empty signals of quality. Uninformed clients could certainly be duped into believing claims that are not supported. Jin and Kato (2006), for example, conducted an experiment on eBay.com auctions for baseball cards and found that while advertised quality was positively related to price, actual quality was not. They conclude that sellers in online markets target uninformed buyers, and that eBay.com's system of universal ratings and anonymous identities allows this situation to persist. In essence, clients could respond to signals that turn out not to truly be signals related to quality. Lewis (2009) contends that Jin and Kato's result may be due to the fact that the stakes are relatively low in the auctions that they study, where the baseball cards in question are not very expensive. It is certainly true that the stakes for misrepresentation are high in the market for male sex work, both in dollar value and the potential negative outcomes from misrepresentation. Furthermore, while buyers in online markets such as eBay.com have some form of formal protection from fraud, the clients of a male escort do not have any formal or implied guarantees against fraud: it is not possible for them to be lulled into a false sense of security by an escort's guarantee. The active policing documented earlier shows that clients are not easily or consistently fooled. As such, while some portion of these results could be explained by the presence of uninformed consumers who are targeted by escorts who use fraudulent face pictures, that portion is likely to be small. Also, nearly every escort advertises that he is of the best quality. Certainly, no escort claims to provide average or mediocre services. While the signal of quality is not used by every escort, claims of quality are made by every escort.

Beauty

One concern with the interpretation of the results is that the face picture premium could be due to a beauty premium and not signaling. Many papers document the premium to beauty in the labor market, and it would be reasonable to conjecture that the premium may be even higher among sex workers.[38] In this sample of sex workers it could certainly be the case that more attractive escorts are more likely to display pictures of their faces and, conditional on displaying any face picture, display more face pictures. It is doubtful, however, that all attractive escorts show their faces since men may not want long-lived evidence of their careers in commercial sex on the Internet.[39]

I tackle the issue of beauty directly by obtaining beauty measures for the escorts in the data. I first address the issue that more attractive sex workers may display more face pictures, conditional on displaying any picture. I then discuss the potential selection issue that more-attractive sex workers might be more likely to display face pictures in general. To do so the beauty of the male escorts was rated independently by a group of men. Beauty was scored from 1 to 5, with 1 being the least attractive, and 5 being the most attractive. These types of rating systems are standard for measures of physical attractiveness. Both openly gay and closeted men were requested to serve as enumerators, since heterosexually identified men likely make up a non-negligible portion of the client base.[40] Nearly 90 percent of the escorts who show their face pictures in the data were given beauty scores; the mean beauty score is 3 and the standard deviation 1.2.[41]

In Figure 2.6 I present results of the value of face pictures where I also include estimates of escort beauty. Since subjective ratings of beauty and other personal characteristics may differ across enumerators, giving rise to a spurious correlation, the estimates include enumerator-fixed effects in all specifications. The first bar shows the estimate of the premium to face pictures for comparison, but in this instance only includes the escorts for

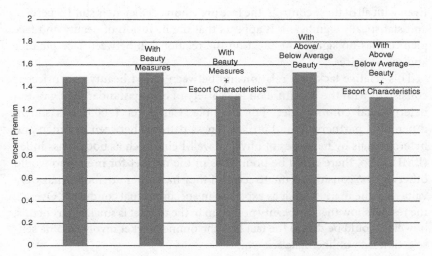

Figure 2.6 The premium to face pictures when beauty is also measured

whom I have beauty scores.[42] Conditional on posting face pictures, the premium for each additional face picture is 1.5 percent, which is similar to the previous estimates. In the second estimate I include the measure of beauty, and find that while positively correlated with log hourly price, the coefficient is not statistically significant and the effect on the value of face pictures is nonexistent. The main face picture result remains statistically significant and has a magnitude of 1.5 percent. Therefore, even after controlling for escort beauty, the main result remains consistent and statistically significant. I then include all the various control measures, such as race, height, weight, body type, and eye color, and the beauty coefficient, though smaller and still positive, is not statistically significant, and the inclusion of beauty and these individual measures (which could be correlated with beauty) does not significantly change the face picture premium.

Perhaps it is not beauty differences between a "2" and a "5" that matter, however. It could be a case of simply being or not being attractive. The next estimate in Figure 2.6 explores whether returns to beauty may be nonlinear by including a dichotomous indicator for above-average beauty (beauty score equals 4 or 5) and below-average beauty (beauty score equals 1 or 2). Again, neither of the beauty measures is statistically significant, although the point estimates show that above-average beauty is rewarded and below-average beauty is not. Last, I include the above- and below-average beauty measures along with the various control measures for escort characteristics.

Even with all of these controls, the face premium coefficient is still 1.5 percent and statistically significant. It appears that the inclusion of beauty and face pictures has no significant effect on the relationship between face pictures and escort prices.

This relative lack of a relationship between escort beauty and prices is consistent with the literature on the variety of beauty standards in gay and heterosexual communities. For example, Carpenter (2003) has shown differential partnership and attractiveness patterns between gay men and heterosexuals by measures of physical well-being such as body mass index (BMI). Also, there could be premiums in the market for men who would otherwise be considered unattractive if they had other attributes that were valued by the market, such as expertise in specific sexual conduct.[43] Overall, the results show that the beauty premium in the market is small – part of this, however, could be due to the fact that the online market involves some self-selection into online male sex work.

Recall that the results in Figure 2.6 show estimates of the effect of face pictures on prices for the men who show their faces in their advertisements. Therefore, there might be selection by beauty into posting – i.e., more beautiful men might be more likely to post face pictures. Ultimately, I cannot rule out this explanation definitively, but I can use the results of Figure 2.6, and the other coefficients in the specifications, to roughly calculate how much beauty could explain the difference between men who do and do not show their face pictures. To estimate the maximum of the proportion of the results that could be due to beauty, assume that all men who do not post their face picture are rated a beauty that is *strictly less* than the *lowest* rated beauty (that men who do not show their faces have a beauty rating of, say, zero, where the lowest beauty rating allowed is one) and that men who do post their faces are rated as the highest beauty score (every man who shows a face picture is a "5"). Even under this implausible assumption, the differences in the beauty premium between the two groups (4.5 percent) could explain, at best, less than one-quarter of the face picture premium (which is 20 percent). Put another way, even the least attractive man is still much better off showing a picture of his face than not, as the "no picture" penalty is more than four times as large as the "unattractive" penalty. This implies that beauty can explain, at best, a small fraction of the estimated face picture premium.

In the data there are also the physical characteristics of the escorts. If more beautiful escorts select into providing face pictures and have different physical characteristics, then a comparison of the distribution of characteristics of escorts who do and do not show face pictures would reveal such differences. Overall, the results show that along nearly every dimension of physical characteristics, the escorts who provide face pictures are statistically similar to those who do not. Out of more than twenty physical characteristics (e.g., hair color, eye color, body type), there are only three instances where escorts who show their face pictures are significantly different from those that do not: escorts who show their face pictures are more likely to be blond (14 percent versus 10 percent) and have an "athletic/swimmer's" build (50 percent versus 42 percent); escorts who do not show their faces are *more* likely to be muscular, however (34 percent versus 28 percent).[44]

This issue is also addressed indirectly by considering second-order implications of the interpretation of the face picture premium. Consider that text reviews reveal information about the quality of the escort, but not the escort's beauty. If the premium to face pictures is due to beauty, then the interaction of face pictures with text reviews should be positive: beauty would be a *complement* to quality as described in the text reviews. If face pictures are a measure of quality, however, the interaction of face pictures and text reviews should be negative, as face pictures are *substitutes* for client descriptions of quality. In essence, this is a test of how the interaction of basic quality and service quality operate. The two should have a negative interaction if face pictures are indeed a signal of quality – but a positive interaction if face pictures are about beauty as opposed to quality. When I include the interaction of face pictures and text reviews in the specification, the interaction is negative in both instances (−0.009 [0.004] and −0.028 [0.031] for number and fraction, respectively). The results do not change when I interact the number or fraction of face pictures with the number of positive text reviews (−0.004 [0.002], −0.009 [0.013] for number and fraction, respectively). I take this as suggestive evidence that face pictures convey similar information about quality text reviews, and therefore are substitutes for quality measures.

If face pictures only conveyed beauty, then the marginal value of additional face pictures would be zero. Otherwise, additional pictures would have value, although, as I argued earlier, that value would decrease with the number of pictures as credibility is established. The results indicate that, on average, additional face pictures come with a 1.5 percent price premium, similar to the estimate in Figure 2.6. The premium I find applies to additional face pictures – two escorts of the same beauty would be paid differently if one supplied one face picture and the other supplied five. This is more consistent with the notion that face pictures establish quality rather than beauty, which can be ascertained from a single picture. Given the evidence presented above, I believe it is unlikely that the majority of the face picture premium is driven by beauty, although this cannot be established conclusively.

A Counterfactual – Signaling without Informal Enforcement

A key to the interpretation of face pictures as a signal of quality is the belief that informal policing by clients causes the signal that escorts send to be credible. Without the informal enforcement, the value of the signal would certainly be suspect. Additionally, informal policing would have little effect on beauty premiums or true quality in the market, since policing would not be related to escort beauty itself or the claims that escorts make about the quality of their services. Unfortunately, the value of informal enforcement is difficult to test directly. The data does give us one unique instance where I can observe the value of the signal when informal enforcement is lacking. As noted earlier, in the advertisement data escorts can choose whether or not they will allow themselves to be reviewed on the website. Disallowing reviews is all-or-nothing: escorts do not have the option of deleting or selectively posting reviews of either type. An escort who disallows reviews cannot establish a reputation in the data source. The vast majority of escorts (nearly 95 percent) allow themselves to be reviewed. In general the issue is moot since there is little variation.[45] There is one exception: the escorts in Las Vegas allow themselves to be reviewed only 40 percent of the time. Las Vegas is unique – there is no other city where fewer than 90 percent of the escorts disallow reviews. Of all escorts who disallow reviews, more than 35 percent are located in Las Vegas. It is doubtful that this is a state effect, since escorts in other Nevada cities allow reviews more than 90 percent of the time. While the exact cause of this curiosity is unknown,[46] I am able to test for the value of the signal in a location with little client policing. As described earlier, client policing allows signaling to be credible, so without client policing, the value of the signal should be negligible.

For comparison, Table 2.2 shows summary statistics for escorts based in Las Vegas and escorts based in five other randomly selected cities with similar numbers of escorts. As the table shows, the cities are all similar in terms of rates and escort attributes such as height and weight. Similarly, escorts in Las Vegas post the same average number of face pictures as those in other cities. In general, the Las Vegas market looks similar to the other markets shown in Table 2.2 and to the overall market, except for the fact that only 40 percent of Las Vegas escorts allow reviews.

Table 2.2 *Escort characteristics for selected cities*

	Summary statistics by city					
	Las Vegas	Chicago	Atlanta	Houston	Dallas	Boston
Observations	65	78	76	65	92	54
Review allowed?	0.40	0.96	0.93	0.98	0.95	0.96
	(0.49)	(0.20)	(0.26)	(0.12)	(0.22)	(0.19)
Price	227.36	231.79	232.74	209.9	207.12	232.13
	(66.95)	(57.20)	(86.38)	(57.93)	(62.65)	(51.74)
No. of pictures	6.44	6.38	6.52	6.18	6.46	6.24
	(2.75)	(2.57)	(2.82)	(2.69)	(2.77)	(2.97)
No. of face pictures	2.80	2.73	3.43	2.41	2.15	2.79
	(2.81)	(2.77)	(3.04)	(3.09)	(2.52)	(3.42)
Age (years)	28.75	27.48	27.33	26.35	29.31	26.7
	(6.97)	(6.02)	(6.19)	(6.29)	(6.91)	(5.88)
Height (inches)	70.88	70.62	70.56	70.06	70.44	69.76
	(2.70)	(2.95)	(2.59)	(2.49)	(2.67)	(2.80)
Weight (pounds)	172.23	166.59	166.46	168.02	169.41	165.43
	(25.02)	(30.16)	(21.77)	(23.48)	(24.47)	(31.31)

Standard deviations in parentheses.

In Figure 2.7 I show estimates for the value of face pictures, where I replicate the regressions presented earlier for each city separately. In every other city I find a large and significant premium to face pictures that matches the population estimates discussed earlier. Both the dichotomous and continuous measures of face pictures yield estimates close to the overall values for each city – except Las Vegas.

While the value of signaling is reasonably stable across markets, the results for Las Vegas are striking. In the Las Vegas market there is no premium to posting face pictures in an advertisement. This is not merely an artifact of statistical significance, the point estimates for the value of face pictures in Las Vegas (−0.09 for the dichotomous measure, 0.007 for the continuous measure) are much lower than for every other city in Figure 2.7. In the one location where client policing is stymied by escorts who do not allow client reviews, the credibility of the signal is in doubt and market prices do not respond to the signal. There appear to be spillovers, as well – even among escorts who allow reviews in Las Vegas, the value of face pictures is not statistically significant.[47] This result conforms to the interpretation of the premium to face pictures in the market. It would be cavalier, however, to suggest that these results for Las Vegas are definitive. Since there is no other location in the data with the same information differences, it is not possible

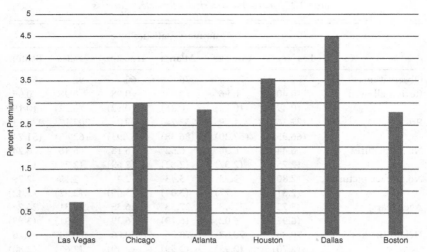

Figure 2.7 The face picture premium by city

to distinguish this effect from a location effect. While there is evidence that clients are aware of the increased probability of encountering low-quality escorts, it is unclear whether the escorts in Las Vegas are aware of the low value of information in their market. These results are inconsistent with either a beauty or true quality interpretation, unless one is willing to argue that escorts in Las Vegas are markedly less attractive than other escorts or are of uniformly different quality than escorts in other cities.

ROBUSTNESS

Prices

Thus far, all of the prices used are the prices in an escort's advertisement. Though the qualitative evidence suggests that the prices posted are the prices paid, it could be that escorts are more willing to price discriminate once they are alone with clients. If this is the case, the empirical strategy will yield biased estimates of the value of the signal. Fortunately, I have spot prices, specific transaction prices recorded by clients from the most recent text reviews of escorts, which I can compare to the prices that escorts post in their advertisements. Additionally, there are a small number of escorts who do not post their price, but have a spot price. As these are prices actually paid by clients in specific appointments, I can check the results with these prices.

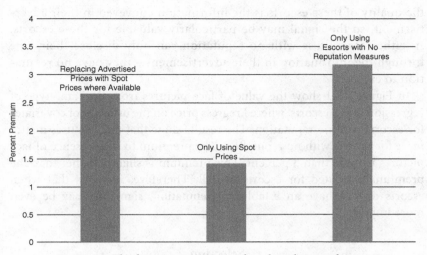

Figure 2.8 The face picture premium for selected types of escorts

Spot prices are well correlated with posted prices (the correlation is 0.89). Even so, I check the results with spot prices in two ways. First, I replace existing prices with spot prices where available. These results are reported in Figure 2.8. Even when actual prices paid replace advertised prices, this does not alter the results. As a more stringent test, I use only spot prices. Using only spot prices as the dependent variable reduces the size of the sample, but I still find that each face picture yields a premium of nearly 1.5 percent. The premium to each face picture is slightly smaller and may be due to the fact that the variation in the number of face pictures is much smaller for men with text reviews.

Another potential concern with the results is that they could be driven jointly by reputation and information. Although I have included measures of reputation in all of the specifications, it could be that men supply higher-quality information once their reputation is established, rather than the reverse. If the market is dominated by clients returning to the same escorts with whom they have had a good first encounter, that will drive the results.

I test for this reverse determination by looking at escorts who have no reputation to speak of; they have neither survey reviews nor text reviews. These could be new escorts in the market or old escorts who are abandoning an older profile. On the one hand, escorts with no reputation are unknown and could be more likely to signal against type. On the other hand, the only information a client can use to determine the quality of these escorts is the information conveyed in their advertisement, so the signal may be particularly valuable for these escorts. In either case, those with no reputation can only disclose their type through the information in their advertisement – they have no reputation to exploit.

In Figure 2.8 I show the value of face pictures from the same type of regression for all escorts, where I regress price on the usual set of covariates for escorts with no reputation. The results show that face pictures matter *more* for escorts with no reputation. The premium to the presence of face pictures is more than 3 percent. This premium is slightly higher than the premium estimated for escorts overall. Therefore, it seems that when escorts do not have an established reputation, signaling may be even more important.

Selection

Escorts do not have to post their prices in their advertisements, although well over 85 percent of the men in the data do. For example, an escort can list that he provides a given service (incall or outcall), but may not post the price for that service. The results could overstate the effects of information if there is selection into posting prices that varies with the information content of the advertisement, which could lead to selection in either direction. It could be that escorts who post more pictures or more face pictures are more likely to post their prices since they have signaled their quality.

These types of arguments could be extended to the reservation wages of escorts who do or do not provide a certain set of information to the market, which itself could alter the estimate of the returns to signaling quality in the market. To test whether the number or type of pictures has any impact on the decision to post prices, I estimated a model where the outcome is whether the escort posts prices. If there is a difference in the likelihood of posting prices based on the presence of face pictures then this would need to be taken into account. The results of these regressions show that the number of pictures, the presence of face and body pictures, and the number of face and body pictures do not significantly predict the decision to post prices or not. This holds when I consider a number of alternative specifications and when I include or exclude additional controls. I take this as evidence that the decision to post prices is not influenced by the other information in the advertisement itself.

CONCLUSION

Male sex workers are unique in illegal markets: they price independently and without intermediaries, they use a rich information environment to solicit clients, and their large number creates a competitive setting where we expect markets to function as if the assumptions of neoclassical economic theory held. Unfortunately, two of those assumptions are that the underlying transaction is legal and that buyers and sellers have similar information. Since formal institutional enforcement is nonexistent, the market could be plagued with adverse selection. Before moving to more systematic analysis of the market, it is important to establish that this market functions well and reacts to information in a manner that suggests that it gets prices right. The illegal nature of online male sex work makes it theoretically unlikely that this market would be well functioning, however. Unlike street sex work, online sex work does not involve a face-to-face negotiation where reputations and personal interactions allow the market to work. Buyers are, in essence, purchasing on faith. This faith would be in short supply if all that clients had to go on were the "word" of a sex worker with whom they had never dealt with. To overcome this problem, buyers have developed a unique solution where they require a specific type of information, face pictures, from male sex workers, which they interpret as a signal of escort trustworthiness.

I find that escorts do convey a great deal of information through their advertisements and that the market rewards this information. Empirically, the reward to face pictures is substantial; it is the driving force behind the premium to information in this market. Not only do I find a sizable information premium in this market, but the magnitude is similar to the premium seen in legal markets. Sex workers who signal their credibility via face pictures earn roughly $10,000 more per year than those who do not. Overall, the result is consistent with a market that functions well despite its illegal nature.

It is important to note some caveats to these results. First, although it would be tempting to argue that the results show that informal institutions such as client-policing are close substitutes for formal institutions such as courts, it could well be true that the premium to information I observe is due entirely to the complementary effects of informal institutions. Even in markets with formal contracts and enforcement, the types of forums created by the clients of male sex workers are common (e.g., AngiesList.com). As I documented, client communication dramatically raises the costs of deception because detection is likely. A dishonest escort may swindle one or two clients, but the possibility of doing so frequently is unlikely. Informal policing is critical to this market. Indeed, without the extensive policing by clients it would have been impossible to identify the signal used by escorts.

Second, although the market does respond positively to information here, it is not necessarily true that the response is of the correct size. For example, the face pictures may be a weak signal to which the market over-responds because there is little additional information to go on. In such a case, the returns to showing a face picture would be larger than the actual value of information it provides. For example, while showing a face picture may increase the likelihood of encountering a high quality escort, it may not increase the likelihood enough to justify the significant price premium. While the theoretical predictions held that the market would not respond to information, client demand could be such that the market responds too much to the relatively sparse information contained in face pictures.

The relationship between formal and informal institutions is inherently complex. I can say little about their interaction, since formal institutions play no role here. More empirical research is needed on the interaction of formal and informal institutions to estimate the degree of substitutability or complementarity between the two. While the results do not address how much the premium to signaling would change if there were formal enforcement in this market, this market shows that rich information environments alone allow escorts and clients to overcome the problems of asymmetric information.

The male sex market functions well despite its illegal nature. While it is easy to see that face-to-face interactions would minimize fraudulent activity, the analysis of the market for male sex work shows that even in online settings illegal markets can function well. The information that one would naturally seek out in face-to-face transactions is substituted with face pictures in the online market for male sex work. The fact that near-anonymous encounters between sex workers and clients takes place in a market where signals of both basic and service quality are well-correlated with prices suggests that the market for male sex work is, in fact, well developed.

3

Market Movers: Travel, Cities, and the Network of Male Sex Work[1]

INTRODUCTION

Prices in a market are only a piece in economic analysis. Economists are primarily interested in overall market structure – the ways that firms in a market interact with one another and how that interaction influences the way the market functions. Interaction in a market for sex workers is, essentially, the way that sex workers compete with one another for clients. Competition is key to consumer welfare – without firm competition, monopolistic or oligopolistic prices would be seen in the market. These prices would be higher than those seen in direct competition, and consumer welfare would suffer as a result. The open question is how competition in the market for male sex work influences the prices in the market. Prices are key for analyzing how competitive the market is, which is related to how much consumer and producer surplus exists. Now that the primitives of market prices have been confirmed to reflect market fundamentals such as the quality of escort services, the effects of competition can be explored.

The basic structure of online male escorting sets it apart from the most common type of sex work practiced. Escorts craft advertisements of their services and directly compete with other escorts on websites. This is rare for a service such as sex work, where usually a client can only choose between the sex workers who are actively seeking clients at the same time that a client is searching for sex workers. For example, given the use of the Internet, it is not possible for a male sex worker to appear on the market only at times of day when demand is high or low – his advertisement is visible at all times.[2] Sex workers are constantly in competition with every other advertisement in

75

their local area – they cannot choose times where the supply is low or demand is high in order to gain an advantage in the market.

This is a very different structure from street-based sex work, in which initial transactions among sex workers and clients (i.e., solicitations) occur in a public setting. Increasing access to and use of the Internet has provided clients with unique opportunities to secure meetings with sex workers outside of public scrutiny for both male and female sex workers. Street-based work is likely the most widespread form of prostitution across the globe and is also the most widely studied form of prostitution among health scholars and social scientists.[3] Findings from a recent study in the United States suggest that online solicitation of female prostitutes is displacing street-based prostitution among certain population subgroups, particularly highly educated female sex workers. Through the analysis of FBI crime statistics, researchers have found evidence of a decreasing prevalence of street-based sex work among younger women (under age 40), which has been attributed to the increasing Internet-savvy client base for sex work.[4]

There are a number of additional differences between online and street-based sex work.[5] The first difference is the scheduling of appointments for sex work as opposed to immediate transactions with clients. Sex workers who solicit clients online have greater control over the pace of their work and its parameters – they can arrange schedules to avoid fatigue, ensure timely appointments, and discuss the terms of the transaction in advance in a way that avoids the rush or pressure of immediate negotiations. This does include the potential downside of clients changing their minds or of finding another sex worker more amenable to their demands between the time of arrangement for a meeting and the time of the actual transaction. Movement to online simultaneously brings more potential clients to the market and increases the scope of market competition among sex workers for clients.

Another significant difference between Internet escorts and street workers is that the former are far more likely than the latter to travel long distances to different cities to meet clients. This is for several reasons. First, it is easier for clients to search for sex workers both inside and outside of their local market. If a client desires a particular sex worker, they can offer to compensate the sex worker to travel to them. Second, the Internet allows sex workers to advertise their services in several different markets – noting one as the "home" location and other areas as "travel" destinations. In other words, the online market expands the number of potential client/escort interactions and the scope of competition. Third, the Internet offers sex workers the ability to change their availability and willingness to serve other local areas quickly and at little cost. This not only allows escorts to change locations as they travel, but also to "test" locations to see if placing advertisements in a given area will be met with client demand in that area.

This type of traveling creates a unique type of competitive structure in the market for male sex work. While street-based and online sex workers compete against local competitors in a spot market, in the online-market sex workers also compete against those in other locations who can enter their market and serve clients. This makes the study of competition among male sex workers one in which traveling adds to the industrial organization of the market. Certain types of escorts may be more prone to travel and, conditional on their traveling, more prone to travel farther distances based on the services provided. The extent to which male sex workers serve multiple markets, how far these markets are from each other, and whether serving multiple markets is related to prices – all of these are unknown. While researchers have investigated the travel patterns of clients of male sex workers, there is very little research on the travel patterns of male sex workers themselves.[6]

Since male sex work does not use intermediaries such as pimps, each sex worker is an independent firm that competes against a number of different firms – other sex workers – for clients. In traditional analysis, the location of firms is quite important: firms should place themselves nearest to their consumers. When analyzing male sex work, the unique feature is that the firm is mobile and so is the competition. Economists usually study firm location as a one-time decision, and for good reason. Firms locating in an establishment do not move often. Sex workers, however, are inherently mobile, and therefore travel is critical in the study of competition in this market.

In the current online structure, sex workers cannot list different prices in different cities. For example, while escort prices may be higher in New York City, an escort serving New York City, a high-priced city, and Philadelphia, which has lower average prices, can only list one price, which applies to both markets. That is, sex workers cannot price-discriminate based on the markets they are serving. This means that the prices and propensity for travel among escorts in one city can influence the prices of male sex workers who do not travel and those who, if they travel, serve different markets than others who travel to different sets of cities. This effect would be a price spillover effect of sex worker travel – the prices of sex workers who do not travel could be influenced by the prices of those who do travel. The extent to which traveling has an effect on prices also shows how mature the market is – price differences between locations would tend to diminish as the market became more integrated. In a completely integrated market, the geographic price differences would disappear and the law of one price would hold.

Travel patterns also have implications for the sexual networks of male sex workers and clients.[7] There are two effects of sexual networks. First, the travel of sex workers and clients has the potential to be a key factor in disease transmission.[8] Second, sexual networks (serving cities with higher or lower prevalence rates for sexually transmitted infections – STIs) may influence the prices that sex workers charge if city-level risk factors affect prices.[9] The ways in which escort travel influences the density of the sexual networks is important in both economical and epidemiological terms.

Differences in travel propensities by sexual behavior have particularly significant implications for sexual disease transmission. If male sex workers who participate in higher or lower risk behavior are more or less likely to travel, such differences could help us determine the transmission propensities for STI epidemics. For example, the relative risk of contracting HIV for receptive versus penetrative anal sex is 7.69, which suggests that penetrative ("top") male sex workers could act as prominent vectors of transmission if they are more likely to travel, as their partners (receptive partners – "bottoms") would be significantly more likely to contract HIV for a given sexual event.[10] We do not know if travel propensity or the distance between travel locations is related to characteristics, sexual behaviors, or prices.

Furthermore, travel among sex workers creates a network of cities that are more or less linked to other cities due to the travel propensities of escorts and the similarity of travel destinations. The centrality of cities has implications for the prices that sex workers charge, for the potential spread of disease, and for the identification of cities in which efforts would be more effective in reaching a large number of sex workers through interventions. At a basic level, the identification of key cities tells us a great deal about the market for male sex work – where sex work is prominent and where there are more service providers. For example, cities that are popular travel destinations for sex workers may be cities where a larger number of sex workers can be reached, and the potential impact on other sex workers could be large.

Traveling is therefore a key component to male sex work. Economically, travel may have direct and indirect effects on the prices observed in the market. To the extent that travel reflects geographic variations in demand, travel may also provide clues to which markets are most lucrative for sex workers. Similarly, the effects that this travel has on the prices in the market are important for understanding market structure. As a result, traveling may create economic and sexual links between cities. Describing those links is critical to understanding how this market works at a national level.

In order to shed more light on this side of male sex work, this chapter examines the travel patterns and economic returns to travel among Internet-based male escorts. This chapter not only provides a description of male escort travel patterns, but also identifies the conditions under which male sex workers are most likely to travel (and thus to serve as potential vectors for STI transmission across cities and to influence the prices of multiple markets) and which travel patterns are most economically rewarding for the escort himself. In this chapter, the online advertisements of male sex workers are combined with city-level measures to derive network measures for the centrality of cities in the market for male sex work in the United States. A central city is a city that is not only popular among sex workers as a home location, but also one to which sex workers who live in other areas are likely to travel.

I begin by noting the traveling frequency of male escorts, which is substantial. In fact, the majority of escorts serve multiple markets. I then find that escort home location is only weakly correlated with the gay male population distribution, which implies that male escorts either see a large number of heterosexually identified clients or that escorts travel to locations with more demand for male sex work services. Building upon this groundwork, the chapter then proceeds with a detailed exploration of male sex worker travel, its network effects, and the price implications of travel. First, analysis of the travel patterns of male sex workers in the United States is used to estimate the degree to which propensities to serve multiple markets are correlated with advertised personal characteristics and sexual behaviors. The question here is whether particular types of escorts are more likely to serve multiple markets. Second, analysis of what factors specific to particular metropolitan areas lead them to be popular travel destinations for escorts is explored. The question here is whether there are particular city characteristics that make particular cities popular destinations for traveling male sex workers, and whether those characteristics are proxies for client demand. Third, I estimate the relationship between the frequency of travel among other male escorts to the home city and male sex workers' travel patterns. This is an attempt to see if a given sex worker's traveling behavior is influenced by the traveling behavior of competitors in the home market. Fourth, I estimate the economic returns to travel among the escorts and the price spillover effects of male sex worker travel.

The impact of sex worker location and travel patterns is shown to have a large impact on the way that this market works. First, sex worker sexual behaviors are related to the likelihood of traveling. Male sex workers who advertise submissive sexual services are more likely to travel than others, for example. Second, sex workers in cities with large gay populations are less likely to travel. This suggests that cities with larger gay populations have sex workers who are less likely to leave the area in search of work, likely because there is higher demand for their services since they are located in cities with substantial gay populations. Third, sex workers who live in cities popular as travel destinations for other sex workers (whether that city has a large gay population or not) are less likely to travel. This implies that cities where the sex work market is thick are cities where sex workers set up and from which they do not travel. Fourth, sex workers who serve multiple markets charge higher prices than others, rates are higher in cities that are central to the network created by sex worker travel (central cities in the network have higher prices overall than other cities), and the spillover effects on the prices of non-traveling male sex workers are significant.[11] The market prices of traveled-to and traveled-from cities are brought closer together through the competition that traveling escorts create by serving areas with high demand.

Taken together, these results imply that the movement of sex workers does impact the market for male sex work in a meaningful way. The movement of sex workers acts to increase prices in the market. This is because sex workers who are likely to travel, travel to cities where prices are higher. This then causes the average price of their home cities to be higher as well. The traveling of sex workers also shows that overall market prices are partially driven by the high demand for male sex work in cities with large gay populations. Indeed, one of the key findings here is that sex worker home locations are not well correlated with the gay population distribution, but sex worker movement is correlated with gay population density. Consistent with the travel patterns, the key cities in the sex worker network are cities with large gay populations. Because of this, the connectedness of a city in the network is related to the prices in the male sex work market. The competition between male sex workers is more complex than the spot market faced by street sex workers, and the market is more integrated and sophisticated as a result.

(GAY) LOCATION, TRAVEL, AND MALE SEX WORK

Given the use of online markets for male sex work and the disappearance of street-sex work, there are new incentives and economic opportunities for sex workers and clients. In the past, male sex work was highly concentrated in cities with large gay populations, where male sex workers could easily secure clients from the local area. If a client lived in a smaller city it may have proved difficult to secure the services of a sex worker. Searches of national print advertisements in earlier periods from the *Advocate Classifieds* show that few escorts were located in cities outside of the twenty largest in the United States as of 1990. Contrast that with today, where literally dozens of cities are served by at least ten male escorts. From Missoula, Montana to Sioux City, Iowa, clients can find sex workers who serve their local area.

The question for the market is the relationship between the size of the gay population and the concentration of male sex workers. It is important to note that the relationship between the size of the gay population and the concentration of male sex workers hinges on identification of the gay population itself. Since the work of Hooker (1956, 1957), psychologists have noted that there is little to distinguish the homosexual and hetero-sexual, other than self-identification. Men who partake in homosexual acts are not distinguishable from the general male population.[12] While early studies of male sex work focused on particular cities with large gay popula-tions, later qualitative research revealed that a significant portion of the clientele of male escorts is heterosexually identified.[13] Indeed, the "breast-plate of righteousness" that Humphries (1970) saw in heterosexually iden-tified men who took part in homosexual behavior has recently resurfaced in the public lexicon as prominent men, many of whom have been active in anti-gay organizations, have been embroiled in controversies regarding their sexual orientation.[14] In the market for male sex work, such behavior may be common – male escorts regularly note that a significant percentage of their clientele is heterosexually identified, and many such clients are married to women. Since these men are hidden from the most common analysis of sexual minorities, the open question is how their presence in the market influences market function and composition.

This is not to say that there are not social distinctions based upon public affirmation of homosexual orientation. There are now a number of studies by demographers and economists that look at the population trends of the gay-identified population. The empirical studies show that openly gay and lesbian individuals do appear to be different on a range of outcomes, from earnings, to partnership status, to general socioeconomic position.[15] It is still difficult to identify all sexual minorities in the data, but it is now possible to identify same-sex couples.[16] Those population trends have been used to note that the geographic distribution of male same-sex couples is different from that of the general population in the United States.[17] Two factors that seem to be related to gay location patterns are city amenities and the ability to congregate and socialize with a critical mass of other gay people, although alternative explanations that emphasize economic factors have been offered by Collins (2004). Whatever the reason for these location differences, this research poses interesting questions into the demography and geography of male sex work, as we know very little about the population size, demographic characteristics, and geographic distribution of male sex workers in the United States.

Given that heterosexually identified men may have much to lose if their same-sex sexual behavior is exposed, it could be the case that male escorts are more prone to locate in places where there are fewer opportunities for men interested in sexual encounters with other men to meet one another. Self-identified heterosexual men are unlikely to frequent gay bars, coffeehouses, or community groups where they would be more likely to encounter gay men for socialization or sex. This would suggest that male escort location might differ from that of the gay-identified population. Conversely, researchers note that gay communities do not attach the same level of stigma to sex work as do heterosexuals, and if gay communities are seen as safer havens for sex workers we would expect their geographic distribution to closely mirror that of the openly gay population.[18]

Research has shown that the geographic distribution of male same-sex couples is different from that of the general US population, and studies of male sex work in the United States focus on cities with large gay populations.[19] If male sex workers can be thought of as independent businesses, they would need to take the market into account when deciding where to set up shop. For example, locating in a place where there are relatively few men seeking sexual services for hire would make little sense. It would be more profitable to locate in an area where there are more clients. On the other hand, every *other* sex worker is making a similar decision. This could lead to a situation where cities with high demand have a large number of sex workers to serve the market. Assuming that clients do not choose to move based on the number of sex workers in the local market, we would expect sex workers to locate optimally – cities with more client demand would have larger numbers of sex workers, but some sex workers would locate in less-popular markets because their services would be dearer to consumers. In the long run, the market would reach an equilibrium and sex workers would have a price that would correspond to the local demand, but since sex workers move in response to local demand (places with too many sex workers would have lower prices than places with too few), in the end there could be few differences in local prices for sex work.

To see how this would work, imagine a sex worker in a given area where there is a fixed number of clients and a fixed number of sex workers. Given this supply of sex workers and number of clients, the market would set the price of sex work at a given level. It could be the case that another sex worker in a different city would move to that city if the prices were higher there. This would serve to increase the number of sex workers, which would increase the supply and, all else being equal, would result in lower prices in the market. Now, if the sex worker were to see that another city had higher prices (because of a local undersupply of sex workers), he would move to that location if the moving cost were sufficiently low. The movement of sex workers would continue until the prices of sex work were no different in one location than in another – that is, there would be no incentive for sex workers to move due to price differences.

Theoretically, the movement of sex workers would correspond to the size of the client base. The location model of Hotelling (1929) predicts that, since the proposed client base is not uniformly distributed, distribution of service providers would be non-uniform; sex workers would need to be located close to the largest mass of potential clients. Tests of this theory for male sex workers are lacking. The unanswered question is whether the openly gay population constitutes the vast majority of the client base, or whether the number of heterosexually identified clients of male sex workers influences location patterns. If heterosexually identified clients are a significant portion of the customer base and if their location patterns are different from those of gay men, male sex workers' location patterns could also differ from those of the gay male population to the extent that the patterns would be related to the non-gay clients they serve. Given that heterosexually identified men may have much to lose if their same-sex sexual behavior were to be exposed, it could be the case that male sex workers are more prone to locate in places where there are fewer opportunities for men interested in sexual encounters with other men. Conversely, researchers note that gay communities in the United States do not attach the same level of stigma to sex work as heterosexuals, and if gay communities are seen as safer havens for sex workers we would expect male sex workers' geographic distribution to closely mirror that of the openly gay population.[20] Therefore, the first area of interest is the home location of male sex workers.

Empirically, we would need to account for the city's gay population in order to analyze the issue. Unfortunately, data limitations make generating reliable estimates of gay population difficult. The most widely used estimate for a gay population is the Gay Concentration Index (GCI). Since

1990, the US Census has included an "unmarried partner" category on the household roster. By examining the genders of primary respondents and their unmarried partners, households that are headed by two male partners can be identified. The proportion of two-male-headed households is traditionally used to estimate the concentration of gay men within cities.[21] I estimate the GCI for each city in the advertisement data. For each city, I divide the number of households that are headed by two unmarried men by the number of two-person headed households (both married or unmarried) within the city. The resulting number represents the proportion of two-person-headed households within the city that are headed by two unmarried men. That number is then divided by the proportion of two-person-headed households that are headed by two unmarried men across the entire United States. The resulting measure, which can be used to measure each city's gay concentration, equals 1 if the city's Gay Concentration Index is equal to the national average, is greater than 1 if the GCI is above the national average, and is less than 1 if the GCI is below the national average.[22] This proxy for the city's gay population can therefore be used to investigate the location of male sex workers and the relationship of their location to gay population distribution.

SEX WORKER HOME LOCATION AND GAY CONCENTRATION

What is the relationship between the size of the gay population and the concentration of male sex workers? Table 3.1 shows the geographic distribution of male escorts who advertise online, where I count the actual number of escorts by the home location given in their advertisements.[23] The size of the escort population varies considerably – there are more than 300 escorts in only one city, New York City, which has long been known in the media to have the largest male escort market.[24] Atlanta, Los Angeles, Miami, and San Francisco each has more than 100 escorts, but most cities have considerably fewer. I also include the rank and size of the populations of each Metropolitan Statistical Area (MSA) as well as the Gay Concentration Index (GCI) to compare the location of escorts with gay male location patterns. To provide a broader picture of the distribution of male sex workers, I list randomly selected cities.

In terms of location patterns, there is a striking trend – the number of gay escorts more closely follows the size of an MSA than it follows gay location patterns. For example, Detroit is the eleventh-largest MSA in the United States, and its gay concentration is 42nd, but there are 51 percent

Table 3.1 *Geographic distribution of escorts – selected cities*

City	MSA Rank	MSA Population	Gay concentration Rank	Gay concentration Index	Number of escorts
New York City, NY	1	18,815,988	13	1.49	309
Los Angeles, CA	2	12,875,587	6	2.11	126
Chicago, IL	3	9,524,673	18	1.31	93
Miami, FL	7	5,413,212	14	1.46	119
Washington, DC	8	5,306,565	2	2.68	99
Atlanta, GA	9	5,278,904	7	1.96	108
Boston, MA	10	4,482,857	9	1.67	53
Detroit, MI	11	4,467,592	42	0.6	50
San Francisco, CA	12	4,203,898	1	4.95	124
Seattle, WA	15	3,309,347	5	2.21	33
Minneapolis, MN	16	3,208,212	10	1.61	33
St. Louis, MO	18	2,808,611	37	0.69	18
Tampa, FL	19	2,723,949	24	1.05	47
Denver, CO	21	2,464,866	12	1.53	41
Portland, OR	23	2,175,113	15	1.45	15
Sacramento, CA	26	2,091,120	8	1.71	17
Kansas City, MO	29	1,985,429	25	1.04	9
Columbus, OH	32	1,754,337	27	0.99	30
Indianapolis, IN	33	1,695,037	19	1.12	19
Charlotte, NC	35	1,651,568	45	0.49	19
Austin, TX	37	1,598,161	3	2.44	26
Nashville, TN	39	1,521,437	32	0.85	14
Oklahoma City, OK	44	1,192,989	34	0.83	3
Buffalo, NY	46	1,128,183	49	0.35	5
Rochester, NY	50	1,030,495	29	0.89	4
Albany, NY	57	853,358	31	0.85	5

Correlation of number of escorts with Gay Concentration Index: 0.39
Correlation of per capita escorts with Gay Concentration Index: 0.69
Correlation of number of escorts with MSA population: 0.92

Counts of number of unique escort advertisements. Gay concentration is the fraction of the Metropolitan Statistical Area (MSA) identified as same-sex male partners in the 1990 Census divided by the national average. See Black, Sanders, and Taylor (2007) for further details. MSA population counts from the Census Bureau. Cities with MSA rank >12 were selected at random from the fifty cities listed in Black, Sanders, and Taylor (2007). The correlations in the lower panel are for all fifty cities listed in Black, Sanders, and Taylor (2007).

more escorts in Detroit than in Seattle, a city with the fifth-highest GCI. A similar finding pertains to other cities such as Chicago and St. Louis. Indeed, the correlation of the number of escorts with MSA population is quite strong ($r = 0.92$), but the correlation with the GCI is much weaker

($r = 0.39$). Also, the correlation of per capita escorts with the GCI ($r = 0.69$) is weaker than the correlation of escorts with MSA.

This result is consistent with the claims that the market for male sex work is national in scope and that it is not driven exclusively by gay-identified participants. If escort services were primarily demanded by self-identified gay men, we would expect the geographic distribution of male escorts to mirror the geographic distribution of self-identified gay men – male escorts would locate in places that have a higher concentration of those potential customers. The results in Table 3.1 imply that male escorts tend to concentrate in cities with substantial populations, as opposed to cities with substantial gay populations. This result holds even when considering mid-sized and smaller cities – it is not driven by cities that have large populations and large gay populations, such as Los Angeles. Overall, the evidence is consistent with the hypothesis that male escorts serve a market that includes a substantial number of heterosexually identified men.

Such analysis, however, is limited. The online market for male sex work is not a spot market and home locations paint an incomplete picture of the market and the locations for male sex work. Since sex workers may serve multiple markets it is possible that the results in Table 3.1, which only apply to home locations, do not describe the entire market and the provision of services more generally. Given the ease of traveling, a full study of the market, which allows for and investigates the likelihood of travel, is needed.

ESCORT TRAVEL AS AN ECONOMIC DECISION

Treating escort travel formally requires that one accept the proposition that escorts would be motivated by pecuniary benefits to travel. This is not to say that other factors could not enter into the decision, but in the case of sex work the economic benefits of travel would be most important when the traveling involved would be for the purposes of sex work. A formal approach would begin with the framework of economic models of migration.[25] The models begin with the idea that migration (as an economic decision) is related to the cost and benefits of migrating. A standard migration model considers the wage that a potential migrant would earn in the current and potential new destination. For male sex workers, this must be modified to reflect the price they charge for their services. An additional factor is that escorts cannot discriminate in their pricing by charging different prices in different markets. This is consistent with the data, in which escorts can only post one advertised price that is seen by all online clients, irrespective of the client's location. The key is the expected wage due to traveling. When sex workers travel to another city, they increase the supply of sex workers in that location, and therefore drive down prices unless demand is perfectly elastic. This implies that the city to which an escort travels has demand that is sufficiently inelastic to cause a wage gap that would still induce them to travel, thus allowing them to charge higher prices overall.

Travel could also be a signal of desirability among clients. To the extent that an escort serves multiple markets, it could be taken as a positive signal of demand for their services or a negative signal that they are very active in the sex work market. This would naturally vary at the individual client level, but how this would aggregate to the market price that a sex worker could charge as a function of travel is unknown. Ultimately, this is an empirical question.

This simple conceptual framework has several implications. First, the wages in the city traveled to must be greater (in expectation) than the wages in the current city.[26] Considering the simple dynamics of supply and demand for escorts, the cities traveled to must be cities where the existing supply of escorts would be sufficiently low relative to demand so that the wages of escorts in those cities would be bid up. This implies that cities that are traveled to will be cities that, on average, have higher wages for male sex workers. In other words, popular cities for travel are hypothesized to be relatively high-wage cities for escorts and, given their higher wages, would make the escorts who travel to those cities higher-priced in their home locations.

Second, the potential for high wages in popular cities (cities escorts are likely to travel to) will cause escorts whose home location is that city to be less likely to travel to other cities. Indeed, to the extent that the wage in popular cities is related to that city's popularity, escorts with those locations as a home base will be less likely to travel to other cities, as they have fewer economic incentives to do so. Third, we would also predict that the wages of escorts in cities that are popular travel destinations earn higher wages on average, since their locations are in cities with relatively higher demand (or less supply). Fourth, those escorts who serve multiple locations will have higher wages, on average, than those who serve only one location. Indeed, the fact that these escorts travel implies that the wage differential they see is large enough to induce them to serve multiple locations.[27]

THE MALE SEX WORKER TRAVEL NETWORK

While the migration framework derives implications for an individual sex worker's travel, it does not speak to the network that is formed when some cities are more popular than other locations. This network would imply that some cities would have stronger links than others since they would "share" more sex workers. For example, cities that are well connected by travel may be more uniform in their pricing than cities that share fewer escorts. In other words, cities that are popular, and the escorts who service those cities, would be more likely to have similar prices than an escort picked at random from a city that was not well linked to other cities. Consideration of the network created by sex worker movement requires some new measures that go beyond prices. Below, I define the key network measures that I incorporate into the empirical analysis to better describe the network created by escort travel.

A network perspective is useful for measuring dimensions of male escort travel patterns as it provides a formal means for measuring influential properties of both city- and individual-level characteristics that are theoretically linked to an escort's likelihood of travel and their economic returns to travel. For instance, the Hotelling model predicts that sex workers would need to be located close to the largest mass of potential clients. Thus, I hypothesize that escorts are less likely to travel to other cities to meet clients when they are situated within cities that have high demand for the services of male sex workers. The question is, how to measure such a characteristic.

A city's degree, which is the number of escorts who are residing or willing to travel to the particular city to meet clients, is indicative of its overall supply of male sex work, both home-based and traveling to that location. It should be the case that escorts who live in cities with high degrees are less likely to travel to other cities for work, as demand for their services is already high, as noted earlier. It should also be the case that travel is associated with higher prices. However, not all travel is equally rewarding. More specifically, escorts who travel to cities where demand for their services is high will experience greater returns to their work than men who travel to less-popular cities. In essence, a network approach captures the features of the extent of network travel in an empirically compact way.

MEASURES OF NETWORK CENTRALITY

In order to measure features of both city and escorts' positions within the travel network, I used the escort advertisement data and the locations noted in the advertisements to link escorts to cities and cities to escorts. In the network literature this is referred to as a two-mode (i.e., affiliation) travel network.

The two-mode travel network consists of escorts who are tied to particular cities through their residence or willingness to travel to the particular city. For instance, one-mode networks are frequently employed in the study of cash transfers between individuals and organizations or in the transfer of information and resources. Conversely, two-mode networks consist of ties between opposing node sets.[28] Within this network, a tie exists between an escort and a city if the escort indicates in his advertisement that he is residing in or traveling to that city. Importantly, escorts are only *directly* tied to cities, and vice versa. This type of network allows for two different notions of centrality, where "centrality" is the network terminology for what we would consider "popularity." An escort can be central to the network and a city can be central to the network. Escorts are central if they travel to several cities. Conversely, cities are central if they are visited by several escorts.

In particular, there are three measures of network centrality. The first measure is degree centrality. An escort's degree centrality is measured by the number of cities he travels to, normalized by the number of cities in the total network. A city's degree centrality is measured by the number of escorts who reside or travel to that particular city, normalized by the total number of escorts in the data.

The second measure of centrality reflects the fact that being tied to other escorts who are themselves tied to several other escorts through their links implies that popularity should incorporate the popularity of those to whom (escorts) or to which (cities) you are linked. Consider two cities that are visited by the same number of escorts. One city should be more central than the other if it is visited by escorts who travel to more places. Similarly, an escort is central if he travels to many cities. However, an escort who is relatively inactive in traveling (say, serving only two cities) could also be important if he should build ties between two or more cities that otherwise would not be connected. This second measure, eigenvector centrality, simultaneously captures the extents to which escorts travel to cities that are popular work and travel destinations among other escorts and the extent to which cities are visited by escorts who travel to other popular cities.[29]

The third measure of centrality is betweenness. Escorts and cities may also be central if it is possible to connect two cities (through an escort) or two escorts (through a city). In other words, a city can be thought of as central if it is the easiest path through which two escorts can be connected (relative to other cities) and an escort can be central is he is the easiest path through which two cities are connected. This means that a city or escort lies on several of the shortest paths that link other cities and escorts.

Another interesting feature to explore in the male sex worker travel network is the diversity of cities' links with escorts. Escorts who travel to a city may be from the same city or from different cities. The former case may imply a special relationship between two cities (e.g., geographical proximity), while the latter case generally implies that the visited city is attractive to escorts. When considering travel it is important to distinguish between these two effects. We can evaluate how diverse a city's links are by the measure of their entropy, that is, the geographic diversity of the escorts who travel to that particular city. Here, the diversity of city links with escorts is hypothesized to be highly correlated with the economic condition of the male sex worker market. A city with higher diversity should sustain higher service rates.

MEASURING THE EFFECTS OF TRAVEL IN MALE SEX WORK

I use two dependent variables related to traveling patterns and one dependent variable for price to estimate the empirical relationships described above. The two dependent variables for traveling are extensive travel and intensive travel. Extensive travel is a binary variable indicating whether the escort is traveling to other cities to meet clients to provide his services (0 = no, 1 = yes). Intensive travel measures the mean travel distance (in miles) between the geographic central point of the city of an escort's home location and the center of the city or cities that he visits. Because this value is highly skewed by escorts with cities far apart from one another, I take the log of the distance to measure distance traveled. It is important to note that the cities are standardized in the data – escorts choose the location from a drop-down menu that best corresponds to their location and travel destinations. This produces a range of distances in a tractable way as opposed to having an escort list a city or area of a city that would be difficult to identify. The third dependent variable is the wage, which is the escort's outcall price. The outcall price represents the hourly rate (in US dollars) that the escort charges his clients for an hour of his services. As noted earlier, the escort can only post one outcall price in his advertisement.

INDEPENDENT VARIABLES

As described earlier, escorts are also able to list a number of personal characteristics through drop-down menus in their advertisements. These might affect the prices charged in a number of ways. Here, these characteristics are used as controls so that the effect of networks on travel is estimated while including the effects that these characteristics may have. In particular, escort race, height, weight, body type, the escort's advertised sexual behaviors, and whether the escort provides massage services in addition to escorting.

City-specific factors related to male sex work would be those related to local demand, the local sexually transmitted infection (STI) rate, and other factors that could influence both ease of access and the escort's ability to provide services. As discussed above, the GCI gives a proxy for demand. For the local disease environment, accurate reporting is difficult, but the reporting for specific diseases is done at the city level. When looking at disease environments, however, it is important to note that STI prevalence itself works through sexual networks. Epidemiologists have noted that syphilis and HIV occur at greater proportions than other STIs among men who have sex with men. As such, syphilis and HIV have been used to measure the underlying STI prevalence of men who have sex with men. Since the two are strongly correlated, I chose the HIV rate as a proxy for the underlying STI environment. Calculation of the HIV rate is the number of HIV-positive individuals in an MSA per 1,000 people in the population. This is calculated by the Centers for Disease Control and Prevention (http://www.cdc.gov).

Lastly, cities may have properties that would structurally make them easier to serve as central locations. For example, a city that serves as a hub for a major airline, by definition, is easier to reach, as there will be a large number of direct flights to that location. I use information provided by 2012 US Bureau of Transportation Statistics to define a city to be an air traffic hub if its largest airport serves at least 0.25 percent of all enplaned passengers in the United States. This is the measure of the degree to which a city serves as a traveling pass-through, which implies a relatively large stream of potential clients for that location, as hub cities are popular business travel destinations as well.

EMPIRICAL RESULTS

Summary Statistics

Table 3.2 provides the summary measures of travel for the network at the escort level. Slightly more than half of the escorts in the data, 55.6 percent, serve multiple markets, which suggests that travel is an important element

Table 3.2 *Summary travel and network measures, individual escorts*

Variable	Mean	Standard deviation
Escort travels?	0.556	0.497
Log travel distance	5.466	1.227
Escort degree	0.009	0.005
Escort eigen centrality	0.011	0.012
Escort betweenness	0.001	0.001

Note: Total sample size is 2,022 for traveling and distance. Sample size for network measures is 1,926.

Table 3.3 *Correlation of escort-level network measures*

	Escort degree	Eigen centrality	Betweenness centrality
Escort degree	1.000		
Eigen centrality	0.359	1.000	
Betweenness centrality	0.653	0.451	1.000

N = 1,926

in online male sex work. Conditional on traveling, the average distance traveled is approximately 240 miles. This implies that escorts are not merely serving other nearby cities, but are traveling relatively long distances when they serve other markets. Given the distance traveled, on average, it would seem likely that the choices of destinations would not simply be matters of convenience but explicit choices about which markets to serve.

Table 3.3 shows the correlations between three measures of network centrality for escorts. The correlations between them are relatively slight, except the correlation between degree and betweenness centralities. Recall that degree centrality measures the number of cities that an escort visits while eigen centrality measures the popularity of those with which an escort is connected. The low correlation between the two implies that the propensity of escorts to travel (which is high, given that roughly half serve multiple markets) is only weakly related to the popularity of the links formed by that travel. This is intuitive: since most escorts travel, only a small fraction could reasonably be expected to be key in terms of popularity. The correlation of betweenness centrality and degree centrality is greater, and reflects the fact that the more connections an escort has, the more likely

Table 3.4 *Summary statistics – city level*

Variable	Mean	Standard deviation
Airline hub?	0.359	0.481
Gay Concentration Index	1.019	0.336
HIV rate	13.163	8.163
City degree	0.015	0.028
City eigen centrality	0.018	0.059
City betweenness	0.015	0.038
City diversity	1.146	0.832

Note: 131 cities are used in calculations

Table 3.5 *Correlation of city-level network measures*

	City degree	City Eigen centrality	City betweenness centrality	City diversity
City degree	1.000			
City eigen centrality	0.918	1.000		
City betweenness centrality	0.983	0.930	1.000	
City diversity	0.716	0.548	0.682	1.000

he is to be a conduit that connects those in the network. The correlations also imply that the measures of connectivity provide different information about the travel network, and each piece of information may play a different role in the market to the extent that escorts play different roles in the travel network under different definitions of centrality.

The summary statistics at the city level are given in Table 3.4. Around a third of the cities in the data, 35.9 percent, serve as air traffic hubs. The average city in the data has a Gay Concentration Index of 1, which should be the case as the GCI measures the number of same-sex male households relative to the national average. On average, each city has an HIV rate of 13.2 per 1,000 people in the population. There is wide variation in the measures of GCI and HIV rate, however.[30]

Table 3.5 shows the correlations between the centrality measures at the city level. Unlike the escort-level measures of centrality, the city measures of centrality are well correlated with each other. The high correlations (between 0.92 to 0.98) among network centralities at the city level suggest that central cities are consistently identified by different network measures. This is intuitive – a city that is well-traveled-to by escorts is highly likely to be a popular city and a city that would be linked to other popular cities. Also, a city's popularity would make it a pathway through which two cities would be linked.[31] Figure 3.1 shows maps of US cities in the male sex worker travel network. In each panel, the relative size of a city represents the corresponding network centrality or characteristics. The figure shows that the major cities in the East and West Coasts, plus Chicago, are central cities in the travel network for all measures of centrality. Detailed information of the top fifteen cities with the highest degree of centrality is provided in Table 3.6. The table shows that nearly all of the popular cities have many sex workers, once travelers are accounted for. In addition, every city in Table 3.6 has a GCI greater than 1, which shows that the city has more gay households than the national average.[32] In general, all of the cities have relatively high HIV rates as well. The national HIV rate is 4.2 per 1,000 persons, and all of the cities in Table 3.6 have higher HIV rates.

THE TRAVEL OF MALE SEX WORKERS

The Likelihood of Sex Worker Travel

To describe the relationship between the *extensive* measure of travel, which is whether an escort travels or not, and personal characteristics, local market competition, and network measures of centrality, I use regression analysis. In particular, the regression analyzes the decision to travel as a function of the escort's individual characteristics and the network measures of their home location.[33] Since the city-level measures of centrality are well correlated with each other, I estimate the relationship between the city centrality measures in separate regressions.

Figure 3.2 reports results without the city-level measures of centrality as a benchmark. From the results, we see that Asian sex workers are less likely to travel than their White counterparts (the excluded race). Indeed, Asians are 10 percent less likely to serve multiple markets. Those with athletic and muscular bodies are 12 percent more likely to travel than thin sex workers (the reference group). Both top and bottom sex workers are more likely to travel, but bottom sex workers are much more likely to travel than tops.[34] While top escorts are 8 percent more likely to travel, bottom escorts are 20 percent more likely to travel. Indeed, in nearly all specifications, the coefficient on bottom sex workers is more than twice the size as that for top sex workers.

The greater likelihood of traveling for bottom sex workers has implications for the spread of STIs. The traditional view among public health

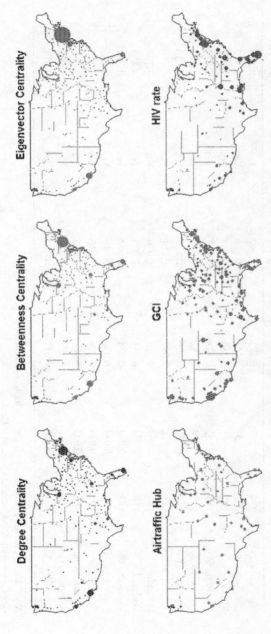

Figure 3.1 City characteristics and network centrality measures

Table 3.6 *Top fifteen US cities visited by male sex workers*

City	Links	Average degree	Eigen centrality	Betweenness centrality	Airline hub	Gay Concentration Index	HIV rate
New York, NY	374	0.203	0.571	0.297	Yes	1.308	29.2
Los Angeles, CA	252	0.137	0.231	0.175	Yes	1.512	13.0
Miami, FL	197	0.107	0.160	0.139	Yes	1.742	41.9
San Francisco, CA	175	0.095	0.123	0.112	Yes	2.414	16.5
Washington, DC	155	0.084	0.168	0.093	Yes	1.404	31.8
Chicago, IL	147	0.080	0.009	0.120	Yes	1.130	12.0
Atlanta, GA	141	0.076	0.058	0.114	Yes	1.590	20.0
Orlando, FL	124	0.067	0.048	0.076	Yes	1.121	26.0
Dallas, TX	118	0.064	0.051	0.080	Yes	1.295	16.0
Houston, TX	107	0.058	0.044	0.072	Yes	1.224	19.7
Las Vegas, NV	100	0.054	0.058	0.049	Yes	1.445	14.5
Boston, MA	90	0.049	0.088	0.046	Yes	1.147	8.0
Philadelphia, PA	80	0.043	0.082	0.036	Yes	1.060	23.1
Riverside, CA	77	0.042	0.055	0.022	No	1.282	7.6
San Diego, CA	74	0.040	0.047	0.022	Yes	1.411	13.1

Note: "Links" includes escorts listing the city as a location they serve.
Gay Concentration Index defined from 2010 Census.
HIV rate defined per 1,000 individuals.

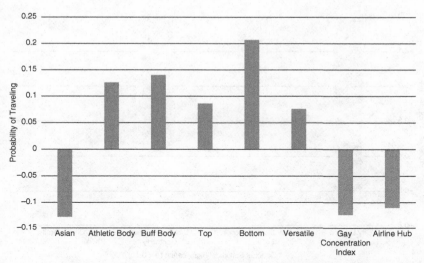

Figure 3.2 Escort characteristics and the probability of traveling

researchers is that sex workers can act as a vector of infection because they could potentially spread diseases to their clients. In the case of male sex work a key element in such an argument would hinge on whether sex workers, should they be infected, would participate in sex acts that would place their clients at greater risk of disease transmission. Those who are receptive in intercourse face a higher likelihood of being infected with STIs from their sexual partners, but this also implies that clients seeing those sex workers would be less likely to be infected. At a basic level, this travel pattern implies that traveling sex workers would be less likely to spread disease, as those who are bottoms are more likely to travel.

In all specifications, the Gay Concentration Index is negatively related to the likelihood that an escort serves multiple locations. A one-standard-deviation increase in the GCI decreases the probability of traveling by more than 3 percent. This is consistent with the idea that cities that have large gay populations have a larger client base for escorts located there, leaving the sex workers who live there less likely to travel to other cities to provide services. The city HIV rate does not have a significant effect on the likelihood of traveling. The indicator for city air traffic hub has a negative effect for traveling, but it is not statistically significant once city network measures are included.

For the centrality measures, displayed in Figure 3.3, the results are somewhat mixed. In the figure, the city centrality results are presented

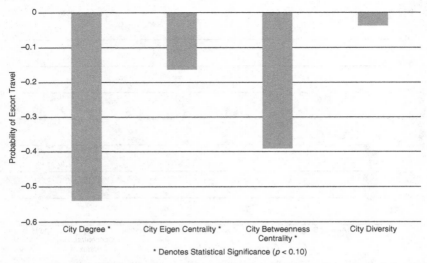

Figure 3.3 City centrality measures and the probability of escort travel

from their separate specifications for comparison. City degree centrality is not found to have a significant influence on a worker's traveling decision. The insignificance of city degree centrality is largely due to its correlation with the Gay Concentration Index.[35] This is intuitive to the extent that cities with a high gay concentration would have relatively larger numbers of gay men (potential clients) and therefore would be cities that would be linked to more escorts, to the extent that escorts travel to those cities where demand is relatively high. The city eigenvector and betweenness centralities do exert a significant and negative effect on the likelihood of traveling.

Recalling that city network centralities reflect cities' popularity in this travel network, they are also proxies for the demand for male work in a city, so male sex workers who live in particular cities with high centralities will have less incentive to travel. In other words, when a worker is located in a city that is central to the network, that condition acts as a disincentive to travel (to serve additional locations). The diversity of city link, measured by entropy, is also found have no significant effect on traveling.

Overall, some personal characteristics are related to the likelihood of traveling, and they run counter to the idea that sex workers would serve as vectors of transmission of diseases. Also, the concentration of gay men in a city is negatively related to the likelihood of travel. The network measures suggest that cities central to the network created by gay travel are correlated with lower travel propensities. That is, cities that are popular among sex

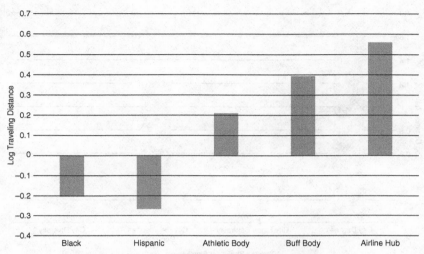

Figure 3.4 Escort characteristics and traveling distance

workers as travel destinations are also cities from which the resident sex workers are unlikely to travel.

The Distance of Sex Worker Travel

Knowledge of the determinants of travel is only one aspect of understanding the decision to serve multiple markets. There is also the question of how far the markets are from each other. For example, the traveling and the results of the previous section could be driven by escorts serving nearby locations. Here, I replace the extensive measure of travel with the intensive measure of travel, the log of the average distance traveled between the home location and the cities visited.

In these results I exclude the sex workers who do not travel. As before, I report results for the characteristics that excluded the city centrality measures, and then compare the effects of the city centrality measures. From the results in Figure 3.4, I find that Black and Hispanic workers travel shorter distances than their White counterparts. Sex workers with athletic and muscular body builds travel longer distances than thin workers. No sexual behaviors have a significant relationship with traveling distance (and they are excluded from the figure). While the behaviors did predict travel, they do not predict the distance traveled.

Similarly, the Gay Concentration Index of the home location does not have a significant effect on traveling distance of sex workers. The HIV rate

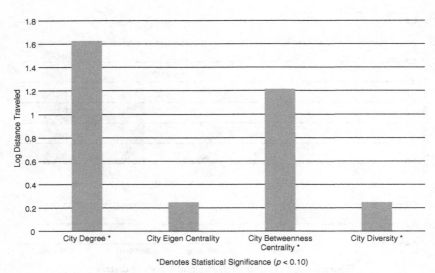

Figure 3.5 City centrality and the distance traveled by escorts

in the home location has no significant effects on male sex workers' travel distance, either. The most significant environmental influence is whether or not the city is an air traffic hub. The positive coefficient for city hub suggests that air traffic convenience significantly contributes to longer traveling distance for workers in those cities. Given that the average sex worker who travels goes a distance greater than 300 miles, the use of air travel (and the ease of air travel when being located in a hub city) does have a positive influence on the distance traveled.

All of the centrality measures have a positive effect on the distance traveled. These are reported in Figure 3.5. Degree and betweenness centralities have statistically significant effects on travel distance. The implication is that traveling workers who live in central cities of the travel network travel longer distances, on average, than workers who live in peripheral cities. The city network diversity is also found to have a positive effect on workers' traveling distance. These results, when combined with the results for the extensive measure of travel, suggest that sex workers in cities central to the network are less likely to travel, but when they do travel, they travel farther distances.

This is intuitive. Imagine two escorts who are similar in every aspect except that one lives in a city that is a popular travel destination and the other does not. The escort who does not live in a popular travel destination is likely to travel to his nearest popular city. The escort who lives in a popular travel destination, is likely to travel a greater distance than the other escort, who is closer to a popular destination but does not live in a popular destination. That is, if living in a popular city and traveling to another popular city, those escorts by definition will travel greater distances than those who are not in popular cities, as escorts whose home location is not popular can select the nearest popular city to serve.

Travel and the Prices of Male Sex Work

While the previous results analyzed the determinants of travel, traveling should be related to remuneration in some way if escorts are indeed acting as business operators. As described earlier, the wages of escorts should be related to the popularity of the cities they live in and their own propensity to travel. Also, the cities that are popular should have higher wages for escorts, which would reflect the fact that traveling by escorts is due to the demand for escort services in those cities. When demand outstrips supply, prices should be higher.

First, I analyze the relationship between the extensive measure of travel and wage rates in Figure 3.6. I find that the effect of travel (extensively measured) on the wage rate is significant and positive, which shows the economic return to travel for male escorts. It is the case that traveling escorts charge higher prices than escorts who do not travel. On average, sex

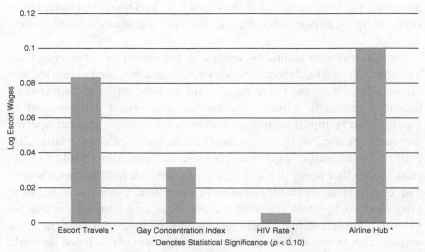

Figure 3.6 Escort travel, city properties, and escort wages

workers who travel charge 8 percent more than sex workers who do not travel.

In some specifications, I interact the traveling indicator with other measures to investigate the possibility that the returns to travel differ by other characteristics.[36] In that model, traveling sex workers charge 20 percent more than non-traveling sex workers. Part of this difference is due to the existence of heterogeneity within the travel premium. For example, Black and Asian escorts who travel do charge more than black and Asian non-traveling escorts, but they charge 2 and 8 percent less, respectively, than white escorts who travel. On the whole, traveling work- ers of non-White races receive lower wages than Whites. The results show that traveling indeed is one way in which a sex worker can earn more, but even here some differences remain.

At the individual level, sex workers who are muscular charge 18 percent more than thin escorts (the excluded group). No other personal character- istic is shown to have a relationship to the wages of travelers. Regarding environmental influences, city GCI does not have a significant effect on rates charged. However, Figure 3.6 shows that city HIV rate shows a significantly positive correlation with wage, which reflects the wage pre- mium for job risk that varies across geographic areas. The results for HIV rates are similar to the wage effects seen for female sex workers, whose wages are positively correlated with STI prevalence.[37] When the risk of HIV infection is greater, the rates for sex work increase. This is consistent with higher disease prevalence being an implicit part of sex worker com- pensation and the disease risk in the market. A city's traveling convenience, captured by the airport hub indicator, also has a significantly positive effect on wage.

Second, traveling should be related to the centrality measures of the locations traveled to, if those centrality measures are related to the demand for sex work services. These results look at how wages are affected by individual and city network centralities. The results are reported in Figure 3.7. It is important to note that both sex-worker- and city-specific measures are used in these specifications to investigate the relationship between a sex worker's network position and wages in addition to the relationship that being in a city of a given network level has with wages. The city-level network measures have consistent correlations with the rates charged by male sex workers. All three city network centralities have significant positive effects on wages, which implies that male sex workers charge more when they live in central cities of this travel network. For example, a one-standard-deviation increase in city degree or city

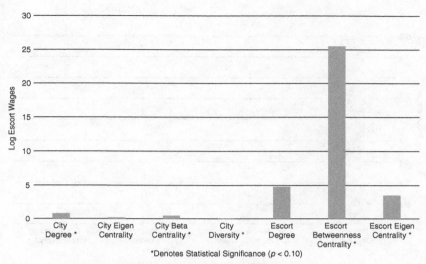

Figure 3.7 Escort and city centrality and escort wages

betweenness increases the wage rate by 2.3 and 1.79 percent, respectively. The result implies that the position of the city of residence for a male sex worker matters in terms of price. The more central a position a city has, the higher the wage rate he charges. I note that this holds for sex workers who travel and those who do not – as such, it is an effect of being in a central location itself, and not of their own propensity to travel. This is consistent with more popular cities being more expensive cities for sex work. As such, these cities have higher wages than others for sex work.

Finally, I focus on male sex workers who travel. There, the centrality of the cities they visit and its relationship to wages is presented.[38] However, after I control city network centralities, the effect of the airline hub seen in Figure 3.6 becomes statistically insignificant. This suggests that the hub acts as a proxy for network centrality, such that the inclusion of network centrality reduces the effect of a hub. The interaction terms of travel indicator with city GCI and HIV rate show that travelers from cities with high HIV and GCI may ask for a lower wage rate, but the estimates are only marginally significant.

I use the result to answer an additional question – travel to cities where demand for services is high results in greater return than travel to less popular cities. The return of traveling to popular cities is captured by including average network centralities and characteristics of destination cities in the wage equation for travelers. The results for destination-city

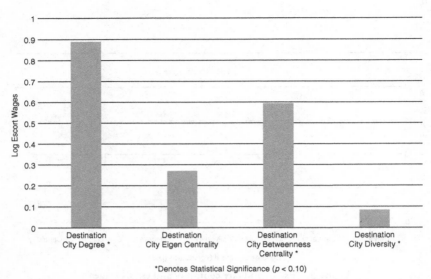

*Denotes Statistical Significance ($p < 0.10$)

Figure 3.8 Destination city centrality and traveling escort wages

network measures are reported in Figure 3.8. The results show that the GCI and HIV rate of destination cities do not affect wage rate. However, all three network centralities and network diversity of destination cities have significant positive effects on the wage rate of travelers. For example, a one-standard-deviation increase in the degree centrality and betweenness centrality of the destination city increases wages by 2.5 and 2.3 percent, respectively. The result provides empirical evidence to support the hypothesis that escorts travel to cities with high demand for male escort services.

There is an additional implication of traveling that can be tested. Cities that are popular destinations for escorts are cities where the average price for escort services is higher than in other cities. Also, the previous results have established that escorts are less likely to travel when their home location is in a popular city. This implies that cities that are not popular contain sex workers who travel (and therefore charge higher rates) and those who do not (and so charge lower rates), while popular cities have escorts who are less likely to travel. Taking both of these into account, there is an implication that there will be less dispersion of prices in cities that are popular, because escorts in those cities are less likely to travel. Using the interquartile range of prices (the difference between the 25th and 75th percentile of prices in a given city) for a city as the measure of price dispersion, I find that network centralities and link diversity are negatively related to price dispersion. The more connected a city is by network, the less dispersion there is in prices. This is consistent with the phenomenon of price dispersion in a city decreasing with a city's centrality – this means that popular cities are high-price cities where a client is less likely to find a low-priced escort. The lack of price dispersion would be consistent with the law of one price, where the price of a good in a market is invariant if the market is competitive. It is also a fact that price dispersion is negatively related to the gay concentration, which implies that in cities with a larger number of potential clients there is less price dispersion. This is consistent with a competitive market in which sex workers lose their ability to price discriminate. Clients in less-popular cities will be more likely to find escorts at a variety of price points, owing to the presence there of both stationary and traveling escorts.[39]

CONCLUSION

This chapter presented the first empirical analysis of male sex worker competition in the form of travel. Serving multiple markets increases the number of potential clients for a given sex worker, and as such this chapter concentrated on travel patterns and their effects on prices in the market. Even more, it adopted a network approach to assess the interlinks that cities have due to the travel of male sex workers. The market for male sex work involves a great deal of movement, and this movement is related to market demand, as opposed to non-market factors. Male sex workers travel to locations where demand is high (and prices are high). I also showed that the movement of male sex workers, a measure of market competition and incentives in the market, has an effect on the price of male sex worker services. The first key finding is that male sex workers who advertise on the Internet have a propensity to serve multiple markets. Traveling escorts are more common than stationary ones. Overall, male sex workers are highly mobile. This mobility causes market prices to be linked through the traveling of male sex workers, since escort travel is related to market demand. The market for male sex work is not a spot market, but rather a mature market with key cities that nationalize the male sex worker market by serving as hubs for male sex workers.

The relationship between the home locations of male sex workers is not strongly related to the location patterns of gay men. It does not appear that male sex workers are concentrated in areas that have relatively dense populations of gay men. At a basic level, this suggest either that a signifi-cant portion of the client base is not gay-identified or that the ease of traveling allows male escorts to locate at home bases that are not correlated with gay location trends. Intuition would suggest that sex workers would locate or serve the markets where there is significant demand, which would presumably come from gay-identified men. Given the high degree of traveling, however, the lack of a relationship between home location and gay population distribution necessitates an analysis of the traveling decisions of male escorts.

While overall location patterns were not related to gay population density, male sex workers in cities with large gay concentrations are less likely to travel than other escorts. Intuition suggests that the reason these escorts do not travel is that their home location is one where demand is reasonably high. This suggests that male sex workers in cities with large gay populations would be less likely to form links between cities, as they are less likely to travel. It is the escorts in low-gay-concentration cities who travel to high-gay-concentration cities. It is these escorts that drive the links between cities that create the network of male sex work in the United States.

I also showed that travel was not equally likely among all types of escorts. Certain personal characteristics of male sex workers are correlated with an escort's willingness to serve multiple locations. Escorts who advertise submissive sexual services are more likely to travel. This traveling behavior has implications for the sexual network inherent in male sex work, which has been the largest area of research since it has implications for disease transmission. As the likelihood of receiving the transmission of certain STIs is more likely for submissive sexual partners, the results would imply that submissive male sex workers who travel could simultaneously be more likely to have an STI and less likely to transmit the STI to clients. This result runs counter to the idea that sex workers could act as vectors of transmission of disease, as the sex workers traveling more are those who are less likely to transmit disease.

Lastly, male sex workers who serve multiple markets charge higher prices than others and rates are higher in cities that are central to the network created by sex worker travel. This suggests that the returns to travel are significant for escorts, that travel is related to demand, and that the market prices overall are connected due to the fact that traveling escorts serve high-priced cities. Sex worker movement is related to market incentives in the form of higher prices. The popular cities appear to be those with high demand for sex work services, and as such the incentive to travel to these cities is that they are lucrative options for sex workers, as the wage differential is significant.

In all instances, the market is broadly consistent with relatively simple models of economic agents responding to incentives provided by the market. Male escorts travel to markets that are high-priced markets, where the demand for their services is high. This leaves the market with a relatively small number of popular cities that escorts travel to provide services. For the escorts who live in these cities, the high wages they enjoy give them fewer incentives to travel. Indeed, when they do travel they travel farther distances as they must seek out more lucrative markets, which are at a greater distance. Beyond this, the cities that are popular from centrality-based measures of sex work are high-priced cities where there are fewer low-priced sex workers working.

It appears that escorts make reasonable economic decisions about their location patterns. They remain in and travel to cities that are high priced, and these cities appear to be cities where demand for their services is high. In particular, the results here suggest that the inclusion of network measures is important to understanding the economic incentives involved in the returns to traveling and sex worker service provision. The market for male sex work is not only a sexual network, but an economic one as well. The connectedness of the market is evidence of the maturity of the male sex work market. Sex workers appear to be aware of the geographic price differences and they respond to them. While the price differential remains between markets, the effects show a degree of market integration that has never been empirically observed for male sex work before. While not a national market with one price, which would occur in a fully integrated market, this integration shows a level of market development and maturity that cautions against treating male sex work as an economic anomaly or as an institution with few market features.

PART II

MALE SEX WORK AND SEXUALITY

4

Illicit Intersections: The Value of Sex Worker Services

Sex work is about more than supply and demand. Economic forces are obviously important in the market, and the economic gains that sex workers see from their labor are likely the primary reason why the industry continues to see men enter the profession. At the same time, the work of sex work involves a very intimate aspect of human behavior. Purchasing sex is similar to purchasing other goods, but also different. Any good or service on the market contains social aspects of consumer demand. For example, luxury items may be priced partially to establish their desirability and exclusivity. Other products are produced and consumed to affirm group affiliations, cultural identity, and other social factors.

When the product being offered is sex itself, there are obvious social functions at play in the market. Sex combines notions of desire, attraction, social acceptability, taboos, fantasy, deviance, power, and sexual stereotypes. Each of these is a socially derived and constructed commodity that becomes packaged in sex work transactions. These have to be packaged by sex workers for sale to clients who will consume them only to the extent that they understand them. Buyers and sellers are not operating in a vacuum, but are instead making decisions that take place within an American gay subculture that gives them guidelines on what the production function should be. This implies that the social context of sex work is just as important as the economic – the product being bought and sold has value only insofar as it matches with what is socially believed to have value.

While social scientists have long had interest in prostitution as a form of exchange (Simmel 1907 [1971]) or a place where cultural values and market logic intersect, the specific ways in which this takes place for male sex work remains under-researched in the social sciences.[1] There is a wealth of research on female prostitution, which uses the fact that female prostitution places women on a market for consumption by men. The ways that women

111

present themselves and how they interact with clients has been informed by gendered notions of power, sexuality, performance, and desire. This litera-ture has produced novel insights into the ways that sex work is a uniquely social-economic exchange.

For the study of male sex work, however, the male/female binary is not a useful conceptual framework. Male sex workers are difficult to concep-tualize in the economic, social, and gender theories of prostitution primar-ily because the participants are of the same gender.[2] For example, recent economic theories of prostitution are based upon the idea that prostitution is well paid (relative to unskilled labor) because female sex workers are compensated for forgoing the marriage market and pursuing paternity.[3] Several gender theories of prostitution see sex work as the commodifica-tion of women's bodies for consumption by men. Neither of these frame-works is appropriate for the study of male sex work. The framework for the social study of male sex work must begin from a different starting point.

There is a qualitative literature on male sex workers, which has informed the theories of sexuality, sexual behaviors, and sex work.[4] One important limitation of the qualitative work is that it does not capture the degree to which the market is affected by social ideals. Questions about the social aspects of the market can only be answered through a market analysis. We stand to increase the understanding of the ways that commerce, sexuality, and masculinity interact by quantitatively analyzing the market for male sex work as a market.

Similarly, the existing qualitative literature is primarily about male sex workers who work the street. Little is known about male escorts who occupy the highest position in the hierarchy of male prostitution, where the freedom offered by escorting would have arguably larger effects on the social value of male sex work.[5] The literature on male escorts that does exist has aged poorly due to technological progress (the Internet).[6] Another factor is the increas-ing social acceptance of homosexuality.[7] The recent qualitative scholarship on male escorts has found that the demographic and social characteristics of male sex workers and the reasons for entry into commercial sex work described in earlier postwar research do not apply today.[8] For example, rather than being young men experiencing homelessness, men struggling with addiction, or men participating in survival sex, many modern male sex workers have professionalized the industry. The chief medium through which this takes place is the online market – the professional aspects of the online market imply that the men in the online portion of the market would be particularly attuned to the social context, giving us more reason to expect social distinctions in value to play a role in the market.

Researchers have also noted the unique social and epidemiological position of male sex workers.[9] They serve numerous social groups – gay-identified men, heterosexually identified men, as well as their own noncommercial sexual partners. Male sex workers interact with groups of men that are unlikely to interact with each other, and therefore can act as an interesting social and sexual conduit between various groups.[10] More important, they must communicate to all of these groups simultaneously in a way that takes advantage of the commonality of what is most desirable and appropriate for a commercial sexual transaction between men. The social context at work for online male sex work is inherently complex.

In contrast to male-female prostitution, we cannot easily assign sexual positions or behaviors to participants based on sex or gender, and this necessitates a discussion of the social value of sexual behaviors among the participants that is not usually required in discussions of female sex work. In particular, we stand to gain by analyzing how and whether men who have sex with men reinforce and critique social constructions of masculinity through their valuation of sexual behaviors. In modern treatments of male homosexuality and masculinity, the masculinity prized (and therefore valued) by men in the market may conscribe to hegemonic, heterosexually focused masculinity. This hegemonic masculinity is, essentially, the ability of a sex worker to inhabit the social masculine ideal. Whether this is valued in the market is especially interesting as gay men are considered counter-hegemonic.[11]

Additionally, scholars have noted that sexual stereotypes interact with racial stereotypes among gay men. This may give rise to unique values for sexual practices among men of particular races. In a market for sex work, sex workers would exploit these stereotypes in order to reap economic gain from socially derived structures on sexual behavior. Put another way, some men, by the nature of racial-sexual stereotypes, could be more valuable than others when advertising the same sexual behaviors. This, too, is related to masculinity insofar as men of certain racial groups are thought to be more inherently masculine than others. Theoretically, this would allow us to see how the intersection of identities further refines the construction of masculinity and sexual desire among men who have sex with men.[12]

This chapter studies the relationship between escort prices, personal characteristics, and sexual behaviors as a social and economic process. This provides a key window into this relatively under investigated social activity.[13] The conceptual framework begins by considering how this type of empirical analysis can shed light on social theories of sexuality, hegemonic masculinity, and gay masculinity.[14] I use the principles of economic theory to motivate the methodological approach, but the motivation for the analysis and the interpretation of findings is done in light of *social theories* of gay male sexuality. Explicit in this framework is the idea that there are economic gains to adhering to socially derived demand, which itself is based upon the social construction of masculinity among gay men.[15]

This type of framework is possible because of the economic structure of the market. Male escorts in the United States do not use intermediaries who could potentially control the prices and earnings of male escorts or distribute sex workers to clients in some deliberate way, and they set their prices conditional on a perception of client demand. Since sex workers advertise to a broad client base, this gives us the opportunity to see how male escorts price their services conditional on their personal characteristics and sexual behaviors. The values attached to those characteristics and behaviors lie at the intersection of social value and market forces. The desire to earn as much as possible would provide market incentives for male sex workers to align their advertisement with the most dominant social cues to desired traits.

This approach allows me to answer heretofore open questions about male sex workers and, in turn, social theories of male sexuality: How does this market value physical characteristics (race, height, weight, etc.) and sexual behaviors? For example, do the clients of male sex workers value hegemonically masculine behaviors and appearance more than their feminine counterparts in a way that we can reconcile with hegemonic masculinity?[16] Furthermore, what are the effects of interactions between characteristics and sexual behaviors? Are men of particular races rewarded more for downplaying or emphasizing certain sexual behaviors than for others, as intersectional theory predicts?[17] How does this square with racial-sexual stereotypes in the gay community at large?

This chapter answers several of the pressing social questions in the literature. The estimated values of sex worker physical characteristics and sexual behaviors provide novel confirmation for social theories of gay male sexuality and also suggest additional ways in which gay masculinity has developed. In terms of physical characteristics, I find a small penalty for being thin and a sizable penalty for being overweight, which is consistent with studies of body image among gay men. For sexual behaviors, those who are "tops" (the penetrative partner) receive a premium to sex work and "bottoms" (the receptive partner) a penalty. The price differential between "tops" and "bottoms" is 17 percent, a substantial difference. A "top" male sex worker could earn nearly $10,000 more annually than a "bottom" sex worker. This difference is consistent with gay men placing a sizable premium on traditionally masculine (dominant) sexual behaviors at the expense of others. Rather than a rejection of traditionally masculine norms, men in this market replicate and reward them.

Surprisingly, race does not affect escort prices by itself. This stands in stark contrast to studies that have documented dating premiums and penalties with respect to race. The *intersection* of race and sexual behavior, however, exerts a very strong influence on prices. Black, Hispanic and White "tops" command a significant premium in the market while "tops" of other races, including Asians, do not. We also find that Black and White "bottoms" incur a significant price penalty while Hispanic and Asian "bottoms" do not. In both instances, the premiums *and* penalties for sexual behaviors are greatest for Blacks—the "top"/"bottom" price differential for Black escorts is more than *twice* the differential for any other racial or ethnic group. This finding is consistent with a particular form of sexualized race role-play practiced in gay communities, which is predicated on a hypermasculine, sexually dominant Black ideal.

The social interpretation of these economic values proves to be a powerful window into the way that sexuality and masculinity are defined in gay communities. While the analysis here is restricted to sex work, the findings are surprisingly consistent with studies of gay dating markets. This, in and of itself, lends support to the idea that sex work markets may be key institutions to study sexual-social values that cannot be estimated in dating markets. I conclude by noting how research on masculinity and sexuality should incorporate more fully the ways that race, physical characteristics, and sexual behaviors play out in the construction of desire, the development of sexual hierarchies, and the general ways in which sexuality constrains social interactions among gay men.

SOCIAL SCIENCE THEORIES OF MALE SEX WORK

Social and economic research on commercial sex work traditionally concentrates on women. While female sex work and the various ways it is institutionalized have been studied, very few studies focus on the differences in the ways that male sex work is organized. This focus has led to neglect of the heterogeneous social structures which give rise to the marked diversity of forms of male sex work around the globe.[18] In the research that surveys male prostitution, both scientific and popular media have pointed out several geographic and cultural distinctions in the practice and forms of male sex work that make it difficult to generalize the phenomena over space or time.[19] As different cultures grapple with the realities of human sexuality and embrace or repress the public expression of same-sex desire and identification, the rules and social norms governing male sex work change as well.

Theories of sexuality have paid particular attention to sexual minorities and marginalized sexualities as these are key for the development of both majority and minority sexualities and sexual identities.[20] The usual theoretical tools of power and gender are altered when we consider male prostitution, and this allows us to explore the dynamics within genders in a novel way.[21] For example, while female prostitution can be viewed as men replicating their dominance as sexual dominance of women in an exchange of sex for money, how this works between men is complicated by the fact that inter-gender relations need not be the same as intra-gender relations. We cannot use gender and its presentation to infer the sources of power and the degree of exploitation in the relationship.

Research on political economy among sexual minorities largely deals with the commoditization of gay desire.[22] As the social acceptability of gay relationships increases, gay consumers and their sexual norms become tools of marketing. This commoditization must exploit existing social norms about what is desired, and usually distinguishes itself from its heterosexual counterpart. Put another way, when men are commodified in contemporary society, there are explicit cues as to whether that commodification is homosexual or heterosexual. Some contemporary commentators even go so far as to state that ambiguous presentations are deliberate attempts to appeal to the largest market.

Commoditization is a market force with supply, demand, quantities, and prices. We can investigate how men in the male sex work market construct identities (commodify themselves) and are influenced by the social factors which lead to market rewards. Not every aspect of desire is commodified, however, and those that are commodified may come with different values befitting different levels of desirability. Importantly, the theoretical predictions about what is valued come from the noncommercial market, in particular what is known in social science as the "sexual field."

Borrowing from the conceptual framework in the physical sciences, social scientists use field theory to study the relations between elements in a given setting, a field. Field theory, in its broadest sense, attempts to explain the regularities of social behavior not only as the product of external (social) forces, but also internal forces (motivation). A key advantage of field theory is that one can analyze similar behavior (relations between elements) in different fields and draw very different theoretical predictions about the meaning of that behavior. For example, a person's action of participating in vigorous physical activity could have very different motivations in one field than in another.[23] This would hinge on the motivations and the relationship between the activity and its purported goal and how the activity allows an individual to relate to others. While field theory in general does not hypothesize about mechanisms, it does derive hypotheses about actions and motivations.

Field theory has not been extended to male sex work. Rather than deriving an entirely new theory to describe actions and motivations in the male sex work field, I use the existing theoretical work on gay sexual fields to derive hypotheses. This serves two purposes. First, scholarship about sexual fields commonly asserts that there is a marked distinction between the commercial and noncommercial sexual fields. Seeing if the hypotheses derived about the noncommercial sexual field hold for the commercial tells us how distinct the two fields are or are not. The degree of overlap between the two fields could be significant and would suggest that, in matters sexual, the distinction could be minimal. Second, by openly positing an overlap between the two fields, I explicitly entertain the possibility that the commodification of gay desire draws primarily not from self-identified gay desire, but from a broader range of men who have sexual desires for other men.

In both the past and present, significant numbers of male escorts and clients do not identify as homosexual.[24] Allen (1980) describes studies of male sex workers who find that fewer than 10 percent identify as homosexual, and since the controversial work of Humphreys (1970), social scientists have noted that men partaking in same-sex sexual behavior are unlikely to be found in surveys unless they choose to publicly reveal their sexual behaviors and desires.[25] As such, the world of male sex work is one of the few where men who adopt and refuse homosexual identity are in intimate contact with one another, and it offers us the opportunity to ask and answer many interesting questions about male sexual identity and homosexual desire. For example, we learn what roles and behaviors escorts must conform to in order to realize the largest economic gains from sex work, and this market extends beyond men who self-identify as gay. The value of these roles has the potential to inform our analysis of the construction of masculinity at the intersection of heterosexual and homosexual identities, since men participating in the market, both clients and escorts, adopt disparate sexual identities. This implies that we can learn more about desire that is not necessarily attached to the politics inherent in a publicly expressed gay identity.

Given the wealth of theories of sexuality, I adopt a broad theoretical view, drawing on the scholarship of social scientists looking at issues of male sexuality and male sex work. I borrow from the literatures in demography, economics and sociology, with additional insights from social psychology and public health to derive predictions. The approach here is not to be all-encompassing, but instead to outline the ways in which a sociologically informed analysis of male sex work emphasizes different dimensions of sex work and suggests alternative mechanisms underlying the market behavior we observe.

Hegemonic Masculinity

Hegemonic masculinity is defined as "the configuration of gender practice which embodies the currently accepted answer to the problem of legitimacy of patriarchy" (Connell 1995: 77). Hegemonic masculinity is about relations *between* genders and *within* genders.[26] In particular, hegemonic masculinity is about the *power relations* between and within genders. While changing over time, the root is a masculine "ideal" whose masculinity is defined not only by the presence of socially constructed "masculine" traits but the absence of socially constructed "feminine" traits. It is equally important for a man to be a man as it is for a man not to be a woman. While this seems somewhat unnecessary in a definition, it is important that masculinity be defined as both possessing some traits and rejecting others. It is the masculinity that epitomizes what a "man" is supposed to be and do. It contains not only physical ideals, but attitudes, beliefs, personality traits, and actions.

Hegemonically masculine practices ensure the dominant position of men over women, and of particular men over other men. The practices can take a number of forms, and research has usually stressed social traits such as drive, ambition, independence, assertiveness, self-reliance, and aggressiveness, which legitimize the power of men over women. This can also include the absence of other traits, such as empathy, communication, sensitivity, cooperation, or displays of emotion. The absence of these traits is important in the construction of the ideal because they come to define who is not masculine. It is not only the presence of traits such as aggressiveness that define the masculine ideal, but the absence of traits such as empathy.

Within genders, there is the subordination of certain masculinities and the marginalization of others.[27] Just as hegemonic masculinity acts to ensure the dominance of men over women, it also works to establish the dominance of some men over other men. For example, gay masculinities are subordinated and marginalized so that patriarchy can be reproduced through heterosexuality. Men who conform to a heterosexual masculine ideal dominate those who do not. Connell's (1995) conception is that hegemonic masculinity is never influenced by non-hegemonic elements – elements of non-heterosexuality in hegemonic masculinity are seen as contradictions or weakness.[28] In other words, the masculinity that gay men seek in sexual partners or in the public response to their own behavior is inherently counterfeit under hegemonic norms.

Scholars have noted the limits of this conceptual binary between hegemonic and non-hegemonic masculinity.[29] Demetriou, Reeser, Levine, and other scholars have suggested that rather than binary, hegemonic masculinity should be viewed as a hybrid, made up of practices and elements of both heterosexual and, for example, homosexual masculinities, giving hegemonic masculinity the ability to change over time to meet historical circumstances with a different set of practices. Masculinity is not a fixed definition; at any point in time the definition is culturally malleable, and over time it must change as the scope of human activity and relations change. Similarly, all men learn culturally specific hegemonic masculine norms because, irrespective of their future identities, these norms shape gendered relations.

Allowing for this broader definition of hegemonic masculinity expands the possibilities for gay and heterosexual masculinities to interact with each other, for masculinities to adapt to developments in subordinate masculinities, and increases the scope for empirical analysis. In the broader definition, the practices of gay men, who are non-hegemonic by design, act not only to reinforce the patriarchal goal of hegemonic masculinity, but also help to define the hegemonic ideal itself.[30] And the heterosexual counterpart need not reject all aspects of gay masculinities. Partly, this could be due to the fact that gay masculinities themselves are based on hegemonic ideals, and hence stem from the same source. If gay men were to reject all aspects of heterosexual masculinities it would threaten their desire to be seen and related to as men in society. In earlier generations this was the social category to which gay men were confined, the invert. Gay liberation sought to broaden the social acceptability of gay men and simultaneously allow them to construct masculinities that would reinforce the maleness of gay men. This required not the rejection of hegemonic masculinity inherent in the invert, but the development of a gay masculinity that incorporated several elements from hegemonic masculinity.

Additionally, drawing from gay masculinities in the refinement of hegemonic masculinity allows for finer distinctions between the two, which may be increasingly necessary in societies that socially accept openly gay individuals. Demetriou, for example, notes the recent construction of the "metrosexual" as one example of gay masculinity influencing the construction of the hegemonic ideal. Grooming practices are now acceptable within a heterosexual masculinity, but with clearly defined limits, and with the goal of pursuing women for sexual conquests. The extent to which gay masculinities contain elements of heterosexual masculinity could also serve to reinforce the power and authority of heterosexual masculinities. For example, if gay masculinities prize muscular physique it can serve to reinforce the notion that muscularity is a defining hegemonic masculine trait since *even gay men recognizes the "inherent" masculinity of it.*

This expansive definition allows some behaviors that may have been rendered contradictions in the past to become part of hegemonic masculinity in the present. The recent proliferation of men's beauty products would, under a binary framework, be labeled a contradiction. Under the hegemonic ideal, masculinity rejects any preoccupation with the finer details of physical appearance. (It is important to note that this is quite different from preoccupation with physique.) When used as a means of attracting women, however, the preoccupation with beauty regimens can fall under hegemonic masculinity, but only to the extent to which it serves the purpose of attracting women. To the extent that they would give some men more sexual conquest with women than others, these practices become a vehicle for establishing their masculinity both with women and relative to other men: in essence, heterosexual hegemonic masculinity explicitly borrowed from gay masculinities for the express purpose of the sexual domination of women.

An additional advantage of the expansive definition is that a hybrid approach opens the possibility of analyzing how gay men define, subordinate, and marginalize masculinities among themselves. In the analysis of sex work it is not male/female relations that are key, but relations among men themselves. Gay men practice a given set of gay hegemonic masculine norms that are used to define gay men's relationships with each other—these within gender relations are most interesting for the study of male sex work, and they require an expansive definition of hegemonic masculinity and a careful consideration of gay masculinity. Some gay masculinities can be accepted as more legitimate constructions of hegemonic masculinity than others, which allows gay men to create their own hierarchy of gay masculinities. These masculinities are interesting in and of themselves because they offer us the opportunity to regard what is considered hegemomically masculine among men who are counter-hegemonic by nature of their sexual orientation. In other words, it allows us to analyze what makes a gay man a "masculine gay man" and what does not.

Levine (1998), Donaldson (1993), and Connell (1992) note that gay men reinforce hegemonic norms – modern masculine gay practices celebrate and exemplify hegemonic ideals such as body building and concentration on physical strength. This reification of masculine norms can create a situation where some gay masculinities are themselves subordinate to others. This is counter to scholars who assert that gay men have developed entirely new norms of masculine behavior. Rather, gay masculinities that are most valued are those that come closest to heterosexual hegemonic masculinity. Donaldson (1993) raises the intriguing point that "it is not 'gayness' that is attractive to homosexual men, but 'maleness.' A man is lusted after not because he is homosexual but because he's a man. How counter-hegemonic can this be?" (p. 649). This becomes a question not only of masculinity but questions of practice, intention, and motivation as well.

While scholars of masculinity have asserted that gay men critique hegemonic ideals through counter-hegemony, it could also be the case that gay men overtly reinforce hegemonic ideals.[31] This may be even more likely sexually. Gay masculinities may be quite aligned with the hegemonic masculinity that marginalizes them. Thinking back to the subject of fields, hegemonic masculinity gives us concrete ideas as to why some men would be motivated to behave as they do. For gay men, the practice of a gay masculinity could be motivated by a number of non-mutually exclusive desires. First, it could reflect the desire to conform, as much as possible, with hegemonic masculinity. This would allow gay men to articulate a masculinity that retains their maleness as opposed to feminizing gay men due to their sexuality. This would confer some dominance over other men (both homosexual and heterosexual), who do not have such traits.[32] Second, it could reflect the desire to appeal sexually to other gay men, who see the hegemonic ideal as the most sexually desirable. Third, it could offer the most protection from heterosexual aggression, as conforming to hegemonic ideals would give one greater ability to "pass" as heterosexual. While there are studies that look at these types of values qualitatively and quantitatively between genders, little quantitative work exists that looks at differences *within* genders and the study of male sex work allows us to consider these within-gender relations in detail.[33]

Gay Masculinity, Heterosexual Masculinity, and Male Sex Work

The question, however, is how masculinity (hegemonic, homosexual, or heterosexual) should inform the analysis of male sex work. The key here is to recognize that masculinity is a collection of traits and practices which sex workers bring together in the market in the form of the persona that they create for clients. Escorts are selling temporary encounters that fulfill client fantasy and desire. As firms, sex workers must pay attention to client demand, and in a gay sexual arena this implies careful attention to masculinity at a number of levels.

One aspect is the basic element of attraction as broadly construed among gay men. While masculinity practiced between heterosexual men can be used to shield them from each other, create a distance, and offer an ordered way of interacting with each other (leader and follower) without the assumption of any sexual relationship, masculinity between homosexual men also acts as a practice to attract sexual partners. The practices may take their cues from the larger social construction of hegemonic masculinity, but their purpose is different and related to the counter-hegemonic practice of sexual relations between men. Rather than marking a territory where men define themselves relative to other men, gay masculinity is designed to bring men together socially and sexually in a way outside of the confines offered by the larger social construction.[34]

Gay masculinity serves a very different purpose within genders than heterosexual masculinity. While gay masculinity may incorporate parts of heterosexual masculinities, the sexual purpose is physical intimacy with another man. The empirical question is the degree to which homosexual men are complicit in hegemonic masculine norms – in Demetriou's language, the degree to which gay masculinities contain significant elements of hegemonic masculinities that legitimize patriarchy, and which may in turn influence hegemonic masculinity itself. Quantitative analysis of male sex work allows us to see how men who have sex with men value hegemonically masculine practices amongst themselves. In an explicitly sexual arena, hegemonic masculinity would extend to physical appearance (muscularity, body size, body hair, height) and sexual behaviors (sexual dominance, sexual aggressiveness, penetrative sexual position). To the extent to which homosexual men conform to and reinforce hegemonic masculine norms, the value of masculine traits and practices should have a direct effect on the desirability and value of a given escort. While the usual function of such "manhood acts" serves to elicit deference from other men and the reinforcement of hegemonic masculinity, in an explicitly homosexual arena it may also elicit sexual desire, fantasy, sexual excitement, and sexual objectification.[35] In this instance, what the sexual field would describe as desirable becomes demand from clients in the market.

This turns the traditional nature of dominance into a sexualized act. While aggression between men would establish the masculinity of one man relative to another, in a homosexual space it could also be a source of sexual power. Specifically, while hegemonic masculinity would presume that men desire to dominate others and establish their position in the hierarchy of men, it could act as a source of sexual desire for other men to the extent that dominance is something they desire in a partner. Masculinity becomes a source of overtly homosexual power.

The function of male sex work in gay communities may heighten the appeal of hegemonic ideals. In a market for sex work, clients are explicitly seeking sexual contact. Clients may choose escorts who would not be like the men that they would interact with socially but do desire sexually, which may act to increase the value of certain masculine characteristics insofar as the hegemonic masculine archetype may be a driving force in purely sexual desire.[36] Is the *lust* of men in this market consistent with hegemonic norms?

It is important to note that, although likely hegemonic, these masculinities are gay masculinities to the degree to which they are practiced among gay men themselves. The masculine presentations offered by the sex workers are done so to secure male clients for sex. In a binary these two masculinities would have little relation with one another, but in a hybrid the gay masculinity would share several features with the hegemonic. Although not directly tested since the entire market is sexual, the related question is how gay masculinity reifies and sexualizes the traits of hegemonic masculinity.[37]

This type of hybrid hegemonic masculinity would have additional implications about gay male body image and the body's use in the construction of masculinity among gay men. Levine (1998) and Sadownick (1996) see the gay liberation movement as a time when gay men began, *en masse*, to idealize hypermasculinity, muscles, and a hirsute body, turning on its head the "flight from masculinity" that Hooker (1957) observed for earlier generations of gay men who sought overtly feminine presentations of themselves to express their sexual orientation.[38] The physical ideal of gay masculinity is typified by muscular physique and other markers of hegemonic masculinity such as height, body hair, Whiteness, youth, and middle-class socioeconomic status.[39] This is not the rejection of hegemonic masculinity, but acquiescence to it as a means of defining a gay masculinity and sexual desire among gay men.

The gay masculine norm has a history that developed largely in urban areas in the United States and became typified by the 1970s as the *Gay Clone*. According to Levine's (1998) classic study of the gay masculine ideal, the currency that gay men began to use with one another was, in fact, masculinity. This came in two related parts, the "butch clone" and the "hot clone." The butch clone was a masculine look while the hot clone was a direct projection of explicitly male sexuality and eroticism. Physically, this referred to muscular bodies, facial hair, and clothing that was related to masculine, manual occupations such as construction worker. To convey sexual prowess, men wore tight clothing, spoke in low, deep voices, and maintained an aloof manner consistent with detached emotions.[40] That is, both the physical representation and the practices were important in the development of gay masculinity. The construction of the clone, one example of the unique interaction between hegemonic masculinity and gay sexuality, allowed gay men to both parody and personify hegemonic masculine norms physically, psychologically, and socially.

This turn of events has molded the gay body into a political representation of masculinity, in part subverting norms that question the compatibility of masculinity and homosexuality, but at the same time reinforcing a quasi-masculine ideal.[41] The reinforcement has powerful effects – even *gay men* believe that this or that is masculine, which serves to reinforce the power of that masculine ideal in society in general. Gay men have shown stronger tendencies to prefer particular body types than either lesbians or heterosexuals, and this can lead to poor psychological and health outcomes for gay men who do not conform to gay standards of beauty.[42] The development of rigid norms regarding the sexual desirability of specific body parts was arguably related to the development of gay masculinity, and that masculinity was further used to define some gay men relative to others as more/less masculine. This helped not only to define the physical traits that a masculine gay man was supposed to possess, but also what traits would be seen as sexually desirable.[43]

In fact, attempts by some gay subcultures to subvert these beauty standards have been critiqued as being agents themselves of hegemonically masculine agendas.[44] For example, *gay bear* culture supplants (in some formulations) muscles as a marker of masculinity, instead offering a hirsute, affable masculinity that is more empathetic and emotional than the stoic clone. Bear culture offers men who do not have muscular physique access to a gay masculinity that retains the maleness through facial and body hair as opposed to physique. Part of the reason for this was to reject gay masculine ideals that prized a muscular physique, and offer an alternative construction of masculinity. Over time, however, this led to the development of "muscle bears" (men who are both muscular and hirsute) who are able to combine both constructions of masculinity and reinforce the underlying hegemonic ideal.[45]

In many ways, the rejection of large and thin men can be seen as the rejection (subjugation) of feminizing features. For example, excess weight in a man visually minimizes the relative size of male genitals, produces larger (and, importantly, non-muscular) male breasts, and so on. At low weights men will appear slight, waifish, and physically weak. Also, given the social norms regarding female body size, thinness is seen as adhering more to a feminized body image than a masculine one. These act to emphasize feminizing traits that are actively discouraged in mainstream gay culture.[46] This suggests that in the market for male sex work, clients would prize physical characteristics such as muscular physiques, body hair, and height, as those would be markers of hegemonic masculinity. It also suggests that excess weight and thinness would be penalized, as these are feminizing features.

According to earlier scholarship on the construction of gay masculinities, the body was explicitly objectified in casual sexual encounters. Personalizing features such as hair color, eye color were not the chief determinants of attraction. In fact, personalizing features were said to be relatively unimportant in the casual sexual arena. While personalized features play a role in the development of romantic relationships, they are not the deciding factors in sexual conquest and the search for casual partners. The most prized features were those body parts most directly linked to maleness and homosexual sex – penis size and musculature of the chest, arms, back, legs, and buttocks.[47]

Both the theory of hegemonic masculinity and the closely related literature on the body in gay communities suggest that clients of male sex workers are likely to prize "masculine" personas and body type. There are several reasons for this. First, numerous scholars have asserted that gay men's relationships with effeminate behavior is complex – while celebrated in many aspects of gay culture (camp, drag shows, diva worship, etc.), it is particularly stigmatized in sexual relationships and as an object of lust.[48] Feminized behavior is not as desirable, as it falls outside of the constructed gay masculinity. For a culture that is defined by sexual orientation, one must pay special attention to the sexual desirability of particular features. While gay men may consume counter-hegemonic representations of masculinity as art and entertainment, their sexual desires may align firmly to the hegemonic ideal. If this is the case, it would be inexact to assert that gay men are counter-hegemonic sexually.

Second, some have noted the ways in which the gay community has commoditized the "authentic" masculinity of self-identified heterosexual men who engage in sex with men, and this has given rise to the distinction between "genuinely masculine gay men" and "posturing masculine gay men" in gay communities.[49] It is unclear how these types are related to the social construction because the definition of "genuine" versus "posturing" is entirely subjective. In popular gay media, this is usually linked to interest in sports and other traditionally masculine recreation and a rejection of camp, drag, and other traditionally gay recreation or interests such as decorating, fashion, and entertaining.

This supposes that at the highest level of gay masculinities are men who may or may not be gay but who participate in homosexual acts. This would be consistent with two concepts. First, the desire for heterosexual men who have sex with men to possess an "authentic" masculinity that homosexual men, by nature of their sexual orientation, do not have access to. Second, it reinforces the motivations of gay men to aspire as much as possible to the hegemonic ideal, as that would have the most appeal among men who are gay and therefore cannot access the heterosexual hegemonic ideal. In male sex work, many men describe themselves as "straight" to the client base.

The construction of multiple masculinities among gay men and the distinctions between the two are used to legitimate the power of "masculine" gay men over "effeminate" gay men, a reproduction of patriarchy.[50] Even more, there are nuanced distinctions between varieties of gay masculinity – and it could be the case that only those masculinities that allow homosexual sex, and who in every other way conform to the hegemonic heterosexual ideal, have the largest sexual desirability in gay spaces. We would expect that men who are interacting primarily for sexual purposes would likely place a premium on masculine sexual practices (penetrative sexual position, aggressive sexual behavior, muscular physique, etc.), and to penalize feminine practices (receptive sexual position, submissiveness, large body size, thinness, etc.) to the degree to which both conform not only to hegemonic masculinity, but also the construction of masculine gay identity among gay men.

Intersectionality and Male Sex Work

The theory of hegemonic masculinity has been critiqued for not considering the ways that gay men can conform to and inform hegemonic masculinity. In fact, the very use of the term hegemon implies a sort of overarching masculinity that is relatively invariant and does not interact with other social processes. At its core, hegemonic masculinity does not allow for other social constructions to create different types of hegemonic masculinity that may have different import in gay sexual spaces. The complex relationship with masculinity in both its physical and sexual manifestations has interesting theoretical interactions with other types of characteristics.

Scholars of gender have long noted that the ways in which masculinity is distributed among and within discrete racial and ethnic groups in society must be explored. Racial and ethnic critiques of hegemonic masculinity (and even the gay masculinity described above) state that it does not account for other identities that have had limited access to hegemonic masculinity. If hegemonic masculinity is restricted in Western society to White men of particular educational and social standing, then many men will not be able to attain the masculine ideal, irrespective of their sexual orientation. This also raises the question of how those masculinities are constructed and sexually desired by gay men. Allowing for racial and ethnic variation in the concept of hegemonic masculinity allows for a fuller and more nuanced analysis of the masculinity that would be valued in gay sexual interactions.

There is a burgeoning literature that looks at the racial variation in social value among gay men and a literature that looks at how masculinity and its representations are influenced by other social stereotypes.[51] At heart, this nuanced approach to hegemonic masculinity is not concerned with sexual orientation *per se*, but with ways that racial ideals about masculinity are reformulated by gay men. This requires an intersectional approach to the topic of masculinity and its value. This is necessary for the analysis of male sex work because of the racial diversity of male sex workers. To apply a racially specific form of masculinity (gay or heterosexual) upon these men would be a naïve approach. These questions add greater complexity to the analysis of masculinity in male sex work, as they consider the interplay of hegemonic masculinity with a number of social factors that have been shown to influence sexual desire.

As the theory of intersectionality suggests, the interaction of these social categories is neither cumulative nor additive, but rather independent.[52] The intersection of hegemonic masculinity with racial/sexual stereotypes can create multiple forms of sexual objectification for particular types of gay men that are unique to them. For example, the value of a "top" is not uniform across all tops (as hegemonic masculinity would predict). The value of that particular sexual activity is both a function of its general value as a component of hegemonic masculinity and a function of the type of man presumed to be the most successful at the activity. It follows directly that the value of a White "top" is not simply the addition of the value of Whiteness and "topness," but an independent effect for men in that particular category, who in this instance embody the highest position in the racial and sexual behavior hierarchies among gay men. Most important, occupying this position need not bring the highest value – there may be other men (not at the highest position of the racial hierarchy) who would be more valued for the specific combination of those traits. Markets for sex may reinforce these sexual stereotypes (what Cameron et al. [1999] term "ethnico-sexual stereotypes") in explicitly monetary terms.

Baldwin (1985) has noted that the American ideal of sexuality is rooted in the American ideal of masculinity, which, he argues, necessitates an inherently racial dimension. While white men were historically given the duty to protect White women from Black sexuality, and this supposed threat legitimized the social control of White women by White men (and Whites over Blacks), for the homosexual White man the sexuality of the Black man becomes an object of desire because he is perceived to be sexually dominant and unrestrained, although still under the social control of Whites due to his race, turning the hegemonic ideal on its head.[53] Levine (1998), Robinson (2008), McBride (2005), Reid-Pharr (2001), and others have noted how racial stereotypes interact with notions of masculinity to produce a desire for hypermasculine Black men, particularly among White gay men.

This extends to the representation of Black bodies themselves and even the degree to which Black men can access social categories of gay masculinity. Dyer (1997) notes that the very social construction of "muscle man" is largely confined to Whites, which suggests that the gay Clone/Muscle culture discussed earlier is only accessed by White gay men. The avenues of masculinity afforded to Black gay men are distinct from those available to White gay men. While Black men are allowed to be muscular and are perceived as masculine when adhering to larger social scripts of masculinity, their masculinity must be presented differently than that of White gay men. Indeed, the masculinity of Black men has a different social interpretation.

Levine (1998) notes that Black gay Clones are inherently different from White ones, where Black clones were perceived as being more dangerous than White men. To the extent that Black men had "currency" in gay clone culture, it was due to their association with danger and explicitly rough masculinity. White muscularity, according to Dyer, is related to White supremacy and the product of careful management of their diet and physique. Among Black men, this is stigmatized as being the by-product of time spent in incarceration (a criminalization, where Black muscularity is due to a "prison gym build"), playing sports, or attributed to "genetics" or "natural ability" and therefore not due to mindful and purposeful choices regarding diet and training. The leisure needed to partake in weight training is attributed to affluence in Whites and deviance in Blacks. Similarly, the mental acumen and diligence needed to maintain a strict physical and dietary regimen is attributed to discipline and intelligence in Whites and genetic endowments in Blacks. To Dyer, this works to deprive Black muscularity of the perception that it is due to achievement, which is inherently granted to White muscularity. As such, the same embodiment of hegemonic masculinity, and the gay modifications thereof, are constructed and interpreted along racial lines that limit the ways that Black men can adopt gay masculinities.

The development of gay masculinities took place in gay neighborhoods that developed after the Second World War.[54] These spaces, then and now, are overwhelmingly White. Nero (2005) notes that these locations are places of explicit racial hostility and sexual hospitality to particular types of gay men. While not specifically mentioning earlier ethnographic work, Nero delineates the ways in which Blackness is made incompatible with gayness by White gay men, largely due to Black gay men being savage and violent.[55] This is similar to the ways in which Black masculinity is constructed as being hyper-violent, dangerous, and beyond redemption to the point of pathology.[56] The construction of Black masculinity by White gay men justifies the social exclusion of Black men from gay communities at the time when explicitly gay masculinities were being defined. This social exclusion of Black gay men did not extend to sexual relations, however. In sexual relations the same constructions that rendered them socially unacceptable also made them sexually desirable.

This hypermasculinity among Black men is a direct result of sexualized racial fetishism in gay communities, concomitant with social exclusion.[57] In social surveys of gay men, more than three-quarters of White gay men believed that Black men were the most well-endowed sexual partners. More than 80 percent of Black gay men have reported feeling sexually objectified because of their race by White gay men. More than 60 percent of White gay men believe that Black men are sexually dominant.[58] This objectification is not the generalized fetishism of a dark body, it is the explicit fetishization of the supposed link between race and penis length and girth. In fact, white gay men have adopted an acronym to describe the genitals of black men: "BBC," which stands for "big black cock."[59] The BBC acronym is ubiquitous among gay men on dating sites, in pornography, and in other gay sexual spaces. Its use extends beyond penis size itself to encompass a number of sexual traits that would establish Black men as prized sexual partners. It often includes specific mention of dominance, aggressiveness, and the submission of the White partner. Its use is not in reference to penis size, which may be a sign of masculinity in a general sense, but in particular to *Black* penis size.

The stereotype of the sexually dominant Black men, rather than being an agent of fear, is celebrated for his hypersexual behavior, appearance, and conduct. As noted earlier, the general level of social interaction between Black and White gay men is relatively low, and occurs chiefly over sex.[60] Black men who demonstrate hypermasculine and sexually aggressive behavior are offered entry into White gay spaces, but this entry is limited to sexual liaisons. McBride (2005), for example, notes the limited range to which Black men interact with Whites in gay pornography, where the vast majority of Black performers are "tops" and adopt a "thug" persona. In a strictly sexual space, Black men who adopt an aggressive persona and who convincingly display sexual dominance may be particularly prized for sexual encounters.

It is useful to note how this sexual hierarchy upends a traditional gender interpretation. In a gender theory, the dominance of one over another would, by definition, signal the power of the dominant group. In this sexual space, however, the dominance of Black men is not general. While Black men are seen as sexually aggressive men, they are still socially controlled. The submission of White men to this dominance is entirely voluntary and has as its purpose the sexual fulfillment of White men. Unlike the submission of women, the submission of White men to Black sexual dominance does not negate their higher social standing. In many respects, it reinforces racial hierarchies by allowing White access to Black bodies for White sexual fulfillment. The actual dominance or submission that takes place is still done under a racial hierarchy in which Whites are in control of Black bodies and where White sexual pleasure is prioritized over Black sexual pleasure.

This racially sexualized space is firmly within a racial hierarchy. Many White scholars of gay sexual organization imply that sexual intimacy between Black and White men fosters a sense of sexual kinship.[61] These sorts of claims are at odds with the lack of racial equality in White gay sexuality. In such a racialized space, kinship, to the extent that it exists, is not the same as equality. This sexualized space offers a clear form of racial control and prescribed behavior that is predicted on stereotypical views of Black male bodies, Black sexuality, and the perceived superiority of White sexual partners. Indeed, many scholars of "sexual racism" in gay communities point to the explicit exclusion of non-White partners, but pay little attention to the limits on how non-White men are *included* and the limitations on that inclusion.[62] The inclusion of non-White men in these sexual spaces carries a different, but related, set of racial presumptions. For example, the inherent limitations placed on Black masculinity in White gay spaces requires that any arguments of egalitarian practice in interracial sexual spaces obviate the racial structures that oversee these interactions. Inclusion is *not* the opposite of exclusion.

This racial control extends to those who would seek to defy the stereotype. Since White gay men desire Black men as sexually aggressive partners, those Black men who defy such restrictions would not be desired. This, in and of itself, suggests that there are limits to the sexual pleasure that Black men can expect when operating within gay masculine norms. Such racial stereotypes could also give rise to markedly lower values for men who defy racial-sexual stereotypes, and become in this particular instance counter-hegemonic. Robinson (2008) finds that Black men who do not conform to the stereotype of the hypermasculine Black male are largely ignored and devalued by White gay men, suggesting that the penalties for nonconformity may be particularly harsh. This again is counter to a traditional interpretation of sexual dominance.

The reverse is true for Asians, whose passivity and docility are celebrated. In racialized gay masculinity, Asian men lack the socially constructed "maleness" conferred upon others. In terms of personality, Asian men are perceived to be docile, compliant, and lacking in the hegemonic traits that would confer "inherent maleness" to them.[63] Robinson (2007, 2008), Phua and Kaufman (2003), and Han (2006) describe the persistent stereotype that Asian men should be passive, docile "bottoms." More than half of White gay men believe that Asian men are sexually submissive.[64]

Just as there are stereotypes about Black penis size and masculinity, there exist stereotypes about Asian penis size and masculinity. The racial stereotypes about the sexual submissiveness of Asian men are not independent of the racial stereotypes about Asian penis size. In surveys, more than 75 percent of White gay men believe that Asian men have small penises.[65] The fact that penis size is so related to race and sexual stereotypes for Asian men, but in a different direction than for Black men, shows the way that gay masculinity interacts with racially specific stereotypes and creates distinct rules of masculinity for specific types of men.

Those Asian men who perform in a traditionally submissive role would be seen as conforming to their racially based stereotypes. In this case, the counter-hegemonic activity is for the Asian man to appear sexually dominant or aggressive. As with Black men, this racial-sexual stereotype allows the larger gay community to limit the socially acceptable sexual expressions of Asian men. These authors and others have also noted that Hispanics are celebrated as passionate, virile lovers. Indeed, more than 70 percent of White gay men agree that Hispanic men are passionate. Although this can sometimes be conflated with sexual dominance, it is difficult to discern. It is difficult to reformulate this racial-sexual stereo-type into a specific hypothesis.

The intersection of race with sexual stereotypes shows that racial dom-inance plays itself out in different ways for expectations of sexual dom-inance and submissiveness. None of the sexual dominance or submission, however, acts to upend the racial hierarchy. In this setting, non-White bodies exist for the purpose of sexual pleasure for White gay men to the degree to which they conform to racially specific norms of sexual behavior. The sexual dominance of White men, the submissiveness of Asian men, and the passion of Hispanic men are all socially controlled by Whites. Some scholars would assert that the racial dynamics break the link between sexual dominance and social dominance.

In a market for sex work, these social processes would play out in the returns that sex workers would see for their services. While we may expect White sex workers to be functions of hegemonic masculine norms, Black, Asian, and Hispanic men may see very different realities owing to the intersection of race with gay masculinities and hegemonic masculinities, both of which place restrictions on non-White sexuality. This would be due to the interaction of racial-sexual stereotypes and the fact that the demand side of the market is dominated by White gay men, and specifically, given the prices charged, White middle- and upper-class men who may or may not identify as gay. While the theory posited above presumed that the pleasure of White gay men was the driving force of the racial distinctions, in the market for male sex work there is little doubt that the client's pleasure is directly related to compensation.

Given these racial-sexual stereotypes, it is necessary to consider how the values of particular sexual behaviors differ by race. Phua and Kaufman (2003) find that dating "preferences for minorities often are tinted with stereotypical images: Asians as exotic, docile, loyal partners; Hispanics as passionate, fiery lovers; and Blacks as 'well-endowed,' forbidden partners" (p. 992). If the market for male sex work mirrors the gay community at large, then we would expect Black men who advertise themselves to be "tops" to command high prices in the market, and for Asian men who advertise themselves as "bottoms" to command high prices as well, reflect-ing the value of conforming to racial-sexual stereotypes.

EMPIRICAL STRATEGY

Previous quantitative work analyzing male escorts has not exploited the prices of male escort services.[66] I make use of the prices of male escort services with a hedonic regression, a technique developed by Court (1939), Griliches (1961), and Rosen (1974). The basic technique is to regress the price of a particular good or service on its characteristics. For example, if one were performing a hedonic regression of computers, one would assemble data on the computers in the market and their characteristics, such as processor speed, hard drive size, memory, graphics card, and monitor size. A regression of computer prices on characteristics would then give coefficients for each of the characteristics, which would tell us how much computer prices increase or decrease, on average, for an increase or decrease in hard drive size or monitor quality. This type of regression is widely used in economics and is particularly useful for goods that are inherently unique and/or bundled.

The estimated coefficients from hedonic regressions are commonly interpreted as implicit prices, as they reflect the change in price that one could expect, on average, for a change in that particular characteristic.[67] It is common to refer to positive coefficients as a premium and negative coefficients as a penalty. Using this insight, I regress the price of individual escort i's services (P) on the escort's characteristics (Z), his sexual behaviors (S), and identifiers for his location (X).

$$\ln(P_i) = \alpha + \sum_{j}^{J-1} \beta_j Z_{ij} + \sum_{k}^{K-1} \gamma_k S_{ik} + \delta X + \varepsilon_i \tag{1}$$

The regression gives the implicit prices for each characteristic (each β) and for each sexual behavior (each γ). I control for the escort's location to purge my estimates of geographic differences in prices.[68] As I take the log of price in this specification, my estimates are percentage price changes for each characteristic. In describing the results, I emphasize the percentage differences, but to increase the exposition I also give the dollar value of the differentials based upon an average price of \$200 per session.[69] It is important to emphasize that these differentials are cumulative. For example, a 10 percent (\$20) price differential per session could lead to earnings differences in excess of \$5,000 per year.[70]

EMPIRICAL RESULTS

Physical Characteristics and Male Escort Prices

Given that clients in commercial sex markets generally tend to be older White men, I would expect clients to prize youth and beauty, which is

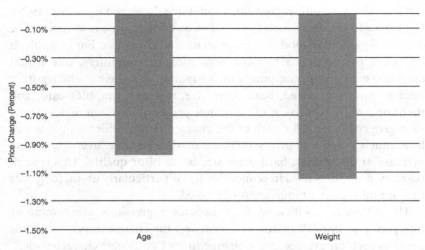

Figure 4.1 Age, weight, and escort prices

consistent with female sex work.[71] The theory of hegemonic masculinity and the related literature on the gay body, however, also predict that hegemonically masculine physical traits would be prized in the market. Figure 4.1 shows the estimates of the value of age and weight on the pricing of male escort services from hedonic regressions of escort prices on these characteristics. There is a penalty for age, with each additional year of age costing an escort 1 percent ($2) of his price. Similarly, there is a penalty for weight, with each additional ten pounds resulting in more than a 1.5 percent ($3) price decrease.[72]

Figure 4.2 shows the results for body build, another characteristic that appears to be important. Men with average body type face a price penalty that exceeds 15 percent ($30), while men who have excess weight face a price penalty of more than 30 percent ($60).[73] Also, men who are thin face a price penalty, although it is not as large as the penalty for those who are average or overweight, being on the order of 5 percent ($10). This is consistent with work that finds that the social penalty for additional weight among gay men is large, theoretical work that describes the codes of body image in gay communities, and the literature on the body, which suggests significant penalties for weight among gay men, as both excess weight and thinness have feminizing features.[74] Men who have a muscular build, however, enjoy a price premium of around 4 percent ($8). Indeed, only men who have muscular builds enjoy a price premium relative to "athletic/swimmer's build," the reference category. As muscularity is a physical signal of maleness

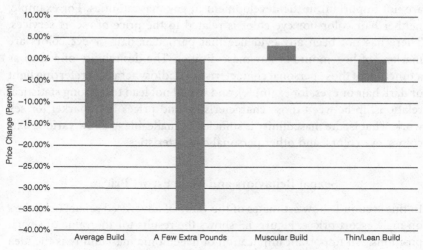

Figure 4.2 Body type and male escort prices

and dominance and can be considered a proxy for strength and virility, the premium attached to muscularity in this market is consistent with hegemonic masculinity.

Surprisingly, race does not seem to play an independent role in escort prices. There is no race that commands higher prices in the market than any other. While some escorts of color have claimed in the media that they are paid less than their White counterparts, I do not see this in the data.[75] Body hair, a masculine trait, does not come with a premium in this market. In general, this result goes against theories stipulating that there is a hegemonic ideal with reference to body hair. On the other hand, gay masculinities have been known to adhere to a manicured look for men, consistent with what is seen for professional bodybuilders, who regularly shave the majority of their body hair to accentuate the appearance of their muscles.[76] It appears that most personal characteristics other than weight and body build are not very important in the male escort market, *per se.* While this is somewhat inconsistent with the theory of hegemonic masculinity, it is also the case that selection of men into sex work could drive the lack of results to a certain extent. If the majority of men selecting into sex work do so conditionally on appealing to hegemonic and/or gay masculine norms, there may not be enough variation between them in certain characteristics that would be statistically related to prices.

Importantly, the lack of any distinction due to other personal characteristics is consistent with Levine's (1998) notion that personal characteristics are not important in the development of gay masculinities. For example, neither hair color nor eye color is related to the price of escort services. There has not been any evidence that particular hair or eye colors are markers of hegemonic or gay masculinities. The desirability of a man as a function of those personal characteristics is idiosyncratic (preferring light or dark hair or eyes, for example), and would not lead to a strong statistical relationship between those characteristics and prices in a market for sex work. That is, the masculinity is sufficiently malleable to allow various hair colors, eye colors, and other personal characteristics.

Sexual Behaviors and Male Escort Prices

In this section I show estimates of the value of advertised sexual behaviors on male escort prices. Figure 4.3 shows the results for the value of sexual positions. An important implication of hegemonic masculinity is the idea that dominant sexual behaviors would be rewarded in the male escort market. Consistent with hegemonic masculinity, the premium to being a "top" is large, more than 9 percent ($18), and the penalty for being a "bottom" is substantial – in some specifications it is nearly as large as the premium to being a "top," on the order of –9 percent ($18). The price differential for men who are "tops" versus men who are bottoms – the "top"/ "bottom" differential – is substantial, ranging from 14.1 percent ($28) to 17.6 percent ($35), depending on how the model is specified.[77]

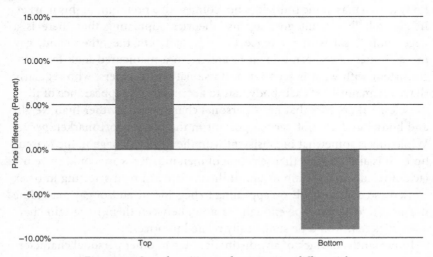

Figure 4.3 Sexual position and escort price differentials

Since there is little in the production function or inputs that would necessitate a difference in prices, the marked price differences between tops and bottoms is difficult to economically discern. These results can be interpreted sociologically, however, as the premium attached to masculine behavior in gay communities. The premium for "tops" is consistent with the literature, which notes that gay men prize traditionally masculine behaviors and sexual roles, and that the penetrative partner in sexual acts is canonically considered more "masculine." The fact that men who act in the "dominant" sexual position charge higher prices for their services is also consistent with the social acceptance of quasi-heteronormativity within groups of men who have sex with men. As described earlier, gay communities prize behavior that can be described as hegemonically masculine, and this would extend to sexual acts themselves.[78]

There are other alternative explanations for the "top" premium that bear mentioning. One possibility is that the premium may derive from the biology of being a "top." If "topping" requires ejaculation and "bottoming" does not, this could limit the number of clients that "tops" could see in a given period of time and could therefore drive the premium. Essentially, there could be a "scarcity premium" for "top" services that would be consistent with supply and demand. The search of escort advertisements, however, revealed that "top" escorts who mention "bottoming" also mention that they charge a significant premium for "bottoming" services.[79] Similarly, a detailed analysis of client reviews and online forums did not show that clients demand ejaculation more from "top" escorts than "bottoms." I take this as evidence of the *social* penalty of "bottoming" and premium of "topping." While biology could certainly play a role, the social position of "tops" appears to be the dominant force behind the "top" premium observed in this market

The Intersection of Race and Sexual Behaviors

As I described earlier, the intersection of race and sexual behaviors could shed quantitative light on many of the concepts at the intersection of hegemonic masculinity and racial-sexual stereotypes. In particular, Black men are expected to be dominant sexually and Asians, passive. I investigate these intersections by looking at the interaction of race and sexual behaviors. Figure 4.4 shows estimates of the value of advertised sexual behaviors for men by race, where each entry shows the implicit prices of the interaction of that race and sexual behavior (e.g., the premium or penalty to being a White "top" or "versatile" White).

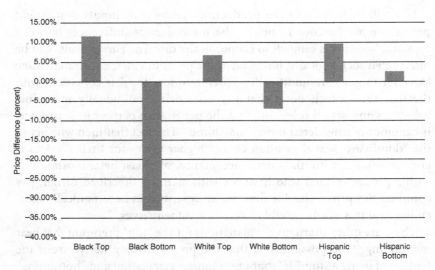

Figure 4.4 Sexual position and race price differentials

The results are striking. Black, Hispanic, and White men each receive a substantial premium for being "tops," but the largest premium is for Black men (nearly 12 percent [$24]). The premium for Hispanics is greater than 9 percent ($18), while for Whites the premium is less than 7 percent ($14). There is no statistically significant "top" premium for Asian escorts.[80] The penalty for being a "bottom" also varies by race – White "bottoms" face a penalty of nearly 7 percent ($14), while Black "bottoms" face a penalty that is nearly 30 percent ($60), the largest penalty seen in any of the results in Figure 4.4. Also of note is the lack of a "bottom" penalty for Asians or Hispanics.

The "top"/"bottom" price differential also varies by race. While the differential for Whites and Hispanics is close to the overall "top"/"bottom" differential (13.2 percent [$26] and 12.3 percent [$25], respectively, while the estimates of Figure 4.3 put the differential between 14.1 and 17.6 percent), the differential for Blacks is more than *twice* the differential for any other racial group, 36.5 percent ($73). These results are consistent with the intersection theory outlined earlier, where Black men who conform to stereotypes of hypermasculinity and sexual dominance are highly sought after, and those who do not conform are severely penalized. These types of stereotypes appear to carry over to the male escort market, and they influence the premiums and penalties for sexual behaviors. The predictions for

Asians, however, are not borne out in the data – I found no "top" premium or "bottom" penalty for Asian escorts in the data.[81]

DISCUSSION AND CONCLUSION

This chapter sheds important quantitative light on questions pertaining to male sex work, and in doing so we learn a great deal about gay male sexuality in general. Drawing on the literature from a broader swath of social science research, I highlighted some important questions about male sex work that could be answered through quantitative methods. These were not economic questions, but were related to how the social informs the economic. I uncovered a number of facts that should stimulate further research into male sex work and the related areas of gender, sexuality, masculinity, race, and crime. In general, the results highlight the fact that male sex work is markedly different, socially, from its female counterpart, and also shows how some of the concepts of ethnographic, qualitative, and theoretical work in social science can be subjected to quantitative empirical approaches, including statistical tests of hypotheses.

Gender and sexuality, particularly cultural constructions of masculinity, inform this market process a great deal. I found that personal characteristics were largely unrelated to the prices of male escorts, except for those pertaining to body build. I found that muscular men enjoy a premium in the market, while overweight and thin men see a penalty, which is consistent with hegemonic masculinity and the literature on the body and sexuality. Conformity to hegemonic and gay masculine physical norms is well-rewarded in the market.

I found that the premium to being a "top" was substantial, as was the penalty for being a "bottom," again consistent with the theory of hegemonic masculinity and possibly an extension to the value that gay masculinity places of sexual dominance. When interacting these behaviors with race, I found that Black men were at the extremes – their premiums for "top" and penalties for "bottom" behavior were the largest. This is consistent with the intersection theory that gay communities prize Black men who conform to racialized stereotypes of sexual behavior and penalize those who do not. While the sexually dominant Black male is feared in heterosexual communities, he is rewarded handsomely in gay communities. The variation of the penalties and premiums also points to the possibility that hegemonic masculinity is much more malleable than others have suggested. The concept of gay masculinity must also grapple with the matter of who is allowed to be masculine within a gay context and whether or not that masculine presentation is controlled by another process, such as racial stereotypes of sexual behavior. Here, I found that the racial hierarchy exerts strong pressure on masculine sexual representations in male sex work.

Given these results, the ways in which desire interacts with racial stereotypes should be given focused and significant attention in masculinity studies, particularly the ways that racial hierarchies influence the construction of gay masculinity and its presentation. Theoretically, these results should focus renewed attention on the complex construction of masculinities among gay men, in which counter-hegemonic groups adopt and reiterate hegemonic masculine norms among themselves, and explicitly reinforce hegemonic norms as a result. This is not only a reification of hegemonic masculinity, but also an importation of racially restrictive codes of sexual behavior. In particular, further work at the nexus of the construction of gay masculinity, its interaction with hegemonic masculinity, and the interlocking forces of racial inequality would be a fruitful area of research. While this appears in the market for sex workers, it could have stronger or weaker effects among gay men more generally.

This chapter has made use of novel data to test theories of male sex work, but several limitations should be noted. First, I have analyzed only the largest website for escort advertisements, and it is not certain that the results I present would hold for other website competitors. For example, if certain types of escorts are more likely to congregate at different websites, I would not be able to capture them here, and this would limit this survey's ability to describe the market in general. While the travel of male escorts certainly links markets, it could be the case that the values here do not correspond to the values recorded elsewhere, even by the same escort. Second, the information in the advertisements is posted by the escorts and therefore constitutes a self-report. While I have exploited independent data to confirm the precision of the price measure, it is not possible to say with certainty that there are not omitted confounders in the data. This is important, since the conclusions here are about perceived market values of certain masculine characteristics. Third, there may be omitted variables that would influence the price of escort services that are not included in these data, such as endowment, the escort's education level, and expertise in specific sexual conduct.

These limitations, however, should not be viewed as deficiencies, but rather calls for future quantitative research on male sex work. For example, future studies should look to analyze competing websites with a similar methodology to confirm or dispute the results of this chapter. Similarly, detailed analysis of client-operated websites that review escort services could act as an independent check on the veracity of the information posted in escort advertisements. Panel data on male escorts that would allow us to track escorts over time to see how and whether their behaviors, identities, advertisements, and personas change, would add an important dimension to this literature. Unfortunately, the new policing of male escort websites, which led to the closure of Rentboy.com in August 2015, make it difficult to replicate the data collected and analyzed here. Also, with the new policing by federal authorities, the remaining websites have made pricing data more coarse or nonexistent, which makes it difficult to estimate value.

The work also calls for new research on the interaction of race, sexuality, and commerce, which can address issues unexplored here. For instance, due to data limitations I cannot discuss the class dimensions that are inherent in male sex work and feature prominently in hegemonic and gay masculinities. An important question for intersectionality, in light of the results presented here, is how race and sexual behavior interact with class masculinities to yield premiums and penalties in this market. Further developments along those lines would allow us to demonstrate whether class distinctions also play a significant role. As this chapter has shown, there is much to be gained from an integrated, interdisciplinary approach to male sex work that seeks to use an economic approach to uncover the economic premiums and penalties that stem from social behaviors. The results here speak to the power of masculinity in the commerce of male sex work, the values that men have in gay sexual markets, and the strong links between gay and hegemonic masculinities.

5

Show, Tell, and Sell: Self-Presentation in Male Sex Work[1]

How do male sex workers use social cues to present themselves to the market? In street prostitution, the study would extend to the places where sex workers congregate, how they distinguish themselves from others, and how they signal to clients that they are available for hire. In the online market for sex work, the presentations are inherently more technologically advanced but must still communicate the same information to clients, and perhaps more. This is even more important online since there is no conversation to reassure clients that they will have a satisfactory experience. Also, a presentation online must be explicit enough to entice a client but not so direct as to be off-putting. The advertising strategy in the online market must be sophisticated, taking cues from social norms about how gay sex is advertised and how to most effectively communicate one's desirability and specific sexual expertise. Online sex workers must communicate their ability to fulfill client demand without personal contact.

Given the need to communicate nonverbally through digital media, the study of online sex work provides an opportunity to analyze how culture and society regulate the presentation of sexual services. Sex work is, at a minimum, a performed exchange.[2] This performance goes beyond simple marketing of a known product, because sexual experiences are inherently unique. The sale of male sexual services online requires that sex workers construct images that should be studied in light of the ways male sex workers develop an online persona to secure clients. In a strict marketing sense, sex workers present themselves to clients and advertise what they will do. But in sex work, sex workers are advertising a personalized, experiential service. This includes not only sex acts, but sexual persona, fantasies, and the ability to have an experience that can many times be at odds with the reality of the sexual exchange. For example, a sex worker who advertises himself to be a "boy next door" is fulfilling a very different role than one who advertises himself to be a "bad boy" or some other sexual archetype. Clients are seeking not simply money for sex in a pure transaction, but an intimate experience with a particular man who is desired both for who he is specifically and for what he represents generally to a client. It is an odd combination of needing to be an individual (lest a client hire another sex worker) but simultaneously a commodity (creating an image that clients will intuitively interpret correctly, sexually).

Both clients and sex workers adopt certain roles to fulfill client demand for fantasy, intimacy, and other nonsexual services.[3] These desires exert pressures on the ways sex workers present their physical selves to clients. Part of what is being exchanged is access to a sex worker's physical body and sexual performance, which includes a sexual persona. The body and its presentation are part of the exchange, and therefore informed by societal notions of desire, attractiveness, and sexual stratification. The issue here is not how (or even if) the persona is related to prices, but what the crafting of that persona represents in and of itself about client desires.

The social study of prostitution has a long tradition of analyzing these effects, but the current literature suffers from two significant shortcomings. First, most of the literature has focused on female sex workers.[4] It is unknown whether or how similar patterns of performance hold for gay men in general or male sex workers in particular. When men are interacting with men for commercial sex work, the forms of presentation and their desired effects on the audience are very different. A female sex worker is offering a different body under a different set of circumstances and to a different audience than a male sex worker. For example, male sex work allows us to consider how masculinity, broadly construed (other than those of the normative heterosexual dyad), shapes the construction and presentation of sexual selves in general, and in commercial sexual transactions in particular. While this has been analyzed among gay men generally, the social forces at play could differ from the sexual-social forces that would be more prominent in sex work.

Second, and more important, the social theories pertinent to sex work have been used in isolation. When studying the interactions of clients and sex workers with respect to their social performance, theorists have not considered how social theories may be used in concert with one another to explain the regulation of the presentation of self. The study of sex work draws upon a broad base of theories that highlight the ways in which market forces interact with social norms regarding sexuality, producing socio-economic presentations of sexuality, sexual behavior, and sexual fantasy. The lines between the market and personal desire are blurred for sex work. Sex workers must exploit entrenched social conventions about sexuality and sexual behavior for profit. This means social stereotypes, norms, and taboos regarding sexual behavior and desire are codified and explicitly marketed for consumption.

For instance, Goffman's (1959, 1963) concepts of stigma and the presentation of self have been applied to analyze the lives of sex workers. Sex work is inherently stigmatized due to its illegal nature and the long-standing cultural taboo against sex for compensation. In male sex work, there are the additional stigmas of homosexuality and men providing and receiving compensation for sexual behaviors. Sex workers must balance the desire to advertise an intimate experience with an attractive partner against the reality that some clients may be attracted or repelled by its clandestine nature, the deviance assigned to sex work, and the social implications of paying for sexual favors.

Queer theorists such as Butler (1990) and Connell (1992, 1995) offer additional insights that can be integrated with Goffman's theories to better define sex work as a nexus where, in addition to stigma, gender relations are made explicit on sex workers' bodies. A sex workers' sexual presentation must be seen and acknowledged as a *sexual* presentation by the intended audience, and this acts to filter the salience of the presentation. Put another way, clients must perceive that they are engaging with a sex worker for sexual acts, and this is usually communicated implicitly. Gender norms and stereotypes inform the ways in which sex workers present their sexuality to the market. At the same time, sex workers have to be mindful of the experiential nature of sex work – they are not just offering their physical bodies but a persona and an interpersonal experience – the constructed person that the client will interact with in the appointment.

One of the most basic market forces, product differentiation, requires sex workers to tap into distinctions. Sex workers must offer a product (themselves) that is unique and differentiated from others and at the same time must share a range of attributes that would allow clients to categorize the sex worker appropriately so that clients offer compensation consistent with the product class. This is usually a neglected aspect of the sale of sexual services. By uniting these theoretical approaches, I investigate which distinctions are most salient for sexual presentations between men.

Furthermore, theories of sexual fields show how features of collective erotic life may lead sex workers to accentuate certain aspects of themselves in their self-presentations.[5] The collective (social) field gives us general clues as to what behavior or sexual personalities are most desired and by whom. While sexual field theory has sought to limit the prospects of market behavior in the sexual field, in the case of sex work the market and the field are inherently linked.[6] Since sex workers are seeking the employ of a client, they should be particularly sensitive to adhere to the broadest and most general presentations that would enhance their appeal to a large client base. At the same time, no sexual persona can be all-encompassing. Sex workers must choose which features to accentuate and what archetypes they will use to guide client perceptions.

To reach the largest market (client base), sex workers must engage with the broader sexual field and take their marketing cues from nonmarket sexual behavior. Whatever distinctions there are between the market and nonmarket sexual fields, it is doubtful that they extend to what is erotic and desired. For example, it is difficult to imagine the case where one type of sexual presentation would be acceptable for sex work but unacceptable for a private, nonmarket liaison.[7] Indeed, it is the privacy that draws the two together – a sexual presentation is inherently about private sexual behavior. To the extent that clients desire an imagined, genuine sexual connection, sex workers must promise and fulfill desires rooted in non-market sexual desire.

Even more, sex work is not only a performance, but also relational. Dominant narratives about race, gender and sexuality likely inform the performances sex workers give and what specific relations are most frequent in the market. Because of this, intersection theory, too, can provide a framework for understanding sex work as an arena where racial stereotypes are perpetuated through explicitly sexual interaction.[8] The way sex workers present themselves must take into account the ability of clients to properly interpret the presentation as valid. For example, just as a thin sex worker would be hard pressed to present himself as physical embodiment of masculinity, an Asian sex worker may find it difficult to convince clients of his sexual dominance, as it would run counter to prevailing racial stereotypes about Asian sexual submissiveness.

The discussion above shows that a great deal of information must be conveyed in an escort's advertisement. It must communicate on a number of levels, each of which is informed by societal notions of sex, sexuality, masculinity, and sex work. Given the fact that sex workers are successful in doing so, this raises the question of *how* sex workers do so. This, of course, requires that we consider the ways that sex workers use societal cues in presenting their sexual selves to clients. Does that presentation match with what the theories above predict?

The study of sex work in this instance is a novel opportunity to bring empirical analysis to the relationship between sexual, gender, and race narratives in a specific social activity. Integration of the insights from these multiple theoretical perspectives generates useful empirical predictions and greatly enriches the sociological understanding of sex work and the sexual spaces it informs and by which it is informed.[9] Sex work is not only an economic activity; it is also a social one. The sex worker is constructing an image for clients, but is not alone in doing so. Being an image, it is a particular form of social construction which, in order to be successful, must be influenced by a large range of socially acceptable ideals about what is being offered.

Because sex workers are likely compelled to present a self that leads to the most financial return through the attraction of clients, they will be attuned to the norms and values that dictate how they should present themselves.[10] Escorts face clear, market incentives that govern their physical presentations. At the same time, escorts' personal attributes (e.g., body type, race) and sexual proclivities constrain which stylized presentations of self may be construed as both genuine and fitting for the escort, as assessed by potential and actual clients. Presentations are inherently directed toward a financial return, and as such reflect an escort's attempt to maximize marketability, given the societal values and norms that apply in sexualized spaces. Accordingly, the aspects of the self that online escorts accentuate and de-emphasize for economic gain are fundamentally of social origin and require sociological investigation and interpretation.

In this chapter, the focus shifts from being about the economic returns to the presentations to being about the mechanisms by which those presentations are made and how they differ among sex workers depending upon which social narratives they adopt about sexual persona. I combine relational (gender and economic exchange), performative, and intersectional theories of sex work into a cohesive core that produces novel hypotheses about *how* and *why* male sex workers may differ in their physical presentations to the market. I adopt an empirical approach to test hypotheses that stem from integrating these theoretical perspectives. Specifically, I analyze the posted photographs of male sex workers to assess how they present their physical bodies to potential clients. In doing so, I closely align the predictions about the presentation of physical bodies, which are generated from multiple social theories in concert with one another.

This chapter provides a new means of linking performative, relational, gender, and economic theories together, which then permits us to conceptualize other social relations as affecting how male sex workers who have sex with men present their bodies. Specifically, this integrated theoretical approach illustrates the utility of simultaneously employing

Goffman's (1959) concept of the presentation of self, Butler's (1990, 1993) idea of the body as a site of performance, Connell's (1995) hegemonic masculinity, Collins' (2004) intersection theory, and Green's (2008b, 2008c) field theory of erotic capital in understanding male sex work.[11] By using the photographs male escorts provide to advertise for their services, I am able to test features of these theories, and implications that can only be derived from their interaction, by focusing on the performativity and economic relations of sex work, eliminating many of the exogenous factors (e.g., desire for romantic attachment, assortative mating) that are potentially important in analyses of noncommercial sexual relationships.

I hypothesize that male sex workers will largely adhere to dominant narratives related to gender, race, and sexuality in their presentation of self. For example, advertised dominance should display nudity in way that conveys sexual dominance. The same would apply to submissive sexual behavior. Statistical analysis of the data compiled from male escorts' pictures demonstrates that social and economic forces influence male escorts' presentation of self.

I find that the escorts largely adhere to racial and gender stereotypes in crafting their public erotic persona in an effort to secure clients. For example, escorts who advertise dominant sexual behaviors have a larger fraction of frontal nudity pictures, while those who advertise submissive sexual behavior have a larger fraction of rear nudity pictures. Also, I find that this dominant/submissive distinction is even larger when interacted with race – black men who advertise dominance show the largest fraction of frontal nudity pictures and the lowest fraction of rear nudity pictures. This suggest that the confluence of racial sexual stereotypes and the masculine ideals creates a situation where sex worker bodies are decomposed into parts that much be accentuated to adhere to client notions of sex worker behavior.

Perhaps most important is what is not found. There is no relationship between this variation in presentation of erotic persona and prices in the market. In other words, even though sex workers of different types present themselves in different ways in the market, there are no economic returns to doing so. This emphasizes the point that the pictures serve a social purpose in tapping into social narratives about sexual behavior that must be discerned by clients to make the escort sexually credible, but which, by themselves, are not related to prices. The pictures assure clients that the escort can perform the stated task, and they supplement the description by painting the appropriate picture of the sexual persona claimed by the escort.

The synthesis of multiple theories applied to the arena of sex work demonstrates the maintenance of gendered, racialized, *and* sexualized hierarchies in the presentation of self among sex workers. The lack of relation to prices shows this to be largely a social function. Further, the findings demonstrate how dominant narratives about gender and race may manifest themselves within the broader online community of men who have sex with men (MSM), indicating how these narratives are taken up and reinforced by gay men.

The Position of Online Male Escorts and Self-Presentation

Male sex workers' online advertisements provide data on a group that occupies a unique position at the nexus of masculinity, gay male sexuality, and the commodification of the body. Given the interest in masculinity and male sexuality, the analysis of male prostitution offers insights into theoretical areas that cannot be explored with female sex workers. The limited existing research has identified notable differences between the working conditions of male versus female prostitutes.

First, compared to their female counterparts, men's involvement in prostitution tends to be more transitory and sporadic.[12] Additionally, men tend to leave the profession earlier than women, although it is unclear whether their departures are related to the fact that male sex workers are much less likely to use brokers or other intermediaries who could increase their tenure in the profession.[13] Research also suggests men are less likely to be dependent upon prostitution as a sole source of income or survival. Male prostitutes also maintain greater autonomy in their general working conditions, in large part because they exercise greater physical strength in comparison to their clients than do women.[14] Finally, some argue that men derive more sexual gratification from their encounters with customers, with males tending to reach orgasm with clients more often than their female counterparts. Indeed, research on male escorts suggests for many male escorts, prostitution represents another form of recreational sex that just so happens to entail compensation.[15]

Research also highlights differences in the nature of sex work between Internet male sex workers and street male sex workers, or men whose initial transactions occur within public settings such as sidewalks, parks, or truck stops.[16] Mimiaga et al. (2008) report that while substance use occurred in association with many Internet escorts' sexual encounters with clients, obtaining money for drugs and alcohol was not the primary motivation for their involvement in prostitution. Mimiaga et al. also found that street workers often used words such as "desperation" and "survival" when describing their motivations for participating in sex work. Conversely, Internet male sex workers often indicated that they engage in sex work in order to pay for school or for supplemental income and that they view prostitution as a form of casual sex that entails a financial reward. Given these facts, it seems likely that online male sex workers would adhere to noncommercial social cues in their sex work, as they see it largely as an extension of their noncommercial sexual behavior.

Another advantage of studying male Internet sex work as compared to other forms is that online advertisements allow sex workers to procure *stylized* presentations of self that aim to entice a particular clientele. This is a function of both the greater autonomy of male sex work and the competition created by the online sex work industry. Through the careful presentation of photographs, escorts present their bodies in ways that inform potential clients of the type of sexual experience they are best equipped to offer (exploiting their autonomy) and to differentiate themselves from other escorts from whom clients could choose (product differentiation).

This differentiation stems from a source other than the face pictures that male escorts use to overcome the problem of asymmetric information. The use of face pictures is about the establishment of trust for the sex worker, irrespective of the sexual conduct they offer. The pictures of their bodies that sex workers use, however, are directly tied to the sexual persona they create. It is in these photographs that they establish their legitimacy as being authentic to the type of sexual behavior in which they are willing to engage.

Importantly, escorts may (purposefully or unwittingly) manipulate stereotypes from both the gay community and the larger society in their advertisements in order to more effectively entice clients with particular sexual proclivities. Accordingly, online advertisements of male escorts provide a unique opportunity for the sociological examination of how structures of inequality inform the presentation of self. Indeed, in order to seek the largest financial gain, escorts face clear incentives to fit themselves into sexual roles that are believable and widely popular. They have clear incentives to turn themselves into a sexual archetype that is widely acknowledged in the gay community. Put another way, escorts face clear economic incentives to exploit, to the best of their ability, existing sexual norms and stereotypes that best fit to their physical selves.

Online male sex workers enjoy a unique and arguably advantaged position in the sex work industry. The advantages afford Internet male sex workers more freedom to procure presentations of self that not only entice a particular clientele, but also reflect their sexual proclivities. Despite the centrality of advertising in online male sex work, to date no research has employed sociological theories and quantitative analysis to explain differences in presentations of self among online advertisements of male sex workers. I synthesize a number of sociological theories to formulate and test hypotheses regarding the stylized presentations of self among male sex workers in an attempt to better understand how sex work reflects larger social narratives about gender, race, masculinity, sexuality, and intelligibility.

Theoretical Framework

I build on Goffman's (1959) approach to the presentation of self in order to identify the theoretical linkages between general interactional processes and male sex workers' self-presentations. Since I am using male sex workers' online advertisements to investigate how this population crafts a public sexual persona while upholding larger social norms, Goffman's (1959) understanding of the presentation of self provides the theoretical foundation on which I build the integrative approach. However, Goffman's theory does not speak to how the presentation of self is moderated by social norms as they relate to stratification – the differentiation that would lead to different perceptions among clients and among sex workers themselves. This is of particular concern given the interest in how these advertisements reflect larger social narratives related to race, gender, and sexuality. In other words, while Goffman is the natural starting point for thinking about self-presentation generally, insights from additional theoretical approaches are needed to refine the hypotheses that develop. I first detail Goffman's theory and how male sex workers' online advertisements act as a means of operationalizing the presentation of self. Following this, I provide an overview of several other theories – sexual scripts, sexual capital, and theories related to queer and racialized bodies – to argue that the presentation of self of this population is moderated by additional social forces, thereby reflecting and reinforcing social norms and inequalities.

Presentation of self. Goffman describes the presentation of self as akin to a dramatic performance. Goffman's (1959) dramaturgical theory is the natural base for a theory of self-presentation because it affords a number of "sensitizing concepts" that provide "a general sense of reference and guidance in approaching empirical instances."[17] To that end, humans endeavor to play various roles as well as possible, and engage in processes of impression management so as to influence the impression that others have of us. In this way, self-presentation is inherently contextualized. It may be calculated or subconscious, practiced or spontaneous. Performances are successful insofar as others accept the presentation that an individual puts forth and act in accordance with it, which may or may not be part of a performance on the recipient's part. The effectiveness of one's presentation in turn is measured more by the resulting behaviors of others than by the nature of the performance itself.

Male sex workers who post their pictures on a website to advertise their services to clients are actively engaging in a carefully crafted presentation of self. This is an online advertisement of sexual services. Through what they choose to display in the photographs in their advertisements, men in this market create narratives about themselves and their sexual proclivities and expertise, all to the end of enhancing their desirability to the ultimate end of securing a financial transaction. Because male sex workers are selling a service, their clients must be sufficiently enticed by their presentation of self to motivate a transaction. Therefore, it is in sex workers' best interest to craft a presentation of self that will appeal to as many potential clients as possible, thus leading to the greatest return.[18]

It is also critical that the presentation be read as authentic. Goods and services can be deemed inappropriate and disregarded if they are not imbued with qualities the seller or provider claims they embody.[19] For instance, a White escort would find great difficulties in securing a clientele base if he were to attempt to appeal to clients who desire men of color as sexual partners. A large escort will have difficulty appealing to client demand for lithe physiques. Accordingly, sex workers must make their performances *intelligible* to potential clients by expressing certain qualities that they actually possess, or would be presumed to possess. Sex workers thus consider the type of desirable experiences and services they can *reliably* provide to their customers, and would appear authentic to customers, when crafting their online persona. For the escort, this process entails taking the role of potential clients, identifying their sexual proclivities, and assessing which types performances would be deemed intelligible (from the standpoint of the client), given demographic, bodily, and behavioral characteristics. It is through this process that one maximizes sexual desirability by developing a self-presentation that accentuates the types of services one is best equipped to perform.

Since the focus is on images male sex workers post of themselves to generate a particular reaction – that is, an exchange of sex for money – I focus these men's *fronts,* which Goffman defines as "the part of an individual's performance which regularly functions in a general and fixed fashion to define the situation for those who observe the performance."[20] Goffman does make a distinction between what is being presented versus the backstage, where confidants or insiders may be given a less polished, less rehearsed – that is, more intimate and authentic – presentation of self. This study's design draws strength from its exclusive focus on the front as opposed to the backstage. Advertisements are deliberate acts by the seller to pique the interest of potential buyers unknown to the escort. As such, they are inherently front, and indeed, may entice buyers by offering the possibility of viewing the backstage. For example, Bernstein (2007) sees sex work as a type of "bounded authenticity" (p. 6) wherein sex workers maintain a façade of emotional investment for the client's pleasure while also maintaining the commercial, transactional nature of sex work.

The study of male sex workers provides a unique opportunity to employ Goffman's theory, as the preponderance of male sex workers secure clients through independent efforts and without intermediaries such as pimps or strip clubs.[21] For example, other research has shown that male escorts take great care to convey their honesty and scrupulousness to clients, which is necessary as there is no intermediary who can guarantee the veracity of the information conveyed.[22] Because the respondents maintain control over their fronts, it is assumed that they will do their utmost to create whatever reality will be the most desirable to clients, therefore making the most money.

While Goffman's theory offers a number of sensitizing concepts that inform the approach, it does not provide *definitive concepts,* which refer "precisely to what is common to a class of objects, by the aid of a clear definition in terms of attributes or fixed benchmarks."[23] Importantly, individual sexual desire is socially constructed and shaped by larger structures of inequality as well as meanings of sexual behavior and personal attributes that are shared by actors who are differentially situated within sexual fields.[24] Goffman's concept tells us that the men in this market will craft presentations to elicit an erotic response from clients, but how that response would be elicited (what that performance would contain) requires further development. Further theoretical analysis must distinguish *what* will be presented and *why.* Accordingly, I draw upon a number of sociological theories in order to construct informed hypotheses that point to what strategies male sex workers might use in selecting their photographic images in their online presentations of self.

Sexual scripts. Sexual scripting theory provides insight into processes involved in the ordering of events within individual sexual encounters.[25]

Building on Goffman's theory of the presentation of self, which includes dramaturgical theory and social learning theory, Gagnon and Simon note that individuals enact social scripts throughout sexual situations. Among other things, sexual scripts allow actors to demonstrate a learned competence regarding the meaning of internal states (i.e., sexual desire), provide cultural templates for the sequencing of action in sexual exchanges, and help individuals identify proper contexts for sexual practice and set limits on sexual responses. Sexual scripts also allow for the disclosure and expression of desired acts within sexualized encounters, which facilitate sexual satisfaction and the realization of biological events (i.e., sexual stimulation, orgasm) through the fulfillment of individualized desires.[26]

In the case male sex workers, the client/escort dialogue regarding interpersonal scripts to be performed begins when a potential client first views an escort's advertisement. Escorts profess knowledge regarding the roles and ordering of events of particular sexual scripts in part through expressing certain aspects of their erotic personas in their advertisements. In an escort advertisement, escorts note their prices or services, the sexual services they provide, and further details about their persona through text. Equally important, the advertisements are accompanied by pictures, as many as 12 in the data source.

Photographs serve as concrete evidence that an escort is who he purports to be. Such expressive actions are important precursors to exchange, as they help persuade clients that the price of the exchange is appropriate and ensure that both parties involved are aware of, and will subsequently agree upon, the interpersonal script that is to be enacted in the sexual encounter. They can also encourage a client to schedule an appointment, as they act as a bond – a client can quickly ascertain whether an escort is "as advertised" before becoming further entangled. Ultimately, the expression of one's erotic persona is an important mechanism through which escorts assure clients that they will be able to enact the desired script that is most likely necessary for customer satisfaction. The script that the men follow is inherently one that is social, as they must appeal to a large group of men from which their clients will be selected.

Importantly, the script used by male sex workers must simultaneously serve two distinct purposes. It must give the client some insight into escort personality and disposition while at the same time clearly communicating about sexual expertise. The script must form a cohesive core where the personality advertised ("laid back" or "aggressive" for example) matches with the sexual behaviors that the escort has indicated that they provide. Experiences assured to be "fun" may well be accompanied by different pictures than those advertising "aggression," and sex workers must navigate how much play they will allow themselves between extremes. The most important part of this is that, irrespective of the escort's claim, the clients reviewing the advertisement must immediately recognize it and authenticate it.

Erotic capital. Emphasizing "erotic capital" provides additional motivation for strategically presenting one's erotic persona in escort advertisements. Green (2008b, 2008c) conceives of erotic capital as "the quality and quantity of attributes that an individual possesses, which elicit an erotic response in another" (2008b, p. 29). Green describes erotic capital as consisting of a variety of eroticized personal features, including bodily characteristics (e.g., breast size, height, hair color) and eroticized cultural styles (e.g., the archetypal sexual fantasy centered on the Catholic schoolgirl). Most important to the present analysis, erotic capital is expressed through affective presentations that signal the embodiment of desirable qualities, such as dominance, submissiveness, or sexual versatility. Building on this notion, Hakim (2011) proposes that erotic capital consists of a number of other elements, including social charm and physical beauty, as well as sexuality itself, which comprises sexual competence, stamina, erotic imagination, playfulness, and other personal characteristics that partners find sexually satisfying.

Erotic capital is both inherent and constructed, and is limited by one's characteristics and social position. For example, if one is lithe, his or her erotic capital would be constrained as it would be difficult to parlay that physical presentation into one of dominance. The same may be true of a man with a muscular physique. Similarly, a man with a large number of tattoos may find it difficult to enact the schoolboy fantasy. That is, while some men may have more erotic capital than others, one can enhance their erotic capital by capitulating to the erotic norms that best emphasize their own physical, psychological, and erotic selves.

Escorts must be acutely aware of both the erotic capital they possess and the sexual scripts that their potential customers desire to perform. Even more, escorts must be aware of how best to effectively transmit their erotic capital through their presentations. The ultimate aim of their advertisements is to formulate and convey an erotic persona that best highlights their erotic capital in a way that convinces potential clients that they will be able to perform interpersonal scripts in a desired manner. This implies that escorts emphasize certain aspects of their personas that command the most erotic capital among the generalized "other" that makes up their client base. Thus, while an escort may actually possess erotic capital that is desirable to a certain clientele (e.g., aptitude in fulfilling the bottom role), he likely accentuates other, often opposing, forms of erotic capital if it will result in a more profitable exchange or greater market share. In other words, escorts will emphasize the sexual roles that they can authentically convey and that have the most marketability and believability among a naïve client base. This is at the heart of presentation – the muscular escort may in fact be quite submissive, but that performance may not be perceived as authentic. Escorts are advertising to the largest possible market. As a result, larger social narratives about what is sexually desirable – or sexually desired – should influence how these sex workers choose to craft their erotic personas in an attempt to secure clientele.

A specifically gay embodiment of erotic capital is what Levine (1998) referred to as "hotness" in gay sexual spaces.[27] To be "hot" was to have an overtly sexual persona that articulated the ability to be skilled in sexual behaviors while at the same time being desired as a sexual object. The most interesting aspect of "hotness" was that it was specified by and for gay men. While erotic capital can be thought of as general, "hotness" is the capital with specifically high returns among gay men. For obvious reasons, male escorts need to communicate "hotness" to their clients, as it simultaneously signals their ability to provide an exceptional sexual experience to clients and their condition as the type of man whom clients would prefer to have the experience with. Since both are important, the impression management that escorts engage in must effectively communicate both aspects of the experience to the client base.

Queer bodies. Green (2008c) notes that sexual field theory situates micro-level processes within macro-level structural factors. In particular, Green notes that power relations pertaining to gender and race shape the valuation of certain forms of erotic capital across temporal and spatial contexts. As an example, Green discusses Levine's (1998) study of the "gay clone," a subculture where hypermasculine gay men were found sexually desirable. Although Green mentions the role of hegemonic masculinity in determining what forms of erotic capital carry more value at any particular time and place, a more comprehensive exploration of various forms of hegemony as conceptualized by other theorists leads us to specific, testable hypotheses of sexual fields in online male sex workers' advertisements.

The body is a site of discipline on which society enforces norms regarding what is acceptable and desirable.[28] Society constantly acts on the body, demarcating the borders of who is intelligible and how we should make sense of particular bodies.[29] The line between the body and the perfor-mance of gender is blurred. Butler (1993) discusses how our embodiment, our physical presence in our own bodies, is interpreted through a social lens. How the body is conceived, made material within the context of the social, is influenced by dominant ideas about gender – what bodies *should* be and how they *should* look.

Gay male culture in particular places a high premium on the body.[30] Although gay men interact with the cultural messages about the ideal body in complex ways, the dominant narratives of the muscular, toned physique as a signifier for masculinity and the slender, waifish "twink" body as a signifier of youth and femininity are still held up as desirable.[31] Kane states that these two types of body may constitute an orthodoxy within the literature precisely because they conform to preexisting nar-ratives about gay male bodies and masculinity. Bodies that more closely resemble extreme poles of gender performance – the hypermasculine gym body and the hyperfeminine twink body – may command the most erotic capital within the gay sexual fields.[32] These bodies also inhabit idealized sexual performances – the muscular man as dominant and the thin man as submissive.

The desirability of specific bodies varies with the context. While gay men have shown consistent attraction to muscular physiques, this is not a universal.[33] The physical features of sexual partners, particularly those for temporary and anonymous encounters, have usually been associated with greater adherence to the polarity between muscular and thin.[34] In contemporary gay social networks, partners have shown a rejection of men who are not "height-weight proportionate," a phrase that, while appearing to encompass a broader number of men, is most exclusionary of men perceived to be overweight.[35] In general, large men are least likely to be sexualized in gay culture.

The politics of gay male bodies are extended through the negotiation of behavior within sexual exchanges. For example, gay sexual encounters often entail a differentiation of roles, in which one serves as either the "top," or insertive partner during anal intercourse, or the "bottom," the receiving partner. Penetration is often connoted with masculinity, and being penetrated is thought to be a loss of masculinity.[36] This negotiation of roles may manifest itself in the context of online male sex work. For instance, because the twink body is associated with boyishness and effemi-nacy, male sex workers advertising themselves as bottoms may use online advertising to emphasize parts of their body, such as their waist and buttocks, that are more closely associated with femininity.[37] Conversely, because the mesomorphic, muscular ideal is closely tied to masculinity, sex workers exemplifying this body type may be more likely to display their genitalia.[38] Because these men are trading on their bodies and sexuality rather than qualities that may be desirable in a long-term romantic partner, sex workers may rely on masculine narratives to determine which position they should occupy during the physical act of sex with (paying) clients. Clients, too, may actively seek out sex workers who adhere to gender norms they find sexually desirable.

Racialized presentations of sexual selves. Green's approach to sexuality points out that erotic capital is unequally distributed among actors who are embedded in particular *sexual fields*, which represent mutually constitutive "socially stratified, institutionalized [matrices] of relations" within which actors navigate, and onto which individual and collective sexual desires are transposed.[39] Sexual fields, as well as the structure of social relations among actors within them, facilitate sexuality in part by helping actors assign meaning and value to specific presentation styles and personal attributes that constitute one's erotic capital. In turn, structural features of sexual fields largely determine the hegemonic "currency" of erotic capital that characterizes a particular sexual field. Individual self-presentations of our respondents are in large part an effort to express that they embody specific currency of erotic capital that dominates sexual fields in which they navigate.

Green (2008c) suggests that sexual actors encounter fields of relations that are constituted by "positions anchored to histories of marginality and racialization."[40] Sexual fields are thus largely informed by, although not entirely isomorphic with, stratification systems of other fields. Following Green and others, it is important to acknowledge the potential for racialized stratification systems of other fields to permeate constitutive elements of the sexual fields in which sex workers are embedded. In other words, racial stratification within nonsexual fields shapes structures of desire of sexual fields, which in turn inform the ways our respondents construct their erotic personas.

Long before the development of the Internet, Baldwin (1985) noted the strict sexual codes for the Black body in gay masculinities. To him, a Black man became the physical embodiment of a hypermasculinity that is inherently relational as it truly reflected the insecurity of White men. The social expectation that Black men enact and embody this hypermasculinity is filtered through a gay masculinity that seeks to sexualize the image and attach a phallic orientation to it. The penis – a representation of masculinity, is enhanced if it is Black due to stereotypes of both Black penis size and Black masculinity. This becomes the dominant, sexualized "big black cock" that is prized in both the commercial and noncommercial markets. This practice explicitly eroticizes Black men and their bodies, and has long been a feature of White urban gay sexual behavior. For example, Levine (1998) notes that Black men were seen as exotic sexual partners and the masculinity of the White man securing a Black dominant sexual partner was enhanced because he (the White partner) was able to secure a Black man. As noted by Baldwin, this allows the Black man to become a conduit through which White gay men attain greater masculine credentials. In essence, the White gay man who can be a successful sexual partner with a dominant Black gay man has revealed a type of sexual stamina and prowess relative to other White gay men. Escorts would be certain to pay attention to these cues as they would be a source of desirability among clients, and to accentuate these features.

As being the top is considered to be the more masculine or dominant role, and as Black masculinity is commonly conceived of as overly aggressive and hypermasculine, it would follow that Black escorts would likely engage in a presentation of self that reflects stereotypes emphasizing masculine characteristics.[41] As noted earlier, the racialized sexual stereotypes practiced among White gay men have rendered the Black male body a collection of pieces that symbolize masculinity. In particular, White gay men have fetishized Black male genitalia for its alleged size. The "big black cock" is desired as the epitome of masculinity, and in this setting for use by other men for their sexual pleasure. For a Black man with outward masculine presentation, adopting a persona that assumes that they possess a "big black cock" would be one with significant rewards. If this is true, than a Black escort advertising as such must make this known to clients through his advertisement. The advertisements therefore combine the notion of intelligibility (they must provide the client with evidence that the body presented is a body that can be interpreted as such) with the very real need that escorts face to adhere to dominant social narratives regarding racialized sexuality (which places social restrictions on whose body can be rendered intelligible).

At the same time, Black men will also be especially likely to de-emphasize cues that express submissiveness in their self-presentations. That is, displays that would run counter to this narrative of dominance and large penis size are likely to be unintelligible if not properly distinctive. There is also the converse, however. Black men who may not wish to adhere to the dominant narrative (in both senses of the term) will need to provide a greater degree of assurance to potential clients that they can fulfill the submissive role, given that they may be more likely expected by clients to fulfill the sexually dominant role. In this way, escorts act to reaffirm and also distance themselves from particular narratives in ways that would lead to discernible differences in presentation.

Another example of this would be Asians, who are presumed to be docile and submissive. A related stereotype is that Asian men are not well endowed. These stereotypes are the opposite of those for Black men, and the result is a social emasculation of Asian men in gay sexual sociality.[42] This renders Asian bodies as less masculine than others, and may cause Asian escorts to emphasize their femininity as opposed to their masculinity to adhere to these norms. The stereotype of Asian men as having small penises would need to be actively counteracted by Asian escorts who promise clients an above average endowment. Acting against these dominant narratives would require effort to assert a counterintuitive sexual persona.

The dual needs for definition and differentiation are key. Escorts must first define themselves relative to the dominant narrative given their own physical selves. While escorts adhering to dominant narratives would theoretically predominate, those of a given type who are seeking a nondominant narrative would need to be particularly sensitive in how they present themselves. For a given sex worker, the differences in presentation would need to be substantial enough to be discernable by clients.

In the data used here, escorts record their own race. This is important, as the presentation that an escort will employ should be internally consistent with their self-identified (presented) race, as opposed to another form of racial classification. Escorts may endogenously choose a racial classification that would suit to best advantage their sexual presentation and vice versa. In other words, the objective for the escort is to present a cohesive sexual presentation that is consistent with the racial classification he would adopt in an attempt to be intelligible and desirable to potential clients.

Hypotheses for the Self-Presentation of Male Sex Workers

The analysis of advertisement pictures allows for specific predictions regarding the particular selves male sex workers choose to present to potential clientele. These sex workers' presentations of self are largely influenced by preexisting social norms. The presentation of (sexual) self that escorts partake in their profiles serves two primary functions. First, it enables these men to express their mastery of certain sexual scripts that clients desire to perform in their sexual encounters with escorts.[43] Second, escorts' presentations of self also enable the men to express components of their *erotic personas,* which the men must situate within larger structures of masculinity, race, gender, and sexuality.

Male escorts' online advertisements, then, provide a unique opportunity to study the presentation of self as it relates to larger sexual scripts of desirability and intelligibility. Goffman's theory suggests that the escorts will present themselves in a manner to elicit an erotic response from potential clients. This takes place within a script, where the escort's advertisement and the pictures displayed therein form the beginning of the script that will result in an exchange of money for sexual services. In crafting these personas, sex workers use and display their erotic capital to their best advantage, which is informed by narratives of desire and sexual hierarchy in the noncommercial sexual field. Doing so requires that they take into account specific narratives of the body and racial-sexual stereotypes that act as a constraint on the amount and type of erotic capital they possess and how they present their bodies to the market. In general, these men's advertisements will adhere to dominant conceptualizations related to race, masculinity, and sexuality. The combination of the aforementioned theories leads to predictions that the presentation of self of male sex workers' bodies through their posted photographs will conform to particular stereotypes.

Based on the literature, body type plays an important part in the sex workers' presentations of self. Waifish, "twink" bodies connote a feminized erotic persona within gay popular narratives, which in turn is strongly associated with fulfilling the receptive role during anal intercourse. I thus hypothesize that men with thin or lean body types will display a greater portion of pictures that display their buttocks, compared to men with more muscular body types. I also hypothesize that thin men will display a smaller portion of pictures featuring their bare fronts or the penis. Conversely, toned, muscular bodies are more likely signify hypermasculinity. Men with muscular bodies will likely desire to express masculine erotic personas, which entail fulfilling the penetrative role during anal intercourse. Accordingly, I hypothesize that men with muscular physiques will display greater proportions of pictures featuring the penis and smaller proportions of pictures featuring the buttocks.

Sexual scripting theory points to the importance of the ordering of sexual encounters, much of which takes place prior to actual sexual exchanges. I propose that expressing knowledge of roles within sexual scripts prior to the sexual exchange helps escorts convince clients that they will be able to execute the scripts that they desire to enact. Accordingly, I hypothesize that men who advertise as tops or bottoms emphasize different features of themselves so as to express intimate knowledge of their role within enactments of sexual scripts. Accordingly, I hypothesize men who advertise as bottoms will display greater proportions of pictures featuring their buttocks and smaller proportions of their bare fronts. Conversely, I hypothesize that men who advertise as tops, or the penetrative partner during intercourse, will display a greater proportion of pictures that display their penis than of pictures displaying their buttocks.

Finally, following insights from Green's theory of sexual fields, I generate hypotheses regarding differential patterns of self-presentation on the basis of race and sexual positioning. First, expecting that Black men advertising as tops bank on hypermasculine conceptions Black male sexuality within popular narratives, I hypothesize that the positive association between top positioning and the proportion of pictures featuring the penis would be accentuated among Black escorts. At the same time, I expect Black tops to be especially careful to deemphasize submissiveness in their advertisements. Thus, I hypothesize that that the negative association between top-positioning and proportion of pictures displaying the buttocks to be accentuated among Black escorts. Conversely, we expect that Black men who advertise as bottoms would have to exert extra effort to assure potential clients that they can fulfill the bottom role because of racial stereotypes surrounding African American male sexuality. I therefore hypothesize that the positive association between bottom positioning and the proportion of pictures featuring the buttocks would be accentuated among Black escorts, and the negative association between the proportion of pictures featuring the penis and bottom positioning would be stronger among Black escorts.

For Asian men, we would predict that the sexual script would work in the opposite direction than for Black men. Asian men would be more likely to emphasize pictures of the buttocks to adhere to the dominant narrative, and these men would de-emphasize frontal nudity. Those Asian men defying the stereotype would need to show an abundance of frontal nudity pictures in order to counteract the narrative of Asian submissiveness.

Data and Methods

Male escorts' online advertisements

In addition to written information provided in the advertisements, men could provide up to twelve pictures of themselves, for which they may display any feature of their bodies, including the penis and buttocks. I constructed the dependent variables from visual inspection of these pictures.

In addition, comparisons of the website from which the data were collected to other large websites for male sex workers suggest the chosen site provides sufficient coverage of the online escort market in addition to racial and sexual behavior variation necessary to empirically ascertain the role of pictures in escort advertisements.[44]

Dependent variables. The hypotheses are concerned with the association between body type, race, sexual positioning, and eroticized presentations of self. I examine two particular dimensions of eroticized presentations in advertisements, namely one that emphasizes dominance and another that emphasizes submissiveness. An escort wishing to emphasize sexual dominance within male-to-male sexual encounters will feature a greater proportion of pictures that display his penis. The dependent variable is the proportion of pictures, since the proportion controls for differences in the number of pictures that an individual escort may display.[45] Importantly, some pictures feature both the penis and buttocks. Pictures featuring both the penis and buttocks were counted in both categories, meaning the two categories are not mutually exclusive.[46]

It is important to stress that the pictures analyzed here are not in themselves related to the prices that escorts charge for services. For this reason, I do not use escorts' prices in the analysis. While face pictures are related to prices, all other picture types are not.[47] This does not mean that there are not economic incentives involved, just that a direct link to prices is not evident. Indeed, given that picture composition of frontal and rear nudity is not related to prices, we might expect for there to be little variation in the type of nudity shown. While the underlying sexual behavior advertised has been shown to be related to prices, here the concern is with the performance and presentation of those advertised roles. The presentations that I analyze here are about how the escorts fulfill the expectations of the market, and how that differs based on their self-descriptions.

The key independent variables include race, sexual position, and body type. I include five binary variables that indicate whether the respondent is *White, Black/African American, Hispanic, Multiracial,* or *Asian.*[48] Body type is measured by four binary variables indicating *Average, A few extra pounds, Muscular/buff,* or *Thin/lean.*[49] Finally, I measure sexual positioning with three indicators for the escorts' advertised sexual behavior. First I include two variables that signify whether the escort indicated that they serve as a *top* (i.e., the penetrative partner in anal sex) or *bottom* (i.e., the receptive partner in anal sex). Men who indicated that they are both a top and bottom were coded as *versatile.* In addition, versatile and top, as well as versatile and bottom, are not mutually exclusive categories, meaning escorts may be both versatile and top, or versatile and bottom.[50] Such men would have values of 1 for both versatile and top or versatile and bottom.

Empirical strategy. I use ordinary least-squares (OLS) regression to test the hypotheses. The modeling strategy analyzes the relationship between body size, race, sexual position, and race and sexual position and the *proportion* of pictures featuring the penis and the *proportion* of pictures featuring the buttocks. Specifically, I estimate the regression

$$\frac{T_{ij}}{N_i} = \alpha + \beta X_i + \varepsilon_i \tag{1}$$

where i indexes an escort, T is the number of pictures of type j, N is the total number of pictures, X is the vector of independent variables described above, and ε is a well-behaved error term.

I first test hypotheses regarding the association between presentation and body types. Next, I test the association between sexual positioning and the composition of pictures. Finally I test whether race moderates the association between race and sexual positioning in the composition of pictures for escorts.

Results

The empirical model features two outcomes – the fraction of pictures that show frontal or rear nudity. Since the showing of either type would, theoretically, be driven by different goals of self-presentation, I describe the results by type. I first present the results in which the proportion of pictures featuring the penis serves as the outcome and consider the relationship between frontal nudity and discrete characteristics. I then describe the results in which the proportion of pictures featuring the buttocks is the dependent variable for discrete characteristics. Finally, I consider the implications for the interaction between race and sexual behavior with self-presentation.[51]

Body Type, Sexual Position, and Self-Presentation
Figure 5.1 shows the estimates of the fraction of pictures showing frontal nudity by personal characteristic. The results show that men who advertise as having average build display a greater proportion of pictures featuring the

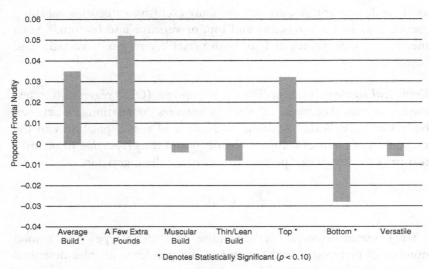

* Denotes Statistically Significant ($p < 0.10$)

Figure 5.1 Escort characteristics and proportion of frontal nudity

penis than those advertising as having an athletic/swimmer's build, which is the excluded category. The result is quite large – men with average builds will show 50 percent more pictures of frontal nudity than men on average. No significant difference between the proportion of pictures featuring the penis were found between athletic/swimmer's build and those advertising as "a few extra pounds," thin/lean build, or muscular build.

Figure 5.1 also presents the results from statistical models testing hypotheses regarding sexual positioning and dimensions of eroticized presentation styles. These results indicate advertising as tops (i.e., men who are the penetrative partner during anal intercourse) is positively associated with the proportion of pictures that display the penis. The result is nearly as large as the result for average body size, where men advertising as tops will show 50 percent more frontal nudity pictures than other men. Bottoms (i.e. men who are the receptive partner during anal intercourse), on the other hand, display a statistically significantly smaller proportion of pictures that feature the penis. This result is also large: men advertising as bottoms will display 40 percent fewer pictures of genitalia than other men. These results provide support for our hypotheses regarding top and bottom positioning and eroticized presentations of self that accentuate sexual dominance. While men advertising dominant or submissive sexual behaviors present their frontal nudity to different degrees, men advertising versatile sexual behaviors

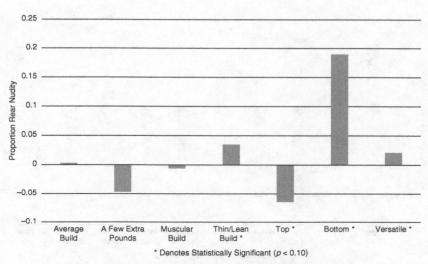

* Denotes Statistically Significant ($p < 0.10$)

Figure 5.2 Escort characteristics and proportion of rear nudity

(able to provide either dominant or submissive sexual behaviors) do not appear to show any statistically different effects.

Figure 5.2 shows the results for the fraction of pictures that feature the buttocks. In support of the hypothesis regarding the association between "twinkish," thin builds and escorts' presentation styles, results show that compared to those with athletic/lean builds, men with thin/lean builds display greater proportions of pictures that feature their buttocks. Men who are thin/lean will show 30 percent more pictures of their buttocks than other men. Figure 5.2 also indicates that advertising as bottom or versatile is positively associated with the proportions of pictures that display the buttocks.[52] In fact, a bottom shows twice the number of pictures of the buttocks as other escorts, while a versatile escort shows roughly 10 percent more pictures of the buttocks. Formal statistical tests reveal significant differences between the proportion for bottom and versatile escorts – although both show more pictures of the buttocks, bottoms show them more systematically.[53] The results for tops are exactly the opposite. Advertising as a top is negatively associated the proportion of pictures featuring the buttocks. Tops show roughly 50 percent fewer pictures of the buttocks than other escorts. The results in Figure 5.2 support the hypotheses regarding the association between sexual positioning and eroticized presentations of self that express submissiveness in male-to-male sexual encounters.

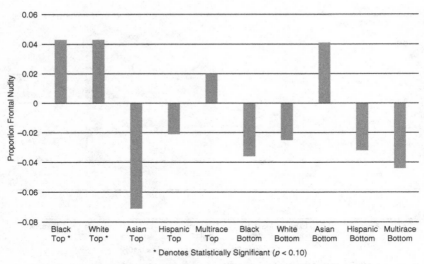

Figure 5.3 Race, sexual position and proportion of frontal nudity

In addition to the body type and sexual position, I also tested for the relationship with race and the fraction of pictures of either type. The results show that there is no statistically significant relationship between race itself and the fraction of pictures portraying one's frontal genitalia. In other specifications I find that there is no statistically significant relationship between race and the fraction of pictures displaying the buttocks. The results imply that race alone does not significantly influence the sexual presentation of escorts. As with the effect of race on prices discussed earlier, there is no independent effect of race itself on the presentations that escorts use in the market.[54]

Race and Sexual Position Interactions with Self-Presentations   I test for interactions between race and sexual positioning in Figures 5.3 and 5.4. In both instances, the "Other" racial/ethnic category serves as the reference category. In support of the hypothesis regarding Black men who advertise as tops and the expression of sexual dominance, results in Figure 5.3 indicate that black tops present greater proportions of pictures that feature their penis than men who indicated they belong to the "Other" racial category. Additionally, White tops display greater proportions of pictures that feature their penis. In fact, both Black and White tops show more than 50 percent more pictures of their penis than other escorts. Thus, while I find support for the hypothesis that Black escorts who advertise as tops

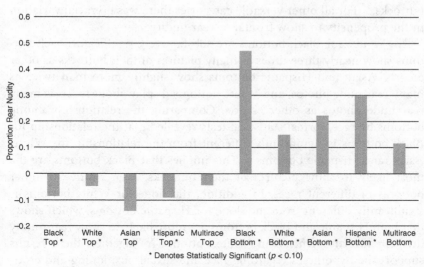

Figure 5.4 Race, sexual position and proportion of rear nudity

would show higher proportions of pictures that feature the penis, I also find these men show roughly the same fraction of pictures of the penis as White men who advertise as tops. Formally, there is no statistically significant different between Black and White tops in the proportion of frontal nudity pictures. For bottoms, there is no racial variation in the propensity to display frontal nudity.

Figure 5.4 shows the results where I test whether race modifies the association between sexual positioning and the proportion of pictures that display the buttocks. Results indicate that Black, Hispanic, and White tops display lower proportions of pictures that feature the buttocks than men who indicate they belong to the "Other" racial category.[55] Black and Hispanic tops show 50 percent fewer pictures of their buttocks than "Other" men, while White tops show 30 percent fewer pictures of their buttocks. Formal statistical tests for differences in the relationship for white, Black, and Hispanic tops failed to reject the hypothesis that they are equivalent to each other, indicating that these three groups are not statistically different from one another in their propensity to show fewer pictures of the buttocks. In addition, Black, White, Asian, and Hispanic bottoms present greater portions of pictures that feature the buttocks than men of "Other" races.[56] For men who advertise versatility, the only group showing any relationship between frontal or rear nudity were Black versatile men, who were more likely to show pictures of their buttocks.[57] For all other versatile categories there was no racial variation in the propensity to show frontal or rear nudity.

The results for Black bottoms are substantively significant. Black bottoms show nearly three times as many pictures of their buttocks as other escorts. Asian and Hispanic bottoms show slightly more than twice as many rear nude photos, and White bottoms display about twice as many rear nude photos as other escorts. Comparing the relationship among bottoms by race, formal statistical tests revealed that the relationship for Black bottoms is significantly different from the relationship for White, Asian, and Hispanic bottoms.[58] This implies that Black bottoms are the most likely to show pictures of their buttocks, even relative to other bottoms of different races. In addition, the slope for White bottoms is significantly different from the slope for Hispanic bottoms, which shows that both Hispanic and Black bottoms are more likely to show rear nudity in their advertisements than White bottoms.[59]. Together, these results support the hypotheses regarding race and sexual positioning and eroticized presentations that accentuate and deemphasize sexual dominance and submissiveness. Comparatively, men of different races do display different personas to the market and present themselves differently based on their sexual position as well as race and body type.

Conclusion

This chapter advances the current understanding of male sex workers by incorporating Goffman's insights into the presentation of self with those from theories of race and gender, queer theory, and theories of sexual fields and sexual scripts. These conceptualizations point to the importance of incorporating multiple sociological theories in a study of male sex workers' erotic personas. In their attempt to convert sexual capital into financial capital, male sex workers present their bodies in such a way as to conform to dominant narratives about masculinity, race, gay male sexuality, and desirability.[60] In this way, the self-presentation of these men tends to uphold social norms, particularly those related to gender, race, and beauty. The manner in which male sex workers craft and present their bodies reflects on dominant sexual narratives within the gay community and larger society.

This analysis tested theoretically informed hypotheses regarding the association between race, sexual positioning, body type, and male escorts' stylized presentations of self in their online advertisements. I find support for the majority of our hypotheses. Male escorts who describe their own bodies as thin or slender are more likely to show pictures of their buttocks, which corresponds with the stereotype of the slender, effeminate gay male. Men who advertise as tops display greater proportions of pictures that display their penis and fewer pictures that display their buttocks. Conversely, I found that bottoms display greater proportions of pictures featuring the buttocks and smaller proportions of pictures that feature their penis.

With regard to race, Black tops were more likely to show pictures of their genitalia in their advertisements when compared to Hispanic, Asian tops, as well as men who advertise as other race/ethnicities, indicating the centrality of the phallus in the construction of an aggressive, racialized masculinity that is typically associated with the insertive position. Black bottoms also displayed greater proportions of pictures that displayed their buttocks. This result is consistent with Black men who defy the racial sexual stereotype seeing a need to provide further evidence than other bottoms about their ability to provide such services.

Perhaps even more interesting, this finding for Black men extended to those who advertised versatility. While Black versatile escorts did not show additional frontal nudity pictures, they did show additional pictures of the buttocks. These findings indicate that, at least to some degree, male sex workers are aware of – and re-enact – dominant cultural narratives related to race, masculinity, and gay male sexuality, which include a cultural terrain in which they are associated with hypermasculinity.

The predictions for Asian escorts were not borne out in the data. One reason for this could be the fact that relatively few Asian men advertise dominant sexual behavior. Indeed, there are twice as many Asian men who advertise as bottoms than as tops. This is somewhat unsatisfying, however, in that ten times as many Black men advertise as dominant as opposed to submissive. At the same time, the very small number of Asian escorts makes it difficult to estimate statistically significant differences.

Beyond the findings specific to sex workers, this chapter demonstrates the utility of integrating insights from multiple theoretical approaches in the study of male sex workers. Intersection theory, the sociology of the body, field theory, and script theory all have important contributions to make to the study of the presentation of self. I expand on Goffman's argument, using other, more contemporary sociological theories, such as queer theory and intersection theory, to demonstrate the importance of dominant cultural narratives in constructing a front within the context of male sex work.

One consequence of the stratification of sexual fields is that particular bodies command more erotic attention than do others in gay male communities, but this depends on not only the body but also on how that body is positioned. Equipped with particular body types, the male sex workers maximize their desirability to the largest number of potential clients by carefully crafting their online presentations of self. Importantly, I argue that the men in this market rely on cultural narratives from the larger gay community to construct erotic personas that will result in the greatest financial return. This return is only indirect, however, which shows the importance of a broader set of theoretical models to predict the role that composition of pictures would play in this market. As is the case for all sexual arenas, exactly what constitutes a desirable body in gay sexual society is intimately linked to larger systems of gender and racial stratification. Gender and racial structures of inequality are thus central in how these men present themselves to their potential clients.

6

Service Fees: Masculinity, Safer Sex, and Male Sex Work

INTRODUCTION

Prostitution is a dangerous business. In addition to the constant threat of arrest and physical violence, sex workers also face the risk of contracting sexually transmitted infections (STIs). Given the large number of sexual partners that a sex worker may have in a given period of time, research in public health has long considered sex workers a potential vector of transmission of STIs. Missing from this analysis is the idea that sex workers become infected from their clients as well. A key question is the relationship between the market rewards for risky sexual behavior and their health implications. If sex workers are better paid to participate in riskier sexual behavior, interventions aimed at STI reductions would need to recognize this economic reality, as the short-term monetary benefits to taking on increased risk of STIs may outweigh the long-term benefits of improved sexual health, depending on the underlying risk, the risk preferences of the sex worker, and the potential loss of clients due to sexual behavior change.

Researchers have found a substantial premium to condomless sex among female sex workers in developing countries.[1] The intuition is that the premium is due to the increased risk faced by female sex workers for condomless sex. These findings are consistent with the market providing a monetary incentive for female sex workers to partake in riskier sexual behavior with clients. Little is known, however, about the market returns to safer sex among male sex workers. This gap in the literature is significant for several reasons. First, the range of STIs that a male sex worker is likely to be exposed to can differ significantly from that for a female sex worker. Men who have sex with men continue to make up the largest segment of the HIV-positive population in the United States, and baseline rates of STI prevalence are significantly higher in the gay community. Estimates suggest that one in five gay men is HIV positive and that as many as 40 percent of HIV-positive gay men do not know their HIV status.[2]

Second, there is evidence that gay men have substantial attachment to the commercial sex industry. Survey evidence suggests that nearly half of self-identified gay and bisexual men in the United States have been involved in the sex work industry, either as clients or sex workers, at some point in their lives.[3] Third, researchers have also found that male sex workers have higher rates of sexually transmitted infections (STIs), including HIV, than men who have sex with men (MSM) in general.[4] Fourth, dynamic models of gay sexual networks suggest that the majority of STI transmissions occur outside of main partnerships and involve men who are undiagnosed and untreated for their STIs.[5] Taken together, these factors show that understanding the dynamics of the market for commercial sex is key for policies that seek to understand gay sexual networks and to reduce the spread of STIs among gay men more generally.

Despite the prominence of commercial sex in the sexual lives of gay men and the greater likelihood of STI transmission in this population, the underlying economic analysis of risk in gay commercial sex is remarkably thin.[6] While there is quantitative work that looks at female sex workers and limited work that looks at male sex work in developing countries, there is very little work that looks at the economic incentives behind sexual behavior among male sex workers.[7] Beyond this, there is very little evidence from the demand side of the market: very few studies of sex work document any aspects of the demand for sex work services. Sexual behaviors and risk in male sex work involve a decision about the perceived economic returns to specific sexual behaviors and the negotiations that clients and escorts engage in regarding sexual conduct and risk management strategies. To focus only on sex workers would paint an incomplete picture of the inherent interaction in sexual conduct in a commercial sex exchange.

In general, gay men have more sexual partners, are more likely to have STIs, and are more likely to negotiate their sexual behaviors in distinct ways.[8] For example, gay men are more likely to use smartphone and online applications to meet sexual partners, and while this is increasing among heterosexuals, it is still more common among gay men.[9] Male sex workers have been identified as men who inform their clients' sexual practices, which opens the possibility not only for STI transmission but for education and change in sexual behavior among clients.[10] If male sex workers have the potential to influence client behavior, the positive spillovers from sex worker interventions would be pronounced if clients would be receptive to it.[11] Naturally, this depends on the extent to which clients show a strong demand for riskier sexual behavior. Behavior change or inertia among sex workers and clients could have significant costs, since treatment for STIs, especially HIV, are non-negligible.[12]

The focus on STIs such as HIV must be undertaken with care, however. The social dynamics of HIV have changed considerably in recent years. Since the debut of antiretroviral treatments in the late 1990s, images of HIV and AIDS in the United States have changed from being images of profound, acute illness to images of a chronic condition that is well managed by medication. The changes with respect to sexual behavior in response to these treatments can lead to higher rates of STI transmission.[13] Rates of unprotected sex and of HIV infection and other STIs among gay men in the United States have begun to increase after years of decline.[14] The number of new HIV/AIDS cases among men who have sex with men increased by 11 percent between 2001 and 2005, and new HIV diagnoses have remained at a constant rate since 2005, even with the increased use of pre-exposure prophylaxis.[15] Irrespective of its cause, the controversy over the increasing normalization of unprotected sex among gay men has ignited a discussion over contemporary gay sex practices that has not been seen since the early days of the AIDS epidemic.[16] What is not known is how this plays out among male sex workers and their clients.

The market for male sex work presents a unique opportunity to consider the dynamics of these changes in a conceptually compact way. We can move from abstract discussions of supply, demand, values and risk to testable implications about the values of sexual behaviors in a way that is not possible with the majority of sexual interactions between men. The theory of compensating differentials hinges on the idea that workers who undertake dangerous or undesirable tasks are appropriately incentivized to do so.[17] This would imply that clients have to compensate sex workers for taking on the increased risk of STIs that comes with condomless (unprotected) sex.[18] We do not know if such a premium exists for male sex workers, nor do we know, if so, how large the premium is.

The social world of male sex work plays an important role in how this risk plays out in the market. Not all clients of male sex workers are gay-identified.[19] Heterosexually identified clients participating in the market have the option of free, anonymous sex with other men in public places, and openly gay clients could find sex partners through gay establishments or their social networks.[20] Today, both types of clients can find sexual partners online and through smartphone applications. These options, however, involve their own risks – especially the possibility of unsuccessful negotiation over sexual behaviors, given the rise in unprotected sex among gay men and the inherent dangers of anonymous public and online encounters.[21] If clients use the commercial sex market to ease the negotiation for *safer* sex, then sex workers would be rewarded with higher wages for condom sex as it removes the need to negotiate over safer sex with a noncommercial sex partner. Put another way, the client's outside option involves a negotiation about safer sex that may not lead to a satisfactory conclusion, so the client is willing to compensate the sex worker for explicitly agreeing to safer sex. The client is paying, in essence, for contractual safer sex practices. Whether there are premiums or penalties for condomless sex depends critically on what it represents, and that depends on client demand, the clients' outside option, and the reasons for engaging with sex workers.

This chapter considers two related issues. First, I analyze the role of attraction and desirability in the propensity to *advertise* safer sex in online sex work advertisements among male sex workers. I find that young escorts, sexually dominant escorts ("tops"), Asians, escorts with established positive reputations, and escorts willing to service a wide variety of clients are strong predictors of the likelihood of advertising safer sex services. I also find that Asians who advertise passive sexual roles are more likely to advertise safer sex. These findings are consistent with sexual field theory and the concept of erotic capital – those most esteemed in the sexual field have greater freedom to limit the terms of their sexual conduct – they are, in essence, trading on their desirability to increase the terms of their control over the sexual encounter and the range of behaviors they are willing to partake in. Other predictions, such as those about dominant Black escorts using their erotic capital to increase the likelihood of advertising condomed sex, are not borne out in the data. In general, the degree to which escorts supply condomed sex is related to their sexual persona in other dimensions.

As noted above, client demand is critical to uncovering the source of premiums or penalties in the market for male sex work. To uncover the returns to riskier sexual practices, I exploit a novel source of information about the male sex worker market to estimate the values of sexual behaviors in the market for male sex work. Using data from over 6,000 client reviews of male escort services, I estimate the value of sexual behaviors for both clients and sex workers. My empirical strategy mirrors the most recent empirical approach applied to female sex workers by using sex worker fixed effects to estimate payoff functions (to the sex worker) for sex work.[22] One key innovation is that I also estimate models with client-fixed effects to estimate the values that clients place on sexual behaviors in the market. To my knowledge, this is the first study to estimate client values (demand) of male sex worker services, either male or female.

I find that clients and sex workers place different values on sexual behaviors and for sex with condoms. While both clients and sex workers value sex worker penetration of the client ("topping") equally, clients place a much higher value on mutual penetration ("versatility") than sex workers. I find that sex workers do not charge more or less for the use of condoms in sex with clients. Clients, however, show a substantial willingness to pay for sex *with* condoms. Estimates suggest that client valuations for sex with a condom are roughly 15 percent more than the average rate of an hourly session ($35). This is exactly the opposite of what has been found for female sex workers. In decomposing the penalty attached to condomless sex, I find that clients compensate sex workers for sex with condoms when they engage in mutual penetration – client valuations are not statistically significant when either the escort or the client is the sole penetrant. Furthermore, the result holds when controlling for a host of sex worker characteristics, which suggest that client willingness to pay for sex with a condom is not a function of the particular attributes of the sex worker involved but rather a general feature of the market. This is consistent with client demand for condomed sex being different from sex worker supply of condomed sex, which was shown to vary significantly by sex worker.

These results are further supported through additional analysis, which finds that advertised safer sex is positively correlated with wages. Sex workers who advertise safer sex earn 5 percent more than those who do not, on average. I find that the evidence is inconsistent with compensating differentials from economic theory. Sex workers who advertise sexual behaviors more prone to escort STI infection are paid less than those that do not – penetrative sex workers who advertise safety enjoy a premium of more than 13 percent. To the extent that there are differences in STI prevalence among sexual minorities by race, those from groups with higher rates of infection should be compensated less for undertaking riskier sexual activity. I find that there is indeed a racial and sexual behavior gradient to this premium; Black and White sex workers who advertise safer sex enjoy substantial premiums of 9 and 6 percent, respectively. These premiums are also inconsistent with compensating differentials.

This chapter shows that economic and social forces combine in the area of sexual practices among sex workers. In doing so, there are several innovations that advance the ways in which sex work can inform larger debates about sexual health. First, the study adopts a novel approach to empirical analysis of commercial sex by using online reviews to estimate the values of sexual behaviors. The extensive online reviews allow me to produce client and sex worker fixed-effects estimates of the value of sex worker services. Doing so allows me to properly distinguish the values that clients and sex workers place on sexual behaviors, respectively. Such analysis would be much more difficult, and conclusions more tenuous, if we used information such as advertisement data. While Logan (2010) has investigated the returns to sexual behaviors and Pruitt (2005) the socio-economic status of escorts, no study exists that looks at the market value of sexual behaviors using transaction-level data for male sex work in the United States. Second, the results show that, contrary to female sex work clients, the clients of male sex workers place a premium on condomed sex. While the positive correlation between prices and condom use is consistent with findings reported using cross-sections of male escort advertisements, the results here reveal that the client valuation of safer sex is the key source of the premium. Third, the results here allow us to begin to consider the ways that interventions with male sex workers may yield changes in sex worker behavior that can lead to declines in STIs among men who have sex with men. Indeed, the results here suggest that sex workers could well be induced to provide safer sex irrespective of their own risk preferences, since it is clients who place a value on sex with condoms.

SOCIETY, THE SEX WORK ECONOMY, AND SEXUAL BEHAVIOR

Before considering the particulars of sex work, the context of male-male sexual behavior needs to be delineated. There is now a large literature that looks at the causes and consequences of sexual risk taking among gay men and how they negotiate over safer sex practices, but many implications remain unexplored.[23] Earlier work looked at the ways HIV changed the sexual scripts of casual and relationship sex that gay men follow, but more recent scholarship notes how technology and the social organization of gay life in urban centers encourages gay men to compartmentalize their sexual sociality.[24] There are relationships, which may or may not be monogamous, there are casual encounters with the same person, and there are casual encounters that are not repeated. Each of these relationship types comes with a different set of expectations regarding behaviors, communication, and disclosure of STI status.[25]

While the period of the mid-1980s to late 1990s saw gay men moving largely in lock-step to normalize safer sex practices in response to the HIV epidemic, the rise of unprotected sex ("barebacking") has been well documented over the last decade.[26] Some have argued that the rise in unprotected sex is the result of "condom fatigue," a revolt against the institutional drumbeat of safer sex messages that public health services routinely target at gay men.[27] In this view, the public health messages act as a form of social control that implicitly reinforces negative stereotypes of gay sexual behavior as uncontrolled and dangerous and simultaneously reinforces heterosexual norms of mating and dating by encouraging gay men to minimize the number of partners and limit their sexual behaviors. Recently, some activists have called for "counter-public health" in response to these public health messages, and some have suggested that gay men re-organize their sexual behaviors in ways that accommodate unprotected sex, such as engaging in unprotected sex with men of similar HIV status.[28] The recent dialogue over pre-exposure prophylaxis has highlighted this as men using the treatment have not seroconverted but alter their condom use in light of significantly decreased likelihood of HIV transmission.[29]

Others have argued that as the risks of HIV infection declined with new treatments the "cost" of unprotected sex declined – not only are those who are HIV positive better able to partake in sexual activity (and due to the new treatments, highly unlikely to transmit the disease if they adhere to a treatment regimen), but those who are HIV negative may no longer fear infection.[30] Indeed, to the extent that the preventative prescription medication is itself a HIV medication, gay sexual behavior may place less value on consistent condom use. Some have noted that HIV-positive gay men have created their own subcultures and HIV negative men may long for the intimacy that HIV-positive men have created for themselves to overcome the stigma associated with their HIV status.[31] Irrespective of its cause, the controversy over unprotected sex has ignited a discussion over the morality and reality of gay sex and the sexual organization of the gay community that has not been seen since the early days of the HIV epidemic.[32]

At the same time that breakthroughs in HIV treatment hit the market, the concurrent explosion in the availability of Internet service produced a virtual world where men could connect with other men for sex in more convenient ways than ever before.[33] Sex work is a part of this online landscape, but the largest segments involve men meeting other men for casual sexual encounters. An open question is whether the Internet brought more men into gay sexual networks or influenced the sexual behavior of gay men generally, but it is beyond question that the sexual organization of gay communities changed substantially due to these technological innovations.[34] It is now easier than ever for men to contact other men for casual or anonymous sexual encounters, yet at the same time it is more difficult to negotiate safer sexual activity, in light of new treatments, the difficulty in beginning a conversation about HIV status and safer sex practices, and the reality of clandestine encounters that may not encourage STI reduction best practices.

EROTIC CAPITAL AND THE ABILITY TO NEGOTIATE FOR SAFER SEX

Against this change in gay sexual sociality, there exist dominant structures that sexually empower some men more than others. When men have more desirability in the sexual market, they may be better able to control the terms of their interactions with others over sex. Public health research has regularly shown that gay men with poor self-image and self-esteem are more likely to engage in higher-risk sexual behavior.[35] The same could be true among sex workers, to the extent that some sex workers will be more desired than others. The question is how desirability among sex workers is related to sexual behaviors.

Qualitative research on male sex workers has informed our theories of sexuality, sexual behaviors, and sex work.[36] These studies have addressed the sexual behaviors of escorts and their reasons for entering the profession. Little systemic data has been exploited, however, to look at potential variations in the propensity to advertise safer sex by male escorts or the nature of client and male escort negotiation. Just as escorts themselves have different reasons for entering the profession, they may apply different rationales to partake in different types of sex in the market.

Social scientists have documented the importance of self-labels for men who have sex with men, which are strongly related to their actual sexual practices.[37] Escorts regularly use sexual behavior labels to advertise their services to clients. This is a form of advertising – using the labels that apply to noncommercial sex work to define themselves in a way that will be discernable to clients. Little is known, however, about whether such self-labels or other characteristics are related to advertised safer sex among male sex workers. For example, men who advertise sexual behavior that increases the client's risk of HIV infection (such as a "top" – penetrative sex on the part of the escort) may be prone to advertise safer sex as a way of allaying clients' fears about STI transmission. Conversely, sex workers who advertise behavior that increases their own risk of STI infection (a "bottom" – receptive sex) may advertise safer sex for their own protection. Similarly, researchers have found that safer sex practices among gay men vary by race, with Black men more likely to partake in safer sex than White men, but we do not know if this extends to commercial sexual encounters.[38]

Beyond the gains of applying statistical analysis to this issue, the determinants of safer sex advertisements among sex workers speak directly to theoretical insights about gay sexuality and sexual organization. Green (2008b) has recently developed a sexual field theory to describe the ways that gay men navigate and compartmentalize their sexual networks in modern society. As noted by Martin (2003), field theory emphasizes the regular interactions between people in different social positions. Building on the work of Goffman (1959) with regard to situational negotiation and Bourdieu's (1977, 1980) model of routine practice, Green's theory outlines how erotic schema become structured practice in gay communities. Green's sexual field theory explicitly considers how the interactions between men having sex with men are regulated in explicitly sexual spaces, as opposed to more general social situations. In other words, his work takes as given the fact that gay men organize their sexual spaces differently from other social spaces, which gives rise to a unique "erotic field" that governs the interactions between these men. Such a theory is useful for thinking about gay sexual relationships, given the different norms in gay sexual behavior that have been well documented by social scientists.[39]

Green's theory is a nuanced approach the issue of how eroticism is socially organized, structured, and constructed by gay men. The key insight is that modernity gives rise to specialized, focused erotic spaces that can be disconnected from other aspects of gay social life, but where the participant's behavior is structured by the social elements they are disconnected from in these erotic spheres. Gay men seeking sexual contact, as opposed to romantic relationships or friendships, must still adhere to social norms regarding racial, gender, and sexual hierarchies – although these hierarchies themselves may be different in erotic fields. That is, social structures give structure to these uniquely sexual spaces, but the structure itself may change, privileging a different set of men in sexual spaces since these spaces are compartmentalized and held distinct from the larger social environment. For example, the type of man that is privileged for a sexual encounter may or may not be the type of man that is privileged for romantic relationships, friendships, professional networks, or other social interactions. This theory is therefore quite well suited to addressing the questions of sexual negotiations because it considers how the social structures create sexual-social structures, and in looking at male sex work we can test the hypotheses that derive from the theory.

Rather than being open or freeing, Green sees the sexual field as one with clearly defined roles, hierarchies, and ritualized practices that apply to this specific sexual field. These sexual structures must then be navigated by men partaking in gay sexual behavior. A key strength of Green's approach is that it is explicitly intersectional – he carefully considers how the intersections of race, class, gender, and sexuality give rise to the unique structures that gay men of particular types must navigate in sexual spaces. The purpose here is not to restate Green's theory, but to use its conceptual framework to think about how this theory can be used to develop hypotheses about who provides safer sex in the male escort market, since male sex workers are working in a sexual arena that will adhere to the larger social structures in which gay men negotiate sexual behavior. Also, the hierarchies that exist in the larger gay social structure would likely carry over to the practice of sex work, giving some male sex workers greater control (less client negotiability) over their sex worker practices than others.

The key conceptual framework in Green's sexual fields theory is the notion of erotic capital. Erotic capital is similar to other types of human capital – it is a personal attribute that one can make investments in and that may increase or decrease over time. Like education in the labor market, erotic capital gives those well-endowed with it a higher standing in the sexual hierarchy – they are more esteemed, have greater partner choice, and generally have more control over the terms of their sexual liaisons. In short, erotic capital translates into power in the sexual fields that gay men navigate. When considering commercial sexual encounters, this power translates into greater authority over the terms of sexual conduct. Escorts with larger amounts of erotic capital would have greater leeway to place restrictions on their sexual behaviors as they would face relatively fewer sanctions for doing so. In essence, men can exchange their erotic capital for restrictions on sexual behaviors. This power is highly variable, however, and depends on the specific type of erotic capital and the sexual field in which the man is operating.

There are two important features of erotic capital that distinguish it from other types of human capital and are key when thinking about the predictors of advertised safer sex among male sex workers. Consideration of each feature leads to hypotheses about who would be more likely to advertise safer sex services. Green claims that erotic capital (1) gives rise to structures in the way that gay men navigate their sexual landscape and

(2) is simultaneously dependent on historical processes that overlay race, class, and gender in gay sexual spaces. These two features are related – the structures that develop are themselves functions of the historical processes that give rise to differences in erotic capital. In the following paragraphs, I begin with the hypotheses that derive from the structure and then discuss the hypotheses that derive from the intersectional historical processes.

STRUCTURAL HYPOTHESES

The first distinguishing feature of erotic capital is that it structures the sexual interactions of gay men. While historical dimensions tell us who may have higher amounts of erotic capital, the structure that it gives rise to tells us which roles gay men must play to realize the full potential of the their erotic capital. A first layer of this structure is the well-known hierarchy of sexual roles among gay men, where men who are penetrative sex partners ("tops") enjoy larger amounts of erotic capital than men who are receptive sex partners ("bottoms"). This goes hand-in-hand with the reification of traditional gender norms among gay men, and also the particular penalties for sexual behavior that is considered feminine.[40] The historical gender norms give us a structure where men who are penetrative sexual partners are looked upon to be initiators of sexual contact, to control the terms of sexual liaisons, and to have greater choice in terms of the sexual conduct in which they will participate (for example, penetrative sex partners have greater leeway in whether they will kiss or perform receptive oral sex). We would therefore expect men who are penetrative partners to be more likely to advertise safer sex services – they have greater amounts of erotic capital than other men, giving them more leeway to control the terms of their sexual conduct.

The same reasoning applies to age and sexual experience. Gay men have well-known and well-researched tendencies to value youth and younger physical appearance in sexual partners.[41] For example, cohabiting male same-sex couples have larger differences in partner ages than any other type of pairing.[42] Younger escorts would therefore be more desirable – have larger amounts of erotic capital – and would be better able to control the terms of their commercial sex encounters. In some ways, this hypothesis turns on its head the idea that young sex workers are more easily exploited than older sex workers, but this is exactly due to their greater amount of erotic capital in the sexual field.

Similarly, men with greater attachment to the escort industry – which could be measured by positive reputation, length of time in the industry, or popularity – would likely have greater amounts of erotic capital. Gay men are known to have different norms about promiscuity (they are less likely to shun those with large numbers of sexual partners), and others have argued that gay sex workers are better integrated into the larger gay community than their heterosexual counterparts.[43] In a sexual field such as male sex work, which I assert is not distinct from the larger sexual field among gay men, experience and success in the profession would lead to large amounts of erotic capital – popular and well-established escorts would have greater choice over the terms of their sexual conduct. In some ways, this would be similar to returns to seniority in the labor market – those with more experience exploit their expertise to avoid conduct in which they would rather not participate.

In sum, the structural aspects of erotic capital predict that men who are penetrative sex partners ("tops"), young men, and men with greater experience and success in the industry would have larger amounts of erotic capital. Theoretically, larger amounts of erotic capital translate into power – these men are more desired and, even as sex workers, can make further demands of their clients than others. We would therefore predict that this power would translate into greater control over sexual behaviors and an increased likelihood of requiring and requesting certain behaviors from their clients, including safer sex.

INTERSECTIONAL HYPOTHESES

The second distinguishing feature of the theory is that erotic capital is situated in historical processes that interlace race, class, and gender norms. Keeping with the human capital analogy, this feature is similar to the idea that historical processes such as discrimination and segregation give rise to differences in human capital that persist, but with erotic capital these historical forces are rooted in explicitly sexual dimensions. The intersection of hegemonic masculinity with racial sexual stereotypes can create multiple forms of sexual objectification for particular types of gay men.[44] For example, the erotic capital of a "top" is not uniform across all tops – the value of a White "top" is not simply the addition of the value of "Whiteness" and "topness," but an independent effect for men in that particular category, who in this instance embody the highest position in the racial and sexual behavior hierarchies among gay men. For these reasons Green takes an explicitly intersectional approach to the development of his theory, and it is in consideration of the intersections that we develop an even finer set of hypotheses about which escorts will be more likely to advertise safer sex.

One key area where erotic capital predicts differences in the propensity to advertise safer sex would be race. Race is a type of erotic capital that is shaped by the historical processes that are key to Green's theory. Scholars have long noted in discussions of American gay sexuality the unique role that race plays.[45] Recent scholarship looks at the racial variation in social value among gay men, but contemplation of Green's theory extends this to the sexual area as well.[46] As Logan (2010) has recently argued, sexual networks among gay men eroticize Black bodies for their stereotypical aggressiveness and dominance. High amounts of erotic capital for Black men are restricted to those who display sexual dominance and aggressiveness. Robinson (2008), for example, finds that Black men who do not conform to the stereotype of the hypermasculine Black male are largely ignored and devalued by White gay men for sexual partnerships.

Asian men are also eroticized for their "exotic" features in the sexual field, and in particular fields would presumably have large amounts of erotic capital that could be exploited. Unlike Black men, Asian men are endowed with large amounts of erotic capital when they present themselves as submissive men. Robinson (2008), Phua and Kaufman (2003), and Han (2006a, 2006b) describe the persistent stereotype that Asian men should be passive, docile "bottoms." The historical stereotype of Asian men as docile works against the structural norm that encourages gay men to present themselves in as masculine a manner as possible, empowering submissive Asian men. This gives Asian men who are docile or submissive greater amounts of erotic capital than other Asian men, and they would be able to exploit that power to control the terms of their sexual relationships.

It is in consideration of these structures that the hypotheses become clearer, and where the intersectionist approach is most useful – while race may be eroticized, it is only eroticized in certain dimensions, consistent with the theory's claim that erotic capital is highly variable. It is not that all Black men have large amounts of erotic capital, but Black men who conform to the stereotype of being aggressive, penetrative sex partners. Phua and Kaufman (2003) note that these stereotypes view Black men as sexually aggressive (and therefore likely to have large amounts of erotic capital only when they are penetrative partners); Asian men as docile (and therefore endowed with larger amounts of erotic capital when they are receptive partners); and Hispanic men as "passionate" lovers. It is unclear how the Hispanic stereotype relates to sexual behaviors – it could well be that Hispanic men are rewarded for either type of sexual behavior, or for being willing to move between the two depending on the desires of their client. The ambiguity of "passionate" makes it difficult to derive specific hypotheses about which types of Hispanic men would have larger amounts of erotic capital.

The hierarchies that develop in these sexual fields, which give certain men more erotic capital than others, can appear counterintuitive until one adopts an intersectional approach to gay sexual organization. This intersectional approach is a key strength of Green's sexual field theory. In an explicitly sexual area, men can exploit their erotic capital to its fullest extent. For example, theories of race and sexuality have long noted that Black men occupy a unique space in the gay sexual landscape.[47] While not sought out for companionship or dating, they are esteemed sexually when they are perceived as or perform as dominant sexual partners.[48] Similarly, men who are sexually aggressive and dominant occupy the highest rung of the sexual behavior hierarchy.[49]

HYPOTHESES FROM SEXUAL FIELD THEORY ABOUT ADVERTISED SAFER SEX

Sexual field theory and the related concept of erotic capital predict that younger men, penetrative sex partners ("tops"), men with greater attachment to the escort market, Black men who are dominant ("tops"), Asian men who are submissive ("bottoms"), and Hispanic men who are "passionate" would be more likely to advertise safer sex, as their higher amounts of erotic capital would give them greater control over the terms of their commercial sexual interactions.

MICROECONOMIC APPROACHES TO NEGOTIATIONS

Sexual Negotiations – Safer Sex as a Game between Clients and Escorts

While the social theory above describes the ways that sex workers may use the power from social structures to better control the terms of negotiating their sexual practices with clients, they must still negotiate with specific clients for transactions. While social theory allows us to derive predictions about advertised sexual behavior from social narratives about who would be most desired, in practice we should consider the reality of sexual negotiations between clients and sex workers. Indeed, clients may seek out sex workers with advertised safer sex and then proceed to negotiate with these sex workers. Similarly, sex workers may not list safer sex practices as a means of eliciting negotiations in order for greater remuneration from clients. A more detailed and economically oriented approach is required when investigating the actual transactions.

This microeconomic approach to the topic brings a number of additional insights but simultaneously requires a different style of analysis. Sex workers and their clients are engaged in economic transactions that take place in specific social contexts. These contexts are usually straightforward – men desire women and compensate them for sexual activity. For most prostitution services these basic dynamics are sufficient to describe the general nature of the profession.[50] The unique social stigmas attached to homosexuality, however, yield different conclusions. Not only are male sex workers more integrated into gay communities, they also serve a clientele with a number of different sexual identities.[51] Add to this the STI risk differences for homosexual and heterosexual sex and we are left with divergent ideas about the ways that risks are mechanized in this market.[52]

Theorizing Client Demand – Client Willingness to Pay for Risky Sex

If the clients in the market desire unsafe sex, and if that sex is inherently riskier for the escort than the alternative (which is inherently true), then clients must compensate sex workers for that additional risk. More generally, the presence of one STI can increase the likelihood of being infected with another, which could potentially compound the compensating differential. For example, even if a sex worker were HIV positive, unprotected sex comes at the risk of re-infection with a different strain of the virus or another STI, which could threaten the effectiveness of their current treatment regimen. In short, irrespective of the escort's STI status, unprotected sex is unambiguously riskier. The existing studies have shown that the premium for unprotected sex work is quite high, which is consistent with the concept of a compensating differential. One drawback of the existing scholarship is that it only applies to female sex workers.

The concept of compensating differentials gives us additional hypotheses with respect to male sex work, which should be tested. The compensating differential should vary with the risks involved. In male homosexual sex, the risk of STI transmission varies considerably by sexual role, and it follows that the compensating differential should as well. Among men who have sex with men it has been well established that particular types of sexual conduct are riskier than others.[53] For example, the relative risk of contracting HIV for receptive versus penetrative anal sex is 7.69, which implies that the compensating differential should be higher for escorts engaged in receptive anal sex.[54]

It could also be the case that compensating differentials could vary by race. According to the Centers for Disease Control and Prevention (CDC), African American males are a disproportionately large share of the HIV population and are nearly twice as likely to contract HIV as their White counterparts, despite higher rates of safer sex activity.[55] Some estimates have suggested that as much as 46 percent of the Black gay population is infected with HIV, more than twice the rate for White men (21 percent) or Hispanics (17 percent).[56] As there is well-documented segregation in gay sexual networks, White and Hispanic men would face lower baseline risks of STI infection. Since Whites and Hispanics face a lower probability of having STIs, they would have to be compensated more for partaking in riskier sexual activity.[57]

Theorizing Client Demand – Client Willingness to Pay for Safer Sex

Even among men who are homosexually identified, negotiating safer sex practices can be difficult.[58] Increasing numbers of gay men are having unprotected sex (barebacking) with men whose HIV status has been disclosed to them. Sociologists and social psychologists have often described the increasing phenomenon of unprotected sex among openly gay men as a form of resistance to safer sex messages in the age of HIV.[59] Eaton et al. (2010), for example, describe a recent survey of gay men and find that more than 50 percent of the White respondents reported that they did not use a condom in their last sexual encounter (compared to fewer than 20 percent for African Americans), although the vast majority (more than 75 percent) of respondents claimed to know the HIV status of their last sexual partner. This implies a growing normalization of sex without condoms among gay men, and a growing number of men who engaging in sex with men whose HIV status is unknown to them.

While public health researchers have noted the phenomena of barebacking and serosorting and their potential impact on HIV transmission, the possibility of having unprotected sex with someone whose status is uncertain is problematic at the individual level.[60] The average man surveyed in Eaton et al. (2010) had not had an HIV test in the past year. Although men claimed to know the HIV status of their partners, it is unlikely that the current status of their partners was known with a large degree of certainty since most men did not know their own HIV status. Further,

Wolitski et al. (1998), Marks et al. (1994), Simon Rosser et al. (2008), and Horvath et al. (2008) have shown that up to one-third of HIV-positive men have unprotected sex without disclosing their status to their partners. This poses risks to both homosexually and heterosexually identified men who navigate these sexual networks. In essence, casual sexual encounters in the contemporary gay community appear to require explicit discussions of condom usage that may have been less likely only a decade earlier.

There is some evidence that male sex workers are more likely to practice safer sex in their commercial sexual encounters, but this evidence is limited. Prestage et al. (2007) found that men who were paid for sex were less likely to engage in unprotected sex in their paid sexual encounters (less than 20 percent of the time) as opposed to their casual sexual encounters (more than 60 percent of the time). This implies that, for risk-averse gay men, the market for male sex work may allow them to see the type of sexual partner they would prefer, not only in terms of physical appearance, but also in terms of sexual behaviors, given the relative prominence of unprotected sex among gay men. To state it another way, irrespective of sexual identity, we cannot say with certainty that condomless sex will be preferred in the market. There is suggestive evidence that men may use the market as a means to overcome the difficulty in negotiating safer sex practices with other men.

DISTINCTIONS

The distinction here lies in the desire of the clients. If there is a compensating differential, then the outside option for the client is protected sex and he uses the sex worker market to avail himself of opportunities to partake in unprotected sex. Given that this is risky for the sex worker, the client must compensate the sex worker for that risk. An additional implication is that the size of the incentive would have to be conditioned on the type of sexual behavior desired by the client (receptive versus penetrative) and the type of escort in question (perhaps in terms of race). If clients are willing to pay for safer sex, the outside option of the client is unprotected sex and he uses the sex worker market to solicit and partake in protected sex or to ease the negotiation for safer sex.[61]

DATA AND EMPIRICAL STRATEGY

The few existing large-scale studies of the male sex worker market have used cross-section data and hedonic regression.[62] This data is limited, however, because it is based on advertisements for male sex worker services, contains no information from the demand side of the market, and is not transaction-specific. Transaction-level data gives us a finer description of the specific sexual conduct and interactions of male sex workers and clients. The few transaction-based studies of male sex workers have used diaries with limited recall times and small sample sizes, limiting their scope and their results' capacity for generalized application.[63]

Recent research in female sex work in developing countries has used the method of sex worker fixed-effects to identify the sex worker payoff function.[64] This is an improvement over cross-sectional analysis of the market since we can now estimate the value of services while controlling for individual-level heterogeneity, which can seriously bias cross-sectional estimates. Analysis of the demand side of the market has been more generally lacking in studies of sex work. Evidence from the demand side is particularly important for male sex work, as different sex acts imply vastly different probabilities for disease transmission among gay men.[65] It is therefore important to estimate client values of sexual behaviors, as knowledge of the price sensitivity of male sex workers and clients is key for developing interventions for behavior change.

DATA

The data come from the online reviews hosted by Daddy's Reviews (www .daddysreviews.com), the oldest and most popular client-based forum for reviews and discussions of male sex workers. This website has been in existence since 1998 and provides a rich structure for clients to review male sex worker services. The website contains both a forum (message board) for clients to discuss male sex workers and a review feature where clients provide detailed reviews of their specific encounters with male sex workers. The individual reviews of male sex workers are the data used here. A key for this data is that all reviews of male sex workers are held in a holding tank and individually verified by the website administrator before they are posted. Male sex workers cannot remove reviews, and reviews are flagged if they are suspicious (for example, if they appear they may have been entered by a competing sex worker). As described by Logan and Shah (2013) and discussed earlier, this website acts to police male sex workers, allowing clients to inform each other about the quality of male sex workers. This function minimizes the opportunity that male sex workers have to exploit clients. Logan and Shah (2013) also note that it is extremely difficult for an escort to create new identities for himself as clients track them over time using this source. If an escort changes his location, over time all of his previous reviews are retained and linked to him, and the same holds if the escort changes his professional name. Male sex workers who have retired are not removed from the website, but they are listed as retired. Male sex workers do have the ability to post comments on reviews. Escort reviews can be searched by individual sex worker name or by geographical location.

For each review page, the contact information is listed as well as all reviews, which are listed in reverse chronological order (newest to oldest).[66] Reviews were collected using a script that pulled the information from the website into a database organized by the fields in the advertisement. Reviews detail the date and location of the transaction, the length of the appointment, the price paid, the client's perception of features of the escort (height, weight, age, etc.), and the sexual behaviors that took place in the given transaction. The reviews also allow clients to enter free form text that describes their encounter in more detail. This field is read manually and coded for sexual behaviors not categorized in the reviews. In addition, clients also rate the experience. At the end of the review, clients identify themselves with a unique "handle" username.

EMPIRICAL STRATEGY – ADVERTISING SAFER SEX

The advertisement of safer sex is a dichotomous indicator – either the escort notes in the text of his advertisement that he practices safer sex or he does not. Since I am interested in differences in the probability of advertising safer as opposed to odds ratios, I use a statistical model that estimates the probability associated with advertising safer sex. I estimate a probit model where the outcome is the escort's advertisement of safety to analyze the predictors of advertised safer sex. Specifically, the model is

$$Pr(Safe = 1|X = x) = \Phi(x'\beta) \tag{1}$$

where Φ is the cumulative distribution function (cdf) of the normal distribution, *Safe* is the indicator for advertising safer sex (1 if advertised, 0 otherwise) and X is a vector of covariates that may potentially be related to the decision to advertise safer sex.[67] The model is estimated using maximum likelihood.[68] The model is nonlinear, and raw coefficient estimates of β must be transformed for interpretation. For ease of interpretation all coefficients are reported at the margin – that is, they give the change in the *probability* (percentage points) of advertising safer sex for a unit change in the corresponding variable.[69]

EMPIRICAL STRATEGY – CLIENT AND SEX WORKER NEGOTIATIONS

We would like to estimate the client and sex worker payoff functions. Any transaction agreed to by the client and the sex worker must hold where the wage offered by the client is agreeable to the sex worker. Using this fact, we can map out sex worker and client payoff functions, the returns they receive to successful negotiations.

Transaction data gives us the equilibrium price for a specific transaction in addition to the characteristics of that transaction (the specific sexual conduct, location, etc.). Simply regressing prices on quantities will not uncover either the supply or the demand function. We can, however, exploit the transaction-level nature of the data by noting that both clients and sex workers are uniquely identified in the data. Since clients in the data potentially review several sex workers, and since sex workers are reviewed by several clients, we can estimate the payoff functions by using client- and sex worker-fixed effects. To use fixed effects there must be a sizeable number of multiple reviews for sex workers and multiple reviews posted by clients. Without this it is not possible to exploit the within-person variation that is critical for fixed-effects estimates. As would be expected when using data that reviews sex worker services, sex workers have more reviews per sex worker than clients have reviews per client. In the data, 72 percent of the escorts have more than two reviews and 34 percent have more than four reviews. For clients, 39 percent have posted more than two reviews and 14 percent have posted four or more reviews in the data.[70]

The standard approach in recent studies of sex workers is to use sex worker-fixed effects to identify the sex worker's payoff (supply) function. For example, Gertler, Shah, and Bertozzi (2005) survey sex workers and obtain information about their last three transactions. We usually know little, however, about the demand for sex services. The data here allows us to estimate the client's payoff function as well. Indeed, because we have detailed information on the characteristics of the sex workers and the sexual behaviors that took place in a given transaction, the payoff function for the client can identify not only the values of sexual behaviors but also the values of sex worker characteristics. In contrast, the sex worker payoff function can only identify the values of sexual behaviors, as client characteristics are not available. Caution should be used in interpreting the sex worker payoff function – if sexual behaviors are correlated with client characteristics it will not be possible to distinguish between the two in the data.

The transaction-level data fits nicely to the assumption of revealed preference; identification of the escort and client payoff functions is straightforward since within-client (i) variation for escorts (j) (the clients' payoff function) and within-escort variation for sexual conduct with clients (the escorts' payoff function) can be estimated from the same data. Since sex workers are independent owner-operators, they are treated as firms. This would not be possible if there were intermediaries or other types of distortions in the market. Specifically, I estimate

$$P_{ij}^{Client} = \lambda + \sum\nolimits_m \beta_m Z_m + \sum\nolimits_k \delta_k S_k + \phi_i + \varepsilon$$

$$P_{ij}^{Escort} = \rho + \sum\nolimits_k \eta_k S_k + \theta_j + \varepsilon,$$

where Z is sex worker characteristics, S is sexual behaviors, ϕ is a client-fixed effect, and θ is a sex worker-fixed effect.[71] The fixed effects in the client (escort) equation control for the bias in both unobserved client (escort) heterogeneity and escort (client) selection based on unobserved client (escort) characteristics. Key for this analysis is the use of client-fixed effects controls for a client's propensity to describe (or not describe) specific sexual behaviors in their reviews of escort services.

One critique of the estimates is that they require within-person variation and are only identified for the "changers" who exhibit within-person variation. While fixed effects estimates do control for individual hetero-geneity, they require that we assume that those who change are equivalent to those who do not, for generalization purposes. In this case, the value of sexual behavior to the sex worker or client is only identified by those sex workers or clients who engage in different types of sex. Clients or sex workers who always or never partake in a given sexual behavior cannot be used to identify the value of that behavior. These may be the sex workers are clients most susceptible to behavior change as they already show a propensity to engage in a variety of types of sex.

RESULTS – THE PROPENSITY TO OFFER SAFER SEX

I begin by considering the physical predictors of advertised safer sex: age and body size. Figure 6.1 shows estimates for the physical predictors of advertised safer sex. Age is negatively related to the probability of advertis-ing safer sex. For example, a 20-year-old escort would be at least 3 percen-tage points more likely to advertise safer sex than a 30-year-old escort. The other physical measures considered, height and weight, are not related

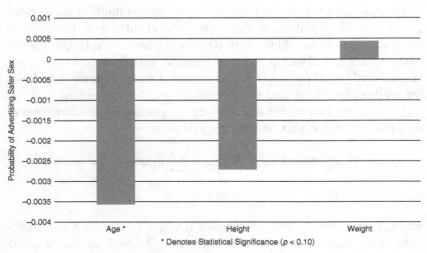

Figure 6.1 Physical characteristics and probability of advertising safer sex

to the advertisement of safer sex services.[72] This result for age is consistent with erotic capital theory, where younger escorts have larger amounts of erotic capital, and therefore greater control over the terms of their commercial sexual encounters, making them more likely to advertise condomed sex with clients.

Figure 6.2 presents estimates of the sexual behavior predictors of advertised safer sex. Being a penetrative escort ("tops") increases the probability that one will advertise safer sex by more than 8.5 percentage points, being a versatile escort increases the probability by more than 10 percentage points, and being a bottom is not significantly related to advertised safer sex. The distinct categories of versatility, as gay men commonly use expressions such as "versatile top" to denote a versatile sexual performer who prefers to be the penetrative partner and "versatile bottom" to denote a versatile sexual performer who prefers to be the receptive partner, were added to see whether there might be a further distinction in the propensity to advertise condomed sex.[73] While being a generic versatile performer increases the probability one will advertise safer sex by more than 10 percentage points, being a versatile top decreases the probability by more than 8 percentage points. Being a versatile bottom is not significantly related to advertised safer sex. Overall, the results are consistent with erotic capital theory. Men who are perceived to have larger amounts of erotic capital in structural aspects (younger men and penetrative sexual position) are more likely to advertise safer sex.

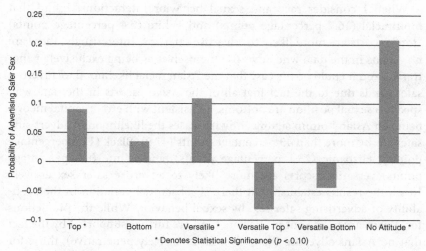

Figure 6.2 Sexual behaviors and probability of advertising safer sex

Figure 6.2 also adds a proxy for sexual adventurousness – whether the escorts claims to have "no attitude." A "no attitude" designation is used in the escort market to inform clients that the escort is willing to engage with clients irrespective of age, race, and physical appearance. This proxy of sexual adventurousness would, in theory, be related to larger amounts of erotic capital. The estimates predict that being a "no attitude" escort increases the probability that one will advertise safer sex by more than 20 percentage points. This result, too, is consistent with erotic capital theory. Escorts who serve a larger clientele would be more likely to have experience and sexual maturity, giving them larger amounts of erotic capital to exploit in their commercial sexual negotiations. This is also an example of the unique intersectional fields approach. Men who are adventurous are actually able to exercise greater control over certain aspects of their sexual behavior, capitalizing on their sexual adventurousness and expertise.

I also considered race and the interaction of race and sexual behavior on advertised safer sex. The results are interesting with respect to race. Being an Asian increases the probability of advertising safer sex by 15 percentage points. There are no other racial distinctions in the likelihood of advertising safer sex. Formal tests of the hypothesis that all other (non-Asian) racial effects are equal to each other cannot be rejected. From race alone, it appears that Asians are an outlier in terms of being more likely to advertise safer sex to clients.

When I consider race and sexual behavior interactions, I find that multiracial (16.7 percentage points) and White (7.4 percentage points) "top" escorts are more likely to advertise safer sex. Interestingly, there are no Asians in the data who advertise themselves as being exclusively penetrative, and it could be the case that the Asian racial likelihood to advertise safer sex is due to the fact that all of the Asian escorts in the data who specify a sexual position are bottoms. Consistent with erotic capital theory, being an Asian bottom significantly increases the likelihood of advertising safer sex by more than 45 percentage points (47.9). Black (11.6 percentage points), Hispanic (25.1 percentage points), and White (6.6 percentage points) versatile escorts are more likely to advertise safer sex as well. In all, the results establish that there is substantial variation in the probability of advertising safer sex, by sexual behavior. While the predictions for Asians are borne out in the data (and are further supported by the fact that no Asians advertise themselves as exclusively penetrative), those for Blacks are not. The Hispanics' results are mixed: versatile Hispanic escorts are more likely to advertise safer sex, but it is unclear if this corresponds to the erotic capital that derives from them adopting a "passionate" persona in the sexual field. As noted earlier, "passionate" erotic persona is ambiguous in terms of sexual behaviors.

Interestingly, the erotic capital that Black "tops" possess is not translated into greater control over the terms of their sexual behaviors with regard to condom usage. This stands in contrast to the higher wages they demand in the market. Thus, Black men participating in the market, even when they possess the masculine traits that would give them erotic capital, are unable to translate this into greater control of sexual behaviors. In terms of intersectionality, this result is consistent with the idea that while "top" (masculine) behavior does allow one greater control of the terms of his sexual conduct, it is limited when interacted with racial hierarchies. That is, Black male sexual autonomy violates the racial structure of the market, where Black male bodies exist primarily for White male pleasure.

It could certainly be the case that other advertising features are related to other features of advertising behavior. If these are correlated with sexual behavior (for example, a Black top may show fewer pictures, and pictures may be related to propensity to advertise condomed sex), then the results described above would be due to differences in advertising and not necessarily elements of erotic capital. I therefore considered the effects of other advertising features on the propensity to advertise safer sex. Recall that erotic capital theory predicts that escort popularity and reputation will lead to larger amounts of erotic capital. Popular and well-regarded escorts will be more likely to advertise safer sex. Earlier we saw that adventurousness was related to advertising safer sex, but adventurousness may be a poor proxy for popularity or expertise. Fortunately, the data gives us several proxies for popularity and reputation that are less tied to sexual dexterity and more closely aligned with popularity as a sexual performer. Escorts provide pictures in their advertisements, and more attractive escorts may be more likely to provide more pictures and to have larger amounts of erotic capital. Additionally, the website used for analysis allows clients to review escorts in two ways. The first review method is a short review (I term this a "survey review"), which is similar to feedback on ebay.com. Clients simply rate escorts on a four-star scale. The data records both the number of reviews and the fraction of total reviews that are four-star. There are also text reviews, where clients enter detailed, free form reviews of their specific experiences with the escort. Since the text reviews are more detailed, they give a better measure of an escort's quality than survey reviews.

The results show that survey reviews are unrelated to the probability of advertising safer sex. While the number of text reviews of client services (which could serve as a proxy for the number of clients for a given escort) are negatively related to the propensity to advertise safer sex (−10.4 percentage points), the number of positive text reviews of escorts (which could be a proxy for quality of escort services) is positively related to advertising safer sex (10.8 percentage points). Indeed, the two effects are nearly identical. This suggests that the more negative reviews an escort collects, the less likely he is to advertise safer sex services. For example, if two escorts both had ten reviews, and one escort had all positive reviews whereas the other had five positive and five negative reviews, the escort with the negative reviews would be 50 percent less likely to advertise safer sex than the other. This is consistent with erotic capital theory – well regarded and popular escorts are more likely to advertise safer sex. This result holds even when controlling for sexual adventurousness itself.[74]

RESULTS – CLIENT AND SEX WORKER NEGOTIATIONS

Constrained Client and Sex Worker Estimates

Figures 6.3 and 6.4 show estimates of client and sex worker payoff functions where the two functions are constrained to contain the same information. Specifically, the estimates do not include sex worker characteristics in the client payoff specification, leading to a set of payoff functions of the following form:

$$P_{ij}^{Client} = \lambda + \sum_k \delta_k S_k + \phi_i + \varepsilon$$
$$P_{ij}^{Escort} = \rho + \sum_k \eta_k S_k + \theta_j + \varepsilon$$

This specification allows us to consider the differences between the value of sex worker services where the only difference is the client- and sex worker-fixed effects. These specifications are similar to those of studies of female sex work that use fixed effects to estimate the payoff functions but where the attributes of the client are unknown. The guiding assumption in these models is that sex worker behavior is not a function of client characteristics. In the data used here, I will relax this assumption for estimates of the client payoff function.

Figures 6.3 and 6.4 show the results for a limited set of sexual behaviors.[75] The first set of results reveal that clients and escorts place similar values on escort penetration of clients ("topping") – both escort and client specifications suggest that escort penetration is valued at roughly $35, a premium of around 15 percent. The results also show that clients place a high value on versatility (mutual penetration). The client value of versatility is nearly the same as the premium for escort penetration (around $35). Escorts, however, do not place such a high value on

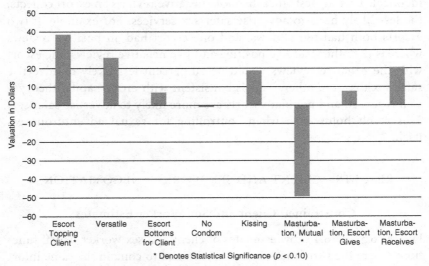

Figure 6.3 Sex worker valuations of sexual behaviors

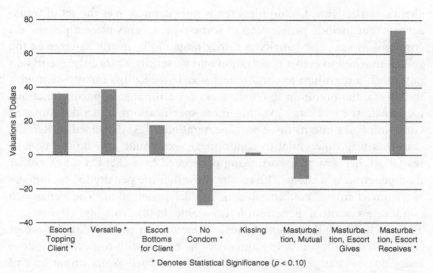

Figure 6.4 Client valuations of sexual behaviors

versatility – the point estimate is less than half as large as the client valuation and is not statistically significant. For client penetration ("bottoming"), neither escorts nor clients place a high value on the behavior, and the point estimate for escorts is actually negative, but not statistically significant. It is important to note that escort penetration comes with significantly lower probabilities of the escort contracting an STI, and the high (low) value placed on escort (client) penetration is not consistent with a compensating differential because it is the less (more) risky activity for the escort in terms of contracting an STI.[76]

The results also show that neither escorts nor clients place a large value on kissing, and the point estimate for clients is much smaller than for escorts. Escorts place a large and negative value ($50) on mutual masturbation; a penalty of more than a 20 percent is attached to the behavior. Clients place a negative value on mutual masturbation as well, but the point estimate ($13) is not as large as that for escorts and is not statistically significant. The results also show that clients do place a large and positive value ($74) on masturbating the escort. Indeed, masturbating the escort comes with a price premium of roughly 30 percent. Escorts also place a positive value on receiving masturbation, but the estimate is not as large ($20) and is not statistically significant.

The main implications for negotiation had to do with condomless sex. Figures 6.3 and 6.4 show the value of condomless sex for sex workers and

clients, respectively. Condomless sex is only defined over the set of transactions that include penetration of some type. Clients place a penalty on
condomless sex. The penalty is rather large ($30), nearly as large as the
values attached to escort penetration and versatility. Curiously, escorts do
not attach a premium to condomless sex. This result is inconsistent with
the substantial premium to condomless sex estimated in payoff functions
for female sex workers.[77] Within these specifications I also decomposed
condomless sex into its three possible iterations.[78] As discussed earlier, the
compensating differential to condomless sex should vary by the type of
sexual activity. For an escort, being penetrated by a client is much riskier
than penetrating a client. The results show that the penalty to condomless
sex from clients is concentrated in mutual penetration. The penalty to
condomless mutual penetration is sizable ($48), roughly 20 percent.
The results show that clients place a premium on penetrating the escort
($18), but it is not precisely estimated. The results with respect to condom
usage do not change when other sexual activity such as masturbation and
kissing are included in the specification.

Client Estimates with Full Sex Worker Characteristics

As discussed earlier, one key advantage of the data used here is that the
client payoff function can be estimated with respect to a host of sex
worker characteristics. Previous research has found that sex worker
characteristics are related to the prices that they advertise for their
services, but it is not known how or whether clients value these
characteristics.[79] Similarly, escorts of certain types are more likely to
advertise safer sex than are others. It is difficult to know from the results
in Figure 6.4 whether part of the results are due to clients' selecting
escorts for condomed or condomless sex. Escort characteristics may be
correlated with sexual behaviors or the sex worker's bargaining power, or
both. Figure 6.5 shows results of the specification that includes sex worker
characteristics Z:

$$P_{ij}^{Client} = \lambda + \sum\nolimits_m \beta_m Z_m + \sum\nolimits_k \delta_k S_k + \phi_i + \varepsilon$$

In general, the results show that escort race is not related to client
valuations, consistent with results from analysis of escort advertisements.
Contrary to escort advertisement pricing functions, the results here show
that age and physical size (BMI) are not related to client payoffs, either.

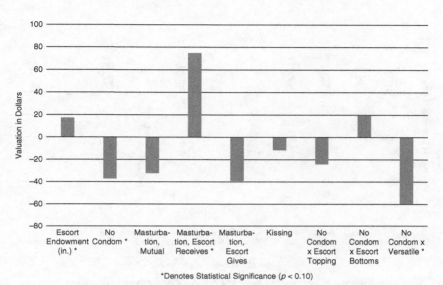

Figure 6.5 Client valuation of sexual behaviors, controlling for sex worker characteristics

The escort's endowment, however, is strongly related to client valuations. This may be one reason why masturbation is highly valued by clients. Client valuation of escort penetration and mutual penetration is not robust to the inclusion of individual escort characteristics. The point estimates are reduced substantially and are no longer statistically significant. This suggests that some of the premiums attached to sexual behavior in Figure 6.4 are correlated with sex worker characteristics, which would likely include beauty and other individual-specific characteristics. The penalty attached to condomless sex, however, is robust to the inclusion of sex worker characteristics. In fact, the result for condomless sex is robust to the inclusion of other sexual behaviors such as masturbation. The client's high valuation of masturbating an escort is also robust to the inclusion of sex worker characteristics. Figure 6.5 shows that the decomposition of condomless sex into its three components reveals values similar to those estimated in Figure 6.4 and is robust to the inclusion of sex worker characteristics. The penalty to condomless sex is concentrated in mutual penetration. Overall, the results imply that individual sex worker characteristics do influence client willingness to pay for most sexual behaviors, but do not influence client willingness to pay for safer sex.

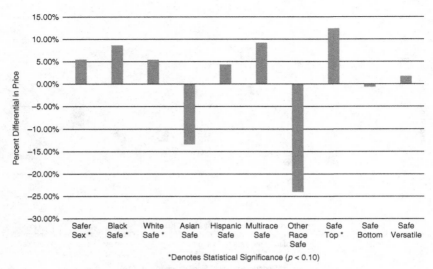

*Denotes Statistical Significance (p < 0.10)

Figure 6.6 Sex worker safer sex behavior and advertised prices

Additional Evidence on Value from Escort Advertisements

Turning to the market returns to safer sex, Figure 6.6 provides estimates of
the hedonic regression of escort price on advertised safer sex. Prices and
advertised safer sex are positively correlated, with a price premium for
safety greater than 5 percent. This result is also inconsistent with the notion
of a compensating differential for riskier behavior for unsafe sex. Men who
advertise safer sex could earn more than $2,500 more per year than men
who do not.

The basic result for safety is intriguing, but as described earlier the theory
of compensating differentials implies that the result should vary by race and
sexual behavior. To investigate these issues I decompose the safe effects by
race and sexual position. The aim here is not to see if there is an independent
effect for race and sexual behavior interactions with safer sex advertisements
net of advertising itself, but to decompose the safety effect by regressing the
prices on permutations by race and sexual behavior.

The results show the interaction of safer sex advertising with every race to
decompose the safe effect by race. Interestingly, the premium to safer sex
does not apply evenly to male escorts of all races. The results show that only
Black and White men enjoy a premium to safety, which is larger for Black
men (9 percent) than for White men (5.5 percent). The additional premium
to Black safety is certainly inconsistent with the notion of compensating

differentials – openly gay Black men have higher baseline rates of HIV infection, which would imply that their compensating differential would be lower than that of other racial groups. According to the Centers for Disease Control and Prevention (CDC), African American males are a disproportionately large share of the HIV population, and are nearly twice as likely to contract HIV as their White counterparts. Some estimates have suggested that as much as 46 percent of the Black gay male population is infected with HIV, more than twice the rate for White men (21 percent) or Hispanics (17 percent).[80] The result is consistent with the social theory, however, in that clients may use the sex work market to engage in safer sex with Black men. In the social theory, clients compensate Black men for removing the need to negotiate for safer sex. Indeed, given the higher rates of HIV prevalence among Black men, clients would likely compensate Black men more for easing this negotiation as it secures the client's sense of safety.

Figure 6.6 also decomposes the safe effect of sexual behaviors by interacting safer sex advertising with sexual behaviors. The results show that there is substantial variation in the return to safer sex advertisements by sexual behavior. Men who advertise as "safe tops" enjoy a premium that is substantial, more than 13 percent. The transmission probabilities by sexual behavior would suggest that it is "bottoms" who should enjoy the price premium, as the risk of disease transmission is much higher for the receptive partner. In the theory of compensating differentials, clients would have to compensate "bottom" escorts for the increased risk of STIs that comes with the receptive sexual position. While these results are inconsistent with compensating differentials, they are consistent with the social theory. If clients have demand for sex that could increase their risk of STI exposure, they would be willing to compensate escorts for providing that sexual conduct as safely as possible. This implies that it would be penetrative ("top") escorts who would enjoy a premium to advertising safer sex. The results are consistent with such an interpretation.

CONCLUSION

It has been difficult to distinguish between the social and sexual structures that mediate the sexual interactions between men who have sex with men. Researchers have long noted that gay men form distinctions between their social and sexual interactions, and the confluence of both in the existing scholarship about gay sexual-socialization has limited our ability to speak to either issue with its proper import.[81] The inability to draw clear distinctions has limited the development of theoretical and empirical approaches to the sexual sociality of gay men. This is problematic for researchers and health policy makers. The changing sexual landscape of the gay community is not only of interest to those whose scholarship considers social organization, modernity, and social change, but also to those to seek to design health policy that promotes STI prevention among gay men.

The sophisticated social structures that give rise to sexual negotiations between gay men have been discussed in the literature, but the nuances of these structures have resisted detailed, rigorous analysis. This chapter attempted to break through this roadblock by combining new field theoretical approaches to gay sexuality with a specific sexualized social setting that allows us to test the hypotheses about gay sexual organization. Green's sexual field theory yields unique predictions about which men have greater amounts of erotic capital in gay sexual spaces, giving them greater control over the terms of their sexual encounters. How this translates into actual sexual behaviors is unknown. Both the emergence of HIV more than two decades ago and the recent antiretroviral treatments have altered the ways in which gay men have organized and navigated their sexual landscape. I used data from the market for male sex work to test these predictions, drawing on the fact that male sex work is a unique sexual field that allows us to look at the sexual organizations that Green's theory speaks to. This chapter offered a unique quantitative test of field theory by exploiting a particular space that conforms to the field being theorized – allowing us to test the effects of the field in terms of personal interaction.

Green's theory yielded both structural and intersectional hypotheses about which men would have larger amounts of erotic capital in gay sexual spaces. Structurally, gay men who are dominant, young, and sexually experienced are endowed with larger amounts of erotic capital. Intersectionally, submissive Asian and dominant Black men would have larger amounts of erotic capital. The quantitative results confirmed that young, dominant, popular and Asian submissive escorts were more likely to restrict the terms of their sexual behavior. The data did not support the hypotheses regarding dominant Black men. Similarly, the data showed that sexual versatility was positively correlated with greater control over the terms of sexual relations, which was not a prediction of the theory, but could be considered consistent with the theory if versatility is considered a type of sexual maturity that would be related to erotic capital.

The results here also show that the nature of safer sex negotiations in the male sex work market are very different from the nature of negotiations seen in female sex work. Rather than a compensating differential for condomless sex, clients pay less for condomless sex. Furthermore, decomposition of the price penalty for condomless sex reveals that the penalty is concentrated in mutual penetration. While inconsistent with the theory of compensating differentials, the result is consistent with theories that postulate that men use the male sex work market as a means of ensuring that they will be able to successfully negotiate for safer sex with escorts. If the clients' outside option is unsafe sex with other men, clients in the commercial sex market may attach a premium to condomed sex. The results here show that clients are willing to pay for safer sex with escorts.

The estimates here should stimulate further research into the dynamics of male sex work and gay sexual health in general. As is generally true of research in this area, there are significant trade-offs. Despite the advantages of this analysis, there are several limits to the approach adopted here. While I can investigate the values of sexual behaviors, it is important to note that the fixed effects estimates may not be generalizable to the entire population of sex workers and clients. This data only allows us to consider successful negotiations between clients and sex workers – extending these findings to the entire population would require a number of assumptions that will be difficult to justify without more basic research into the male sex work market.

While the mechanisms behind the valuations cannot be investigated here, the valuations do produce interesting findings that should spur further research into the sexual behaviors of male sex workers and their clients, and stimulate further discussion about the social and health implications of sexual negotiations among gay men. For example, policies may target sex workers by informing them of the premium attached to safer sex in the market. If this would encourage a larger fraction of male sex workers to engage in condomed sex, the rate of STI transmissions in this population could slow substantially. Even more, if sex workers can influence their clients' noncommercial sexual behaviors, the positive externalities from these interventions could be considerable.

7

Conclusion

Every Man a Sex Worker? Commercial and Noncommercial
Gay Sexuality

INTRODUCTION

Sex work does not take place in a vacuum, divorced from the world around it. The key components of sex work, desire and sexual attraction, feature in dating and marriage markets. It is therefore intuitive to think that sex work would draw from the same social cues as those in dating, marriage, and other intimate relationships. Economists have traditionally seen links between the commercial and noncommercial sexual markets and commonly view them as being driven by the same forces of supply and demand. In a marriage market, for example, those with abilities in high demand will have more choices of partners and, theoretically, better outcomes such as relationship stability. In fact, recent economic theories have posited that female sex workers earn high wages due to the marital stigma attached to sex work.[1] Just as in the marriage market, scholars have documented beauty premiums in markets for sex work and the fact that more attractive sex workers are better able to control the terms of their work.[2] This is intuitive, as one basis for self-arranged marriage markets is attraction – those who are more attractive will have the most options in the dating market and, presumably, better working conditions and compensation in the sex work market. This is not to say that economists view them as equal or that preferences are isomorphic between the two, but that features of the noncommercial market would be similar in the commercial market.

This idea of symmetry between commercial and noncommercial markets has not been accepted across the social sciences. In sociological field theory, for example, scholars have asserted that the fields of commercial and noncommercial sex work are distinct enough that the actors in them are motivated by a different set of intentions. Economically, this would imply different preferences and therefore utility functions in both markets. This is certainly true to some extent. The features one would look for in a temporary commercial sexual transaction would be different from those sought in long-term relationships or even casual encounters. At the same time, the sharp disconnect between the two stands at odds with some of the basic features of both markets – to the extent that sex is an important aspect of a romantic relationship, some attractions in the sex work market would likely be similar to those in the noncommercial market. As a lever to find what is sexually appealing, markets for sex provide valuable information about one important input into romantic partnerships – sexual attraction.

When considering the gay sexual landscape, making a distinction between the two markets may be even more inappropriate. Histories of gay sexual organization have long held that casual sexual encounters are a non-negligible part of gay sexual relations.[3] Gay sexual networks are more connected than heterosexual sexual networks, they feature more casual encounters, and gay men attach less of a social stigma to those encounters.[4] Indeed, in gay cinema, literature, and media these casual sexual encounters are celebrated and seen as source of distinction between gay and heterosexual sexual relations. In the early years of the gay rights movement, this distinction was both a cause for celebration (showing the possibilities of more relaxed sexual norms) and consternation (for fear that gays would be stigmatized due to their sexual norms) among gay political leaders. Indeed, the early years of the AIDS epidemic revealed the high level of connectedness of gay sexual networks and the political problems this caused in mobilizing responses to sexually transmitted diseases.[5]

Casual sexual encounters between men and, more importantly, the cultural institutions that allow them to flourish, share several features that are similar to those of commercial sex work. First, both markets feature men engaged in temporary sexual encounters. By social convention, a casual sexual interaction between two men is explicitly meant to be of short duration. The most important aspect is that both parties are assumed to know of the temporary nature of the encounter – there is no expectation of continued contact or communication beyond the sexual encounter. While noncommercial encounters feature the possibility of a long-term relationship, as structured and defined a "hookup" is, by definition, temporary. While this has increasingly become standard among younger heterosexuals as well, it is a long-standing norm among urban gay men.[6]

Second, these temporary encounters allow men to engage in the fantasy, role-playing, and self-presentations that are seen in the commercial market. Given that there is little to no substitution between the sexual and

nonsexual features of a long-term partner (intelligence, common nonsexual interest, family background, etc. are not being considered along with
sexual desirability in a casual encounter), the casual sex market would
feature sexual encounters that could share in the excitement, immediacy,
and clandestine features of commercial sex work. They offer the distinct
possibility for men to have very specific sexual desires fulfilled. In a casual
sexual encounter men can adopt sexual personas, sexual behaviors, and
proclivities that they may not practice with a long-term partner or even
display in other settings. For example, men can be more restrictive about
the physical features and other characteristics that they desire in their
casual encounters, can try new sexual roles or behaviors, and can encounter men they would not consider as dating partners.[7]

   Third, these temporary encounters are now facilitated by the same
technology as undergirds modern male sex work. Gay men in the United
States use smartphone applications and the Internet to secure these temporary sexual encounters. This is not to say that gay bars and other social
settings do not perform the same function, but the new mediums for sexual
connections are quite explicit in their purpose – they are designed to allow
gay men to meet each other for sexual encounters. The advantage of the
smartphone applications is that they minimize the chance that parties will
misunderstand the nature of the encounter. This form of interaction is
incredibly popular – Grindr, arguably the most widely used smartphone
application for this purpose, has reported more than 2.5 million users in
the United States, and the average Grindr user spends one hour per day
logged into the service. It is safe to say that this application has wide use
among gay men in the United States, particularly those in urban areas.[8]

   For all of these reasons, the noncommercial market for casual sexual
encounters, the hookup, may share many similar features with commercial
sexual markets for gay men. Due to this similarity, I consider several of the
findings that applied to male sex work and investigate the extent to which
they hold in the noncommercial sexual market. If the two markets are
indeed distinct, as argued by field theorists, then the findings seen for sex
work would not be found for the noncommercial market. If there is
significant overlap, it is likely that the preferences seen in commercial sex
work apply to noncommercial casual sex, or at least that it is not possible to
distinguish empirically between the preferences.

   To conclude this study of sex work, I investigate the degree of similarity
and difference between the commercial and noncommercial sexual markets for gay men. First, I analyze the role of face pictures in the gay
smartphone application Grindr, one of the most popular among men

seeking temporary sexual encounters. I find that men consistently note that they require face pictures to enter into and/or continue discussions with other men. In fact, the request for face pictures is quite ubiquitous on the application. Given the strong demand for face pictures among men in the smartphone application, the potential returns to face pictures may be similar. Further analyses of the context in which face pictures are mentioned reveals that they appear to serve a similar purpose in the two markets – they are similar to the bond-posting feature noted earlier in the analysis of sex worker face pictures and they also serve as a marker that a man is not in the closet regarding his sexuality.

Second, I analyze the supply and demand for masculinity in the Grindr noncommercial sexual market. Similar to the market for male sex work, men on Grindr place a high premium on masculinity. Indeed, masculinity is the most commonly mentioned personality description on the application. Masculinity is mentioned more than humor, sexual position, or other factors that may be pertinent to a casual sexual encounter. Similarly, men are most apt to describe themselves as masculine in describing their own personality, which suggests that men note it as a key personality trait worth mentioning to attract potential partners. One of the next most popular features is muscularity, a physical analog to masculinity.[9] Similar to the return to masculine sexual behavior among sex workers, the market for temporary sexual encounters places a high premium on self-described masculine behavior. Masculinity is in high supply and high demand in the noncommercial market.

Third, I consider the way that bodies are disciplined and stigmatized in the noncommercial market. I do so in two ways. First, I look at the presence of body type preferences among men seeking encounters on Grindr. I find that men have strong preferences for men who are "physically fit" or are "height-weight proportionate," and very few men express desire for men who are large. Indeed, men express an extreme distaste for men who are large, and the expression "no fats" is reasonably common among men in the data. To the extent that this conforms to the way the body is disciplined among sex workers (which influences the ways that sex workers present themselves and the wages seen by sex workers of particular body types), similar features are seen in the noncommercial world. Second, I look at the way racialized bodies are discussed and desired in the noncommercial market using both Grindr and Craigslist, an online forum that contains advertisements for men seeking "casual encounters" with other men. I find that the market is highly racialized in two specific but related ways. Men express a strong preference for White partners on the Grindr smartphone application. On Craigslist, men are very likely to mention Black men only when large penis size is also mentioned. When Black men are mentioned in Craigslist advertisements, large penis size is mentioned more than 85 percent of the time. In fact, there is an expression for this, the acronym "BBC," for "big black cock," which was described earlier with respect to the racialized masculinity of gay men. This expression is especially prominent on Craigslist, but not as popular on Grindr. Just as the interaction of race and sexual position worked in the market for male sex work, effectively giving men of different races who present the same masculine behaviors different wages and creating racial differences in how the same men presented their bodies to the market, men in the noncommercial sexual market express a strong demand for specific sexual performances from men by race. This is particularly true for Black men.

The evidence presented here suggests that the market for male sex work and the noncommercial market for hookups share much in common. At one level, this is quite intuitive – most of the theories applied to the study of male sex work are not specific to male sex work but were developed to describe gay social-sexual behavior. At another level, however, the results point to the thin line that exists between the commercial and noncommercial aspects of sexuality and the marketing of gay masculinity among gay men. Men in both markets desire to see the faces of the men they are interacting with, both place a premium on masculinity, both adopt discipline to the bodies they see as desirable, and both practice a racialized type of sexual performance that is based, at least in part, upon racial-sexual stereotypes. This is not to say that gay dating markets are similar to sex work markets, but rather that gay casual sexual markets share a number of common features, whether commercial or noncommercial. Male sex work is one area that provides empirical insight into much larger social forces that govern gay male sexual behavior and the development and refinement of gay masculinities in the new millennium.

THE NONCOMMERCIAL MARKET FOR CASUAL GAY SEX

I use two data sources to investigate the casual sexual market among gay men: a large sample of both the individual accounts on the Grindr smartphone application and advertisements for "men for men casual encounters" on Craigslist. Both of these sources are used for noncommercial social networking with an explicit sexual nature to the contacts being sought. The Grindr application began in early 2009, and as of 2015 claimed for than 2.5 million members in the United States.[10] In the New York metropolitan area alone there are more than 400,000 unique Grindr accounts, and metro areas such as Chicago (200,000+), Philadelphia (125,000+), and Detroit (100,000+) have significant numbers of accounts. Despite a number of competitors and similar applications in the market, Grindr remains one of the most popular social smartphone application among gay men seeking social connections with one another.

The application is specifically developed for men seeking social connections with other men. The application is free for download and use – the developers derive income from the advertisements that appear at the bottom of the screen in the application. Figure 7.1 displays a prototypical profile on the application as of the time of data collection. As Figure 7.1 shows, profiles feature a description of the man and his characteristics – age, height, weight, body type, race, relationship status, gay sub-communities he self-identifies as

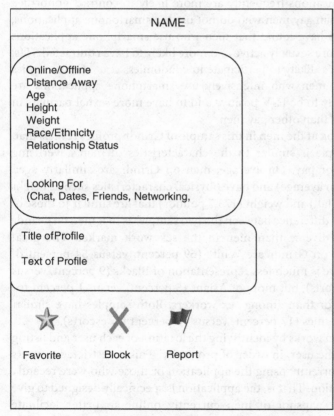

Figure 7.1 Example of a Grindr profile

being a member of, and what types of connections he is seeking from other men. Beneath that, a man has the option of including more detail about himself and what he desires in a partner. As with escort advertisements, these are free form responses. This sample consists of 5,000 Grindr profiles that were collected from 2011 to 2013 from a stratified sample of cities.[11]

The sexual nature of these types of applications has been an active area of study among public health researchers. Public health officials have only begun to investigate the ways in which these smartphone applications are changing gay sexual networks, and there is less work that analyzes the social organization of these applications, although research is accelerating.[12] One area of agreement is their widespread use. Nearly two-thirds of gay men in urban areas report using smartphone applications to find sexual partners in a 12-month period.[13] The fact that they are used for sexual encounters has been documented. For example, gay men who use the smartphone applications frequently are more likely to contract gonorrhea and chlamydia than gay men who do not use the smartphone applications, and other studies have found that men who use smartphone applications were generally more sexually active and more likely to have contracted STIs, but no more or less likely to participate in condomless sex.[14] Other studies have found that men who intensively use smartphone applications are younger, less likely to be HIV positive and to have more sexual partners in the previous year than other gay men.[15]

A summary look at the men in this sample of Grindr profiles reveals that, overall, the sample is similar to the characteristics of men advertising sexual services for pay. On average, men on Grindr are similarly aged (29.7 years old, on average) and have physical characteristics such as height (5 feet, 10 inches tall) and weight (173.7 pounds) that are similar to those of sex workers. One difference between the two samples is that men on Grindr are less racially diverse than men in the sex work market. The great majority of men on Grindr are White (69 percent, versus 54 percent of escorts), and there is much less representation of Blacks (9 percent, versus 22 percent of escorts), but more of Asians (5 percent, versus 1 percent for escorts) on Grindr than among sex workers. Both samples have similar numbers of Hispanics (17 percent, versus 14 percent for escorts).

The application works by identifying the location of each user and listing those closest to the user, in order of proximity. This is restricted to users who are either currently using the application or those who were recently using the application. That is, the application is specifically designed to give users a current snapshot of men currently online to better facilitate immediate meetings. Users have the option of contacting specific profiles through a within-application messaging system. Within this messaging feature, members can exchange messages and pictures with one another as well as send details of their location. Members also have the option of blocking the profiles of others or reporting harassing behavior to central administrators.

There are several features of the profiles on Grindr that are similar to the advertisements used by male sex workers. First, men list their physical characteristics in a way that is similar to the way they are presented among sex workers. Second, men have the option of creating free form profiles where they can discuss aspects of their personality and what they are seeking from their encounters. Third, the photos that men use in their profiles are self-presentations similar to the ones used by male sex workers. These profiles are concise when compared to the more verbose profiles that one would see on a dating service such as Match.com or dating websites where parties list more about their background, personal histories, and other aspects that would be important in a dating market. The profiles on Grindr are not designed to elicit detailed information, as opposed to a basic impression of someone.

There are also important differences between the Grindr profiles and the advertisements of male sex workers. For example, Grindr profiles are restricted to one photo, which is displayed with a profile. Although men can send photos to other men in private messages within the application, the public only sees one photo. Compared to male sex workers, this greatly restricts the possibility of variation in self-presentation. Also, nudity is not allowed in profile pictures, which limits the overt sexual presentation that men may wish to use in their profiles. Another important distinction is that non-response is more likely in Grindr profiles than among the men in sex worker advertisements. There are a non-negligible number of profiles that contain no information at all. The most commonly missing values are for age and body type, although race is also missing from many profiles. Similarly, while the male sex worker data requires the posting of at least one photo in an advertisement, Grindr does not. This means there is a set of profiles that have no pictures at all. More than 10 percent of profiles in our Grindr sample had no photo attached.

Given these distinctions, it is not possible to analyze the Grindr profiles as if they were sex worker advertisements. While that may have certain conceptual advantages, it is also flawed to the extent that the commercial sex worker market comes with a different set of expectations for advertisements. The distinctions are significant enough to make it impossible to treat the sources as if they were the same. At the same time, certain similarities are apparent and can be exploited. In particular, I analyze the self-reported characteristics of Grindr profiles in a manner similar to those for sex workers, the role of pictures *as men describe them in their profiles*, mentions of masculinity in profiles, and restrictions on dating as recorded in the text of Grindr profiles.

The Craigslist data source is a sample of advertisements from the online service craigslist.org, which hosts a section in the personals for "casual encounters" and which is further restricted to "men seeking men." The advertisements in this forum are specifically those of men seeking short-duration meetings with other men. In these advertisements, men respond to an anonymized email service for further contact. These advertisements bear little resemblance to the profiles on Grindr and the male sex worker advertisements, but they serve as an additional data source with which to investigate the noncommercial sexual market. Since there is no instance in which men are required or compelled to list any specific information, only the text of these advertisements can be analyzed for content. The Craigslist sample consists of 2,000 advertisements for "casual encounters" from the same cities as the Grindr sample.[16]

FACE PICTURES IN NONCOMMERCIAL ADVERTISEMENTS

The role of face pictures among sex workers was a source of significant price differences. This occurred because clients who policed the market rewarded self-disclosure among sex workers. Face pictures were seen as a mark of trustworthiness and prices reflected this. Although beauty may also be involved in the premium, clients and sex workers also noted the significant role that face pictures played as a sign of quality of the escort. Face pictures contained information about the truthfulness of the escort, distinct from information with respect to sexual behavior. In the sex work market, face pictures allowed clients to overcome the problem of asymmetric information.

Among the men on Grindr, face pictures play a similar role. Rather than being a signaling device, however, face pictures serve as a screening device used by men in the application.[17] Theoretically, screening is the analogous activity to signaling. While sex workers actively signal with face pictures, the same outcome with respect to face pictures would occur if clients could be explicit about their desire to see face pictures on the same websites escorts use to advertise. As noted earlier, the websites for clients to review sex worker services are independent of the websites, which stymied any attempts that clients could have to screen sex workers.

In the Grindr application, screening is possible because the demand side of the market can explicitly articulate their requirements. While sex workers show pictures of their face to earn client trust, men in the Grindr application use face pictures as first condition of contact. That is, they require a man contacting them to display a picture of his face should he wish to initiate contact or as a condition to respond to contact. A man who chooses not to display a picture of his face is doing so with full understanding that a significant number of men using the application will not be interested in contacting him or being contacted by him.

In a search of the text of profiles, men are explicit in noting that they require face pictures in order to respond to a request for contact. For example, men explicitly mention "Please have a face pic if you want to chat with me" or "No face pic = no chat" or "If your profile is a headless pic, I won't respond." Some men describe the consequences of not having a face picture, with phrases such as "messages from people without a face pic are deleted without reading." These types of notices in profiles are quite typical in reference to face pictures. Men are explicitly restricting their contacts to men who show their face pictures in their profiles. Somewhat surprisingly, this occurs among men who themselves do not show face pictures in their own profiles – more than 5 percent of the men requesting face pictures do not provide them in their own advertisements.

Another type of profile picture restriction allows for men to not have face pictures in their profiles but requires the sending of a face picture if further contact is desired. These stipulations commonly feature expressions such as "No pic no reply. Please send a face pic." "Send a face pic in your first message." That is, this type of restriction allows for the discretion that some men may require when using a forum like Grindr (which is unrestricted – anyone with a smartphone may download the application and begin using it, and the only restriction is geographic proximity), but it requires a face picture before further contact.

Among all of the profiles in the sample from Grindr, more than one-third mention a face picture restriction such as the two described above. When restricting only to those profiles that are complete, the percentage rises to over 40 percent. That is, men in the Grindr data are very specific that face pictures are required for their noncommercial encounters. Men who do not provide face pictures will have a much smaller pool of men to choose from, given the widespread use of this screening device. Just as face pictures were related to better remuneration in the male sex work market, face pictures here allow men to have a larger number of potential contacts.

The face picture requirement sets a bar that men seeking noncommercial sexual contact must meet. From the text of the profiles, one cannot discern the purpose of this requirement, but further discussion in the profiles does point to some clues. Some men mention that face pictures are a screen for a man's acceptance of his sexuality. For example, profiles mention, "If you can't show me your face, we can't meet," or "If you're ashamed to be here, don't bother." While one cannot properly categorize all of these statements, they do appear to fall within the general category of saying that, to some men on Grindr, face pictures are a signal of a man's openness with respect to his sexuality. This would seem to be particularly compelling for those who require a face picture in the profile, as it is always possible to send pictures privately between individual account holders.

Another common mention of face pictures is the indication that other pictures render men "headless torsos," and thus lacking in authenticity. Here, the role of the face picture is to explicitly imbue the contact with individuality, something that may be difficult to establish with pictures of other body parts alone. Men commonly decry the number of "headless torsos" or landscape photos in the profile pictures of others. The responses here are more in keeping with the idea that the casual encounters sought do entail a level of intimacy that requires the exchange of face pictures. Men with "headless torsos" are taken to be indistinguishable from each other. In matters of intimacy, faces are seen as a key to the inherent interpersonal exchange, even in temporary sexual encounters. Men are explicit about wanting to know whom they are corresponding with, and this, to many men on Grindr, requires that a face picture be shown.

Interestingly, beauty is rarely mentioned as a reason for requiring face pictures. Fewer than 5 percent of the mentions for face pictures make any mention of beauty. Given that these encounters are noncommercial, it would seem obvious that both parties would seek partners by mutual selection and that beauty would be of primary importance. In the case of face pictures, however, this is not the case. While that does not imply that face pictures do not also serve this purpose, the lack of explicit mention of beauty suggests that, as a screening device, face pictures serve a different purpose.

As discussed in earlier chapters, the role of face pictures among sex workers is related to market function and the problems of asymmetric information. Face pictures appear to play a similar role among men in the noncommercial market. In commercial interactions, face pictures signal quality. In the noncommercial market they are a screen for self-acceptance, authenticity, and trustworthiness. In both the commercial and noncommercial markets, it appears that face pictures are also evidence of individuality.

Neither a client nor a man on Grindr is seeking men who cannot be easily distinguished as being genuine. Even in the noncommercial market, the role of face pictures is to screen/signal a behavior or personality that is not related to the *content* of the face picture itself, but rather to features of one's behavior and personality that are related to credibility and authenticity.

MASCULINITY IN NONCOMMERCIAL SEX

Among sex workers, masculinity was rewarded by clients. In the analysis of sex workers this was restricted to their sexual behaviors. Among the profiles on Grindr, there is less discussion of sexual behaviors in profiles but more explicit discussion of masculinity. While client demand for masculinity in sex workers was deduced from the correlation of prices with masculine behaviors such as sexual position, in Grindr profiles men are more explicit about their desires for masculine partners. One additional advantage of the Grindr profiles is that the participating men discuss their own, self-reported masculinity in their profiles. As such, the analysis of profiles in the Grindr application allows us to investigate both the supply *and* demand for masculinity in the noncommercial sexual market. Importantly, this is self-described masculinity, although it undoubtedly speaks to specific notions that would be assumed to be common among the men using the application. For the purposes of analysis, the key is that the term is explicitly used by men as both a description of themselves (supply) and as a quality sought in partners (demand).

Analysis of the text in Grindr profiles reveals that masculinity is in very high demand. Of the men who list text in their profiles, more than 20 percent make explicit reference to desiring masculine partners. A sizable portion of men who describe their desire for masculinity desire it exclusively, as "masc only" or "only interested in masc guys" are commonly used among men who state masculinity preferences. No other trait is so frequently mentioned in the Grindr profiles. To be clear – the most-discussed trait for men in Grindr is masculinity. While other traits such as intelligence are occasionally noted, masculinity is the most sought after characteristic in this market. Consistent with the findings from the male sex market, masculinity is the most desired trait among men in the Grindr application. Mentions of masculinity are more than twice as likely as those of any other characteristic mentioned in the smartphone application.

Masculinity is also the most-supplied characteristic among men on the Grindr application. When describing themselves, men are more likely to describe themselves as masculine than as possessing any other trait. Features that refer to human capital, sociality, personality, humor, and the like are much less frequently mentioned. Indeed, masculinity is mentioned more frequently than sexual conduct in self-descriptions. Masculinity is mentioned 1.5 more times than any other trait in men's self-descriptions. With the supply of masculinity so high, there is the common expression "masc4-masc," which denotes men who are self-described as masculine who are seeking connections with other masculine men.[18]

Masculinity is mentioned in several different ways in Grindr profiles. In addition to explicit use of the term, profiles commonly use phrases such as "real men" or "manly" when describing partners. Others are more explicit, requiring that those who seek to contact them "act like men" or "be a real dude" if they expect a response. In the Grindr application, masculinity must be presented or self-professed in some discernable way in order for a participant to meet the masculinity standard that is established in the application. It is difficult to gauge how this masculinity can be assessed, given the limited information allowed in a profile – but the masculinity requirement from others may be one reason for masculinity's being the most common attribute that men apply to themselves.

Masculinity is mentioned so frequently that a non-negligible number of profiles actually *mock* the ubiquitous mention of it in profiles. For example, profiles declare "not into that masc shit" or "I'm prolly not masc enough for you" or "Oh my God! I'm so totally masc! Way too masc for you! Totes masc" and similar send-ups of the frequency to which men declare their own masculinity and declare it as a search characteristic. While this sort of profile is relatively rare, it speaks to the fact that the online profiles have evolved to the point where the discussion of masculinity can now be a target of parody. This, of course, requires that the audience (the other users of the application) understand the frame of reference and note that this is, in fact, a parody of this specific constriction and use of masculinity. This speaks to the fact that Grindr has become a place where gay men, in seeking to connect to other gay men, enforce a rigid code of masculine behavior. Those who present as masculine will likely have more choices than those who do not. Similarly, men see fit to describe themselves as masculine as a means of piquing the interest of other men. While one may think that a gay sexual place would be one where gender norms are not as rigid as in a heterosexual setting, the ubiquitous mentions of masculinity serve clear notice that masculine presentation and self-definition are highly prized in the noncommercial sexual market.

In stark contrast, there are very few mentions of men seeking feminine men for encounters (fewer than 1 percent of Grindr profiles make positive mention of feminine men). In fact, men are much more likely to note that they are not interested in being contacted by feminine men. Men use phrases such as "masc only" or "no fems" to note that they are only seeking connections with non-feminine men. This extends to a branding of feminine men as women and even explicit homophobia, with phrases such as "real men only" or "no sissies" or "no queens" in their profiles. Others are more explicit in desiring men who "act like men" without further definition. When femininity is mentioned in profiles, it is placed in a negative connotation more than 90 percent of the time, consistent with strong distaste for feminine behavior among gay sexual partners.

In terms of sexual behavior, men who openly describe submissive sexual behavior are much more likely to couch it in terms of masculinity. For example, men who are bottoms are much more likely to refer to themselves as "masculine bottoms" than men are to refer to themselves as "masculine tops." Men who are bottoms are more than twice as likely to include the modifier "masculine" than men who are tops. This is consistent with bottom sexual activity being taken to be inherently more feminized than top sexual behavior. Just as escorts had to present themselves to the market in a way assured clients they were as described, bottom men in the Grindr community feel the need to attach a description of their masculinity to sexual behaviors that would be taken as feminine.

The noncommercial market appears to value masculinity to an extent similar to that seen in the commercial market. Masculinity is the single most discussed trait in the application. Men are both claiming to be masculine and desiring connections with masculine partners. At the same time, this is not only a desire for masculinity, but masculinity presented as a strict requirement, with the explicit notice that femininity is not desired. Overall, the form and function of masculinity in the noncommercial market is quite similar to the way masculinity functions in the market for sex work. It is a highly desired trait, and men who profess masculine personas will have more options among potential partners than will other men.

DISCIPLINE OF THE BODY IN NONCOMMERCIAL SEX WORK

Body Size

In the market for male sex work, bodies were presented in specific ways to conform to standards of beauty. In analyzing sex worker presentations, the assumption was that sex workers would choose presentations that conformed to the ways gay men have sexualized male bodies and that also highlighted features that, conditional on given characteristics, would place a man higher in the hierarchy. Gay men have a well-documented desire for bodies that conform to socially accepted norms for masculine bodies. In particular, gay masculinities prize muscularity and penalize men who are larger, but there is little work that analyzes the way this is represented in smartphone applications. Does the noncommercial market exhibit the same values?

Unfortunately, given the limited number of photos in a profile on Grindr, I am unable to explore variations in the ways that men present themselves in the noncommercial market. I can, however, analyze what they do say about what they desire in terms of physical attractiveness. Men describe both their own physical features and also note the physical features they would like to see in others. As with masculinity, men reveal a great deal about what they desire in the noncommercial market, and also what they do not desire in their sexual partners, in their profiles.

In terms of the body, muscularity reigns supreme. Muscularity is the most commonly described physical attribute among men in the Grindr application. Men are more prone to describe themselves as muscular or fit than by any other descriptor of physical features. Men also demand muscularity, but one issue is that there are other terms for the body that are more ambiguous. In particular, the demand for "fit" or "height-weight proportionate" partners is the greatest and most commonly noted on the application. There are also several mentions of being familiar with gyms as a desirable trait, with expressions such as "know your way around a gym" and "works out regularly" relatively common in profiles. The desire to have a casual sexual encounter with a man based on his gym-going behavior is interesting in and of itself, insofar as a man may present the desired physique without belonging to a gym and a regular gym-goer may not have a particular physique, depending on the type of training he practices. There are two ways of reading such demands. First, it could be directly related to the bodies being desired – athletic bodies would require regular training. Second, gym-going is also a type of masculine behavior that could be correlated with physique, but is not necessarily causal. For example, Levine (1998) describes the different types of gyms that gay men frequent – some of which are more conditioned for cardiovascular training as opposed to muscular development and intensive weightlifting.

As with desirable traits, men also reveal what they do not wish to find in their casual encounters. There is a strong distaste for overweight men, but not for thin men. Some men are quite explicit in noting that "no fats" should contact them for private messaging. Another very common description is that men must be "height-weight proportionate," and this has been seen by scholars as more punitive to large men than to small men. Also, Robinson (2016) notes that such terms allow for muscular men (who will, for example, have high BMIs), since the body is regulated by a symmetry of appearance. In general, there is a strong distaste for large men. In more than 95 percent of the references to weight, men are explicit that they do not want a partner who is overweight.[19]

This policing of the body is quite similar to what was observed among sex workers. There is strong demand for body types that are consistent with traditional masculine norms. Muscularity and the presentation of a physically fit physique are important in the noncommercial market. Men who are fit or height-weight proportionate will have more options in the noncommercial market than will others. Men who are muscular, however, will have the most desired physical physique in the noncommercial market. At a general level, the body types seen as most desired in the noncommercial market are the same as those desired in the commercial market.

Race and the Body

Earlier, the commercial sex market was shown to be a place where racial and sexual stereotypes operated in concert with one another. Men who conformed to racial sexual stereotypes were rewarded. Also, men were expected to present themselves in ways that conformed to those stereotypes. Overall, the findings with respect to masculinity and sexual behavior were consistently mediated by race and racial-sexual stereotypes.

In the noncommercial market, men are explicit about their racial preferences in a way that we cannot determine from the commercial sex market. In the Grindr application, the most popular race for a sexual partner is White. Profiles explicitly note that men are "mostly into White guys" or "prefer White guys" when noting race. Roughly 75 percent of all racial preferences noted in the application are for Whites, while in fewer than 25 percent of instances where a racial preference is given, the race other than White. There are men who also mention that they have "no racial hangups" or are "open to all races," but the number of men placing racial exclusions is 1.5 times the number of men mentioning racial openness. In terms of a racial hierarchy, it appears that White will have a larger range of potential partners from which to choose.

As with masculinity and body size, men are also explicit about what races they do not prefer on the Grindr application. Men frequently mention "no Asians" or "no Blacks" in their profiles, evidence of strong racial exclusion. Racial exclusion, however, is less than half as likely as racial preference in profiles. Although racial exclusion has received more popular press and scholarly attention, it is actually much less common than men stating the race of men they desire. This is not to say that all men can be assumed to have these racial views and to recognize a resulting hierarchy of partners. Also, since the men with open racial preferences are open to all, even where there are men who do not have strict racial preferences, White men will find the largest number of potential partners.

One curiosity among men on the Grindr application is that they show some degree of racial self-exclusion. For example, among Black men stating racial preferences, more than a third (34 percent) note that they prefer White or Hispanic partners. The number is slightly higher among Asians (39 percent), who also note that they prefer White partners. Hispanics are less likely to note racial preferences overall, but among those who do they are similarly likely to restrict the race of their partners (37 percent). As such, the racial exclusion practiced in the market is not simply the racial preferences of White men, but the racial preferences of Asian and Black men as well. The preference for Whiteness is less intense among other races, but it is still prominent among all races.[20]

While the evidence from Grindr points to a racial hierarchy, the analysis of male sex work showed that there were more specific interactions of race and sexual behavior that were rewarded in the market. In particular, the literature on race, gay masculinities, and the gay body identified Black male penis size as one component of a racialized Black male sexuality that restricted attention to specific aspects of Black male sexual behavior.[21] With the Grindr profiles it is not possible to investigate this issue due to the paucity of explicit mentions in the profiles that speak to racial-sexual stereotypes, given the strong racial preferences in the application. However, I can use online advertisements from Craigslist to investigate the interactions of race and sexual behavior stereotypes. Unlike Grindr, where men post a profile to pique the interest of other men, the Craigslist forum is one where men are more specific about the sexual behaviors and type of men they are seeking. Put another way, the Grindr profiles are general appeals while the Craigslist profiles are more specific about what men desire.

One unique feature of the Craigslist advertisements is the degree to which penis size is mentioned in reference to Black men. In a text search of the posts in the profile, Black men were almost exclusively desired for their stereotypically large penises. In fact, the shorthand for this on the website is

"BBC," the acronym for "big black cock" that is used in pornography and other sexualized media.[22] In contrast to the discussion of any other racial group, Black men were described by penis size more than 85 percent of the time (88 percent). No other racial group had penis size (or any other anatomical description) noted nearly as frequently – in fact, there was no other racial group with any discussion of penis size nearly as common as for Black men. This is consistent with the concept of restrictive codes of sexual behavior among Black men in White gay masculinities. While the Grindr application shows that Black men are largely excluded from sexual-social interaction, the Craigslist listings show that where Black men *are* included it is when they conform to the racial stereotype of sexual domination and hypermasculinity in the form of a large (Black) penis. As noted earlier, while many scholars and the popular press have focused on exclusion, the racial stereotypes that govern the inclusion of Black men in gay sexual sociality are quite problematic on their own. Among sex workers, Black men conforming to the stereotype were well-rewarded, and the results from Craigslist show that sexual domination is the most sought-after trait for Black men.

This discussion of Black male penis size also contained restrictions on sexual conduct. In discussions of profiles where Black men were desired, they were sought as "top" partners at a ratio of more than 5 to 1. There was no other racial-sexual position combination that approached even a 2-to-1 ratio among all possible combinations in Craigslist. As with sex workers, Black men who conform to the sexual stereotype of sexual aggression and large penis size will have more potential partners than Black men who do not. As with the commercial market, the noncommercial market places strong restrictions on the sexual expressions of Black men, and reifies racial-sexual stereotypes of Black bodies. The racial-sexual nexus for Black men that is so common in sex work is not unique to male sex work, but rather is a continuation of what is seen in the noncommercial sexual market.

MALE SEX WORK AND GAY MALE SOCIETY

Male sex work is both an economic and social practice. As an economic practice, there are specific institutions that underscore its function. It is, after all, a market that must get prices right and provide a consumers with a service (which much be priced lower than or equal to its value – consumer surplus) and producers with profit (which must be priced higher than or equal to the their cost of production – producer surplus).

This book investigated two aspects of the economic aspects of the market: (1) the ways in which the market overcomes the problems of asymmetric information and (2) the price effects of sex worker movement, which is a unique form of competition in the sex work market.

We saw that the community of clients worked to police the market and enforce an interesting type of market discipline through the use of face pictures. Clients are exposed to a number of threats from escorts because the market is illegal. While this includes their physical well-being, an arguably larger threat is simply that they might be scammed by escorts who dupe clients into issuing payments without rendering services. Since the market is illegal there is no way that clients can make any appeals to traditional means of enforcing contracts, and they therefore come together to collectively agree that face pictures are the marker of escort responsibility and escort trustworthiness. Escorts who post pictures of their faces in their advertisements are rewarded with higher prices in the market. We saw that the price effect of face pictures is not driven by factors such as beauty or empty claims of quality. In fact, face pictures had no value in cities where clients were not able to effectively police the market. The male sex worker market solves the tricky issue of asymmetric information by forming a collective of clients who demand a consistent signal of quality that successfully causes more trustworthy escorts to signal their quality and at the same time discourages less scrupulous escorts from doing so. This is one way in which the market works to get the prices right.

In the noncommercial sex landscape of smartphone applications, face pictures played a similar role. There, the asymmetric information problem is the same, and rather than having face pictures work as a signal, men use them as a screen. The screen has the same effect as the signal – men who show pictures of their face will have a larger range of choices for casual sexual encounters than those who do not. Men are also specific in noting what face pictures signify to them – that the man who presents the picture is secure enough in his sexuality to be willing to show his face. This is arguably related to trustworthiness, but primarily related to a man's self-acceptance of his sexuality. While there are no prices here to show the magnitude of the effect, the fact that the discussion is so prominent on the smartphone applications shows that face pictures are also important in the noncommercial sex world of smartphone applications.

Male sex workers' practice of working in multiple markets creates some price effects that are driven by client demand. We saw that male escorts are quite likely to travel – more than half serve multiple locations. While the home locations of male escorts were not related to gay location patterns, the travel locations were related to gay location patterns and likely reflect higher demand in cities with significant gay male populations. The men who live in cities with large numbers of gay men charge more for their escort services than do others, and the price difference is one factor that may lead male sex workers to travel to those cities to provide sex worker services. In doing so, these men raise the prices in their home markets as well because the technology in the market does not allow sex workers to price discriminate. This traveling behavior therefore creates a nationally linked network of male sex work that is driven by the prices in the cities with high demand for male sex worker services. This national linking of the market shows it to be highly developed and, unlike street prostitution markets, deeply connected. As a basic measure of market maturity, the connectedness of the market shows male sex work to be well developed, particularly for an illegal market.

Male sex work is not divorced from the larger forces that shape gay masculinity and gay sexuality. In turning to the social aspects of male sex work, I focused on three issues: (1) the ways that social forces worked in the prices of male sex worker services, (2) the ways that the social discipline of the body in gay communities worked to influence the ways that escorts presented their bodies in the market, and (3) the role that client and sex worker negotiation impacted the role of condomed sex in the market. Each of these social explorations was concerned with both gay masculinities and the related intersections those masculinities have with race. As we saw, these influences had a dominating influence on the way that the market for male sex work operated.

Since men in the market are selling sex to other men, the ways the market values that sex are key windows into gay sexual organization. We saw that gay men prize masculinity in various forms. Dominating sexual behaviors were rewarded in the market. Even more, it was not simply masculinity that mattered: who was offering the masculinity mattered as well. Gay masculinities are deeply intertwined with racially restrictive codes about who is more masculine, who has more legitimate claims on authentic masculinity, and how that masculinity is embodied (which also implies who will be punished more severely for not conforming to that ideal). We saw that Black gay men were rewarded to conforming to racially stereotypically Black hypermasculine behavior – much more than the general premium for sexually dominant sexual behaviors. Along the same lines, Black men offering submissive sexual services were the most punished in the market for not conforming to their racial stereotype of sexual domination.

This carries over to the noncommercial sexual market. The men in the noncommercial market place a very distinct value on masculinity, to the point that the masculinity requirement has become a subject of parody. They are most likely to describe themselves as masculine and also to couch presumably non-masculine sexual behaviors in masculine terms. For example, being sexually submissive is commonly accompanied by the modifier "masculine." Femininity was expressly disdained and routinely discouraged. Also, we saw that the expectation of Black domination is ubiquitous in the noncommercial market. Black men in noncommercial gay sexual space are expected to provide sexually dominant behavior to men in their sexual encounters. While others have noted the general exclusion of particular races in smartphone application profiles, we saw that the inclusion of men could be just as problematic since it is situated on a racially informed expectation of bodies, sexual behaviors, and masculinity.

Gay masculinity also has a direct impact on the body and on which bodies are deemed desirable. Among sex workers, we saw that men took these cues and used them in constructing their erotic personas. Men were not likely to act against the gay masculine requirements that certain types of men (muscular men or Black men, for example) were more likely to provide sexually dominant or submissive sexual services. This informed the very way that the men presented their bodies to the market. Men whose physical body size was unlikely to be seen as masculine in gay masculinities emphasized feminizing features of their bodies such as the buttocks. The reverse was true for men whose physical descriptions fit with traditional gay masculinities – they were more likely to show frontal nudity. For men who defied those conventions there was evidence that they provided even more pictures of frontal or rear nudity to assure clients that their counterintuitive descriptions of their behavior were matched by their physical selves. Perhaps most interesting, these presentations were not related to prices – they served the market function of advertising, but were not themselves related to the prices of escort services.

Among men in the noncommercial market, the same type of body discipline was seen. Men showed a strong distaste for large men and feminine men and preferred muscular men. Along the same lines, men in the noncommercial market expected Black men to possess oversized genitals. When men discussed desiring Black sexual partners they were specific that they desired "big Black cock" and sexual domination, which shows that the presentations among Black male sex workers were expected of Black men in general. The presentations that men need to craft in gay sexual spaces did not appear to differ dramatically between the commercial and noncommercial markets.

Lastly, we saw that escorts used gay masculinity to their advantage to control the terms of their sexual conduct with clients. Sex workers who adhere to gay masculine norms are more likely to advertise condomed sex. We also saw that the growth of condomless sex among gay men in the noncommercial market had a peculiar effect on the male sex work market. Rather than rewarding men for condomless sex, as expected in the theory of compensating differentials, the market rewards condomed sex. This is likely due to the fact that condomless sex is much easier to secure in the noncommercial market, and therefore clients use the sex work market to secure condomed sex, and they reward escorts hand-somely for providing the service. In turn, this alters the way that sex work is viewed from a public health perspective – rather than being a source of disease transmission, the male sex work market works to provide and reward sex workers for safer sexual behaviors. Sex workers actually earn less if they provide condomless sex.

The social and economic forces of sex work offer an interesting and slightly disheartening window into contemporary gay sexual organization. Social constructions of gay masculinity play a strong role in both the male sex worker market and casual sex among gay men. In both instances, men market, supply, and demand sex in relatively strict adherence to gay masculine norms. This masculinity, and a desire to conform to a gay construction of masculinity that features few departures from its hetero-sexual counterpart, forms part of a hierarchy where masculinity is not critiqued among gay men, but is morphed into an ideal that has a direct influence on desirability. Behavior must be modified to fit into this mascu-line ideal in ways that seem odd, such as men needing to adopt modifiers to their "non-masculine" sexual behaviors in such a way that all behaviors become masculine. This gay masculinity also places severe restrictions on the body, accepting and rejecting men for how they adhere to a body norm that idealizes muscularity and rejects feminizing features such as thinness or large body size.

This gay masculinity also contains a significant number of racial restrictions that place significant limits on the sexual representations available to Black men, specifically. Black men in gay masculinities embody a hypermasculinity that is overtly physical. Black men must supply domination, sexual hyperactivity, and oversized genitals in this gay masculinity. Indeed, the full range of sexual exploration is, more or less, not allowed for them. It is unclear whether this applies fully to other racial-sexual stereotypes, but the evidence here suggest that Black men occupy a highly racialized existence in gay masculinities, which reduces them to specific sexual behaviors and physical representations.

The picture of gay sexual organization that emerges suggests that gay men are tied to masculinities in a way that restricts the sexual liberation that was a hallmark of, and one cause for, gay political organization. There is very little in the way of gay masculinity that appears to free gay men from the social restrictions on heterosexual men. While gay masculinities allow for same-sex attraction and sexual desire, they are deeply intertwined with an anti-feminism, which causes gay men to be particularly self-conscious about the way their sexuality is presented to other gay men. The deification of the masculine ideal is, in some respects, an attempt to approach the heterosexual ideal as closely as possible, with the only exception being same-sex physical attraction. As argued by earlier generations of scholars of sexuality and masculinity, gay masculinities have not freed gay men to any large extent relative to their heterosexual counterparts. Indeed, they are restricted in largely the same way with respect to presentation, expectations, and body discipline.

To the extent that the features of commercial sex work feature prominently in the casual encounters of gay men, gay masculinities have caused gay men to market their sexual attraction as transactions in a way that blurs the lines between the commercial and noncommercial. Perhaps the economic forces themselves, hinging upon utility maximization, profit maximization, and rational decision making, tie into masculine norms about behavior in capitalist systems that gay men have placed in both their market and their nonmarket sexual behavior. Feminist economists have noted that the conceptual frameworks of neoclassical economic framework are gendered in ways that prize a masculine approach to distribution, trade, and welfare. While a treatise on the possibility that market forces themselves are masculine traits that gay men would emulate in their sexual behavior is beyond the scope here, those market forces are not restricted to the men seeking prostitution services. Given this possibility, the question that remains is whether the commercial male sex market, with its ingenious solution to asymmetric information, tightly connected network, rewards for masculine behavior, discipline on the body and self-presentation, and complicated negotiations over sexual practices, is a window into gay sexual sociality or a mirror that reflects the rigid social forces at play in gay masculinities.

Appendix 1

Data for the Analysis of Male Sex Work

DETAILED DESCRIPTION OF MALE SEX WORKER ADVERTISEMENT DATA

The data is the universe of men advertising on the site in the United States at the time of data collection, and, by agreement, the website name is not disclosed. Since the data is the entire population, I collected the data by searching through every geographic listing in the United States during the period of data collection. Each escort has a page specific to him that I used to gather the information. The website generates income from escorts only; clients do not pay to access any ads and no portion of the site is restricted from the public. All information collected was publicly and freely available on the website at the time of collection. There are other websites available for clients of male sex workers. A comparison of the website with two competitors, which establishes that the data source is the most comprehensive website in terms of coverage of the male escort market, is shown in Appendix 1.3.

I am able to identify each escort uniquely using the following information (see Figure 1.2 for an example of an escort advertisement):

User ID: Each escort account on the site has a unique user ID. This allowed me to check against the possibility of double-counting escorts who may change location over the data collection period.

User Name: Each escort has a user name that is displayed next to the ID number at the top of the ad.

The measures used are described below:

Services Provided: Under this heading each escort has the option of noting the following services, which are recorded:

Incall: Escort responds "yes" or "no."

Outcall: Escort responds "yes" or "no."

227

Incall Price: The price (by the hour) that incall services are provided at if incalls provided.

Outcall Price: The price (by the hour) that outcall services are provided at if outcalls provided.

Contact Information: Under this heading each escort has the option of noting the following:

Phone: Phone number with area code (I record if a number is listed Yes/No)

Cellular: Cellular number with area code (I record if a number is listed Yes/No)

Pager: Pager number with area code (I record if a number is listed Yes/No)

Prefers Phone Contact: Listed if escort prefers for clients to contact him by phone (Yes/No).

Prefers E-Mail Contact: Listed if escort prefers for clients to contact him by e-mail (Yes/No).

Location: The location listed under the heading is the primary location; the locations with suitcase icons next to them are cities the escort is willing to travel to. In some instances, exact dates are listed under specific travel cities, and this means that an escort is traveling to that city on those dates and will serve clients in those cities on those dates. I record all of these locations.

Age: Age is recorded in years.

Height: Height is reported in feet and inches; I record height in inches. For BMI the inches are converted to centimeters.

Weight: Weight is listed in 20-pound intervals beginning at 130 pounds and ending at 200 pounds (e.g., 150–170 lb.). I took the midpoint of the range given by an escort. If the escort's text ad listed a weight, I recorded that exact weight in place of the midpoint range. For calculation of BMI the weight is converted to kilograms.

Race: White, Black/African American, Asian, Hispanic, Multiracial, Other

Hair Color: Black, Blond, Brown, Grey, Red

Eye Color: Black, Blue, Brown, Green, Hazel

Body Type: Athletic/Swimmer's Build, Average, A few extra pounds, Muscular/buff, Thin/lean

Body Hair: Hairy, Moderately hairy, Shaved, Smooth

For the text of escort ads, I record the mention of the following: (Note: Since the ads were read as opposed to scripts, I do not record the instance of the word but its meaning, which can be inferred from the context of the advertisement.)

Top: The escort stated that he is a top (the penetrative partner in anal sex).

Bottom: The escort stated that he is a bottom (the receptive partner in anal sex).

Versatile: The escort indicated that he is versatile (both top and bottom).

No Attitude: The escort noted that he has "no attitude"/is willing to see clients without regard to race, body type, physical appearance, disability, etc.

Safe: The escort noted that he is disease and drug free/only participates in safer sex.

Note: In American gay society, men may not only be tops, bottoms, or versatile, but also "versatile tops" and "versatile bottoms." The meaning of such terms is the distinction between one man who would rarely or never partake in an activity (a "top" would never perform as a "bottom" and vice versa), and a man who occasionally partakes in an activity (a "versatile top" would occasionally perform as a "bottom" and vice versa). These terms are well established in gay society.

DETAILED DESCRIPTION OF CLIENT REVIEW DATA

Below, all variables from the data are defined. (Yes/No indicates a dichotomous variable. See Figure 1.3 for an example of an escort advertisement.)

Review Number: The chronological review number at the top of the review

Review Date: This is the date when the review was posted to the website after being verified by the webmaster.

Escort Name: The name of the MSW being reviewed. Note that for MSWs who change their names, their old reviews are retained but listed under their most recent name. For uniformity, the most recent escort name being used is the name in the data.

Escort E-Mail: If the MSW has an e-mail address (Yes/No)

Escort Phone: If the MSW has a phone number (Yes/No)

Escort Website: If the MSW has a website or advertisement on a male escort website (Yes/No)

Escort Permanent Location: This is the MSW's home location at the time of the review.

Ethnicity/Race: This is the client's perception of the MSW's race/ethnicity. From this, racial measures for White, Black, Asian, Hispanic, and "other race" are created.

Age: Age is noted in decades (e.g., 30s).

Height: Reported in feet and inches. Height is also transformed to centimeters in the data for the calculation of BMI.

Weight: Weight is noted in 10-pound intervals (e.g., 190–200 lb.). The mid-point of the interval is converted to kilograms for the calculation of BMI.

Build: Client's perception of the body build of the MSW.

Eye Color: MSW's eye color is recorded.

Hair: Both hair color and hair style are noted in separate fields.

Cock Size: Penis size refers to erect member and is noted in 1-inch intervals (e.g., 9–10). The measure is converted to a midpoint of the range in inches for use in the regressions.

Cock Size Description: This is two fields. The first describes circumcision status (Yes/No). The second field records descriptors noted by clients as a text field (e.g., thick).

Smoking: If the MSW smoked during/immediately before or after the appointment (Yes/No)

Drinking: If the MSW drank alcohol during/immediately before or after the appointment (Yes/No)

Tattoos: If the MSW has tattoos (Yes/No)

Orientation: This is the client's perception of the MSW's sexual orientation ("Straight," "Gay," "Bi")

Calls: Whether the MSW performs in (client goes to MSW) or out (MSW goes to client) services, or both

Roles: Roles can include escort, masseur, stripper, etc. This refers to the role or roles that were being performed during that particular appointment.

Masturbation: Records whether the MSW was masturbated by the client, masturbated the client, or both

Anal: Records whether the MSW penetrated the client, was penetrated by the client, or both

Oral: Records whether the MSW performed fellatio on client, had fellatio performed by the client, or both

Kink: Whether the MSW participated in any kinky activity such as bondage, domination, leather, etc. Due to the difficulty of knowing the specific type of sexual activity that the measure refers to, this is not incorporated into the empirical model.

Date of Appointment: Month and year of the transaction being reviewed

Type of Appointment: Appointment length in time

Location of Appointment: The city and state where the transaction took place

Rate: Rate paid by the client for this specific transaction

Rating: The client chooses between Highly Recommended, Recommended, and Not Recommended.

Hire Again: The client enters yes/no as to whether they would use this escort in the future.

Where Found: How the client found the MSW; could be listed as the data source itself (daddysreviews.com), another website, advertisement, or MSW's personal webpage.

Match Description: The client notes if the MSW appeared as advertised (Yes/No).

Lived Up: The client notes if the experience was as expected (Yes/No).

Experience: This is where the client records the activities of a specific encounter, allowing us to encode the sexual behaviors (including safer sex practices, oral sex, anilingus, masturbation, etc.) and sexual positions of both clients and MSWs. The experience measures are text-analyzed for the mention of specific sexual conduct words (e.g., "suck," "pounded," etc.), and variables are created where the mention of that word was included in the experience measure, and further refined to refer to specific conduct (anal sex, oral sex, etc.). Since the true meaning of the terms used can only be inferred from the context, the experience measures were read and coded separately by two analysts (the author and a research assistant) and cross-checked for consistency, which noted the meaning of the word (e.g., transaction contained anilingus by client on escort, transaction contained penetration by escort on client).

Handle: This serves as the unique identifier for the client.

Submissions: The number of other reviews the client had performed at the time of the current review.

About Client: The client enters a brief self-description. Age, height, weight, race, and will be recorded as separate categories if noted by the client (see Figure 1.3 for an example).

COMPARISON OF MALE ESCORT ADVERTISEMENT DATA

It is important to establish that the data source provides sufficient coverage of the online escort market. Appendix Table 1.1 compares escorts on the chosen website with two of the most prominent competitor websites for a random sample of smaller cities. As described earlier, I can uniquely

Appendix Table 1.1 *Comparison of male escort advertisement websites*

City	Number of escorts:				
	Data	Comp 1	Comp 2	Data / Comp 1	Comp 1 / Data
Albany, NY	5	0	3	—	—
Austin, TX	26	3	15	2/3	2/26
Buffalo, NY	5	0	0	—	—
Charlotte, NC	19	3	4	2/3	2/19
Columbus, OH	30	3	13	3/3	3/30
Denver, CO	41	5	19	5/5	5/41
Detroit, MI	73	10	14	9/10	9/73
Indianapolis, IN	19	0	5	—	—
Kansas City, MO	9	1	7	0/1	0/9
Minneapolis, MN	33	2	15	2/2	2/33
Nashville, TN	14	1	8	1/1	1/14
Oklahoma City, OK	3	1	0	1/1	1/3
Portland, OR	15	1	12	1/1	1/15
Rochester, NY	4	0	0	—	—
Sacramento, CA	17	7	5	5/7	5/17 •
St. Louis, MO	18	3	6	2/3	2/18
Seattle, WA	33	14	23	11/14	11/33
Tampa, FL	47	15	22	11/15	11/47
Total	411	69	171	55/69	55/378

Notes: Comp 1 = Rentboy.com, Comp 2 = MaleEscortReview.com
Counts of number of escorts by home base (from advertisement data) or number of advertisements (Comp 1 & 2)

identify the men in the chosen website and their home locations. This is impossible with the competitors, and potential double-counting by city on competitor webites would have biased upward the number of escorts listed on competing websites. Even with this bias, the chosen website's coverage of the male escort market is greater than those of its two competitors. The last two columns of Appendix Table 1.1 show the number of escorts on the chosen site that I could locate on the most prominent competitor's site, and vice versa. I found that the majority of escorts who advertise on competing websites also advertised on the chosen website, but only a small fraction of escorts in my chosen website could be identified on the competitors' websites.

Appendix 2

A Simple Signaling Model

A SIMPLE SIGNALING MODEL

I describe a simple signaling model in the spirit of Spence (1973, 2002). To increase the exposition, I use the simple two-type model where escorts are of two quality types and attempt to signal to a potential client, but also note below how this model is consistent with a disclosure model. I construct a simple one-shot model, but the central result holds in repeated signaling games, since signaling and reputation act as substitutes for one another in repeated games.[1]

To begin, assume that escorts are either high- or low-quality escorts, which are noted as θ_H and θ_L, respectively. In the population of escorts, some fraction λ are type H, and $(1-\lambda)$ are type L. The cost (c) of signaling (s) is a function of the type of escort and the signal itself $c(s, \theta)$, which by assumption has the traditional properties of a signal: the high-quality escort can signal more easily than the low-quality, and the single crossing property holds, such that $c_s(s, \theta) > 0$, $c_{ss}(s, \theta) > 0$, $c_\theta(s, \theta) < 0$, and $c_{s\theta}(s, \theta) < 0$.[2] Escorts can either signal/disclose $(s > 0)$ or not signal/disclose $(s = 0)$. As noted earlier, if one signals and is exposed as a low type, he must incur the costs of creating an entirely new identity, which are non-negligible costs in both time and money. The policing described earlier implies that there is a high probability of being detected. This increased probability of detection increases the cost of signaling for the low type, justifying the assumption.

While policing raises the probability of detection, policing in the market will not lead every high-quality escort to show his face, nor will it lead every low-quality escort to hide his. Disclosure is not always truthful in this market, as the client forums attest. There are several reasons why a high-quality escort may choose not to show his face in escort advertisements. Since sex work is illegal, disclosure could draw unwanted attention to the escort. If an escort plans to escort for only a certain length of time, or if

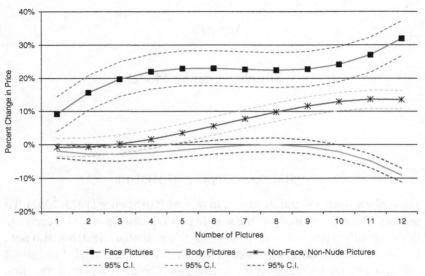

Appendix 2.1 Price premium of pictures by picture type

escorting is not his full-time occupation, he may not want long-lived, easily identifiable evidence of his previous occupation to hound him. News stories abound of men who had been sex workers, and for whom the discovery of their previous life of prostitution had serious consequences.[3] Exposure as a male sex worker could bring into question one's sexual orientation, which could bring about further negative consequences. There is evidence of wage discrimination against gay and lesbian people, and when compounded with a history of sex work this could be even more pronounced. To capture this fact, assume that the cost function contains a random element ε that is unrelated to type:

$$c(s, \theta, \varepsilon) = c(s, \theta) + \varepsilon \; where \; \varepsilon \sim N(0, \sigma^2) \qquad (A1)$$

This new term in the cost function still allows all of the conditions to hold as before, but now in any perfect Bayesian equilibrium the client would have to take into account that a certain fraction $(1 - \alpha)$ of signalers would be low quality, and a certain fraction of non-signalers $(1 - \beta)$ would be high quality. The variance of the random term will cause the client to revise his expectations of α and β ($\partial \alpha / \partial \sigma^2 < 0$ and $\partial \beta / \partial \sigma^2 < 0$). Another way of modeling this feature would be to have two dichotomous nodes: one for escort type as either high/low quality ($q \in \{H, L\}$) and another for disclosure/signaling ($s \in \{Y, N\}$), which can be yes or no. The key point is that in either model, disclosure/signaling does not fully reveal type, and the model hinges on how well disclosure/signaling and quality are believed to be correlated, in the view of the client.

I assume that an escort's utility is a function of the earnings he receives from escorting (w), less the cost of signaling $u(w, s|\theta) = w - c(s, \theta)$.[4] In any pure strategy, perfect Bayesian equilibrium, the client must assign a wage that is equal to the escort's expected productivity, and the wage of the high-quality escort is greater than the wage of the low-quality escort, $w(\theta_H) > w(\theta_L)$. As described earlier, if a client observes the signal (the escort discloses), then with probability α he will expect the worker to be of type H. If no signal is observed (the escort does not disclose), the client will expect the worker to be of type H with probability $(1-\beta)$. This gives the belief structure for the client:

$$\mu(\theta|s > 0) = \alpha\theta_H + (1 - \alpha)\theta_L; \quad \mu(\theta|s = 0) = \beta\theta_L + (1 - \beta)\theta_H.$$
$$(A2)$$

The wages offered by the client are therefore a function of the signal

$$w|s > 0 \rightarrow \alpha w(\theta_H) + (1 - \alpha)w(\theta_L);$$
$$w|s = 0 \rightarrow \beta w(\theta_L) + (1 - \beta)w(\theta_H). \qquad (A3)$$

This wage offer is consistent with the escort's strategy when two conditions hold. First, for the high-quality type, the utility of disclosure/signaling must exceed the wage offered when no signal is observed:

$$w|s > 0, \theta_H \rightarrow [\alpha w(\theta_H) + (1 - \alpha)w(\theta_L)] - c(s > 0, \theta_H, \varepsilon) > \beta w(\theta_L)$$
$$+(1 - \beta)w(\theta_H). \qquad (A4)$$

If this does not hold, then high-quality types would have no incentive to disclose/signal. Second, for low-quality types, the utility of signaling must be less than the wage offered when not signaling,

$$w|s > 0, \theta_L \rightarrow [\alpha w(\theta_H) + (1 - \alpha)w(\theta_L)] - c(s > 0, \theta_L, \varepsilon) < \beta w(\theta_L)$$
$$+(1 - \beta)w(\theta_H), \qquad (A5)$$

or else the low-quality type would always signal. The model is informative, but ultimately the issue of whether the signal leads to different prices in the market is an empirical question.

The results from the estimates in Chapter 2 can be used to estimate the cost of signaling for each type of sex worker. Recall from the model presented above that for both high and low types, the utility of signaling must exceed the wage offered when no signal is observed (Equations A4 and A5). Rearranging terms in equations (A4) and (A5) and simplifying the expression yields

$$(w|s > 0) - (w|s = 0) > c(s > 0, \theta_H, \varepsilon) \qquad (A6)$$

$$(w|s > 0) - (w|s = 0) < c(s > 0, \theta_L, \varepsilon). \qquad (A7)$$

We know the value of the difference between the signal and no signal, $(w \mid s > 0) - (w \mid s = 0)$, is a 20 percent difference in hourly price. Taking \$200 as the average hourly price of escort services in the data, the difference is roughly \$40. This implies that \$40 is greater than the cost of signaling for the high type and lower than the cost of signaling for the low type in this market. This amount seems reasonable, as the price of posting a new advertisement is roughly \$80 for the least expensive type of advertisement on the website analyzed here, which is greater than the amount identified here.

Appendix Table 2.1 *Information, reputation, and the price of male escort services*

	(1)	(2)	(3)	(4)	(5)
Number of pictures	0.0168***	0.0165***	0.0156***	0.00777***	0.00969***
	[0.0024]	[0.0029]	[0.0029]	[0.0021]	[0.0022]
Log of no. of reviews		0.00352	−0.0111	−0.00943	−0.00762
		[0.010]	[0.010]	[0.0096]	[0.0098]
Log of no. of text reviews			0.0881***	0.0925***	0.0918***
			[0.014]	[0.012]	[0.012]
Has face pictures?				0.195***	0.180***
				[0.046]	[0.048]
Has body-only pictures?					−0.0632***
					[0.014]
Additional Controls	X	X	X	X	X
Observations	1475	1475	1475	1475	1475
R-squared	0.22	0.22	0.23	0.31	0.32

Robust standard errors in brackets are clustered at the state level (***$p < .01$, **$p < .05$, *$p < .1$).
Notes: Each Column is an OLS regression where the dependent variable is the log of the price. Each column includes controls for race, age, height, weight, state, top, bottom, versatile, whether the escort was available all day, body type, body hair, whether the escort advertised safer sex, eye color, review allowed, and whether the escort preferred phone contact.
See the Appendix 1 for variable definitions.

Appendix Table 2.2 *Quality of information and the price of male escort services*

Panel A: Number of types of pictures

	(1)	(2)	(3)	(4)	(5)
No. of face pictures	0.0317***	0.0305***	0.0293***	0.0286***	0.0283***
	[0.0060]	[0.0055]	[0.0058]	[0.0057]	[0.0056]
No. of body only pictures		−0.00468	−0.00617	−0.0069	−0.00493
		[0.0039]	[0.0042]	[0.0042]	[0.0037]
Log of no. of reviews			0.0146	−0.0037	−0.0104
			[0.0089]	[0.010]	[0.0096]
Log of no. of Text reviews				0.103***	0.0913***
				[0.018]	[0.014]
Additional controls					X
Observations	1475	1475	1475	1475	1475
R-squared	0.22	0.22	0.22	0.24	0.29

Robust standard errors in brackets are clustered at the state level (***$p < .01$, **$p < .05$, *$p < .1$).

Panel B: Composition of pictures

	(1)	(2)	(3)	(4)	(5)
Number of pictures	0.0139***	0.0140***	0.0126***	0.0114***	0.00987***
	[0.0021]	[0.0021]	[0.0026]	[0.0026]	[0.0022]
Fraction face pictures	0.241***	0.191***	0.190***	0.194***	0.216***
	[0.050]	[0.057]	[0.058]	[0.058]	[0.056]
Fraction body-only pictures		−0.0806**	−0.0821**	−0.0768**	−0.0318
		[0.034]	[0.035]	[0.034]	[0.031]
Log of no. of reviews			0.0133	−0.00338	−0.0234**
			[0.0091]	[0.010]	[0.0099]
Log of no. of text reviews				0.0961***	0.0575***
				[0.017]	[0.018]
Fraction 4-star reviews					0.0396
					[0.026]
Fraction positive text reviews					0.0424
					[0.030]
Additional controls					X
Observations	1475	1475	1475	1475	1475
R-squared	0.24	0.25	0.25	0.26	0.32

Robust standard errors in brackets are clustered at the state level (***$p < .01$, **$p < .05$, *$p < .1$).
Notes: Each Column is an OLS regression where the dependent variable is the log of the price. Each column includes controls for state. Column 5 includes controls for race, age, height, weight, top, bottom, versatile, whether the escort was available all day, body type, body hair, if the escort advertised safer sex, eye color, review allowed, and whether the escort preferred phone contact. See Appendix 1 for variable definitions.

Appendix Table 2.3 *Is the data consistent with a beauty interpretation?*

Panel A: Beauty and face pictures

	(1)	(2)	(3)	(4)	(5)
No. of face pictures	0.0149***	0.0153***	0.0132***	0.0153***	0.0131***
	[0.0034]	[0.0034]	[0.0038]	[0.0035]	[0.0039]
Beauty		0.0089	0.007		
		[0.0063]	[0.0063]		
Above-average beauty				0.0076	−0.0006
				[0.0249]	[0.0247]
Below-average beauty				−0.0155	−0.0195
				[0.0253]	[0.0251]
Additional Controls			X		X
Observations	849	849	849	849	849
R-squared	0.04	0.03	0.02	0.04	0.14

Panel B: The interaction of escort reputation and information

	(1)	(2)	(3)	(4)
No. of face pictures* text reviews	−0.00922**			
	[0.0035]			
No. of face pictures* positive text reviews		−0.00373**		
		[0.0015]		
Fraction face* text reviews			−0.0278	
			[0.031]	
Fraction face* positive text reviews				−0.0092
				[0.013]
Additional controls	X	X	X	X
Observations	1475	1475	1475	1475
R-squared	0.29	0.29	0.32	0.32

Robust standard errors in brackets are clustered at the state level (***$p < .01$, **$p < .05$, *$p < .1$).
Notes: Each Column is an OLS regression where the dependent variable is the log of the price.
Beauty is measured on a 1-to-5 scale with 5 being the most beautiful. Above-average beauty is a
beauty measure greater than 3, and below-average beauty is a beauty measure less than 3.
In panel A, each column includes fixed effects for each beauty enumerator.
In panel B, columns 1 and 2 also include the number of face pictures and number of body pictures.
In panel B, columns 3 and 4 also include the number of pictures and fraction of face and body
pictures.
Columns 3 and 5 in Panel A and all columns of Panel B include controls for race, age, height,
weight, state, top, bottom, versatile, whether the escort was available all day, body type, body hair,
whether the escort advertised safer sex, eye color, review allowed, whether the escort preferred
phone contact, number of survey reviews, number of text reviews, and the fraction of highly rated
survey and text reviews, respectively. See the Appendix 1 for variable definitions.

Appendix Table 2.4 *Enforcement proxy and the value of the signal*

Panel A: Estimates of the value of any face or body pictures in escort advertisements

	Las Vegas	Chicago	Atlanta	Houston	Dallas	Boston
Has face pictures?	−0.086	0.257***	0.221**	0.350***	0.347***	0.253**
	[0.097]	[0.056]	[0.090]	[0.080]	[0.049]	[0.093]
Has body pictures?	−0.141	−0.114*	−0.0706	−0.0834	−0.0407	−0.0314
	[0.092]	[0.060]	[0.097]	[0.093]	[0.069]	[0.091]
R-squared	0.4	0.39	0.16	0.53	0.6	0.35

Panel B: Estimates of the value of face and body pictures in escort advertisements

	Las Vegas	Chicago	Atlanta	Houston	Dallas	Boston
No. of face pictures	0.00742	0.0300***	0.0285*	0.0355**	0.0449***	0.0279*
	[0.017]	[0.011]	[0.016]	[0.015]	[0.011]	[0.014]
No. of body-only pictures	0.00208	0.00228	−0.0262	−0.0105	−0.00726	0.00243
	[0.024]	[0.015]	[0.022]	[0.021]	[0.013]	[0.021]
R-squared	0.33	0.18	0.19	0.27	0.48	0.22

Robust standard errors in brackets (***$p < .01$, **$p < .05$, *$p < .1$)
Panels A and B include the following additional variables in the regressions: number of survey reviews, number of text reviews, fraction of survey and text reviews that are positive, age, height, weight, and race. Panel A includes the total number of pictures. See Appendix 1 for variable definitions.

Appendix Table 2.5 Robustness checks for information quality and the price of male escort services

	Spot prices			Spot prices only			Escorts with no reputation		
	(1)	(2)	(3)	(4)	(5)	(6)	(7)	(8)	(9)
Number of pictures	0.00901*** [0.0023]		0.00970*** [0.0021]	0.00724 [0.0079]		0.00976 [0.0076]	0.00695 [0.0047]		0.00927* [0.0046]
Has face pictures?	0.177*** [0.048]			0.168*** [0.061]			0.188*** [0.059]		
Has body-only pictures?	−0.0587*** [0.014]			−0.0293 [0.035]			−0.0431** [0.020]		
No. of face pictures		0.0266*** [0.0054]			0.0142* [0.0074]			0.0318*** [0.0084]	
No. of body-only pictures		−0.00469 [0.0038]			−0.0041 [0.013]			−0.00995 [0.0078]	
Fraction face pictures			0.213*** [0.056]			0.089 [0.064]			0.234*** [0.084]
Fraction body-only pictures			−0.0272 [0.032]			−0.11 [0.092]			−0.0158 [0.053]
Log of no. of reviews	−0.00909 [0.0100]	−0.0115 [0.0098]	−0.0099 [0.0098]	−0.0405 [0.025]	−0.0333 [0.031]	−0.0358 [0.031]			

(continued)

Log of no. of text reviews	0.0941***	0.0934***	0.0917***	0.0811**	0.0662	0.0614			
	[0.013]	[0.017]	[0.016]	[0.032]	[0.042]	[0.039]			
Additional controls	X	X	X	X	X	X	X	X	X
Observations	1533	1533	1533	243	243	243	610	610	610
R-squared	0.32	0.28	0.31	0.51	0.46	0.48	0.32	0.3	0.32

Robust standard errors in brackets are clustered at the state level (***$p < .01$, **$p < .05$, *$p < .1$).

Notes: Each column is an OLS regression. In columns 1–3 the dependent variable is the log of the spot price. If an escort has both a spot price and a posted price, or no posted price and a spot price, the spot price replaces the posted or missing price. Dependent variable in columns 4–6 the dependent variable is the log of the spot price only. The dependent variable in columns 7–9 is the log of the price (for escorts with no reviews only). Each column includes controls for race, age, height, weight, state, top, bottom, versatile, whether the escort was available all day, body type, body hair, whether the escort advertised safer sex, eye color, review allowed, and whether the escort preferred phone contact. See Appendix 1 for variable definitions.

Appendix Table 2.6 *Information and selection into posting escort prices*

	(1)	(2)	(3)	(4)	(5)	(6)	(7)
Number of pictures	0.00245 [0.0036]	0.0024 [0.0034]	0.00286 [0.0031]	0.00304 [0.0031]			
Has face pictures?		0.00112 [0.017]	−0.00181 [0.018]	0.00007 [0.019]			
Has body-only pictures?			−0.012 [0.022]	−0.0154 [0.021]			
No. of face pictures					0.00448 [0.0030]	0.0058 [0.0038]	0.00634 [0.0040]
No. of body-only pictures						0.00473 [0.0054]	0.00372 [0.0054]
Additional controls				X			X
Observations	1932	1932	1932	1932	1932	1932	1932
Pseudo R-squared	0.0517	0.0517	0.052	0.055	0.0528	0.0535	0.0566

Robust standard errors in brackets are clustered at the state level (***$p < .01$, **$p < .05$, *$p < .1$).

Notes: Each column reports results of a probit regression where the dependent variable is: Does Escort Post Prices? (Mean of dependent variable = 0.85, Standard Error of dependent variable = 0.36)

The coefficients reported are the marginal effects of the probit regressions. For continuous variables (such as "Number of pictures"), the effect is evaluated at the mean. For dichotomous variables (such "Has face pictures?"), the effects calculate the change in probability from moving from 0 to 1. Columns 4 and 7 include controls for race, age, height, weight, top, bottom, versatile, whether the escort was available all day, body type, body hair, review allowed, whether the escort advertised safer sex, eye color, and whether the escort preferred phone contact. Each column includes controls for state. See Appendix 1 for variable definitions.

242

Appendix Table 2.7 *Decomposition of picture premium for all picture types*

	(1)	(2)	(3)	(4)
No. of face pictures	0.0295***	0.0303***	0.0288***	0.111***
	[0.0057]	[0.0056]	[0.0058]	[0.033]
(No. of face pictures)^2				−0.0170***
				[0.0059]
(No. of face pictures)^3				0.000837***
				[0.00029]
No. of body-only pictures	−0.0041	−0.00382	−0.00522	−0.0258*
	[0.0034]	[0.0035]	[0.0038]	[0.015]
(No. of body-only pictures)^2				0.00658
				[0.0049]
(No. of body-only pictures)^3				−0.000433
				[0.00038]
No. of non-face, non-nude pictures		0.00379	0.00161	−0.0139
		[0.0037]	[0.0035]	[0.021]
(No. of non-face, non-nude pictures)^2				0.00551
				[0.0059]
(No. of non-face, non-nude pictures)^3				−0.00027
				[0.00037]
Log of no. of reviews			−0.01	−0.0078
			[0.010]	[0.0098]
Log of no. of text reviews			0.0935***	0.0946***
			[0.014]	[0.014]
Additional controls	X	X	X	X
Observations	1475	1475	1475	1475
R-squared	0.27	0.27	0.28	0.31

Robust standard errors in brackets are clustered at the state level (***$p < .01$, **$p < .05$, *$p < .1$).
Notes: Each column is an OLS regression where the dependent variable is the log of the price.
Each column includes controls for race, age, height, weight, state, top, bottom, versatile, whether the escort allowed himself to be reviewed, body type, body hair, whether the escort advertised safer sex, eye color, and whether the escort preferred phone contact.

Appendix 3

Measuring the Male Sex Worker Network

CENTRALITY MEASURES

This travel network, W, may be represented by a triplet (Z_1, Z_2, E), where Z_1 represents a group of escorts with size equal to n_1, Z_2 indicates a group of n_2 cities, and E represents a collection of edges $w(i,j)$. The value of $w(i,j)$ equals 1 if escort i is willing to travel to city j, and 0 if otherwise. Importantly, I maintain the duality of the travel network data by measuring the centrality of one node set (e.g., escorts) as a function of its ties to the other node set (e.g., cities). Accordingly, I do not project the network into two one-mode networks consisting of only cities or escorts, as the centrality of one node set must be defined in reference to the other node set.[5] The centrality of actors in one node set will quantify the importance of the collection of actors belonging to the opposing node set. I use the resulting network to construct three measures that capture different aspects of centrality that are of theoretical interest in the analysis of the travel network of male sex workers.

Degree centrality reflects the duality of escort and city centrality and is measured as

$$d_{1i} = \frac{\sum_{k \in z_2} w(i, k)}{n_2}$$

$$d_{2i} = \frac{\sum_{k \in z_1} w(i, k)}{n_1}.$$

The degree of an escort i (d_{1i}) is equal to the number of cities that he travels to, normalized by the number of cities in the network, while the degree of a city i (d_{2i}) equals the number of escorts who travel to city i, normalized by the number of escorts in the travel network. As previously mentioned, a city's degree centrality is representative of the overall demand for male sex work. However, a major criticism for the degree centrality is that it treats all escort-city ties equally.

The eigenvector centrality overcomes this criticism of degree centrality.[6] Bonacich (1972) points out that in certain situations, being tied to other actors who are themselves tied to several other actors entails numerous social advantages. Traveling to cities that are frequently traveled to by other escorts could entail greater financial rewards if escorts travel to these cities precisely because demand for sexual services in those cities is higher than in cities that are less frequently visited. The eigenvector centrality of escort i in node set Z_1 is expressed as a function of the centralities of the cities to which he travels:

$$C_e^{Z_1}(i) = \frac{1}{\lambda} \sum_{k=1}^{n_2} C_e^{Z_2}(k) w(i, k),$$

where $C_e^{Z_2}(k) w(i, k)$ is the centrality score of city k in node set w, λ is the largest eigenvalue of the $n \times m$ incidence matrix representing the escort/city travel network, and $w(i,k) = 1$ if escort i travels to city k and 0 if otherwise. Higher values on the index indicate that escorts travel to popular destination cities

$$C_e^{Z_2}(i) = \frac{1}{\lambda} \sum_{k=1}^{n_1} C_e^{Z_1}(k) w(i, k),$$

where λ is the largest eigenvalue from either ww' or $w'w$, where w is the $n1 \times n2$ incidence matrix of the escort/city network. As shown explicitly above, the eigenvector centralities incorporate the duality between escort and city centralities. As noted by Mariolis (1975), Mintz and Schwartz (1985), and Bonacich (1991), among others, the measure of eigenvector centrality has an inevitably high correlation with the sheer number of connections (i.e., degree centralities) for nodes in both types. It is recommended to remove the size effect from the eigenvector centrality if the size of links does not reflect the position of the node, but just some arbitrary rules, as in the case of interlocking directorates. In this analysis, the size of links for both escorts and cities are indicative of their positions in the network, so I do not adjust the eigenvector centrality for its size effect.

Third, escorts and cities may also be central if they lie on several of the shortest paths that link other cities and escorts. A node's *betweenness centrality* is measured by first estimating the number of geodesic paths that include the node, inversely weighted by the number of equally short paths between the same two nodes. In the case of two-mode betweenness centrality, paths can originate and end at nodes from either node set. To measure node betweenness centrality for cities and escorts in our network, I first measure

$$b_i = \sum_{j \neq k \neq i} \frac{\sigma_i(j,k)}{\sigma(j,k)},$$

where $\sigma(j,k)$ represents the total number of geodesics that link node j and node k, where j and k may be either escorts or cities. Among escorts, the value of b_i is divided by the theoretical maximum betweenness $2(n_1 - 1)(n_2 - 1)$, given $n_1 > n_2$. Conversely, the betweenness of cities is divided by its maximum betweenness, $\frac{1}{2} n_2(n_2 - 1) + \frac{1}{2}(n_1 - 1)(n_1 - 2) + (n_1 - 1)(n_2 - 1)$, given $n_2 \leq n_1$. Duality in betweenness centrality is implicit because escorts are always on geodesics between cities, and cities are always on geodesics of escorts.

Diversity is captured by Shannon entropy. Let $p(ij)$ denote the proportion of city i's links with the escorts from city j, where $i,j=1, \ldots, n_2$. Shannon entropy for city i is calculated by $-\sum_{j \neq i}^{n_2} p_{ij} \log(p_{ij})$. It equals zero if all escorts who travel to the city are from a same place. A higher Shannon entropy implies that the city is visited by escorts from different locations more evenly, increasing the diversity of a city's links. The highest value for the diversity measure is $ln(n_2)$, and it is achieved when a city is visited by an equal number of escorts from all other cities. Eagle, Macy, and Claxton (2010) use national communication network data in the United Kingdom to show that the diversity of individuals' relationships is correlated with economic development of communities. Along the same lines, the diversity of traveling escorts to a given city could reflect the market's maturity as a site for male sex work.

REGRESSION MODELS

The extensive travel regression model takes the form:

Extensive Travel$_{ig}$
$$= \alpha + \beta X_i + \gamma GCI_g + \delta HIVRate_g + \eta Hub_g + \lambda NetworkMeasure_g + \epsilon_{ig},$$

where i stands for individual I, g stands for city g, and X contains personal characteristics. All standard errors are clustered at the escort's home city to construct the t-statistics for parameters. To test if there exists a city-wise heteroskedasticity on the error term, I implement Levene test and Brown and Forsythe test of groupwise heteroskedasticity and reject the hypothesis of homogeneity of the error term variance across male sex workers' home cities.

The regression for the distance traveled by sex workers was conditional on travel and took this form:

$Travel\ Distance_{ig}$

$$= \alpha + \beta X_i + \gamma GCI_g + \delta HIVRate_g + \eta Hub_g + \lambda NetworkMeasure_g + \epsilon_{ig}.$$

The model used to describe the relationship between rates of services and explanatory variables are of the form

$Service\ Rate_{ig}$

$$= \alpha + \beta X_{ig} + \rho Extensive\ Travel_{ig} + \xi(Extensive\ Travel_{ig} \times X_{ig}) + \gamma GCI_g$$
$$+ \tau Network\ Measure_{ig} + \lambda Network\ Measure_g + \delta HIVRate_g + \eta Hub_g + \epsilon_{ig}.$$

Appendix Table 3.1 *Regression on travel indicator for escorts*

Age	-0.000824	-0.00083	-0.000786	-0.000811	-0.000779
	(-0.35)	(-0.35)	(-0.33)	(-0.34)	(-0.33)
Height	-0.00111	-0.000981	-0.00103	-0.000943	-0.00095
	(-0.52)	(-0.46)	(-0.48)	(-0.44)	(-0.45)
Weight	0.000491	0.000499	0.000496	0.000488	0.000459
	(0.27)	(0.27)	(0.27)	(0.26)	(0.25)
Black	-0.0112	-0.00944	-0.00973	-0.00857	-0.00779
	(-0.36)	(-0.30)	(-0.31)	(-0.27)	(-0.25)
Asian	-0.128*	-0.115+	-0.114+	-0.115+	-0.123*
	(-2.07)	(-1.94)	(-1.90)	(-1.91)	(-2.01)
Hispanic	0.0141	0.0191	0.0184	0.0195	0.0178
	(0.35)	(0.46)	(0.44)	(0.47)	(0.44)
Multiracial	-0.0252	-0.0206	-0.0209	-0.0207	-0.0238
	(-0.67)	(-0.53)	(-0.53)	(-0.53)	(-0.62)
Other race	-0.0322	-0.0263	-0.0263	-0.0249	-0.0279
	(-0.58)	(-0.45)	(-0.45)	(-0.43)	(-0.48)

(continued)

Appendix Table 3.1 *(continued)*

Athletic body	0.126*	0.125*	0.125*	0.125*	0.126*
	(2.44)	(2.39)	(2.38)	(2.38)	(2.41)
Average body	0.0727	0.0659	0.0658	0.0655	0.0684
	(1.14)	(1.02)	(1.02)	(1.01)	(1.06)
Large body	0.0139	0.0117	0.0114	0.0121	0.0133
	(0.09)	(0.08)	(0.07)	(0.08)	(0.09)
Buff body	0.140*	0.140*	0.141*	0.140*	0.141*
	(2.38)	(2.38)	(2.39)	(2.38)	(2.37)
Top	0.0859*	0.0884*	0.0879*	0.0888*	0.0877*
	(2.02)	(2.04)	(2.01)	(2.05)	(2.05)
Bottom	0.207***	0.205***	0.205***	0.205***	0.204***
	(4.93)	(4.82)	(4.79)	(4.82)	(4.77)
Versatile	0.0757*	0.0757*	0.0768*	0.0764*	0.0761*
	(2.11)	(2.15)	(2.18)	(2.17)	(2.15)
Massage	0.0425	0.0463	0.0466	0.047	0.0448
	(1.22)	(1.32)	(1.32)	(1.34)	(1.28)
GCI	−0.124***	−0.114***	−0.128***	−0.118***	−0.108**
	(−4.28)	(−4.02)	(−4.62)	(−4.18)	(−3.36)
HIV rate	−0.000423	0.00123	0.00111	0.00138	0.000652
	(−0.25)	−0.72	−0.81	−0.88	−0.41
Airline hub	−0.110*	−0.0836+	−0.0941*	−0.0821+	−0.0818
	(−2.41)	(−1.74)	(−2.01)	(−1.72)	(−1.55)
City degree		−0.540+			
		(−1.69)			
City eigen centrality			−0.163*		
			(−2.33)		
City betweenness				−0.391*	
				(−2.16)	
City diversity					−0.0373
					(−1.18)
Constant	0.892**	0.842*	0.860**	0.833*	0.884**
	(2.81)	(2.55)	(2.64)	(2.52)	(2.76)
Observations	1797	1797	1797	1797	1792
R-squared	0.038	0.041	0.04	0.041	0.039

Note: t-statistics in parentheses. + $p < .10$, *$p < .05$, **$p < .01$, ***$p < .001$
Standard errors are clustered on home cities.

Appendix Table 3.2 *Regression of log average travel distance*

Age	−0.0119	−0.0121	−0.0121	−0.0121	−0.0127+
	(−1.58)	(−1.61)	(−1.62)	(−1.63)	(−1.67)
Height	−0.00138	−0.00178	−0.00161	−0.00181	−0.00163
	(−0.20)	(−0.25)	(−0.23)	(−0.26)	(−0.23)
Weight	0.00329	0.0029	0.00316	0.00282	0.00314
	(0.58)	(0.50)	(0.55)	(0.49)	(0.55)
Black	−0.203*	−0.210*	−0.206*	−0.212*	−0.227*
	(−2.27)	(−2.35)	(−2.30)	(−2.38)	(−2.57)
Asian	−0.178	−0.229	−0.204	−0.231	−0.22
	(−0.39)	(−0.50)	(−0.45)	(−0.51)	(−0.49)
Hispanic	−0.266*	−0.288*	−0.276*	−0.290*	−0.273*
	(−2.43)	(−2.59)	(−2.49)	(−2.63)	(−2.44)
Multiracial	−0.000933	−0.0197	−0.0107	−0.0205	−0.0383
	(−0.01)	(−0.16)	(−0.09)	(−0.17)	(−0.32)
Other race	0.0923	0.0782	0.0847	0.0728	0.0714
	(0.65)	(0.55)	(0.59)	(0.52)	(0.51)
Athletic body	0.210+	0.224+	0.218+	0.225+	0.208+
	(1.79)	(1.95)	(1.87)	(1.97)	(1.90)
Average body	0.0383	0.0711	0.054	0.0751	0.0918
	(0.26)	(0.49)	(0.37)	(0.52)	(0.65)
Large body	−0.105	−0.108	−0.106	−0.108	−0.119
	(−0.25)	(−0.25)	(−0.25)	(−0.25)	(−0.28)
Buff body	0.394*	0.408*	0.401*	0.411*	0.401*
	(2.11)	(2.20)	(2.16)	(2.21)	(2.19)
Top	−0.145	−0.158	−0.151	−0.161	−0.158
	(−0.87)	(−0.95)	(−0.90)	(−0.96)	(−0.95)
Bottom	0.0403	0.0409	0.0414	0.041	0.0539
	(0.24)	(0.24)	(0.24)	(0.24)	(0.31)
Versatile	0.138	0.135	0.134	0.133	0.145
	(0.89)	(0.86)	(0.86)	(0.85)	(0.91)
Massage	0.0398	0.0259	0.0327	0.0223	0.024
	(0.50)	(0.32)	(0.40)	(0.27)	(0.30)
GCI	0.177	0.133	0.178	0.142	0.0687
	(1.29)	(0.95)	(1.32)	(1.05)	(0.49)
HIV rate	−0.00252	−0.00693	−0.00457	−0.00745	−0.00949
	(−0.43)	(−1.12)	(−0.72)	(−1.21)	(−1.60)
Airline hub	0.560***	0.488**	0.539**	0.482**	0.394*
	(3.51)	(2.91)	(3.30)	(2.89)	(2.37)
City degree		1.626+			
		−1.73			

(continued)

Appendix Table 3.2 *(continued)*

City eigen centrality			0.247		
			(1.08)		
City betweenness				1.214+	
				(1.79)	
City diversity					0.247*
					(2.64)
Constant	4.990***	5.173***	5.068***	5.196***	4.925***
	(4.48)	(4.53)	(4.47)	(4.57)	(4.46)
Observations	1027	1027	1027	1027	1023
R-squared	0.059	0.063	0.06	0.064	0.069

Note: t-statistics in parentheses. $+ p < .10$, $*p < .05$, $**p < .01$, $***p < .001$
Standard errors are clustered on home cities.
Only escorts who serve multiple locations used in regressions.

Appendix Table 3.3 *Regression of log wage on travel and escort characteristics*

Age	−0.0106***	−0.0106***	−0.0105***	−0.0107***	−0.0106***
	(−7.34)	(−7.32)	(−7.30)	(−7.39)	(−7.29)
Height	0.00264	0.00247	0.00243	0.00236	0.00176
	(1.49)	(1.39)	(1.37)	(1.33)	(0.99)
Weight	−0.00104	−0.000892	−0.000913	−0.000959	−0.000661
	(−0.71)	(−0.61)	(−0.62)	(−0.66)	(−0.45)
Black	−0.00892	−0.00814	0.00311	−0.0125	0.00114
	(−0.33)	(−0.30)	−0.08	(−0.47)	−0.03
Asian	−0.0577	−0.0581	−0.0226	−0.0629	−0.0347
	(−0.95)	(−0.95)	(−0.30)	(−1.03)	(−0.45)
Hispanic	−0.0244	−0.0221	−0.0602	−0.0258	−0.0745+
	(−0.87)	(−0.78)	(−1.45)	(−0.92)	(−1.78)
Multiracial	0.0119	0.0119	0.0331	0.00906	0.0311
	(0.38)	(0.37)	(0.74)	(0.29)	(0.69)
Other race	0.140***	0.136**	0.224***	0.137***	0.210***
	−3.39	(3.29)	−3.93	−3.33	(3.67)
Athletic body	0.0856**	0.0745+	0.0870**	0.0841**	0.0721+
	(2.67)	(1.75)	(2.71)	(2.63)	(1.69)
Average body	−0.0318	−0.0257	−0.0338	−0.0312	−0.0204
	(−0.78)	(−0.47)	(−0.83)	(−0.77)	(−0.38)

(continued)

Appendix Table 3.3 *(continued)*

Large body	−0.228*	−0.392**	−0.214*	−0.229*	−0.406**
	(−2.17)	(−2.81)	(−2.03)	(−2.18)	(−2.91)
Buff body	0.209***	0.198***	0.210***	0.209***	0.194***
	(5.40)	(4.06)	(5.43)	(5.40)	(3.96)
Top	0.02	0.0187	0.0192	0.0812	0.0692
	(0.54)	(0.48)	(0.50)	(1.23)	(1.04)
Bottom	−0.0644	−0.0625	−0.0643	−0.134+	−0.139+
	(−1.46)	(−1.42)	(−1.46)	(−1.70)	(−1.76)
Versatile	0.0444	0.0432	0.0462	0.0117	0.00958
	(1.55)	(1.51)	(1.61)	(0.25)	(0.20)
Massage	−0.130***	−0.130***	−0.129***	−0.187***	−0.190***
	(−5.39)	(−5.40)	(−5.34)	(−5.23)	(−5.28)
Travel	0.0834***	0.0647	0.0933***	0.0608**	0.216*
	(4.58)	(1.15)	(3.80)	(2.81)	(2.41)
GCI	0.032	0.0325	0.0324	0.0309	0.0710*
	(1.22)	(1.24)	(1.24)	(1.19)	(2.01)
HIVrate	0.00581***	0.00586***	0.00585***	0.00585***	0.00807***
	(6.02)	(6.06)	(6.06)	(6.04)	(5.57)
Airline hub	0.1000**	0.0988**	0.103**	0.102**	0.112***
	(3.13)	(3.09)	(3.22)	(3.18)	(3.47)
Travel * athletic body		0.0228			0.0232
		(0.36)			(0.37)
Travel * average body		−0.0105			−0.0234
		(−0.14)			(−0.30)
Travel blarge Body		0.357+			0.398*
		(1.78)			(1.98)
Travel * buff body		0.0204			0.0245
		(0.31)			(0.38)
Travel * Black			−0.0209		−0.0232
			(−0.40)		(−0.44)
Travel * Asian			−0.0909		−0.0849
			(−0.74)		(−0.69)
Travel * Hispanic			0.0633		0.0884
			(1.15)		(1.60)
Travel * multiracial			−0.0406		−0.0426
			(−0.65)		(−0.68)
Travel * other race			−0.175*		−0.159+
			(−2.15)		(−1.94)
Travel * top				−0.0964	−0.0838
				(−1.19)	(−1.03)

(continued)

Appendix Table 3.3 *(continued)*

Travel * bottom				0.106	0.115
				(1.12)	(1.21)
Travel * versatile				0.0526	0.0507
				(0.89)	(0.85)
Travel * massage				0.105*	0.112*
				(2.21)	(2.32)
Travel * GCI					−0.0761
					(−1.53)
Travel * HIV rate					−0.00360+
					(−1.85)
Constant	4.815***	4.844***	4.830***	4.874***	4.857***
	(17.62)	(17.59)	(17.66)	(17.79)	(17.53)
Observations	1283	1283	1283	1283	1283
R-squared	0.192	0.194	0.197	0.197	0.209

Note: t-statistics in parentheses. $+ p < .10$, $*p < .05$, $**p < .01$, $***p < .001$
Standard errors are clustered on home cities.
Only escorts who post prices are used in each regression.

Appendix Table 3.4 *Regression of escort wages on escort characteristics and network centrality measures*

Age	-0.0105***	-0.0105***	-0.0104***	-0.0104***	-0.0104***	-0.0105***
	(-7.30)	(-7.29)	(-7.39)	(-7.39)	(-7.37)	(-7.41)
Height	0.0026	0.00267	0.00242	0.0024	0.00252	0.00229
	(1.47)	(1.51)	(1.39)	(1.39)	(1.45)	(1.32)
Weight	-0.00103	-0.0011	-0.00123	-0.0012	-0.00121	-0.00118
	(-0.71)	(-0.76)	(-0.87)	(-0.84)	(-0.85)	(-0.83)
Black	-0.00652	-0.00654	-0.0106	-0.0115	-0.0101	-0.015
	(-0.24)	(-0.24)	(-0.40)	(-0.44)	(-0.38)	(-0.57)
Asian	-0.0535	-0.0525	-0.0799	-0.0766	-0.079	-0.0734
	(-0.88)	(-0.87)	(-1.34)	(-1.28)	(-1.32)	(-1.23)
Hispanic	-0.0213	-0.0176	-0.0322	-0.0316	-0.0303	-0.027
	(-0.76)	(-0.63)	(-1.17)	(-1.15)	(-1.10)	(-0.98)
Multiracial	0.0113	0.0123	0.0103	0.0109	0.00976	0.0104
	(0.36)	(0.39)	(0.33)	(0.35)	(0.31)	(0.34)
Other race	0.139***	0.137***	0.115**	0.115**	0.116**	0.114**
	(3.39)	(3.35)	(2.86)	(2.85)	(2.88)	(2.84)
Athletic body	0.0846**	0.0844**	0.0887**	0.0888**	0.0893**	0.0877**
	(2.64)	(2.64)	(2.84)	(2.84)	(2.85)	(2.80)
Average body	-0.0333	-0.0306	-0.00732	-0.00741	-0.00711	-0.00958
	(-0.82)	(-0.76)	(-0.18)	(-0.19)	(-0.18)	(-0.24)
Large body	-0.231*	-0.251*	-0.228*	-0.228*	-0.229*	-0.225*
	(-2.20)	(-2.39)	(-2.22)	(-2.22)	(-2.23)	(-2.19)

(continued)

Appendix Table 3.4 *(continued)*

	(1)	(2)	(3)	(4)	(5)	(6)
Buff body	0.208***	0.205***	0.211***	0.211***	0.210***	0.212***
	(5.39)	(5.33)	(5.59)	(5.58)	(5.56)	(5.60)
Top	0.02	0.02	0.01	0.01	0.01	0.01
	(0.53)	(0.42)	(0.35)	(0.36)	(0.39)	(0.34)
Bottom	−0.0656	−0.0689	−0.0619	−0.0626	−0.0629	−0.0622
	(−1.49)	(−1.57)	(−1.44)	(−1.46)	(−1.46)	(−1.43)
Versatile	0.0434	0.0448	0.0413	0.0404	0.0404	0.0402
	(1.52)	(1.57)	(1.48)	(1.44)	(1.44)	(1.44)
Massage	−0.129***	−0.131***	−0.148***	−0.148***	−0.148***	−0.148***
	(−5.38)	(−5.47)	(−6.25)	(−6.26)	(−6.24)	(−6.26)
Travel	0.0429	0.0541**	0.0623**	0.0604**	0.0584**	0.0533**
	(1.36)	(2.64)	(3.16)	(3.06)	(2.94)	(2.81)
GCI	0.0319	0.0329	0.0212	0.029	0.0401	0.0136
	(1.22)	(1.26)	(0.82)	(1.13)	(1.57)	(0.52)
HIVrate	0.00572***	0.00566***	0.00154	0.00174	0.00196+	0.00157
	(5.91)	(5.87)	(1.39)	(1.58)	(1.79)	(1.44)
Airline hub	0.0978**	0.0934**	0.039	0.0434	0.0564+	0.0182
	(3.06)	(2.93)	(1.20)	(1.34)	(1.78)	(0.53)
Escort degree	4.82					
	(1.58)					
Escort betweenness		25.51**				
		(3.05)				
Escort eigen centrality		3.551**	3.832***	3.964***	4.565***	
		(3.09)	(3.36)	(3.31)	(4.85)	

(continued)

254

	(1)	(2)	(3)	(4)	(5)	(6)
City degree			0.818**			
			(3.25)			
City betweenness				0.473**		
				(2.93)		
City eigen centrality					0.204*	
					(2.51)	
City diversity						0.0703***
						(3.59)
Constant	4.802***	4.820***	4.922***	4.918***	4.886***	4.864***
	(17.57)	(17.69)	(18.40)	(18.36)	(18.26)	(18.19)
Observations	1283	1283	1283	1283	1283	1279
R-squared	0.194	0.198	0.231	0.23	0.229	0.232

Note: t-statistics in parentheses. + $p < .10$, * $p < .05$, ** $p < .01$, *** $p < .001$.
Standard errors are clustered on home cities.
Only escorts who post prices are used in each regression.

Appendix Table 3.5 *Log wage regressions for traveling escorts only*

Age	−0.00779***	−0.00804***	−0.00777***	−0.00778***	−0.00773***
	(−4.39)	(−4.60)	(−4.41)	(−4.41)	(−4.37)
Height	0.00127	0.00114	0.00133	0.00139	0.00137
	(0.59)	(0.54)	(0.63)	(0.65)	(0.64)
Weight	0.000259	0.000197	0.000275	0.000287	0.000256
	(0.15)	(0.11)	(0.16)	(0.16)	(0.15)
Black	0.00745	0.00234	0.00972	0.00929	0.00954
	(0.24)	(0.08)	(0.31)	(0.30)	(0.30)
Asian	−0.113	−0.117	−0.102	−0.101	−0.103
	(−1.28)	(−1.34)	(−1.16)	(−1.15)	(−1.16)
Hispanic	0.019	0.0223	0.0236	0.0249	0.0225
	(0.56)	(0.67)	(0.70)	(0.73)	(0.66)
Multiracial	0.0121	0.00904	0.008	0.00776	0.00837
	(0.31)	(0.23)	(0.20)	(0.20)	(0.21)
Other race	0.0351	0.0224	0.0313	0.0314	0.0353
	(0.69)	(0.45)	(0.62)	(0.62)	(0.70)
Athletic body	0.0621	0.0577	0.0613	0.06	0.0613
	(1.41)	(1.33)	(1.40)	(1.37)	(1.40)
Average body	−0.0564	−0.0396	−0.0503	−0.0523	−0.0513
	(−1.02)	(−0.73)	(−0.91)	(−0.95)	(−0.93)
Large body	0.0315	0.0222	0.0288	0.0253	0.035
	(0.22)	(0.16)	(0.20)	(0.18)	(0.24)
Buff body	0.183***	0.176***	0.182***	0.181***	0.183***
	(3.53)	(3.45)	(3.54)	(3.52)	(3.55)
Top	−0.0174	−0.0156	−0.0134	−0.0145	−0.0139
	(−0.41)	(−0.37)	(−0.31)	(−0.34)	(−0.33)
Bottom	0.0266	0.0335	0.0285	0.0276	0.0283
	(0.55)	(0.70)	(0.59)	(0.57)	(0.58)
Versatile	0.0173	0.00999	0.0148	0.0145	0.0164
	(0.54)	(0.32)	(0.47)	(0.46)	(0.52)
Massage	−0.0963***	−0.0960***	−0.0989***	−0.0982***	−0.0999***
	(−3.31)	(−3.35)	(−3.42)	(−3.40)	(−3.45)
Travel	0.0202	0.0472	0.0221	0.0243	0.0203
	(0.59)	(1.37)	(0.65)	(0.71)	(0.59)
GCI	0.00405**	0.00469***	0.00483***	0.00489***	0.00470***
	(3.14)	(3.67)	(3.69)	(3.73)	(3.59)
HIV rate	0.0715**	0.0679+	0.0698+	0.0703+	0.0713*
	(1.97)	(1.90)	(1.93)	(1.95)	(1.97)
Airline hub	0.0654+	−0.0148	0.0153	0.0252	0.0461
	(1.72)	(−0.36)	(0.37)	(0.63)	(1.19)
Destination HIV rate	0.0000115	−0.00242	−0.00214	−0.00218	−0.00177
	(0.01)	(−1.58)	(−1.33)	(−1.36)	(−1.11)

(continued)

Appendix Table 3.5 *(continued)*

Destination diversity	0.0839*** (4.51)				
Destination degree		0.889** (3.08)			
Destination betweenness			0.594** (3.11)		
Destination eigen centrality				0.270** (2.68)	
Constant	4.982*** (15.10)	4.959*** (15.26)	5.005*** (15.27)	4.990*** (15.23)	4.980*** (15.17)
Observations	640	640	640	640	640
R-squared	0.154	0.181	0.167	0.168	0.164

Note: t-statistics in parentheses. $+ p < .10$, $*p < .05$, $**p < .01$, $***p < .001$
Standard errors are clustered on home cities.
Only escorts who post prices and travel are used in each regression.

Appendix Table 3.6 *Regression of city escort price dispersion on city network measures*

GCI	−0.0407 (−0.48)	−0.0262 (−0.29)	−0.0345 (−0.39)	−0.0322 (−0.37)	0.00147 (0.02)
HIV rate	−0.00298 (−0.89)	−0.00239 (−0.66)	−0.00269 (−0.75)	−0.00236 (−0.66)	−0.00162 (−0.48)
Airline hub	−0.00513 (−0.09)	0.00383 (0.06)	−0.000919 (−0.02)	0.00093 (0.02)	0.0422 (0.67)
City degree		−0.426 (−0.41)			
City betweenness			−0.156 (−0.22)		
City eigen centrality				−0.203 (−0.51)	
City diversity					−0.07 (−1.56)
Constant	0.473*** (5.38)	0.455*** (4.62)	0.464*** (4.80)	0.458*** (4.94)	0.489*** (5.58)
Observations	74	74	74	74	74
R-squared	0.022	0.024	0.022	0.025	0.055

Note: t-statistics in parentheses. $+ p < .10$, $*p < .05$, $**p < .01$, $***p < .001$
City price dispersion is measured as the interquartile range of prices in the city.

Appendix 4

Empirical Estimates of Escort Valuation

IS THE PREMIUM TO DOMINANCE DRIVEN BY BIOLOGY?

I elaborate here on the biological interpretation for the top premium, which is a potential explanation for the premium tops seen in the market. The biological interpretation says that the premium for tops is driven by the fact that top escorts are expected to ejaculate as part of their services. If this is true, it may not be possible for top escorts to see as many clients in a given period of time as could a bottom escort. The scarcity of sperm, then, could drive the higher prices observed for top escorts. This would be a plausible explanation and would therefore imply that biological, as opposed to social, factors lay behind the premium. I found that, although intuitive and plausible, one must make a number of additional assumptions before such an interpretation can be accepted. I attempted to find evidence consistent with the assumptions of such an interpretation. Unfortunately, the evidence, which I detail below, moved in the opposite direction.

1. First, the "biological interpretation" (BI) requires that clients compensate escorts for the scarcity of their sperm. This implies that escorts' sperm is dear to the clients (otherwise a client would not compensate an escort for it). In some sense, one could argue that bottoms would be more pressured to ejaculate to show their top clients they were having a pleasurable experience. Similarly, bottom clients may be more selfishly concerned with their own pleasure (ejaculation) from a top escort. For the BI to hold, we would need evidence from clients that they desire escort sperm when the escort is a top (and that they require ejaculations of tops more so than bottoms or escorts who engage in oral sex only). I searched client review websites and found a discussion of the necessity of escort ejaculation on the website Daddy's Reviews (http://www.message-forum.net/index.php). In discussion on the forum, clients repeatedly mentioned they had a strong desire for the

escort to ejaculate, and this desire was not expressed as being more for either top or bottom escorts. The forum reveals that nearly all clients felt a satisfactory experience included an escort ejaculating, regardless of sexual position. From the client forum, it seems that tops and bottoms would have the same limits in terms of bodily function. If clients desire that escorts show they are having a satisfying sexual experience (which could be related to a client feeling wanted or desired by an escort), then both top and bottom escorts would be required to ejaculate.

2. Second, key for the BI is the idea that it is easier to serve as a bottom than as a top. I investigated the medical literature and found that bottoming comes with its own costs, which can impede the ability of a bottom to service large numbers of clients in a day. Many client reviews mention escort hygiene as being very important (bad hygiene is a frequent complaint of clients about escorts). Given the hygiene requirements of receptive anal intercourse, bottoms would need significant amounts of preparation time to see multiple clients in any set period of time. As the health literature notes, some of this preparation can be harmful to escorts and can lead to inability to perform. For example, repeatedly giving oneself an enema (anal douching) can lead to sore and painful rectums and anal canals, which can leave escorts unable to participate in receptive anal sex and increase their disease risk. In addition, there is risk of anal tearing and other health problems from repeated and successive anal intercourse, and the hygiene requirements (e.g., repeated anal cleanses) are well known and could certainly limit the ability of bottom male sex workers to service clients. Indeed, I found several instances of client reviews of bottom escorts who could not perform due to anal tearing caused by anal sex with other clients. It is unlikely that top escorts face similar problems that would limit their ability to perform over long periods of time. The following client review provides an example of a bottom escort who was unable to perform due to receptive anal sex several weeks prior (taken from http://www.daddysreviews.com/finder.php? loc=B-13-150-10&who=bryan_wilder_atlanta):

> In the bedroom, because I am normally a top ... knowing that Bryan was not going to be able to bottom for me ... we just spent a lot of time doing oral and mutual masturbation. Although Bryan could not bottom for me (he had some anal tearing from a particular large and rough client several weeks back, and it should have healed nicely now ... guys ... treat Bryan nicely please!) ...

3. Implicit in the BI is an assumption that escorts desire to earn a fixed amount of income – say, a target salary. The question becomes what

the optimal strategy would be for the average escort, given such an earnings target. If there are limitations to being a top, consistent with the BI, and additional clients could be secured if escorts were willing to bottom, it would stand to reason that escorts would advertise as tops, with a discount for bottom activity. This would allow escorts to see more clients and earn more income (reach a higher earnings target). If the premium were due to sperm scarcity, it would seem to imply that top escorts would offer a discount if asked by a client to bottom, because bottoming, in the BI, is less taxing than topping and does not require the compensated activity of ejaculation. Evidence from escort advertisements suggest that top escorts charge higher fees for their bottoming, which is exactly the opposite of what we would expect if the top premium were driven by sperm scarcity or if only top escorts were expected to ejaculate. In the instances I located of top escorts mentioning bottoming in their advertisements (and this is rare, as escorts who both top and bottom would list themselves as versatile), they mention that they either do not do it at all or charge higher rates for bottoming. I think the evidence for a "top as bottom premium" is inconsistent with the idea that biological limitations are driving the top premium observed in the data. Here are a few examples taken from the escort website Rentboy.com:

Only will bottom for 400.00 flat fee. Please don't ask for a discount on it. [Escort's posted rate is $250 to be a top.]

I'm 27 yrs old, 177 lbs, 5'/10" tall, all non-negotiable top only!! No amount of $$ can [expletive for receptive sex] *me! Don't ask!!*

Top guy here. Please let me know if you would like me to bottom. Advance notice required and an extra $150.

While the BI is intriguing and I have carefully considered it, I believe it requires much more information about what clients demand from escorts and whether their expectations with regard to ejaculation differ by sexual behavior. I could not find evidence that sexual fatigue varies by escort sexual position; in particular, I found evidence that clients require ejaculation of all escorts for a satisfactory experience. I also believe that bottoming is quite taxing as well, and it is difficult to argue, a priori, that topping is more taxing than bottoming. Indeed, escorts who are normally tops ask to be notified if a client would like them to bottom, presumably because of the required preparations. I conclude that the BI is inconsistent with the suggestive evidence. Perhaps with better data, particularly as it pertains to client demand for escort ejaculation and whether that demand differs by the sexual role played by the escort, this issue can be fully addressed in future work.

REGRESSION ESTIMATES OF ESCORT VALUATION

Appendix Table 4.1 *Physical characteristics and male escort prices*

I		II		III	
Age and Body Type		Race		Hair Color	
Age	−0.00975***	Black	0.0433	Blond hair	0.000365
	[0.00119]		[0.0658]		[0.0248]
Height	−0.00224	Hispanic	0.045	Brown hair	−0.0186
	[0.00331]		[0.0668]		[0.0167]
Weight	−0.00114***	Multiracial	0.0882	Gray hair	−0.0475
	[0.000394]		[0.0687]		[0.292]
		Other	−0.0337	Other color hair	0.118
			[0.101]		[0.0852]
		White	0.0277	Red/auburn hair	0.0857
			[0.0646]		[0.0719]
Observations	1476		1476		1476
R-squared	0.044		0.004		0.004

IV		V		VI	
Eye Color		Body Build		Body Hair	
Blue eyes	−0.072	Average build	−0.147***	Moderately hairy	−0.163
	[0.0556]		[0.0230]		[0.292]
Brown eyes	−0.0682	A few extra pounds	−0.300***	Shaved	−0.113
	[0.0535]		[0.0869]		[0.290]
Green eyes	−0.05	Muscular build	0.0319*	Smooth	−0.11
	[0.0573]		[0.0173]		[0.290]
Hazel eyes	−0.0679	Thin/lean build	−0.0479*		
	[0.0561]		[0.0288]		
Observations	1476		1476		1476
R-squared	0.002		0.045		0.019

Robust standard errors are listed under coefficients in brackets (***$p < .01$, **$p < .05$, *$p < .1$).
Each category is a separate regression in which the log of escort prices is the dependent variable.
Each regression includes controls for city location and an intercept.
For II: The omitted race category is Asian. For III: The omitted hair color is black.
For IV: The omitted eye color is black.
For V: The omitted body build is athletic/swimmer's build.
For VI: The omitted body hair is hairy.
All tests of statistical significance are two-tailed.
See the Appendix 1 for variable definitions.

Appendix Table 4.2 *Sexual behaviors and male escort prices*

	I	II	III	IV	V
Top	0.0803***	0.0968***	0.0938***	0.0936***	0.0890***
	[0.0202]	[0.0224]	[0.0224]	[0.0224]	[0.0247]
Bottom	−0.0596**	−0.0773**	−0.0788**	−0.0798**	−0.0865**
	[0.0302]	[0.0355]	[0.0355]	[0.0355]	[0.0385]
Versatile	0.00536	0.0142	0.0089	0.0074	0.00806
	[0.0186]	[0.0214]	[0.0215]	[0.0216]	[0.0216]
Versatile top		−0.0881*	−0.0833	−0.0816	−0.0824
		[0.0515]	[0.0515]	[0.0515]	[0.0516]
Versatile bottom		0.0589	0.0654	0.0675	0.0674
		[0.0673]	[0.0672]	[0.0673]	[0.0673]
Safer sex			0.0510***	0.0488**	0.0420*
			[0.0192]	[0.0195]	[0.0227]
No attitude				0.0147	0.015
				[0.0224]	[0.0224]
Safe top					0.0221
					[0.0490]
Safe bottom					0.0352
					[0.0771]
Observations	1476	1476	1476	1476	1476
R-squared	0.015	0.017	0.022	0.022	0.023

Robust standard errors in brackets (***$p < .01$, **$p < .05$, *$p < .1$).
Dependent variable is the log of the escort's price in all regressions.
Each regression includes controls for age, city location, and an intercept.
All tests of statistical significance are two-tailed.
See Appendix 1 for variable definitions.

Appendix Table 4.3 *Race, sexual behavior, and male escort prices*

	I	II	III
		Sexual behavior	
Race	Top	Bottom	Versatile
Black	0.110***	−0.286***	0.036
	[0.0321]	[0.110]	[0.0476]
White	0.0655**	−0.0667*	−0.01
	[0.0297]	[0.0348]	[0.0234]
Asian	0.311	−0.0729	0.00786
	[0.291]	[0.206]	[0.131]
Hispanic	0.0930*	−0.0258	0.0251
	[0.0537]	[0.0882]	[0.0400]
Multirace	0.0645	0.112	−0.00291
	[0.0556]	[0.131]	[0.0591]
Other race	0.0662	−0.332	−0.25
	[0.206]	[0.206]	[0.207]
Observations	1476	1476	1476
R-squared	0.013	0.009	0.002

Standard errors in brackets (***$p < .01$, **$p < .05$, *$p < .1$)
Each column is a separate regression where the log of the price is the dependent variable.
Each entry is the coefficient on the interaction of the row and column. For example, the "Black top" coefficient is the coefficient of the Black*top interaction term in the regression. All regressions include controls for race, city, sexual behaviors, other personal characteristics, and an intercept. All tests of statistical significance are two-tailed.
See Appendix 1 for variable definitions.

Appendix 5

Empirical Estimates of Self-Presentation

Appendix Table 5.1 *Descriptive statistics for self-presentation*

	Mean	SD	Min	Max
Pictures				
Number of pictures	6.136	(2.84)	1	12
Proportion of pictures featuring the penis	0.073	(0.14)	0	1
Proportion of pictures featuring the buttocks	0.147	(0.19)	0	1
Sexual behavior				
Top	0.16		0	1
Bottom	0.06		0	1
Versatile	0.21		0	1
Race				
Asian	0.01		0	1
Black	0.22		0	1
Hispanic	0.14		0	1
Multiracial	0.08		0	1
Other	0.01		0	1
White	0.54		0	1
Race*sexual behavior				
Black top	0.055		0	1
White top	0.069		0	1
Asian top	0.001		0	1
Hispanic top	0.02		0	1
Multirace top	0.015		0	1
Black bottom	0.004		0	1
White bottom	0.047		0	1
Asian bottom	0.002		0	1
Hispanic bottom	0.007		0	1
Multirace bottom	0.003		0	1
Black versatile	0.026		0	1
White versatile	0.124		0	1
Asian versatile	0.003		0	1
Hispanic versatile	0.036		0	1
Multirace versatile	0.015		0	1

N = 1,932

Appendix Table 5.2 *Regression estimates of self-presentation measures by body type*

	Proportion of pictures featuring the penis		Proportion of pictures featuring the buttocks	
Average build	0.035 ***	(0.01)	0.003	(0.01)
A few extra pounds	0.052	(0.04)	−0.047	(0.05)
Muscular build	−0.004	(0.01)	−0.006	(0.01)
Thin/lean build	−0.008	(0.01)	0.035 **	(0.02)
Constant	0.07 ***	(0.01)	0.145 ***	(0.01)

Note: ***$p < .001$, **$p < .01$, *$p < .05$; N = 1,932
Omitted category: Athletic/swimmer's build

Appendix Table 5.3 *Regression estimates of self-presentations by sexual positioning*

	Proportion of pictures featuring the penis		Proportion of pictures featuring the buttocks	
Top	0.032 ***	(0.01)	−0.064 ***	(0.01)
Bottom	−0.028 **	(0.01)	0.19 ***	(0.02)
Versatile	−0.006	(0.01)	0.021 **	(0.01)
Constant	0.071 ***	(0.00)	0.141 ***	(0.01)

Note: ***$p < .001$, **$p < .01$, *$p < .05$; N = 1,932

Appendix Table 5.4 *Regression estimates of self-presentations by race*

	Proportion of pictures featuring the penis		Proportion of pictures featuring the buttocks	
Black	0.059	(0.03)	0.013	(0.04)
White	0.002	(0.03)	0.022	(0.04)
Asian	−0.009	(0.04)	0.106	(0.06)
Hispanic	0.007	(0.03)	0.036	(0.04)
Multirace	0.019	(0.03)	0.011	(0.05)
Constant	0.056	(0.03)	0.124 **	(0.04)

Note: ***$p < .001$, **$p < .01$, *$p < .05$; N = 1,932
Omitted category: Other race

Appendix Table 5.5 *Regression estimates of self-presentations by race and sexual positioning*

	Proportion of pictures featuring the penis		Proportion of pictures featuring the buttocks	
Top (penetrative partner)				
Black top	0.043 ***	(0.02)	−0.085 ***	(0.02)
White top	0.043 ***	(0.01)	−0.047 ***	(0.02)
Asian top	−0.071	(0.14)	−0.141	(0.18)
Hispanic top	−0.021	(0.02)	−0.09 ***	(0.03)
Multirace top	0.02	(0.03)	−0.043	(0.03)
Bottom (receiving partner)				
Black bottom	−0.036	(0.05)	0.47 ***	(0.06)
White bottom	−0.025	(0.02)	0.149 ***	(0.02)
Asian bottom	0.041	(0.09)	0.222 **	(0.11)
Hispanic bottom	−0.032	(0.04)	0.297 ***	(0.05)
Multirace bottom	−0.044	(0.06)	0.116	(0.07)
Versatile (receiving and penetrative partner)				
Black versatile	0.012	(0.02)	0.044 *	(0.03)
White versatile	−0.012	(0.01)	0.017	(0.01)
Asian versatile	−0.051	(0.07)	−0.04	(0.08)
Hispanic versatile	0.015	(0.02)	0.033	(0.02)
Multirace versatile	−0.037	(0.03)	−0.012	(0.03)
Constant	0.071 ***	(0.00)	0.141 ***	(0.01)

Note: ***$p < .001$, **$p < .01$, *$p < .05$; N = 1,932

Appendix Table 5.6 *Selection regressions by body type*

	Number of pictures in advertisement		Proportion of pictures featuring the face	
Average build	−1.033 ***	(0.20)	0.364 ***	(0.01)
A few extra pounds	−1.318	(0.76)	0.086 *	(0.04)
Muscular build	0.243	(0.15)	−0.034 ***	(0.01)
Thin/lean build	−0.454	(0.24)	0.033 **	(0.01)
Constant	6.247 ***	(0.09)	0.072 ***	(0.01)

Note: ***$p < .001$, **$p < .01$, *$p < .05$; N = 1,932
Omitted category: Athletic/swimmer's build

Appendix Table 5.7 *Selection regressions by sexual positioning*

	Number of pictures in advertisement		Proportion of pictures featuring the face	
Top	0.058	(0.18)	−0.012	(0.01)
Bottom	−0.507	(0.27)	−0.005	(0.01)
Versatile	0.534 ***	(0.16)	−0.006	(0.01)
Constant	6.048 ***	(0.08)	0.074 ***	(0.00)

Note: ***p < .001, **p < .01, *p < .05; N = 1,932

Appendix Table 5.8 *Selection regressions by race*

	Number of pictures in advertisement		Proportion of pictures featuring the face	
Black	−0.515	(0.65)	0.046	(0.03)
White	−0.175	(0.66)	0.05	(0.03)
Asian	0.023	(0.84)	0.02	(0.05)
Hispanic	−0.135	(0.66)	0.051	(0.04)
Multirace	−0.487	(0.67)	0.032	(0.04)
Constant	6.4 ***	(0.63)	0.023	(0.03)

Note: ***p < .001, **p < .01, *p < .05; N = 1,932
Omitted category: Other race

Appendix 6

A Model of Sex Worker and Client Negotiation

I consider the negotiations that sex workers and clients engage in with the bargaining structure offered by Gertler, Shah, and Bertozzi (2005). Let V be the value (willingness to pay) of a particular sexual contact to a client with a specific sex worker. Let B be the value (willingness to pay) to engage in a specific type of sexual conduct. For example, if a client prefers to have unprotected sex, $B > 0$, while if a client prefers to have sex with a condom, $B < 0$. For convenience, let P be the price of the transaction. The client's payoff, then, is $V - B - P$.

For the sex worker, consider W, which is their next best alternative (another customer, or the participation constraint), and γ, which is the disutility from having a specific type of sex with a particular client (exposing themselves to disease, etc.). If the sex worker would prefer to have sex with the client, $\gamma < 0$, while if they would not, $\gamma > 0$. The sex worker's payoff is therefore $P - W - \gamma$.

Sex workers and clients may have different amounts of bargaining power in any specific transaction. Sex workers may be able to use certain features such as beauty, sexual expertise, reputation, or other features to improve their bargaining position. One important feature of this approach is that it allows one to conceptualize erotic capital into the negotiation model. An escort with a greater amount of erotic capital is likely to have more bargaining power in the negotiation with a client than would an escort with less erotic capital. Let α be the client's power in the transaction and $1 - \alpha$ be the sex worker's power in the transaction, such that α is decreasing in the erotic capital of the escort (note that this implies $1 - \alpha$ increases with erotic capital). Within this framework the equilibrium price will solve

$$max_P(V - B - P)^\alpha (P - W - \gamma)^{1-\alpha}.$$

Any transaction agreed to by the client and the sex worker must hold with $P \in [W + \gamma, V - B]$. Using this, one can map out sex worker and client payoff functions:

$$P^{Client} = (1 - \alpha)(V - B)$$
$$P^{Escort} = \alpha(W + \gamma).$$

It is important to note that this model allows for clients and sex workers to place a greater (or lower) value on particular types of sex. For example, I do not assume that sex workers prefer to have condomed sex and clients prefer to have condomless sex. For concreteness, consider the case where a condom is used in a given transaction. If a condom is used, then it holds that either $\beta < \gamma$ or $-\gamma > \beta$. That is, either the client's willingness to pay *not* to use a condom is less than the minimum compensation offered to an escort to take the increased risk of disease transmission ($\beta < \gamma$), or the escort's willingness to pay not to use a condom (γ is negative) is greater than the client's willingness to pay ($-\gamma > \beta$).

If a condom is not used in a transaction, it must hold that either $\beta > \gamma$ or $\gamma < -\beta$. That is, either the client's willingness to pay to use a condom (β is negative) is larger than the compensation needed to induce the sex worker to take the increase risk of disease transmission ($\gamma < -\beta$), or the client is willing to pay more for not using a condom than the sex worker's minimum compensation to take the increased risk of STI infection ($\beta > \gamma$).

Since the compensating differential requires that the escort be compensated for increased risk of STI infection, it would not hold that $\gamma < 0$, since the sex worker would not have to be compensated for the increased risk of unprotected sexual activity, and therefore $\beta > 0$ or $\gamma > 0$. If $\beta < 0$, then the client uses the sex worker market to ensure that he can have the type of sex he prefers. (This precludes the possibility that $\gamma < 0$, since if a condom is used in a transaction, the client's willingness to pay to not use a condom is positive.) A key question is the average value of β for clients and γ for sex workers with respect to specific sexual behaviors such as condom usage. For example, if sex workers gain utility from not using condoms in their commercial sex transactions (which is the same as condoms yielding disutility), then it may be difficult to get sex workers to change their sexual risk behavior. Knowledge of the demand side of the market, however, could be used to encourage condom usage even if sex workers were not inclined to, if the clients' valuation of sexual behaviors were known. For example, if clients actually prefer to have safer sex with escorts and are willing to compensate sex workers for condom usage, then this could be used to encourage male sex workers to practice safer sex for the monetary gain involved.

Appendix Table 6.1 *Physical predictors of advertised safer sex*

	I	II	III	IV
Age	−0.00303**	−0.00357**	−0.00351**	−0.00339**
	[0.00133]	[0.00148]	[0.00147]	[0.00148]
Height		−0.00271		
		[0.00407]		
Weight		0.000437		
		[0.000477]		
BMI			0.00266	−0.02189
			[0.00338]	[0.02802]
BMI^2				0.00049
				[0.00055]
Observations	1932	1932	1932	1932

Robust standard errors are listed under coefficients in brackets (***$p < .01$, **$p < .05$, *$p < .1$).
Each column reports results of a probit regression where the dependent variable is "Is the Escort Safe?" (Mean of dependent variable = 0.19, Standard Error of dependent variable = 0.39).
The coefficients reported are the marginal effects of the probit regressions. For continuous variables (such as "Age"), the effect is evaluated at the mean.
All tests of statistical significance are two-tailed.
See Appendix 1 for variable definitions.

Appendix Table 6.2 *Sexual behavior predictors of advertised safer sex*

	I	II	III
Top	0.0657**	0.0941***	0.0894***
	[0.0263]	[0.0307]	[0.0305]
Bottom	0.0234	0.0516	0.0351
	[0.0382]	[0.0502]	[0.0484]
Versatile	0.104***	0.134***	0.109***
	[0.0243]	[0.0289]	[0.0283]
Versatile top		−0.0943**	−0.0807**
		[0.0370]	[0.0393]
Versatile bottom		−0.0689	−0.0434
		[0.0561]	[0.0626]
No attitude			0.208***
			[0.0316]
Observations	1932	1932	1932

Robust standard errors are listed under coefficients in brackets (***$p <.01$, **$p <.05$, *$p <.1$).
Each column reports results of a probit regression where the dependent variable is "Is the Escort Safe?" (Mean of dependent variable = 0.19, Standard Error of dependent variable = 0.39).
The coefficients reported are the marginal effects of the probit regressions. For dichotomous variables such as "Top"), the effects calculate the change in probability from moving from 0 to 1.
All tests of statistical significance are two-tailed.
See Appendix 1 for variable definitions.

Appendix Table 6.3 *Race and sexual behavior predictors of advertised safer sex*

	Race only I	Race And		
		"Top" II	"Bottom" III	"Versatile" IV
Black	−0.043	−0.0109	0.0626	0.116*
	[0.034]	[0.039]	[0.15]	[0.066]
Hispanic	0.0233	0.111	0.12	0.251***
	[0.040]	[0.075]	[0.13]	[0.060]
Asian	0.151*	–	0.479*	0.239
	[0.09]	–	[0.27]	[0.22]
Multirace	−0.042	0.167*	−0.0211	0.00358
	[0.083]	[0.090]	[0.15]	[0.075]
White	0.00202	0.0740*	0.00126	0.0663**
	[0.033]	[0.039]	[0.042]	[0.030]
Observations	1932	1931	1932	1932

Robust standard errors are listed under coefficients in brackets (***p <.01, **p <.05, *p <.1).

Each column reports results of a probit regression where the dependent variable is: Is the Escort Safe? (Mean of dependent variable = 0.19, Standard Error of dependent variable = 0.39).

"Other race" is the omitted racial category in all regressions.

"Asian top" is excluded from the regression in Column II, due to lack of variation.

The coefficients reported are the marginal effects of the probit regressions. For dichotomous variables such as "Race") the effects calculate the change in probability from moving from 0 to 1.

Each entry in Columns II–IV is the coefficent on the interaction of the row and column.

For example, the "Black top" coefficient is the coefficient of the Black*top interaction.

Asians are excluded from the regression in Column II because "Asian top" perfectly predicts the dependent variable.

All tests of statistical significance are two-tailed.

See Appendix 1 for variable definitions.

Appendix Table 6.4 *Advertising and reputation-based predictors of advertised safer sex*

	I	II	III	IV
Number of survey reviews	0.00207	−0.0180	−0.0168	−0.0143
	[0.00127]	[0.0148]	[0.0149]	[0.0149]
Number of pictures	0.00538*	0.00514	0.00209	0.00114
	[0.00322]	[0.00324]	[0.00323]	[0.00328]
Number of text reviews		−0.0897*	−0.102**	−0.104**
		[0.0484]	[0.0485]	[0.0496]
Number of 4-star survey reviews		0.0205	0.0185	0.0151
		[0.0151]	[0.0152]	[0.0153]
Positive text reviews		0.0965*	0.112**	0.108**
		[0.0503]	[0.0506]	[0.0535]
No attitude			0.221***	0.220***
			[0.0322]	[0.0322]
Fraction 4-star				0.0330
				[0.0212]
Fraction positive text				0.0146
				[0.0371]
Observations	1932	1932	1932	1932

Robust standard errors are listed under coefficients in brackets (***p <.01, **p <.05, *p <.1).
Each column reports results of a probit regression where the dependent variable is "Is the Escort Safe?" (Mean of dependent variable = 0.19, Standard Error of dependent variable = 0.39.)
The coefficients reported are the marginal effects of the probit regressions. For continuous variables (such as "Text reviews"), the effect is evaluated at the mean. For dichotomous variables (such as "No attitude"), the effects calculate the change in probability from moving from 0 to 1. All tests of statistical significance are two-tailed.
See Appendix 1 for variable definitions.

Appendix Table 6.5 *Escort and client payoff functions, sexual behaviors*

	I		II		III		IV	
	Escort	Client	Escort	Client	Escort	Client	Escort	Client
Topping	34.78*	38.64*	33.47*	40.79**	39.26**	42.49**	38.54**	37.03*
	[17.9]	[19.9]	[18.3]	[20.6]	[18.3]	[20.6]	[18.3]	[20.8]
Versatile	15.9	34.15*	14.02	37.17*	26.12	41.67**	25.8	38.59*
	[17.8]	[19.4]	[18.6]	[20.8]	[18.8]	[20.9]	[18.8]	[21.0]
Bottom	-2.53	12.89	-4.308	15.54	7.312	20.56	7.018	17.33
	[27.9]	[27.6]	[28.4]	[28.3]	[28.5]	[28.5]	[28.5]	[28.5]
Kissing			5.97	-7.63	18.04	-0.0172	18.83	3.033
			[16.8]	[18.6]	[17.1]	[19.3]	[17.1]	[19.3]
Masturbation, mutual					-51.97***	-28.48	-49.28***	-13.84
					[13.1]	[18.1]	[13.8]	[21.7]
Masturbation, gives							7.671	-3.381
							[34.5]	[35.2]
Masturbation, receives							20.54	74.77**
							[29.7]	[35.1]
Observations	4865	4871	4865	4871	4865	4871	4865	4871
R-squared	0.47	0.93	0.47	0.93	0.47	0.93	0.47	0.93

Notes: Standard errors are clustered at the state-year level and reported in brackets (***p <.01, **p < .05, *p <.1).
Each column is a regression that uses the standardized hourly rate as the dependent variable.
Column headings signify whether escort- or client-fixed effects were used in the specification.
Sexual behaviors are defined from the perspective of the escort.

Appendix Table 6.6 *Escort and client payoff functions, condom usage*

	I		II		III		IV	
	Escort	Client	Escort	Client	Escort	Client	Escort	Client
Topping	34.82*	37.33*	33.48*	43.15**	38.56**	36.23*	37.10*	41.44*
	[17.9]	[19.9]	[18.6]	[20.4]	[18.4]	[20.7]	[19.0]	[21.2]
Versatile	15.93	33.77*	16.51	43.44**	25.81	38.84*	26.14	48.32**
	[17.8]	[19.4]	[18.4]	[19.9]	[18.8]	[20.9]	[19.3]	[21.4]
Bottom	-2.575	12.62	0.0355	9.506	6.996	17.62	9.199	14.6
	[27.9]	[27.5]	[29.3]	[29.6]	[28.5]	[28.5]	[29.8]	[30.4]
No Condom	-1.684	-29.58**			-0.905	-29.37**		
	[13.3]	[14.5]			[13.3]	[14.5]		
No-condom * topping			5.986	-27.78			6.608	-24.79
			[22.6]	[24.4]			[22.6]	[24.4]
No-condom * bottom			-14.02	18.47			-11.87	17.21
			[46.9]	[53.8]			[46.9]	[53.8]
No-condom * versatile			-2.81	-48.20**			-1.559	-48.21**
			[21.1]	[22.7]			[21.1]	[22.7]
Kissing					18.81	1.455	18.75	2.166
					[17.1]	[19.3]	[17.1]	[19.3]
Masturbation, mutual					-49.28***	-13.76	-49.16***	-14.68
					[13.8]	[21.6]	[13.8]	[21.6]

(continued)

Masturbation, gives					7.629	−2.626	7.885	−4.135
					[34.5]	[35.1]	[34.6]	[35.2]
Masturbation, receives					20.48	73.98**	20.94	72.05**
					[29.7]	[35.0]	[29.8]	[35.1]
Observations	4865	4871	4865	4871	4865	4871	4865	4871
R-squared	0.47	0.93	0.47	0.93	0.47	0.93	0.47	0.93

Notes: Standard errors are clustered at the state-year level and reported in brackets (***p < .01, **p < .05, *p < .1).
Each column is a regression that uses the standardized hourly rate as the dependent variable.
Column headings signify whether escort- or client-fixed effects were used in the specification.
Sexual behaviors are defined from the perspective of the escort.

Appendix Table 6.7 *Client payoff functions with full escort characteristics*

	I	II	III	IV	V	VI
White	−19.93	−20.28	−23.83	−22.98	−23.27	−23.31
	[31.5]	[31.6]	[31.6]	[31.5]	[31.5]	[31.5]
Black	−15.97	−16.91	−18.37	−25.85	−26.13	−25.63
	[54.0]	[54.1]	[54.0]	[53.9]	[54.0]	[54.0]
Latino	28.74	27.95	32.6	30.99	31.51	28.91
	[38.0]	[38.1]	[38.1]	[37.9]	[38.0]	[38.0]
Age 20s	26.96	29.9	39.93	28.02	29.78	26.1
	[71.8]	[72.0]	[72.0]	[71.9]	[72.0]	[72.0]
Age 30s	54.61	55.41	63.51	50.7	53.12	47.71
	[72.1]	[72.2]	[72.2]	[72.0]	[72.2]	[72.3]
Age 40s	3.957	5.204	16.05	1.427	4.334	0.84
	[75.6]	[75.8]	[75.8]	[75.7]	[75.9]	[76.0]
BMI	−4.151	−4.808	−5.326	−1.765	−1.384	−1.295
	[16.8]	[16.9]	[16.9]	[16.9]	[16.9]	[17.0]
(BMI)^2	0.0386	0.0552	0.0676	−0.0198	−0.0284	−0.0375
	[0.34]	[0.34]	[0.34]	[0.35]	[0.35]	[0.35]
Endowment (in.)	17.75**	16.24**	15.68*	16.94**	16.99**	17.37**
	[7.91]	[8.24]	[8.23]	[8.22]	[8.23]	[8.24]
Circumcized	7.529	7.915	8.39	9.934	9.87	8.99
	[20.0]	[20.1]	[20.0]	[20.0]	[20.0]	[20.0]
Topping		19.56	19.67	14.88	17.29	22.49
		[26.3]	[26.2]	[26.3]	[26.7]	[27.3]
Versatile		16.18	17.6	21.48	25.11	36.61
		[24.8]	[24.8]	[25.0]	[25.9]	[26.7]
Bottom		3.464	4.428	8.951	11.96	6.048
		[34.5]	[34.4]	[34.7]	[35.2]	[38.3]
No condom			−37.11**	−36.40**	−37.11**	
			[17.2]	[17.1]	[17.2]	
Masturbation, mutual				−31.77	−29.94	−32.2
				[29.2]	[29.4]	[29.4]
Masturbation, receives				79.61*	77.53*	74.83*
				[42.7]	[42.9]	[43.0]
Masturbation, gives				−35.64	−36.45	−39.16
				[49.3]	[49.4]	[49.4]
Kissing					−12.57	−11.52
					[24.1]	[24.1]
No-condom * topping						−24.04
						[28.9]
No-condom * bottom						19.74
						[62.6]

(continued)

Appendix Table 6.7 *(continued)*

	I	II	III	IV	V	VI
No-condom * versatile						−59.44** [25.8]
Observations	3735	3735	3735	3735	3735	3735
R-squared	0.93	0.94	0.94	0.94	0.94	0.94

Notes: Standard errors are clustered at the state-year level and reported in brackets (***$p < .01$, **$p < .05$, *$p < .1$).

Each column is a regression that uses the standardized hourly rate as the dependent variable. Each regression includes client-fixed effects.

Sexual behaviors are defined from the perspective of the escort.

Appendix Table 6.8 *Advertised safer sex and escort prices*

	I	II	III
Safer sex	0.0545*** [0.0192]		
Black safe		0.0865** [0.0425]	
White safe		0.0539** [0.0249]	
Asian safe		−0.134 [0.110]	
Hispanic safe		0.0433 [0.0438]	
Multirace safe		0.0917 [0.0589]	
Other race safe		−0.240 [0.206]	
Safe top			0.124*** [0.0397]
Safe bottom			−0.00636 [0.0677]
Safe versatile			0.0175 [0.0344]
Constant	5.327*** [0.00844]	5.327*** [0.00844]	5.332*** [0.00793]
N	1476	1476	1476
R-sqaured	0.005	0.009	0.007

Robust standard errors are listed under coefficients in brackets (***$p < .01$, **$p < .05$, *$p < .1$).

Each column is a separate regression in which the log of escort prices is the dependent variable. All tests of statistical significance are two-tailed.

See the Appendix 1 for variable definitions.

Notes

INTRODUCTION

1. http://www.manhattandigest.com/2015/03/08/the-2015-hookies-march-20th-who -should-win-and-why/, accessed October 25, 2015.
2. https://www.youtube.com/watch?v=gBkpU33QEMw, accessed October 26, 2015.
3. http://www.theatlantic.com/politics/archive/2015/08/a-web-site-for-gay-escorts-gets -busted-by-homeland-security/402343/, http://www.nbcnews.com/tech/tech-news /rentboy-com-ceo-six-employees-arrested-prostitution-charges-n415796, http://www .wsj.com/articles/gay-activists-protest-rentboy-raid-1441327676, accessed October 25, 2015.
4. http://www.nextmagazine.com/content/logos-prince-charming-found-rentboy, accessed August 27, 2016. http://boston.edgemedianetwork.com/entertainment/tele vision///203029/, accessed August 27, 2016.
5. Dennis (2008). See Minichiello and Scott (2014) for a collection that shows the broad sweep and interdisciplinary nature of contemporary scholarship on male sex work.
6. Steele and Kennedy (2006); Pompeo (2009).
7. West (1993); Itiel (1998); Aggleton (1999); Kaye (2003); Friedman (2003); Halkitis et al. (2004); Parsons, Koken, and Bimbi (2007); Minichiello, Scott, and Callander (2013).
8. There are few works in the economics literature on male sex work. Theoretical approaches which focus on female sex workers have been offered by Edlund and Korn (2002) and Giusta, Tommaso, and Strom (2008), and some theoretical predictions for male sex workers have been tested empirically as in Arunachalam and Shah (2008), Logan (2010), and Edlund, Engelberg, and Parsons (2009). The literature on male sex work in the historical, sociological, and public health literatures is many times larger and includes Boyer (1989), Dorias (2005), Ginsberg (1967), Hoffman (1972), Kaye (2003), Luckenbill (1986), McNamara (1994), Pettiway (1996), and Salamon (1989). The use of the term "gay" to describe participants in the market is controversial. Some scholars avoid the use of the term "gay" to describe this market since many participants do not self-identify as gay men. Others use the terms since the sexual behaviors are inherently homosexual. As this book seeks to link the

cultural cues from self-identified gay men to the social function of the male sex work market, the terms are use somewhat interchangeably. See Scott (2003) for more on the semiotics of male prostitution.

1 MALE SEX WORK: ANTIQUITY TO ONLINE

1. Dover (1989).
2. Dover (1989).
3. Martin (1996) and Friedman (2014).
4. Duncan-Jones (1982).
5. Boswell (2005).
6. Boswell (2005) and Friedman (2014).
7. Evans (1979).
8. Boswell (2005).
9. Friedman (2014).
10. Schalow (1989).
11. Boswell (2005).
12. Boswell (2005).
13. Friedman (2014) also notes that this term implied that the male sex worker was sexually submissive.
14. Weeks (1989b).
15. Katz (1976, 1983).
16. Katz (1976, 1983).
17. Chauncey (1994).
18. Friedman (2003).
19. Sadownick (1996).
20. Sadownick (1996).
21. Delany (1999) and Friedman (2003).
22. Even in the earlier era of newspapers, escorts were distinct from erotic massage therapists, who offered only masturbation services to clients. Escorts were listed under their own section in most gay newspapers and their services were noted to include a broader range of sexual services.
23. Tyler (2014).
24. Edlund and Korn (2002).
25. Moffatt and Peters (2004).
26. While nudity is allowed, escorts may not post pictures that display sex acts and may not display pictures that include persons other than the escort. Uploaded pictures are placed in an online holding tank until cleared by the website's management. Every advertisement must be accompanied by at least one picture.
27. The questions are: Did he show up? Did he match his description? Did he provide desired services? Would you recommend him? How hot was he?
28. Approximately 17% of escorts with posted prices have a spot price and 12.6% of escorts for the entire sample have a spot price. Note that 76.4% of escorts have a posted price and 79.5% of escorts have some price measure (either spot, posted, or both).
29. Steele and Kennedy (2006), Pompeo (2009).

30. As the ages in advertisements are reported ages, they may be skewed younger than the actual ages of escorts. In either case, male sex workers are certainly not the "youths" described elsewhere.
31. "Versatile" escorts many times denote themselves as "versatile tops" or "versatile bottoms," terms which denote a preference for one activity, but a willingness to participate in the other. We code both "versatile tops" and "versatile bottoms" as "versatile." See the data appendix for further details.
32. Parsons et al. (2013) find that among young men, 82 percent used condoms with their most recent sexual partner.

2 FACE VALUE: HOW MALE SEX WORKERS OVERCOME THE PROBLEM OF ASYMMETRIC INFORMATION

1. Dynamically, sellers of high-quality vehicles will leave the market, and only poor-quality cars will remain. This leads to lower and lower average car quality in the market, and in the end the market entirely disappears.
2. Akerlof (1970); Spence (1973).
3. Schelling (1960).
4. Hart (1995); Tirole (1999); Greif (1993).
5. Lewis (2009).
6. Brown and Goolsbee (2002); Jensen (2007); Lewis (2009); Goyal (2008); Bajari and Hortacsu (2004); Bakos (2001); Cunningham and Kendall (2011).
7. Steele and Kennedy (2006); Pompeo (2009).
8. Murphy and Venkatesh (2006); Lambert (2007); Friedman (2003); Parsons, Koken, and Bimbi (2007); Halkitis et al. (2004).
9. Critical competitive market assumptions include these: (1) the market contains a significant number of producers, such that no individual producer has market power (all firms are price takers); (2) the firms sell a homogeneous product; (3) free entry and exit is available to firms; (4) the market is subject to no government regulation, rationing, or price floors or ceilings; and (5) market participants behave rationally, where consumers seek to maximize utility and firms to maximize profit.
10. Cameron, Collins, and Thew (1999).
11. Friedman (2003).
12. From Rentboy.com "First Time Hiring an Escort?" Accessed April 28, 2008.
13. This roundtable interview with escorts was accessed at http://www.rentboy .com on April 28, 2008.
14. West (1993); Gertler, Shah, and Bertozzi (2005).
15. Itiel (1998); Hart (1998).
16. As a linguistic (perhaps semiotic) sign of the risk borne by the client, male escorts are also known as "hustlers," a term also used for drug dealers, hoodlums, and thieves (see Scott (2003), Sadownick (1996), Itiel (1998), Friedman (2003), and Dorias (2005)).
17. Steele and Kennedy (2006).
18. Itiel (1998); Friedman (2003).
19. Unless otherwise noted, all further quotes from forums come from the online forum hosted by http://www.daddysreviews.com.

20. Spence (2002); Lewis (2009).
21. Jovanovic (1982).
22. The most popular client-based site has been in existence since the early 1990s.
23. Not all exchanges are negative. Indeed, many clients give glowing recommendations to escorts.
24. Laband (1986); Milgrom and Roberts (1986); Pope and Sydnor (2008); Duarte, Siegel, and Young (2009).
25. Cho and Kreps (1987).
26. One might expect, however, that in any market with some form of communication, that information would be of some value. I noted earlier that face pictures could be interpreted by clients as a commitment device, a type of disclosure, but this would imply that the posting of face pictures determines the commitment, and our institutional analysis revealed that escorts signal against type in both directions. Testing for signaling behavior is also more robust – it is the weaker condition, since signaling is inherently inefficient.
27. Bajari and Benkard (2005) show that the interpretation is still valid even if there is imperfect competition or a small number of products, and prove that even with unobserved product characteristics the price function is identified.
28. I use the hourly outcall price as the dependent variable. Results are unchanged when using the incall price (see the Appendix results). Individual characteristics include race, weight, height, age, and sexual behaviors advertised. See the data Appendix for complete variable definitions. I control for the escort's location, not only because price may vary with geography, but also because specific locations may have more or fewer competitors, as noted in the chapter on geographic mobility. I also use state fixed effects in the regressions and cluster the errors at the state level. Results were similar (but standard errors smaller) when I included city-specific effects and/or clustered the standard errors at the city level.
29. The full set of results on which the figures are based are contained in the Appendix.
30. Lewis (2009) describes the lengths taken by eBay to eliminate fraud in their used car sales, including prosecution.
31. In the specifications, the log of the number of text reviews is used to give an elasticity interpretation to the results. Since the number of escorts with text reviews is quite small (see Table 2.1, the average escort has 0.3 reviews), the effect on prices is actually quite small, but still statistically significant.
32. Since the specification is semi logarithmic, the percentage change is approximated by $\exp(\gamma)-1$ (Halvorsen and Palmquist 1980).
33. Specifications that used the fraction of reviews that were negative were negatively related to escort prices, but were not statistically significant.
34. See Appendix Table 2.3.
35. Note that the omitted category is non-face, non-nude pictures. This omitted category is not related to escort prices. See the Appendix for specifications that include all three picture types.
36. The results for a third-degree polynomial specification in the Appendix.
37. The results of the polynomial specification for all picture types is given in Appendix Table 2.7.
38. See Daniel Hamermesh's website for a summary of findings from a number of studies.

39. It is also important to note that not all high-quality escorts will use the signal. As with any information displayed on the Internet, face pictures would be a permanent sign of an escort's involvement in male sex work.
40. Friedman (2003); Sadownick (1996); Wright (2008).
41. There is substantial baseline variation in escort beauty, even among those who show their faces.
42. The baseline specification with escort beauty that does not include face pictures shows a marginally significant beauty coefficient of 0.0073 (.004).
43. Itiel (1998); Cameron, Collins, and Thew (1999); Friedman (2003).
44. I also estimate a regression where I control for the presence of face pictures with a dichotomous indicator (whether there were face pictures or not) and also estimate the value of marginal pictures. This is similar to the marginal estimates presented in Figure 2.5. In this specification the premium to posting face pictures (the coefficient on the dichotomous indicator) is 15.3 percent. This implies that the beauty calculation described earlier (4.5 percent) explains less than 30 percent of the face picture premium, *even when excluding the marginal value of face pictures from the face picture premium.*
45. In the regressions, I control for whether the escort allows himself to be reviewed.
46. For examples of the narrative evidence that led us to consider the Las Vegas market, see the Appendix. I conjecture that the disproportionate number of tourists in the Las Vegas market leads escorts to place little value in their reputations, or they may feel uniquely prone to poor reviews due to cultural misunderstandings with clients.
47. The coefficient on face pictures among the men who allow reviews in Las Vegas is −0.0037 (.40).

3 MARKET MOVERS: TRAVEL, CITIES, AND THE NETWORK OF MALE SEX WORK

1. This chapter is a revised version of Hsieh and Logan (2014).
2. There are websites that allow sex workers to note that they are "available now" for immediate appointments, but a preliminary look at the use of this feature shows that the number listing themselves as being immediately available is quite small. Indeed, sex workers commonly note that they prefer text and phone calls for appointments to be scheduled.
3. Harcourt and Donovan (2005); Weitzer (2009).
4. Cunningham and Kendall (2009).
5. See Harcourt and Donovan (2005) and Weitzer (2009) for reviews.
6. Aggleton (1999); Padilla (2007).
7. Clients may also be key for STI transmission dynamics. See Hsieh, Kovarik, and Logan (2014).
8. Previous research has shown, through qualitative techniques, the ways in which male sex workers inform and influence their clients' sexual practices: Bimbi and Parsons (2005); Parsons et al. (2007); Estcourt et al. (2000); Minichiello et al. (2014).
9. De Graaf et al. (1994); Marlowe (1997); Varghese et al. (2002).
10. Varghese et al. (2002).
11. See Davis (2006), Houde (2012), and Chisholm and Norman (2012) for examples of spatial competition analysis.

12. Humphries (1970).
13. MacNamara (1994).
14. Frankel (2007); MacDonald (2007).
15. Berg and Lien (2002); Carpenter (2004); Jepsen and Jepsen (2002); Carpenter and Gates (2008); Hewitt (1995); Black, Sanders, and Taylor (2007).
16. Black, Gates, Sanders, and Taylor (2000, 2002); Berg and Lien (2006); Cameron et al. (2009).
17. Black, Gates, Sanders, and Taylor (2000, 2002); Black, Sanders, and Taylor (2007).
18. Sadownick (1996); Koken, Bimbi, and Parsons (2009).
19. Black, Sanders, and Taylor (2007); Black, Gates, Sanders, and Taylor (2000, 2002); Luckenbill (1986); MacNamara (1994); Pleak and Meyer-Bahlburg (1990); Timpson et al. (2007).
20. Sadownick (1996); Koken, Bimbi, and Parsons (2009); Koken et al. (2005).
21. Black, Sanders, and Taylor (2007).
22. Analysis using the 2010 Census did not change the results. Annual estimates using the American Community Survey were less reliable as the smaller sample sizes make it difficult to estimate the Gay Concentration Index (GCI) with any reasonable precision.
23. Table 3.1 is a replication from Logan (2010), which estimated the GCI from 1990 Census data as given in Black, Sanders, and Taylor (2007). The data used here give similar results when using the 2010 Census data to construct the GCI.
24. Pompeo (2009).
25. Sjaasted (1962); Harris and Todaro (1970); Schwartz (1976); Greenwood (1997). Formally, consider the value of temporary migration, which would be the discounted cumulative difference in expected utility between the new and current location, less the cost of traveling to the new city.

$$V(0) = \int_0^T [E[W_a(t)] - W_h(t)]e^{-rt}dt - C(0)$$

Where W_a is the wage in the new (away) location and W_h is the wage in the present (home) location, r is the discount rate, t is time, and C is the cost of travel. When $V > 0$, there would be economic gains to migration.
26. In the model this would imply that $W_a > W_h$.
27. What is not known here is whether the higher prices cause traveling, since they could see lower demand in their home location.
28. These networks are frequently studied in the context of interlocking directorates in organization studies (Mintz and Schwartz, 1985; Robins and Alexander, 2004). An important distinction between two- and one-mode networks is that in the former, a member of a particular node set (e.g., escorts) can only be indirectly tied to a member of its own node set through a shared tie to the other node set (e.g., cities).
29. Bonacich (1991); Borgatti and Everett (1997); Faust (1997).
30. I do not have information of GCI and HIV for all cities in the data. In fact, cities with missing GCI or HIV rate usually are smaller cities and have few escorts traveling from or traveling to. Therefore, I drop observations in cities with missing GCI or HIV rates in the empirical specifications. The number of cities drops from 131 to 82 and the number of escorts drops from 1,926 to 1,797.

31. In two-mode network studies, similar high correlations among event centralities can be seen in Faust (1997) and Valente et al. (2008).
32. To account for changes in the gay population over time, the GCI in Table 3.6 was calculated from 2010 Census data.
33. In each regression I use a linear probability model for ease of interpretation of the coefficients, but results with probit models were similar.
34. Those not noting a sexual position are the reference group.
35. This is confirmed in an unreported regression.
36. The full results are reported in the Appendix.
37. Arunachalam and Shah (2013).
38. Unlike the regression models for extensive and intensive measures of travel, I do not reject the null hypothesis of equal error variance across cities in wage regressions. Following Lee (2007), the *t* statistics are not clustered.
39. The full results are reported in the Appendix.

4 ILLICIT INTERSECTIONS: THE VALUE OF SEX WORKER SERVICES

1. Pruitt (2005); Bimbi (2007); Weitzer (2009); Zelizer (1994).
2. Marlowe (1997); Edlund and Korn (2002); Bernstein (2005, 2007); Giusta, Di Tommaso, and Strom (2008).
3. Edlund and Korn (2002).
4. Parsons, Bimbi and Halkitis (2001); Uy et al. (2004); Bimbi and Parsons (2005).
5. Luckenbill (1986); Cameron et al. (1999); Uy et al. (2004); Koken et al. (2005), Pruitt (2005); Parsons, Koken, and Bimbi (2007).
6. Loftus (2001); Scott (2003).
7. These older works would include Pettiway (1996), McNamara (1994), Hoffman (1972), Ginsburg (1967), Salamon (1989), and Boyer (1989).
8. Joffee and Dockrell (1995); Calhoun and Weaver (1996); Uy et al. (2004); Pruitt (2005).
9. Cohan et al. (2004).
10. Parker (2006).
11. Connell (1987, 1995).
12. Collins (1999, 2000); Reid-Pharr (2001); Han (2006b).
13. Minichiello, Scott, and Callander (2013); Bimbi (2007); Weitzer (2009).
14. Dowsett (1993).
15. I am not claiming that all men participating in the market are gay-identified. I am claiming, however, that the construction of gay masculinities would be more prominent in the market than its heterosexual counterpart. As argued later, this depends on the degree to which gay masculinities and heterosexual masculinities are different. If there are few germane differences then, for the case of male sex work, the two are interchangeable.
16. Connell (1987, 1995); Connell and Messerschmidt (2005).
17. Collins (1999, 2000).
18. West (1993); Bernstein (2007).

19. Itiel (1998); Steele and Kennedy (2006); Pompeo (2009); Smith and Grov (2011); West (1993); Aggleton (1999); Kaye (2001).
20. Weinberg and Williams (1974); Stein (1989); Sedgwick (1990); Epstein (2006).
21. Marlowe (1997).
22. D'Emilio (1997); Cantu (2002).
23. This is a necessarily cursory introduction to field theory. See Martin (2003) and Fligstein and McAdam (2012).
24. Chauncey (1994); Dorais (2005); Bimbi (2007).
25. Black et al. (2000); Black, Sanders, and Taylor (2007); Cameron et al. (2009).
26. Sociologists have noted conflicts within masculinities before the theory of hegemonic masculinity developed (Hooker [1957]; Weinberg and Williams [1974]; Levine [1998]).
27. Bird (1996); Schrock and Schwalbe (2009); Reeser (2010).
28. Demetriou (2001).
29. Levine (1998); Donaldson (1993); Dowsett (1993); Demetriou (2001); Anderson (2002); Connell and Messerschmidt (2005); Reeser (2010).
30. Connell and Messerschmidt (2005) express doubts about this hybrid, but do concede that hegemonic masculinity could be informed by and inform gay masculinities.
31. Connell (1992); Reeser (2010).
32. This allows for the distinction between a sexuality-based masculinity and a practice/trait-based masculinity. As such, heterosexual masculinities may be further refined among heterosexual men in a similar manner to that of homosexual men.
33. Almeling (2007); Arunachalam and Shah (2008); Koken, Bimbi, and Parsons (2009).
34. Alvarez (2008).
35. Bird (1996); Schrock and Schwalbe (2009).
36. See Weinberg and Williams (1974), Cameron et al. (1999), and Pruitt (2005). The advertisements of male escorts commonly note the "rugged" quality or "manliness" of the escort and the "refinement" of their "generous gentlemen" clients.
37. An additional contribution is the fact that quantitative analysis of masculinity has largely concerned opinions about masculine traits as opposed to values/effects of practices.
38. See Hacker (1957) for a contemporaneous discussion of the development of post war masculinity.
39. Atkins (1998); Green (2008b).
40. Levine (1998) notes that this does not imply that there were not deep emotional connections between men who adopted a gay clone persona. The image of emotional detachment was not the reality for the men in Levine's ethnography.
41. Connell (1992); Atkins (1998).
42. Herzog et al. (1991); Bresen et al. (1996); Atkins (1998); Carpenter (2003); Green (2008b).
43. Levine (1998); Lanzieri and Hildebrtandt (2011); Tiggerman, Martins, and Kirkbride (2007).
44. Hennen (2005); Whitesel (2014).
45. The hierarchical relationship between these alternative gay masculinities is an active area of research.
46. Atkins (1998); Hennen (2005); Whitesel (2014).

47. Levine (1998).

48. Levine (1998); Nardi (2000); Ward (2000); Clarkson (2006).

49. Ward (2008); Connell (1992); Clarkson (2006); Pascoe (2007).

50. Levine (1998); Clarkson (2006).

51. Nagel (2000); Han (2006b); Robinson (2007).

52. Collins (1999, 2000); Reeser (2010).

53. Baldwin (1985); Reeser (2010).

54. Levine (1998); D'Emilio (1983).

55. There is a well-developed literature that shows the ways that homosexuality may be incompatible with Blackness, but for the analysis of male sex work it is particularly important to note the ways that Blackness would be incompatible with homosexuality since the market is inherently sexual as opposed to racial.

56. This is quite different from the emasculated Black gay man described in Collins (2005). It is interesting to note that Collins describes the emasculated and feminized gay man while Black gay scholars such as Nero describe the savage Black man as inconsistent with homosexuality. One source of the distinction could be that Collins focuses on the social representations of Black gay men while Nero analyzes them within a more deliberately sexual context.

57. For Black exclusion from dating pools, see Robnett, Feliciano, and Rafalow (2013).

58. http://www.gmfa.org.uk/Sites/fsmagazine/pages/fs148-dear-white-gay-men

59. "Cock" is very rarely used as a euphemism for penis in African American vernacular. As such, it is likely that the terminology developed and is used by White men, as "cock" is a common euphemism among Whites.

60. Levine (1998) notes that Black men were largely excluded from the gay clique, the key socializing institution in White gay enclaves. Numerous studies have documented the exclusion of Black gay men from social establishments such as gay bars.

61. Orne (2016); Robinson (2015a).

62. See Feliciano, Robnett, and Komaie (2009) and Wilson et al. (2009) for recent work that concentrates on exclusion by Whites.

63. Han (2006a).

64. http://www.gmfa.org.uk/Sites/fsmagazine/pages/fs148-dear-white-gay-men

65. http://www.gmfa.org.uk/Sites/fsmagazine/pages/fs148-dear-white-gay-men

66. Cameron et al. (1999); Pruitt (2005).

67. Economists have noted problems with some of the assumptions underlying the hedonic empirical approach. For example, Rosen (1974) assumed that the market for the good or service in question was perfectly competitive and that the range of products would be approximately continuous. Many markets are not perfectly competitive, and even fewer have a continuum of goods (which requires a large variety of products of the same type in the market). Rosen also assumed that all product attributes would be observed by market participants, and this is also not true for some goods, particularly services such as escort services. For these reasons, some have objected to the hedonic approach and its interpretation (Brown and Rosen 1982; Epple 1987; Bartik 1987). Fortunately, recent advances in applied econometrics have shown that the hedonic approach we use is able to uncover the implicit prices of characteristics in markets that are not perfectly competitive, where there is not a continuum of goods, and where all product characteristics are not observed (Bajari and Benkard 2005). In short, we can estimate the implicit

prices in this market without making the rigid market assumptions that have been problematic in the literature.

68. I control for the escort's location not only because price may vary with geography, but also because specific locations may have more or fewer competitors (peers), which can exert an independent effect on prices in a particular market.

69. There are several ways to establish the validity of the prices used. Errors or selection could bias the results I report. First, I note that the correlation of advertised prices with actual transaction prices is quite high (r=0.89). Of greater concern is selection. Not all escorts post prices, although the vast majority of escorts (more than 85 percent) do. It could certainly be the case that escort characteristics are related to the likelihood of posting prices. If this is so, the relationship between prices and characteristics could be biased, as characteristics would predict whether an escort would choose to post prices. To address this potential selection issue, I estimated a model where the dependent variable was whether or not an escort posted a price. The results of the selection regressions are reported in the Appendix. I found no relationship between the information in an escort's advertisement (race, sexual position, body size, etc.) and the decision to post prices. Given these results, I am confident that the price measure is an accurate measure of the prices actually paid in transactions.

70. This calculation assumes that escorts see 25 clients per month.

71. Friedman (2003); Bernstein (2007).

72. These results are robust to the inclusion of age-squared and for substituting height and weight with body mass index (BMI).

73. Since the specification is semi logarithmic, the percentage change of a dichotomous indicator is approximated by $\exp(\gamma)-1$, where γ is the coefficient in the regression (Halvorsen and Palmquist 1980).

74. Carpenter (2003); Atkins (1998).

75. Pompeo (2009).

76. Alvarez (2008).

77. See the Appendix for the complete set of models estimated. The price differential is calculated as $\exp(Top)-\exp(Bottom)$.

78. Clarkson (2006).

79. See the Supplementary Material for a fuller delineation of the biological hypothesis and the evidence gathered to consider its implications.

80. See the Appendix for the full set of results.

81. This could be due in part to the fact that there are relatively few Asian escorts in the data. Only 1 percent of the escorts are Asian.

5 SHOW, TELL, AND SELL: SELF-PRESENTATION IN MALE SEX WORK

1. This is a revised version of Fine, Logan, and Soller (2014).

2. Simmel ([1907] 1971).

3. Hoang (2010); Price-Glynn (2010); Thompson, Harred, and Burks (2002).

4. Bernstein (2007).

5. Green (2008c).

6. Martin and George (2006).
7. This is not to say that men would want those sexual aspects made public for their romantic partners. The point here is that the desirability of certain sexual behaviors and sexual personas would extend to the commercial market.
8. Collins (2004).
9. For example, see Price-Glynn (2010) and Thompson, Harred, and Burks (2002).
10. Logan (2010); Bernstein (2007).
11. See Hakim (2011) for a general introduction to erotic capital.
12. Weitzer (2005).
13. Koken, Bimbi, and Parsons (2009).
14. West (1993), Logan (2010).
15. Boyer (1989), Prestage (1994).
16. Weitzer (2009).
17. Blumer (1954, p. 7).
18. Niche markets of sex workers do exist, e.g., sadomasochist sex workers or sex workers of an older age (Cameron et al. 1999), who arguably narrow their client base. There is no suggestion that male sex workers all conform identically to provide nearly identical, broadly aimed advertisements. Instead, I argue that these MSM sex workers largely do rely on overarching racial, gender, and sexual stereotypes in constructing their advertisements, even while seeking to fill niches related to sexual desire.
19. Douglas and Isherwood (2002).
20. Goffman (1959, p. 22).
21. Logan (2010).
22. Logan and Shah (2013).
23. Blumer (1954, p. 7).
24. Green (2008c).
25. Gagnon and Simon (1973).
26. MacNeil and Byers (2005).
27. See Humphreys (1971) for an earlier discussion of the development of gay masculinity.
28. Foucault (1978); Martin (1998).
29. Butler (2004); Fausto-Sterling (2000).
30. Drummond (2010); Robinson (2015a); Varangis et al. (2012).
31. Kane (2009).
32. Green (2008c).
33. Varangis et al. (2012).
34. Levine (1998).
35. Robinson (2015a); Whitesel (2014).
36. Logan (2010).
37. Hennen (2005); Baker (2003).
38. Kane (2009).
39. Green (2008c, p. 28).
40. Green (2008c, p. 25).
41. Collins (2004)
42. Han (2006a, 2006b).
43. Gagnon and Simon (1973).

44. Logan (2010); Logan and Shah (2013).
45. For completeness, Appendix tables show regressions where the number of pictures in an advertisement is the dependent variable. I also show results where the dependent variable is the fraction of the pictures that display the face.
46. All results we present also hold when I estimate the models with the number of pictures of a particular type as the dependent variable as opposed to the share of all pictures of a particular type as the dependent variable.
47. For completeness, I report results with face pictures in the Appendix.
48. "Other race" is the reference category.
49. "Athletic/Swimmer's build" is the reference category.
50. Some within the MSM/gay community use terms such as "versatile top" and "versatile bottom" to indicate their sexual position preferences, meaning that the category of "versatile" is not mutually exclusive from the categories of "top" or "bottom." For instance, a "versatile top" may be willing to be either the insertive or receiving partner during anal sex, but typically prefers to be the insertive.
51. The full specifications are given in the Appendix.
52. Bottom ($b = 0.190$, $p < 0.001$), Versatile ($b = 0.021$, $p < 0.01$).
53. The Wald test shows ($F_{[1,1928]} = 66.46$, $p < 0.001$).
54. The results of this specification are reported in the Appendix.
55. Black ($b = -0.085$, $p < 0.001$), Hispanic ($b = -0.090$, $p < 0.001$), and White ($b = -0.047$, $p < 0.001$).
56. Black ($b = 0.470$, $p < 0.001$), White ($b = 0.149$, $p < 0.001$), Asian ($b = 0.222$, $p < 0.01$), and Hispanic ($b = 0.291$, $p < 0.001$).
57. These results are reported in the Appendix ($b = 0.044$, $p < 0.05$).
58. White ($F_{[1,1916]} = 22.80$, $p < 0.001$), Asian ($F_{[1,1916]} = 3.86$, $p < 0.05$), and Hispanic ($F_{[1,1916]} = 4.41$, $p < 0.05$) bottoms.
59. $F_{[1,1916]} = 7.36$, $p < 0.01$.
60. Green (2008b).

6 SERVICE FEES: MASCULINITY, SAFER SEX, AND MALE SEX WORK

1. Gertler, Shah, and Bertozzi (2005); Rao et al. (2003); Robinson and Yeh (2011); Arunachalam and Shah (2008, 2013).
2. Eaton et al. (2007); Eaton, Kalichman, and Cherry (2010).
3. Koken et al. (2005).
4. Halkitis et al. (2004).
5. Goodreau et al. (2011).
6. Weitzer (2009).
7. Lillard (1998); Rao et al. (2003); Gertler, Shah, and Bertozzi (2005); Levitt and Vankatesh (2007); Robinson and Yeh (2011, 2012); Arunachalam and Shah (2008); Galarraga et al. (2011); Shah (2013); Cheng and Weng (2012).
8. De Graaf et al. (1994); Marlowe (1997); Varghese et al. (2002); Eaton, Kalichman, and Cherry (2010); Green (2008a).
9. Robinson (2015a).

10. Parsons et al. (2004); Uy et al. (2004); Bimbi (2007); Bimbi and Parsons (2005); Browne and Minichiello (1996); Coutinho et al. (1988); Joffee and Dockrell (1995); Connell (2002).
11. Reisner et al. (2008).
12. For example, AIDS\Drug Assistance Programs (ADAP) cost more than $1.2 billion annually. While ADAP programs only cover those within a range of the federal poverty level (from 200 to 400 percent, depending on the state of residence), nearly three-quarters (72 percent) of those in ADAP programs are uninsured and not eligible for Medicare or Medicaid. It is important to emphasize that the implications extend beyond HIV. For example, gay men are more likely to have HPV infections, which are spread by skin-to-skin contact, and rates of anal cancer are higher for gay men as a result (Epstein 2010). Furthermore, recent research has linked HPV to oral cancers, which implies that STIs among gay men could be linked to other health conditions (Spinelli 2011). Up to 60 percent of oral and pharynx cancers are linked to HPV, and those with more than six oral sex partners face an eight-fold increase in their risk of oral cancer due to HPV exposure.
13. Lakdawalla, Sood, and Goldman (2006), Kremer (1996). Some have argued that gay men have adopted HIV/AIDS optimism, where the negative health implications of HIV have decreased to an extent that they now routinely partake in unprotected sex (Klausner, Kim, and Kent [2002]; CDC [2010a]; Van de Ven et al. [2002]; Stolte et al. [2004]; Adam et al. [2005]). Others have argued that as the risks of HIV infection declined with new treatments, the cost of unprotected sex declined – those who are HIV positive are better able to partake in sexual activity (and due to the new treatments are less likely to transmit the disease with low viral loads), but those who are HIV negative may no longer fear infection (Van de Ven et al. [2002]; Stolte et al. [2004]). Recent advances in the use of pre-exposure prophylaxis (PrEP) has been correlated with decreased likelihood of HIV transmission but increased incidence of other STIs. One factor related to this trend is the decline in condom usage (Volk et al. 2015).
14. Shoptaw et al. (2005); Colfax and Shoptaw (2005); Mattison et al. (2001); Volk et al. (2015).
15. CDC (2010a).
16. Shernoff (2006); Shilts (1987).
17. Rosen (1986).
18. Rao et al. (2003); Gertler, Shah, and Bertozzi (2005); Robinson and Yeh (2011); De la Torre et al. (2010).
19. Logan (2010); Grov et al. (2013).
20. Humphreys (1970); Frankel (2007); MacDonald (2007); Francis and Mialon (2010); Reidy and Goodreau (2010).
21. Dean (2009); CDC (2010a, 2010b); Adam et al. (2005); Van de Ven et al. (2002); Stolte et al. (2004); Hall et al. (2008).
22. Gertler, Shah, and Bertozzi (2005); Robinson and Yeh (2011).
23. Shernoff (2006); Horvath, Oakes, and Simon Rosser (2008); Marks et al. (1994).
24. Simon and Gagnon (1973); Nardi (2000); Sadownick (1996).
25. This is not to say that it is new. Similar distinctions were documented in Levine (1998).

26. Shernoff (2006); CDC (2010b).
27. Dean (2009); CDC (2010b); Adam et al. (2005).
28. Eaton et al. (2007); Cairns (2006).
29. Volk et al. (2015).
30. Van de Ven et al. (2002); Stolte et al. (2004).
31. Dean (2009); Shernoff (2006); CDC (2010b).
32. Shilts (1987).
33. Benotsch, Kalichman, and Cage (2002); Shernoff (2006).
34. Benotsch, Kalichman, and Cage (2002).
35. Klein, Ellifson, and Sterk (2010); Martin and Knox (1997).
36. Uy et al. (2004); Bimbi and Parsons (2005); Parsons, Bimbi, and Halkitis (2001); Weitzer (2009).
37. Hart et al. (2003); Moskowitz et al. (2008).
38. Eaton, Kalichman, and Cherry (2010).
39. Laumann et al. (2004); Weinberg and Williams (1974).
40. Connell (1992); Logan (2010).
41. Atkins (1998); Bresen et al. (1996); Herzog et al. (1991).
42. Heterosexual or lesbian – Schwartz and Graf (2010); Black, Sanders, and Taylor (2007); Carpenter and Gates (2008).
43. Koken, Bimbi, and Parsons (2009).
44. Logan (2010); Fields et al. (2011).
45. Reid-Pharr (2001); McBride (2005); Nagel (2000); Boykin (1996).
46. Nagel (2000); Robinson (2008).
47. Luna (1989); Cochran and Mays (1994); Nagel (2000); Ford et al. (2007); Fields et al. (2011).
48. Ellington and Schroeder (2004); Robinson (2008); Fields et al. (2011).
49. Logan (2010).
50. Edlund and Korn (2002).
51. Reay (2010); Koken, Bimbi, and Parsons (2009).
52. Logan (2011).
53. Mastro and de Vincenzi (1996).
54. Varghese et al. (2002).
55. Fields et al. (2011).
56. Sifikas et al. (2005).
57. Eaton et al. (2010).
58. Mancilla and Troshinsky (2003).
59. Crossley (2004); Shernoff (2006); Dean (2009).
60. Troung et al. (2006); Cairns (2006); Eaton et al. (2007).
61. In the Appendix I adopt a simple model of sex worker-client negotiations to formally capture these distinctions.
62. Logan (2011, 2010); Logan and Shah (2013).
63. Williams et al. (2003, 2006); Timpson et al. (2007); Escourt et al. (2000).
64. Rao et al. (2003); Gertler et al. (2005); Robinson and Yeh (2011).
65. Varghese et al. (2002).
66. See Figure 1.3 for an example of a client review of escort services. Client free-form reviews are sexually explicit. For this reason the field is obscured in Figure 1.3.

67. Logistic models were also estimated and gave qualitatively similar results.
68. The log likelihood function is $\ln L(\beta) = \sum_{i=1}^{n} (y_i \ln \Phi(x'_i\beta) + (1 - y_i)\ln(1 - \Phi(x'_i\beta)))$.
69. For dichotomous indicators, the marginal effect reported is for moving from 0 to 1. For further details on calculation of marginal effects see Ruud (2000).
70. There are fewer than 25 repeat transactions (multiple transactions involving the same client and escort) in the data.
71. In all specifications, standard errors are clustered at the state-year level.
72. Results are similar when Body Mass Index (BMI) is used in place of height and weight. Results are reported in the Appendix.
73. Hart et al. (2003); Moskowitz et al. (2008).
74. The results of the specification are in the Appendix.
75. Sexual behaviors are described from the perspective of the sex worker. For example, "Topping" means that the escort penetrates the client.
76. Varghese et al. (2002).
77. Rao et al. (2003); Gertler, Shah, and Bertozzi (2005); Robinson and Yeh (2011).
78. These results are in the Appendix.
79. Logan (2010).
80. Sifikas et al. (2005).
81. Green (2008a).

7 CONCLUSION

1. Edlund and Korn (2002).
2. Arunachalam and Shah (2012).
3. Levine (1998).
4. Doherty et al. (2005); Laumann et al. (2004).
5. Shilts (1987).
6. Levine (1998).
7. Phua and Kaufman (2003); Kaufman and Phua (2003); Robinson (2015 in press).
8. Grosskopf et al. (2014).
9. Lanzieri and Hildebrandt (2011); Tiggerman et al. (2007).
10. Grindr (2013).
11. The method of sampling used the smartphone application and, at various times of day, opened the application and captured the profiles that were displayed. The specific metropolitan areas included were Detroit, Los Angeles, Boston, New York City, Chicago, Las Vegas, Columbus, Washington DC, San Francisco, Denver, and Dallas. Duplicates were eliminated through successive searches in the same location via the picture used in the profile. The sampling continued until 5,000 unique profiles were collected.
12. See Robinson (2016) for a recent example, but this study uses a website as opposed to a smartphone application.
13. Phillips et al. (2014).
14. Beymer et al. (2014). There were no differences in the likelihood of HIV or syphilis infections between men who used smartphone applications and those

who did not. Lehmiller and Loerger (2014) find that adjusting for time of sexual activity (to control for age differences among users and non-users), smartphone app users have more sexual partners.

15. Phillips et al. (2014).
16. The data collection method was similar to that of the Grindr. At the time of Grindr data collection, the same city Craigslist profiles were searched and recorded. Only the first page of advertisements was recorded for each city for each day in order to minimize the appearance of ads that would be re-posts of older advertisements.
17. Mowlabocus (2010).
18. In noting mentions of masculinity, "masc4masc" is taken as supply and demand for masculinity.
19. See Robinson (2016) for theoretical framework for how the gay body is disciplined in cyberspace.
20. See Wilson et al. (2009) and Paul et al. (2008) for more on racial-sexual stereotypes among men using Internet and smartphone applications to find partners. It could be the case that the racial preferences among non-Whites, and even the Whites on Grindr, are driven partially by selection. Given that Grindr is Whiter than the general population, non-White men using the smartphone application may be doing so due to their racial preferences and White men due to the likelihood of finding White partners through the application. Put another way, it is not possible to extend the racial preferences beyond what is reported to a great extent, since the preferences seen could be endogenous to the racial composition.
21. Perhaps due to the strength of the relationship for Blacks, the mentions of Asian and Hispanics in the Craigslist advertisements were far less frequent.
22. One interesting aspect of the development of "BBC" as an acronym is the fact that "cock" is rarely used as a euphemism for penis in African American vernacular or literature. This dramatically increases the likelihood that "BBC" is used primarily for interracial sexual behaviors, as the terminology itself is not organic to African American people.

APPENDIX 1 DATA FOR THE ANALYSIS OF MALE SEX WORK

1. Kaya (2009) shows that the degree of substitutability will depend on the agent's desire for a smooth payoff stream. There is a test for substitution in the section on beauty.
2. I stress here that the costs of signaling may be both material and psychic. For example, if escorts have negative attitudes towards gays or would be subjecting themselves to negative outcomes if the public knew they participated in gay sex, it would be more costly (psychically) for them to signal to clients.
3. Steele and Kennedy (2006).
4. Since I deal only with men who are escorts, and are not concerned with selection into male escort work, I normalize the standard reservation wage to zero.
5. Bonacich (1991); Faust (1997).
6. Bonacich (1972, 1991).

References

Adam, B.D., W. Husbands, J. Murray, and J. Maxwell (2005) "AIDS Optimism, Condom Fatigue, or Self-Esteem? Explaining Unsafe Sex among Gay and Bisexual Men." *Journal of Sex Research* 42 (3): 238–248.

Aggleton, P., ed. (1999) *Men Who Sell Sex: International Perspectives on Male Prostitution and HIV/AIDS.* Philadelphia: Temple University Press.

Akerlof, G.A. (1970) "The Market for Lemons: Quality Uncertainty and the Market Mechanism." *Quarterly Journal of Economics* 84(3): 488–500.

Allen, D.M. (1980) "Young Male Prostitutes: A Psychosocial Study." *Archives of Sexual Behavior* 9: 399–426.

Almeling, R. (2007) "Selling Genes, Selling Gender: Egg Agencies, Sperm Banks, and the Medical Market in Genetic Material." *American Sociological Review* 72: 319–340.

Alvarez, E. (2008) *Muscle Boys: Gay Gym Culture.* New York: Routledge.

Anderson, E. (2002) "Openly Gay Athletes: Contesting Hegemonic Masculinity in a Homophobic Environment." *Gender and Society* 16: 860–877.

Arunachalam, R., and M. Shah (2008) "Prostitutes and Brides?" *American Economic Review Papers and Proceedings* 98: 516–522.

Arunachalam, R., and M. Shah (2012) "The Prostitutes Allure: The Return to Beauty in Commercial Sex Work." *The B.E. Journal of Economic Analysis and Policy* 12: Article 60.

Arunachalam, R., and M. Shah (2013) "Compensated for Life: Sex Work and Disease Risk." *Journal of Human Resources* 48: 345–369.

Atkins, D., ed. (1998) *Looking Queer: Body Image and Identity in Lesbian, Gay, and Transgender Communities.* New York: Routledge.

Bajari, P., and C.L. Benkard (2005) "Demand Estimation with Heterogeneous Consumers and Unobserved Product Characteristics: A Hedonic Approach." *Journal of Political Economy* 113: 1239–1276.

Bajari, P., and A. Hortacsu (2004) "Economic Insights from Internet Auctions." *Journal of Economic Literature* 42(2): 457–486.

Baker, P. (2003) "No Effeminates, Please: A Corpus-Based Analysis of Masculinity via Personal Adverts in Gay News / Times 1973–2000." *Sociological Review Monograph* 2003: 243–260.

Bakos, Y. (2001) "The Emerging Landscape for Retail E-Commerce." *Journal of Economic Perspectives* 15(1): 69–80.

Baldwin, J. (1985) *The Price of the Ticket: Collected Nonfiction 1948–1985*. New York: St. Martin's.

Bartik, T.J. (1987) "The Estimation of Demand Parameters in Hedonic Price Models." *Journal of Political Economy* 95: 81–88.

Benotsch, E.G., S. Kalichman, and M. Cage (2002) "Men Who Have Met Sex Partners via the Internet: Prevalence, Predictors, and Implications for HIV Prevention." *Archives of Sexual Behavior* 31:177–183.

Berg, N., and D. Lien (2002) "Measuring the Effect of Sexual Orientation on Income: Evidence of Discrimination?" *Contemporary Economic Policy* 20: 394–414.

Berg, N., and D. Lien (2006) "Same-Sex Sexual Behavior: US Frequency Estimates from Survey Data with Simultaneous Misreporting and Non-Response." *Applied Economics* 38: 759–769.

Bernstein, E. (2005) "Desire, Demand, and the Commerce of Sex," in E. Bernstein and L. Schaffner, eds., Regulating Sex: *The Politics of Intimacy and Identity*. New York: Routledge, pp. 101–125.

Bernstein, E. (2007) *Temporarily Yours: Sexual Commerce in Post-Industrial Culture*. Chicago: University of Chicago Press.

Beymer, M.R., R.E. Weiss, R.K. Bolan, E.T. Rudy, L.B. Bourque, J.P. Rodriguez, and D.E. Morisky (2014) "Sex on Demand: Geosocial Networking Phone Apps and Risk of Sexually Transmitted Infections among a Cross-Sectional Sample of Men Who Have Sex with Men in Los Angeles County." *Sexually Transmitted Infections* 90: 567–572.

Bimbi, D.S. (2007) "Male Prostitution: Pathology, Paradigms and Progress in Research." *Journal of Homosexuality* 53: 7–35.

Bimbi, D.S., and J. T. Parsons (2005) "Barebacking among Internet Based Male Sex Workers." *Journal of Gay and Lesbian Psychotherapy* 9: 89–110.

Bird, S.R. (1996) "Welcome to the Men's Club: Homosociality and the Maintenance of Hegemonic Masculinity." *Gender and Society* 10: 120–132.

Black, D., G. Gates, S. Sanders, and L. Taylor (2000) "Demographics of the Gay and Lesbian Population in the United States: Evidence from Available Systematic Sources." *Demography* 37: 139–154.

Black, D., G. Gates, S. Sanders, and L. Taylor (2002) "Why Do Gay Men Live in San Francisco?" *Journal of Urban Economics* 51: 54–76.

Black, D., S. Sanders, and L. Taylor (2007) "The Economics of Lesbian and Gay Families." *Journal of Economic Perspectives* 21: 53–70.

Blumer, H. (1954) "What Is Wrong with Social Theory?" *American Sociological Review* 19: 3–10.

Bonacich, P. (1972) "Factoring and Weighting Approaches to Clique Identification." *Journal of Mathematical Sociology* 2: 113–120.

Bonacich, P. (1991) "Simultaneous Group and Individual Centralities." *Social Networks* 13(2): 155–168.

Borgatti, S.P., and M.G. Everett (1997) "Network Analysis of 2-Mode Data." *Social Networks* 19(3): 243–269.

Boswell, J. (2005) *Christianity, Homosexuality, and Social Tolerance*. Chicago: University of Chicago Press.

Bourdieu, P. (1977) *Outline of a Theory of Practice*. Cambridge: Cambridge University Press.

Bourdieu, P. (1980) *The Logic of Practice*. Stanford: Stanford University Press.

Boykin, K. (1996) *One More River to Cross: Black and Gay in America* New York: Anchor/Doubleday.

Boyer, D. (1989) "Male Prostitution and Homosexual Identity." *Journal of Homosexuality* 17: 151–184.

Bresen, S.E., H.A. Hayden, D.E. Wilfley, and C.M. Grilo (1996). "The Influence of Sexual Orientation on Body Dissatisfaction in Adult Men and Women." *International Journal of Eating Disorders* 20: 135–141.

Brown, J.R., and A. Goolsbee (2002) "Does the Internet Make Markets More Competitive? Evidence from the Life Insurance Industry." *Journal of Political Economy* 110(3): 481–507.

Brown, J., and J. Morgan (2006) "Reputation in Online Auctions: The Market for Trust." *California Management Review* 49(1): 61–81.

Brown, J.N., and H.S. Rosen (1982) "On the Estimation of Structural Hedonic Price Models." *Econometrica* 50: 765–768.

Browne, J., and V. Minichiello (1996) "Research Directions in Male Sex Work." *Journal of Homosexuality* 31: 29–56.

Butler, J. (1990) *Gender Trouble*. New York: Routledge.

Butler, J. (1993) *Bodies That Matter: On the Discursive Limits of "Sex."* New York: Routledge.

Butler, J. (2004) "Undiagnosing Gender," pages 75–101 in *Undoing Gender*. New York: Routledge.

Cairns, G. (2006) "New Direction in HIV Prevention: Serosorting and Universal Testing." *IAPAC Monthly* 12: 42–45.

Calhoun, T.C., and G. Weaver (1996) "Rational Decision-Making among Male Street Prostitutes." *Deviant Behavior* 17: 209–227.

Cameron, S., Alan Collins, and Neill Thew (1999) "Prostitution Services: An Exploratory Empirical Analysis" *Applied Economics* 31: 1523–1529.

Cameron, S., A. Collins, S. Drinkwater, F. Hickson, D. Reid, J. Roberts, M. Stephens, and P. Weatherburn (2009) "Surveys and Data Sources on Gay Men's Lifestyles and Socio-Sexual Behavior: Some Key Concerns and Issues." *Sexuality and Culture* 13: 135–151.

Cantu, L. (2002) "A Place Called Home: A Queer Political Economy," in C. Williams and S. Stein, eds., *Sexuality and Gender*. New York: Blackwell.

Carpenter, C. (2003) "Sexual Orientation and Body Weight: Evidence from Multiple Surveys." *Gender Issues* 21: 60–74.

Carpenter, C. (2004) "New Evidence on Gay and Lesbian Household Incomes." *Contemporary Economic Policy* 22: 78–94.

Carpenter, C., and G. Gates (2008) "Gay and Lesbian Partnership: Evidence from California." *Demography* 45: 573–590.

Centers for Disease Control and Prevention (CDC) (2010a) "HIV/AIDS and Men Who Have Sex with Men." Retrieved April 15, 2011 (http://www.cdc.gov/hiv/topics/msm/index.htm).

Centers for Disease Control and Prevention (CDC) (2010b) "Prevention Challenges." Retrieved on April 15, 2011 (http://www.cdc.gov/hiv/topics/msm/challenges_partner.htm).

Chang, H.H., and Y. Weng (2012) "What Is More Important for Prostitute Price? Physical Appearance or Risky Sex Behavior?" *Economics Letters* 117: 480–483.

Chauncey, G. (1994) *Gay New York: Gender, Urban Culture, and the Making of the Gay Male World 1890–1940*. New York: Basic Books.

Chisholm, D.C., and G. Norman (2012) "Spatial Competition and Market Share: An Application to Motion Pictures." *Journal of Cultural Economics* 36(3): 207–225.

Cho, I.-K., and D.M. Kreps (1987) "Signaling Games and Stable Equilibria." *Quarterly Journal of Economics* 102(2): 179–221.

Clarkson, J. (2006) "'Everyday Joe' versus 'Pissy, Bitchy, Queens': Gay Masculinity on StraightActing.com." *Journal of Men's Studies* 14: 191–208.

Cochran, S.D., and V.M. Mays (1994) "Depressive distress among homosexually active African American men and women." *Am. J. Psychiatry.* 151: 524–529.

Cohan, D.L., J. Breyer, C. Cobaugh, C. Cloniger, A. Herlyn, A. Lutnick, and D. Wilson. (2004) "Social Context and the Health of Sex Workers in San Francisco." Paper presented at the 2004 International Conference on AIDS.

Colfax, G., and S. Shoptaw (2005) "The Methamphetamine Epidemic: Implications for HIV Prevention and Treatment." *Current HIV/AIDS Reports* 2(4): 194–199.

Collins, A. (2004) "Sexual Dissidence, Enterprise, and Assimilation: Bedfellows in Urban Regeneration." *Urban Studies* 41: 1789–1806.

Collins, P.H. (1999) *Black Feminist Thought: Knowledge, Consciousness, and the Politics of Empowerment*. New York: HarperCollins.

Collins, P.H. (2000) "Gender, Black Feminism, and Black Political Economy." *Annals of the American Academy of Political and Social Science* 568: 41–53.

Collins, P.H. (2005) *Black Sexual Politics: African Americans, Gender, and the New Racism*. New York: Routledge.

Connell, J.A. (2002) "Male Sex Work: Occupational Health and Safety." Paper presented at the 2002 International Conference on AIDS.

Connell, R.W. (1987) *Gender and Power: Society, the Person, and Sexual Politics*. Sydney, Australia: Allen and Unwin.

Connell, R.W. (1992) "A Very Straight Gay: Masculinity, Homosexual Experience, and the Dynamics of Gender." *American Sociological Review* 57: 737–751.

Connell, R.W. (1995) *Masculinities*. Sydney, Australia: Allen and Unwin.

Connell, R.W., and J.W. Messerschmidt (2005) "Hegemonic Masculinity: Rethinking the Concept." *Gender and Society* 19: 829–859.

Court, A.T. (1939) "Hedonic Price Indexes with Automotive Examples," in *General Motors Corporation, The Dynamics of Automobile Demand*. New York, pp. 99–119.

Coutinho, R., R. van Andel, and T. Rijsdijk (1988) "Role of Male Prostitutes in Spread of Sexually Transmitted Diseases and Human Immunodeficiency Virus." *Genitourinary Medicine* 64: 207–208.

Crossley, M.L. (2004) "Making Sense of 'Barebacking': Gay Men's Narratives, Unsafe Sex, and the 'Resistance Habitus.'" *British Journal of Social Psychology* 43: 225–244.

Cunningham, S., and T.D. Kendall (2009) "Prostitution 2.0: The Changing Face of Sex Work." *Journal of Urban Economics* 69: 273–287.

Cunningham, S., and T. Kendall (2011) "Behaving Better: How Reputational Mechanisms Change the Behavior of Prostitutes." Working paper, Baylor University.

Davis, P. (2006) "Spatial Competition in Retail Markets: Movie Theaters." *The Rand Journal of Economics*, 37(4): 964–982.

Dean, T. (2009) *Unlimited Intimacy: Reflections on the Subculture of Barebacking*. Chicago: University of Chicago Press, pp. 100–113.

De Graaf, R., I. Vanwesenbeeck, G. van Zessen, C.J. Straver, and J.H. Visser (1994) "Male Prostitutes and Safer Sex: Different Settings, Different Risks." *AIDS Care* 6: 277–288.

Delaney, S. (1999) *Times Square Red/Times Square Blue*. New York: New York University Press.

De la Torre, A., A. Havenner, K. Adams, and J. Ng (2010) "Premium Sex: Factors Influencing the Negotiated Price of Unprotected Sex by Female Sex Workers in Mexico." *Journal of Applied Economics* 13(1): 67–90.

Della Giusta, M., M. L. Di Tommaso, and S. Strom (2008) "Who's Watching? The Market for Prostitution Services." *Journal of Population Economics* 22(2): 501–516.

Demetriou, D.Z. (2001) "Connell's Concept of Hegemonic Masculinity: A Critique." *Theory and Society* 30: 337–361.

D'Emilio, J. (1983). *Sexual Politics, Sexual Communities: The Making of a Homosexual Minority in the United States 1940–1970*. Chicago: University of Chicago Press.

D'Emilio, J. (1997) "Capitalism and Gay Identity," in R. Lancaster and M. diLeonardo, eds., *The Gender/Sexuality Reader*. New York: Routledge, pp. 100–113.

Dennis, J. (2008) "Women Are Victims, Men Make Choices: The Invisibility of Men and Boys in the Global Sex Trade." *Gender Issues* 25: 11–25.

Doherty I.A., N.S. Padian, C. Marlow, and S.O. Aral (2005) "Determinants and Consequences of Sexual Networks as They Affect the Spread of Sexually Transmitted Infections." *Journal of Infectious Diseases* 191: Suppl 1: S42–54.

Donaldson, M. (1993) "What Is Hegemonic Masculinity?" *Theory and Society* 22: 643–657.

Dorais, M. (2005) *Rent Boys: The World of Male Sex Workers*. London: McGill-Queens University Press.

Douglas, M., and B. Isherwood (2002) *The World of Goods: Towards an Anthropology of Consumption*. New York: Routledge.

Dover, K.J. (1989) *Greek Homosexuality*. Cambridge, MA: Harvard University Press.

Dowsett, G.W. (1993) "I'll Show You Mine, if You'll Show Me Yours: Gay Men, Masculinity Research, Men's Studies, and Sex." *Theory and Society* 22: 697–709.

Drummond, M.J.N. (2010) "Younger and Older Gay Men's Bodies." *Gay and Lesbian Issues and Psychology Review* 6: 31–41.

Duarte, J., S. Siegel, and L. Young (2009) "Trust and Credit." Working paper, University of Washington.

Duncan-Jones, R. (1982) *The Economy of the Roman Empire*. London: Cambridge University Press.

Dyer, R. (1997) *White: Essays on Race and Culture*. New York: Routledge.

Eagle, N., M. Macy, and R. Claxton (2010) "Network Diversity and Economic Development." *Science*, 328(5981): 1029–1031.

Eaton, L.A., S.C. Kalichman, D.N. Cain, C. Cherry, H.L. Stearns, C.M. Amaral, J.A. Flanagan, and H.L. Pope (2007) "Serosorting Sexual Partners and Risk for HIV among Men Who Have Sex with Men." *American Journal of Preventative Medicine* 33: 479–485.

Eaton, L.A., S.C. Kalichman, and C. Cherry (2010) "Sexual Partner Selection and HIV Risk Reduction among Black and White Men Who Have Sex with Men." *American Journal of Public Health* 100: 503–509.

Edlund, L., J. Engelberg, and C. Parsons (2009) "The Wages of Sin." Columbia University Economics Discussion Paper No. 809–16.

Edlund, L., and E. Korn (2002) "A Theory of Prostitution" *Journal of Political Economy* 110: 181–214.

Ellington, S. and K. Schroeder (1994) "Race and the Construction of Same-Sex Sexual Markets in Four Chicago Neighborhoods," in E. Laumann, J. Gagnon, R. Michaels, and S. Michaels (eds.) *The Social Organization of Sexuality: Sexual Practices in the United States*. Chicago: University of Chicago Press. pp. 93–123.

Epple, D. (1987) "Hedonic Prices and Implicit Markets: Estimating Demand and Supply Functions for Differentiated Products." *Journal of Political Economy* 95: 59–80.

Epstein, S. (2006) "The New Attack on Sexuality Research: Morality and the Politics of Knowledge Production." *Sexuality Research and Social Policy* 3: 1–12.

Epstein, S. (2010) "The Great Undiscussable: Anal Cancer, HPV, and Gay Men's Health," in K. Wailoo, J. Livingston, S. Epstein, and R. Aronowitz, eds., *Three Shots at Prevention: The HPV Vaccine and the Politics of Medicine's Simple Solutions*. Baltimore: Johns Hopkins University Press, pp. 61–90.

Estcourt, C.S., C. Marks, R. Rohrsheim, A.M. Johnson, B. Donovan, and A. Mindel (2000) "HIV, Sexually Transmitted Infections, and Risk Behaviours in Male Commercial Sex Workers in Sydney." *Sexually Transmitted Infections* 76: 294–298.

Evans, H. (1979) *The Oldest Profession*. Newton Abbot, England: David and Charles Press.

Faust, K. (1997) "Centrality in Affiliation Networks." *Social Networks* 19: 157–191.

Fausto-Sterling, A. (2000) *Sexing the Body: Gender Politics and the Construction of Sexuality*. New York: Basic Books.

Feliciano, C., B. Robnett, and G. Komaie (2009). Gendered Racial Exclusion among White Internet Daters." *Social Science Research* 38: 39–54.

Fields, E.L., L.M. Bogart, K.C. Smith, D.J. Malebranche, J. Ellen, and M.A. Schuster (2011) "Young Black Males' Conflict Between Masculinity and Homosexuality: Implications for HIV Risk." Working paper, Johns Hopkins Bloomberg School of Public Health.

Fine, L.E., T.D. Logan, and B.J. Soller (2014) "Displaying Your Best Assets: The Presentation of (Sexual) Self in Male Sex Work." Working paper, The Ohio State University.

Fligstein, N., and D. McAdam (2012) *A Theory of Fields*. New York: Oxford University Press.

Ford, C.L., Whetten, K.D., Hall, S.A., Kaufman, J.S., and Thrasher, A.D. (2007) Black Sexuality, Social Construction, and Research Targeting "the Down Low" ("the DL"). *Annals of Epidemiology*, 17, 209–216.

Foucault, M. (1978) *The History of Sexuality: Volume 1: An Introduction*, Pantheon, New York.

Francis, A., and H. Mialon (2010) "Tolerance and HIV." *Journal of Health Economics* 29(2): 250–267.

Frankel, T. (2007) "In Forest Park, the Roots of Sen. Craig's Misadventure." *St. Louis Post-Dispatch*, August 31, 2007.

Friedman, M. (2003) *Strapped for Cash: A History of American Hustler Culture*. Los Angeles: Alyson.

Friedman, M. (2014) "Male Sex Work from Ancient Times to the Near Present," in V. Minichiello and J. Scott, eds., *Male Sex Work and Society*. New York: Harrington Park Press, pp. 3–33.

Gagnon, J.H., and W. Simon (1973) *Sexual Conduct: The Social Sources of Human Sexuality*. Chicago: Aldine.

Galarraga, O., S. Sosa-Rubi, C. Infante, P. Gertler, and S. Bertozzi (2011) "Willingness to Accept Conditional Economic Incentives to Reduce HIV Risks among Men Who Have Sex with Men in Mexico City." Working paper, Brown University.

Gertler, P., M. Shah, and S. M. Bertozzi (2005) "Risky Business: The Market for Unprotected Commercial Sex." *Journal of Political Economy* 113: 518–550.

Ginsburg, K. (1967) "The 'Meat Rack': A Study of the Male Homosexual Prostitute." *American Journal of Psychotherapy* 21: 170–185.

Giusta, Marina Della, Maria Laura Di Tommaso, and Steinar Strom (2008). "Who's Watching? The Market for Prostitution Services." *Journal of Population Economics* 22(2): 501–516.

Goffman, E. (1959) *The Presentation of Self in Everyday Life*. New York: Anchor.

Goffman, E. (1963) *Stigma: Notes on the Management of Spoiled Identity*. New York: Simon and Schuster.

Goodreau, S.M., N. Carnegie, E. Vittinghoff, and S. Buchbinder (2011) "The HIV Transmission Network among Men Who Have Sex with Men in the United States: New Insights from Dynamic Demographic Network Models." Working paper, University of Washington.

Goyal, A. (2008) "Information Technology and Rural Market Performance in Central India." Working paper, World Bank Research Development Group.

Green, A.I. (2008a) "Erotic Habitus: Toward a Sociology of Desire." *Theory and Society* 37: 597–626.

Green, A.I. (2008b) "Health and Sexual Status in an Urban Gay Enclave: An Application of the Stress Process Model." *Journal of Health and Social Behavior* 49: 436–451.

Green, A.I. (2008c) "The Social Organization of Desire: The Sexual Fields Approach." *Sociological Theory* 26: 25–50.

Greenwood, M.J. (1997) "Internal Migration in Developed Countries." *Handbook of Population and Family Economics* 1: 647–720.

Greif, A. (1993) "Contract Enforceability and Economic Institutions in Early Trade: The Maghribi Traders' Coalition." *American Economic Review* 83(3): 525–548.

Griliches, Z. (1961) "Hedonic Price Indexes for Automobiles: An Econometric Analysis of Quality Change," in *The Price Statistics of the Federal Government*. New York: National Bureau of Economic Research, pp. 173–196.

Grindr (2013) Advertising Kit. Accessed 10/20/2015 http://www.grindr.com/download/Grindr-Ad-Kit.pdf

Grosskopf N.A., M.T. LeVasseur, and D.B. Glaser (2014) "Use of the Internet and Mobile-Based 'Apps' for Sex-Seeking among Men Who Have Sex with Men in New York City." *American Journal of Men's Health* 8: 510–520.

Grov, C., M. Wolf, M.D. Smith, J. Koken, and J. Parsons (2014) "Male Clients of Male Escorts: Satisfaction, Sexual Behavior, and Demographic Characteristics." *Journal of Sex Research*, 51: 827–837.

Hacker, H.M. (1957) "The New Burdens of Masculinity." *Marriage and Family Living* 19: 227–233.

Hakim, C. (2011) *Erotic Capital: The Power of Attraction in the Boardroom and the Bedroom*. New York: Basic Books.

Halkitis, P.N., J.M. Uy, J.T. Parsons, D.S. Bimbi, and J.A. Koken (2004) "Gay and Bisexual Male Escorts Who Advertise on the Internet: Understanding Reasons for and Effects of Involvement in Commercial Sex." *International Journal of Men's Health* 3: 11–26.

Hall, H.I., R. Song, P. Rhodes, J. Prejean, Q. An, L.M. Lee, J. Karon, R. Brookmeyer, E.H. Kaplan, M.T. McKenna, and R.S. Janssen, HIV Incidence Surveillance Group. (2008) "Estimation of HIV Incidence in the United States." *Journal of the American Medical Association* 300: 520–529.

Halvorsen, R., and R. Palmquist (1980) "The Interpretation of Dummy Variables in Semilogarithmic Equations." *American Economic Review* 70: 474–475.

Han, C. (2006a) "Being an Oriental, I Could Never Be Completely a Man: Gay Asian Men and the Intersection of Race, Gender, Sexuality, and Class." *Race, Gender and Class* 3/4: 82–97.

Han, C. (2006b) "Geisha of a Different Kind: Gay Asian Men and the Gendering of Sexual Identity." *Sexuality and Culture* 10: 3–28.

Harcourt, C., and B. Donovan (2005) "The Many Faces of Sex Work." *Sexually Transmitted Infections* 81(3): 201–206.

Harris, J.R., and M.P. Todaro (1970) "Migration, Unemployment, and Development: A Two-Sector Analysis." *American Economic Review* 60(1): 126–142.

Hart, J. (1998) Gay Sex: A Manual for Men Who Love Men, 2nd ed. New York: Alyson.

Hart, O. (1995) *Firms, Contracts and Financial Structure.* London: Oxford.

Hart, T.A., R.J. Wolitski, D.W. Purcell, C. Greene, and P. Halkitis (2003) "Sexual Behavior among HIV-positive Men Who Have Sex with Men: What's in a Label?" *Journal of Sex Research* 40: 179–188.

Hennen, P. (2005) "Bear Bodies, Bear Masculinity: Recuperation, Resistance, or Retreat?" *Gender and Society* 19: 25–43.

Herzog, D.B., K.L. Newman, and M. Warshaw (1991) "Body Image Satisfaction in Homosexual and Heterosexual Males." *International Journal of Eating Disorders* 11: 356–396.

Hewitt, C. (1995) "The Socioeconomic Position of Gay Men: A Review of the Evidence." *American Journal of Economics and Sociology* 54: 461–479.

Hoang, K.K. (2010) "Economies of Emotion, Fantasy, and Desire: Emotional Labor in Ho Chi Minh City's Sex Industry." *Sexualities* 13: 255–272.

Hoffman, M. (1972) "The Male Prostitute." *Sexual Behavior* 2: 16–21.

Hooker, E. (1956) "A Preliminary Analysis of Group Behavior of Homosexuals." *Journal of Psychology* 42: 217–223.

Hooker, E. (1957) "The Adjustment of the Male Overt Homosexual," *Journal of Protective Techniques* 21: 18–31.

Horvath, K.J., J.M. Oakes, and B.R. Simon Rosser (2008) " Sexual Negotiation and HIV Serodisclosure among Men Who Have Sex with Men with Their Online and Offline Partners." *Journal of Urban Health* 85: 744–758.

Hotelling, H. (1929) "Stability in Competition." *The Economic Journal*, 39: 41–57.

Houde, J.F. (2012) "Spatial Differentiation and Vertical Mergers in Retail Markets for Gasoline." *American Economic Review* 102(5): 2147–2182.

Hsieh, C.S., J. Kovarik, and T. Logan (2014) "How Central Are Clients in Sexual Networks Created by Commercial Sex?" *Scientific Reports* 7: 7540.

Hsieh, C.S., and T.D. Logan (2014) "Men on the Move: The Traveling Patterns of Male Sex Workers in the US." Working paper, The Ohio State University.

Humphreys, L. (1970) *Tearoom Trade: Impersonal Sex in Public Places*. Hawthorne, NY: Aldine de Gruyter.

Humphreys, L. (1971) "New Styles of Homosexual Manliness." *Transaction* 8: 38.

Itiel, J. (1998) *A Consumer's Guide to Male Hustlers*. New York: Harrington Park Press.

Jensen, R. (2007) "The Digital Provide: Information (Technology), Market Performance and Welfare in the South Indian Fisheries Sector." *Quarterly Journal of Economics* 122(3): 879–924.

Jepsen, L., and C. Jepsen (2002) "An Empirical Analysis of the Matching Patterns of Same-Sex and Opposite-Sex Couples." *Demography* 39: 435–454.

Jin, G.Z., and A. Kato (2006) "Price, Quality, and Reputation: Evidence from an Online Field Experiment." *RAND Journal of Economics* 37(4): 983–1005.

Joffee, H., and J.E. Dockrell (1995) "Safer Sex: Lessons from the Male Sex Industry." *Journal of Community and Applied Social Psychology* 5: 333–346.

Jovanovic, B. (1982) "Truthful Disclosure of Information." *Bell Journal of Economics* 13(1): 36–44.

Kane, G. (2009) "Unmasking the Gay Male Body Ideal: A Critical Analysis of the Dominant Research of Gay Men's Body Issues." *Gay and Lesbian Issues and Psychology Review* 5: 20–33.

Katz, N. (1976). *Gay American History*. New York: Thomas Crowell Company.

Katz, N. (1983). *Gay/Lesbian Almanac*. New York: Harper & Row.

Kaufman, G., and V.C. Phua (2003) "Is Ageism Alive in Date Selection among Men? Age Requests among Gay and Straight Men in Internet Personal Ads." *The Journal of Men's Studies* 11: 225–235.

Kaya, A. (2009) "Repeated Signaling Games." *Games and Economic Behavior* 66(2): 841–854.

Kaye, K. (2001) "Male Prostitution in the Twentieth Century: Pseudohomosexuals, Hoodlums, Homosexuals, and Exploited Teens." *Journal of Homosexuality* 46(1/2): 1–77.

Klausner, J.D., A. Kim, and C. Kent (2002) "Are HIV Drug Advertisements Contributing to Increases in Risk Behavior among Men in San Francisco, 2001?" *AIDS* 16(17): 2349–2350.

Klein, H., K.W. Elifson, and C.E. Sterk (2010) "Self-Esteem and HIV Risk Practices among Young Adult 'Ecstacy' Users." *Journal of Psychoactive Drugs* 42: 447–456.

Koken, J.A., D.S. Bimbi, and J. Parsons (2009) "Male and Female Escorts: A Comparative Analysis," in R. Weitzer, ed., *Sex for Sale: Prostitution, Pornography, and the Sex Industry*, 2nd. ed. New York: Routledge, pp. 205–232.

Koken, J.A., J.T. Parsons, J. Severino, and D.S. Bimbi (2005) "Exploring Commercial Sex Encounters in an Urban Community Sample of Gay and Bisexual Men: A Preliminary Report." *Journal of Psychology and Human Sexuality*, 17: 197–213.

Kremer, M. (1996) "Integrating Behavioral Choice into Epidemiological Models of AIDS." *Quarterly Journal of Economics* 111(2): 549–573.

Laband, D.N. (1986) "Advertising as Information: An Empirical Note." *Review of Economics and Statistics* 68(3): 517–521.

Lakdawalla, D., N. Sood, and D. Goldman (2006) "HIV Breakthroughs and Risky Sexual Behavior." *Quarterly Journal of Economics* 121(3): 1063–1102.

Lambert, B. (2007) "As Prostitutes Turn to Craigslist, Law Takes Notice." *New York Times*, September 5, 2007.

Lanzieri, N., and T. Hildebrandt (2011) "Using Hegemonic Masculinity to Explain Gay Male Attraction to Muscular and Athletic Men." *Journal of Homosexuality* 58: 275–293.

Laumann, E.O., S. Ellington, J. Mahay, A. Paik, and Y. Youm, eds. (2004) *The Sexual Organization of the City*. Chicago: University of Chicago Press.

Lee, L.F. (2007) Identification and Estimation of Econometric Models with Group Interactions, Contextual Factors and Fixed Effects. *Journal of Econometrics* 140(2): 333–374.

Lehmiller, J.J., and M. Ioerger (2014) "Social Networking Smartphone Applications and Sexual Health Outcomes among Men Who Have Sex with Men." *PLoS One* 9(1): e86603.

Levine, M.P. (1998) *Gay Macho: The Life and Death of the Homosexual Clone*. New York: New York University Press.

Levitt, S., and S. Venkatesh (2007) "An Empirical Analysis of Street-Level Prostitution." Working paper, University of Chicago.

Lewis, G. (2009) "Asymmetric Information, Adverse Selection and Online Disclosure: The Case of eBay Motors." Working paper, Harvard University.

Lillard, L.A. (1998) "The Market for Sex: Street Prostitution in Los Angeles." Paper presented at the 1999 Population Association of America Annual Meetings.

Loftus, J. (2001) "America's Liberalization in Attitudes toward Homosexuality." *American Sociological Review* 66: 762–782.

Logan, T.D. (2010) "Personal Characteristics, Sexual Behaviors, and Male Sex Work: A Quantitative Approach." *American Sociological Review* 75(5): 679–704.

Logan, T.D. (2011) "Negotiating Intimacy: Gay Men, Safer Sex, and the Sexual Field." Working paper, The Ohio State University.

Logan, T.D. (2016) "The Economics of Male Sex Work" in *The Oxford Handbook of the Economics of Prostitution*, ed. Scott Cunningham and Manisha Shah. New York: Oxford University Press, pp. 255–281.

Logan, T.D., and M. Shah (2013) "Face Value: Information and Signaling in an Illegal Market." *Southern Economic Journal* 79: 529–564.

Luckenbill, D.F. (1986) "Deviant Career Mobility: The Case of Male Prostitutes." *Social Problems* 33: 283–296.

Luna, A. (1989) *"Gay Racism" in Men's Lives*, ed. M.S. Kimmel and M.A. Messner. New York: Macmillan.

MacDonald, L. (2007) "America's Toe-Tapping Menace." *New York Times*, September 2, 2007.

MacNeil, S., and E.S. Byers (2005) "Dyadic Assessment of Sexual Self-Disclosure and Sexual Satisfaction in Heterosexual Dating Couples." *Journal of Social and Personal Relationships* 22: 169–181.

Mancilla, M. and L. Troshinsky (2003) *Love in the Time of HIV*. New York: Guilford Press.

Mariolis, P. (1975) "Interlocking Directorates and Control of Corporations-Theory of Bank Control." *Social Science Quarterly* 56(3): 425–439.

Marks, G., M.S. Ruiz, J.L. Richardson, D. Reed, H.R. Mason, M. Sotelo, and P.A. Turner (1994) "Anal Intercourse and Disclosure of HIV Infection among Seropositive Gay and Bisexual Men." *Journal of Acquired Immune Deficiency Syndrome* 7: 866–869.

Marlowe, J. (1997) "It's Different for Boys," in J. Nagle, ed., *Whores and Other Feminists*. New York: Routledge, pp. 141–144.

Martin, J.I., and J. Knox (1997) "Self-Esteem Instability and Its Implications for HIV Prevention among Gay Men." *Health Social Work* 22: 264–273.

Martin, J.L. (2003) "What Is Field Theory?" *American Journal of Sociology* 109: 1–49.

Martin, J.L., and M. George (2006) "Theories of Sexual Stratification: Toward an Analytics of the Sexual Field and a Theory of Sexual Capital." *Sociological Theory* 24: 107–132.

Martin, K.A. (1998) "Becoming a Gendered Body: Practices of Preschools." *American Sociological Review* 63:494–511.

Martin, T. (1996) *Ancient Greece*. New Haven, CT: Yale University Press.

Mastro, T., and I. de Vincenzi (1996) "Probabilities of Sexual HIV-1 Transmission." *AIDS* 10 (Supplement A): S75–S82.

Mattison, A., M. Ross, T. Wolfson, D. Franklin, and HNRC Group (2001) "Circuit Party Attendance, Club Drug Use, and Unsafe Sex in Gay Men." *Journal of Substance Abuse* 13 (1–2): 119–126.

McBride, D. (2005) *Why I Hate Abercrombie and Fitch: Essays on Race and Sexuality*. New York: New York University Press.

McNamara, R. (1994) *The Times Square Hustler: Male Prostitution in New York City*. Westwood, CT: Praeger.

Milgrom, P., and J. Roberts (1986) "Price and Advertising Signals of Product Quality." *Journal of Political Economy* 94(4): 796–821.

Mimiaga, M.J., S.L. Reisner, J.P. Tinsley, K.H. Mayer, and S.A. Safren (2008) "Street Workers and Internet Escorts: Contextual and Psychosocial Factors Surrounding HIV Risk Behavior among Men Who Engage in Sex Work with Other Men." *Journal of Urban Health* 86: 54–66.

Minichiello, V., and J. Scott, eds. (2014) *Male Sex Work and Society*. New York: Harrington Park Press.

Minichiello, V., J. Scott, and D. Callander (2013) "New Pleasures and Old Dangers: Reinventing Male Sex Work." *Journal of Sex Research* 50: 263–275.

Mintz, P., and M. Schwartz (1985) *The Power Structure of American Business*. Chicago: University of Chicago Press.

Moffatt, P.G., and S.A. Peters (2004) "Pricing Personal Services: An Empirical Study of Earnings in the UK Prostitution Industry." *Scottish Journal of Political Economy* 51(5): 675–690.

Moskowitz, D.A., Rieger, G. and M.E. Roloff (2008) "Tops, Bottoms and Versatiles." *Sexual and Relationship Therapy* 23: 191–202.

Mowlabocus, S. (2010) "Look at Me! Images, Validation, and Cultural Currency on Gaydar," in C. Pullen and M. Cooper, eds., *LGBT Identity and Online Media*. Abingdon, England: Routledge, pp. 201–214.

Murphy, A.K., and S. Venkatesh (2006) "Vice Careers: The Changing Contours of Sex Work in New York City." *Qualitative Sociology* 29 (2): 129–154.

Nagel, J. (2000) "Ethnicity and Sexuality." *Annual Review of Sociology* 26: 107–133.

Nardi, P., ed. (2000) *Gay Masculinities*. London: Sage.

Nero, C.I. (2005) "Why Are the Gay Ghettos White?" in E.P. Johnson and M.G. Henderson, eds., *Black Queer Studies: A Critical Anthology*. Durham, NC: Duke University Press, pp. 228–245.

Orne, J. (2016) *Boystown*. Chicago: University of Chicago Press.

Padilla, M. (2007) *Caribbean Pleasure Industry: Tourism, Sexuality, and AIDS in the Dominican Republic*. Chicago: University of Chicago Press.

Parker, M. (2006) "Core Groups and the Transmission of HIV: Learning from Male Sex Workers." *Journal of Biosocial Science* 38: 117–131.

Parsons, J.T., D.S. Bimbi, and P.N. Halkitis (2001) "Sexual Compulsivity among Gay/Bisexual Male Escorts Who Advertise on the Internet." *Journal of Sexual Addiction and Compulsivity* 8: 113–123.

Parsons, J.T., J.A. Koken, and D.S. Bimbi (2007) "Looking beyond HIV: Eliciting Individual and Community Needs of Male Internet Escorts." *Journal of Homosexuality* 53: 219–240.

Parsons, J.T., Koken, J.A., and Bimbi, D.S. (2004) "The Use of the Internet by Gay and Bisexual Male Escorts: Sex Workers as Sex Educators." *AIDS Care* 16: 1021–1035.

Parsons, J.T., C. Lelutiu-Weinberger, M. Botsko, and S.A. Golub (2013) "Predictors of Day-Level Sexual Risk for Young Gay and Bisexual Men." *AIDS Behavior* 17: 1465–1477.

Pascoe, C.J. (2007) *Dude, You're a Fag: Masculinity and Sexuality in High School*. Berkeley, CA: University of California Press.

Paul, J.P., G. Ayala, and P.R. Johnson (2008) "Internet Sex Ads for MSM and Partner Selection Criteria: The Potency of Race/Ethnicity Online." *Journal of Sex Research* 47: 528–538.

Pettiway, L.E. (1996) *Honey, Honey, Miss Thang: Being Black, Gay and on the Streets*. Philadeplphia: Temple University Press.

Phillips, G., M. Magnus, I. Kuo, A. Rawls, J. Peterson, Y. Jia, J. Opoku, and A.E. Greenberg (2014) "Use of Geosocial Networking (GSN) Mobile Phone Applications to Find Men for Sex by Men Who Have Sex with Men (MSM) in Washington, DC." *AIDS Behavior* 18: 1630–1637.

Phua, V.C., and G. Kaufman (2003) "The Crossroads of Race and Sexuality: Date Selection among Men in Internet 'Personal' Ads." *Journal of Family Issues* 24: 981–994.

Pleak, R.R., and H.F.L. Meyer-Bahlburg (1990) "Sexual Behavior and AIDS Knowledge in Young Male Prostitutes in Manhattan." *Journal of Sex Research*, 27(4): 557–587.

Pompeo, J. (2009) "The Hipster Rent Boys of New York." *New York Observer* January 27.

Pope, D.G., and J.R. Sydnor (2008) "What's in a Picture? Evidence of Discrimination from Prosper.com." Wharton Operations and Information Management Working paper No. 2008-7.

Prestage, G. (1994) "Male and Transsexual Prostitution," pages 174–190 in R. Perkins, G. Prestage, R. Sharp, and F. Lovejoy eds., *Sex Work and Sex Workers in Australia*. Sydney: University of New South Wales Press Ltd.

Prestage, G., L. Mao, F. Jin, A Grulich, J. Kaldor, and S. Kippax (2007) "Sex Work and Risk Behavior among HIV-Negative Gay Men." *AIDS Care* 19: 931–934.

Price-Glynn, K. (2010) *Strip Club: Gender, Power, and Sex Work*. New York: New York University Press.

Pruitt, M. (2005) "Online Boys: Male for Male Internet Escorts." *Sociological Focus* 38: 189–203.

Rao, V., I. Gupta, M. Lokshin, and S. Jana (2003) "Sex Workers and the Cost of Safe Sex: The Compensating Differential for Condom Use in Calcutta." *Journal of Development Economics* 71: 585–603.

Reay, B. (2010) *New York Hustlers: Masculinity and Sex in Modern America*. New York: Manchester University Press.

Reeser, T.W. (2010) *Masculinities in Theory*. Oxford: Wiley Blackwell.

Reid-Pharr, R.F. (2001) *Black Gay Man: Essays*. New York: New York University Press.

Reidy, W.J., and S.M. Goodreau (2010) "The Role of Commercial Sex Venues in the HIV Epidemic among Men Who Have Sex with Men in King County, WA." *Epidemiology* 21(3): 349–359.

Reisner, S.L., M. J. Mimiaga, K. H. Mayer, J. P. Tinsley, and S. A. Safren (2008) "Tricks of the Trade: Sexual Health Behaviors, the Context of HIV Risk, and Potential Prevention Intervention Strategies for Male Sex Workers" *Journal of LGBT Health Research* 4: 195–209.

Richards, T.J., R.N. Acharya, and A. Kagan (2008) Spatial Competition and Market Power in Banking. *Journal of Economics and Business*, 60, 436–454.

Robins, G. and Alexander, M. (2004) "Small Worlds Among Interlocking Directors: Network Structure and Distance in Bipartite Graphs" *Computational & Mathematical Organization Theory* 10: 69–94.

Robinson, B.A. (2015) "'Personal Preference' as the New Racism: Gay Desire and Racial Cleansing in Cyberspace." *Sociology of Race and Ethnicity* 1: 317–330.

Robinson, B.A. (2016) "The Quantifiable-Body Discourse: 'Height-Weight Proportionality' and Gay Men's Bodies in Cyberspace." *Social Currents* 3: 172–185.

Robinson, J., and E. Yeh (2011) "Transactional Sex as a Response to Risk in Western Kenya." *American Economic Journal: Applied Economics* 3: 35–64.

Robinson, J., and E. Yeh (2012) "Risk-Coping through Sexual Networks: Evidence from Client Transfers in Kenya." *Journal of Human Resources* 47(1): 107–145.

Robinson, R.K. (2007) "Uncovering Covering." *Northwestern University Law Review* 101: 1809–1850.

Robinson, R.K. (2008). "Black 'Tops' and Asian 'Bottoms': The Impact of Race and Gender on Coupling in Queer Communities." Working paper, UCLA.

Robnett, B., C. Feliciano, and M. Rafalow (2013) "Racial-Ethnic Exclusion among Gay, Lesbian and Heterosexual White Online Daters." Working paper, University of California, Irvine.

Rosen, S. (1974) "Hedonic Prices and Implicit Markets: Product Differentiation in Pure Competition." *Journal of Political Economy* 82: 34–55.

Rosen, S. (1986) "The Theory of Equalizing Differences," pages 641–692 in O. Ashenfelter and R. Layard, eds., *Handbook of Labor Economics*, vol. 1. Amsterdam: Elsevier.

Ruud, P. (2000) *An Introduction to Classical Econometric Theory*. New York: Oxford University Press.

Sadownick, D. (1996) *Sex between Men: An Intimate History of the Sex Lives of Gay Men Postwar to Present*. New York: HarperCollins.

Salamon, E.D. (1989) "The Homosexual Escort Agency: Deviance Disavowal." *The British Journal of Sociology* 40: 1–21.

Schalow, P.G. (1989) "Male Love in Early Modern Japan: A Literary Depiction of the 'Youth,'" in M. Duberman, M. Vicinus, and G. Chauncey, Jr., eds., *Hidden from History*. New York: New American Library, pp. 118–128.

Schelling, T.C. (1960) *The Strategy of Conflict*. Cambridge, MA: Harvard.

Schrock, D., and M. Schwalbe (2009) "Men, Masculinity, and Manhood Acts." *Annual Review of Sociology* 35: 277–295.

Schwartz, A. (1976) "Migration, Age, and Education." *Journal of Political Economy*, 84(4): 701–720.

Schwartz, C. R., and N. Graf (2010) "Can Differences in Partner Availability Explain Differences in Interracial/Ethnic Matching Between Same- and Different-Sex Couples?" Center for Demography and Ecology Working Paper No. 2010-07.

Scott, J. (2003) "A Prostitute's Progress: Male Prostitution in Scientific Discourse." *Social Semiotics* 13: 179–199.

Sedgewick, E.K. (1990) *The Epistemology of the Closet*. Berkeley: University of California Press.

Shah, M. (2013) "Do Sex Workers Respond to Disease? Evidence from the Male Market for Sex." *American Economic Review Papers and Proceedings* 103(3): 445–450.

Shernoff, M. (2006) *Without Condoms: Unprotected Sex, Gay Men and Barebacking*. New York: Routledge.

Shilts, R. (1987) *And the Band Played On: Politics, People, and the AIDS Epidemic*. New York: St. Martins.

Shoptaw, S., C. Reback, J. Peck, A. Yang, E. Rotheram-Fuller, S. Larkins, R. Veniegas, T. Freese, and C. Hucks-Ortiz (2005) "Behavioral Treatment Approaches for Methamphetamine Dependence and HIV-Related Sexual Risk Behavior among Urban Gay and Bisexual Men." *Drug and Alcohol Dependence* 17(2): 125–134.

Sifikas, F., C.P. Flynn, L. Metsch, M. LaLota, C. Murrill, B.A. Koblin, T. Bingham, W. McFarland, S. Behel, A. Lansky, B. Byers, D. MacKellar, A. Drake, and K. Gallagher (2005) "HIV Prevalence, Unrecognized Infection, and HIV Testing among Men Who Have Sex with Men – Five US Cities, June 2004 – April 2005." *Morbidity and Mortality Weekly Report* 54: 597–601.

Simmel, G. (1907) "Prostitution," in D.N. Levine, ed., *On Individuality and Social Forms*. Chicago: University of Chicago Press [1971], pp. 121–126.

Simon Rosser, B.R., K.J. Horvath, L.A. Hatfield, J.L. Peterson, S. Jacoby, and S. Stately (2008) "Predictors of HIV Disclosure to Secondary Partners and Sexual Risk Behavior among a High-Risk Sample of HIV-Positive MSM." *AIDS Care* 20: 925–930.

Sjaastad, L.A. (1962) "The Costs and Returns of Human Migration." *The Journal of Political Economy* 70(5): 80–93.

Smith, M.D., and C. Grov (2011) *In the Company of Men: Inside the Lives of Male Prostitutes*. Santa Barbara, CA: Praegar.

Spence, M. (1973) "Job Market Signaling." *Quarterly Journal of Economics* 87(3): 355–374.

Spence, M. (2002) "Signaling in Retrospect and the Informational Structure of Markets." *American Economic Review* 92(3): 434–459.

Spinelli, F. (2011) "Oral Sex and Cancer." *The Advocate* May 2011: 46.

Steele, B.C., and S. Kennedy (2006) "Hustle and Grow." *The Advocate*, April 11, 2006.

Stein, A. (1989) "Three Models of Sexuality: Drives, Identities, and Practices." *Sociological Theory* 7: 1–13.

Stolte, I., N. Dukers, R. Geskus, R. Coutinho, and J. Wit (2004) "Homosexual Men Change to Risky Sex When Perceiving Less Threat of HIV/AIDS since Availability of Highly Active Antiretroviral Therapy: A Longitudinal Study." *AIDS* 18(2): 303–309.

Thompson, W.E., J.L. Harred, and B.E. Burks (2002) "Managing the Stigma of Topless Dancing: A Decade Later." *Deviant Behavior* 24: 551–570.

Tiggerman, M., Y. Martins, and A. Kirkbride (2007) "Oh to Be Lean and Muscular: Body Image Ideals in Gay and Heterosexual Men." *Psychology of Men and Masculinity* 8: 15–24.

Timpson, S.C., Ross, M.W., Williams, M.L., and Atkinson, J. (2007) "Characteristics, Drug Use, and Sex Partners of a Sample of Male Sex Workers." *American Journal of Drug and Alcohol Abuse* 33: 63–69.

Tirole, J. (1999) "Incomplete Contracts: Where Do We Stand?" *Econometrica* 67(4): 741–781.

Truong, H.M., T. Kellogg, J.D. Klausner, M.H. Katz, J. Dilley, K. Knapper, S. Chen, R. Prabhu, R.M. Grant, B. Louie, and W. McFarland (2006) "Increases in Sexually Transmitted Infections and Sexual Risk Behavior without a Concurrent Increase in HIV Incidence in San Francisco: A Suggestion of Serosorting?" *Sexually Transmitted Infections* 82: 461–466.

Tyler, A. (2014) "Advertising Male Sexual Services," in V. Minichiello and J. Scott, eds., *Male Sex Work and Society*. New York: Harrington Park Press.

U.S. Bureau of Transportation Statistics (2012) *The Transportation Statistics Annual Report*. Washington, DC: Government Printing Office.

U.S. Census Bureau (2010) *Census of Population 2010*. Washington, DC: Government Printing Office.

Uy, J.M., J.T. Parsons, D.S. Bimbi, J.A. Koken, and P.N. Halkitis (2004) "Gay and Bisexual Male Escorts Who Advertise on the Internet: Understanding Reasons for and Effects of Involvement in Commercial Sex." *International Journal of Men's Health* 3: 11–26.

Valente, T.W., K. Coronges, C. Lakon, and E. Costenbader (2008) "How Correlated Are Network Centrality Measures?" *Connections*, 28 (1): 16–26.

Van de Ven, P., P. Rawstorne, T. Nakamura, J. Crawford, and S. Kippax (2002) "HIV Treatments Optimism Is Associated with Unprotected Anal Intercourse with Regular and with Casual Partners and Australian Gay and Homosexually Active Men." *International Journal of STD and AIDS* 13(3): 181–183.

Varangis, E., N. Lanzieri, T. Hildebrandt, and M. Feldman (2012) "Gay Male Attraction to Muscular Men: Does Dating Context Matter?" *Body Image* 9: 270–278.

Varghese, B., J.E. Maher, T.A. Peterman, B.M. Branson, and R.W. Steketee (2002) "Reducing the Risk of Sexual HIV Transmission: Quantifying the Per-Act Risk for HIV on the Basis of Choice of Partner, Sex Act, and Condom Use." *Sexually Transmitted Diseases* 29: 38–43.

Volk, J.E., J.L. Marcus, T. Phengrasamy, D. Blechinger, D.P. Nguyen, C. Follansbee, and C.B. Hare (2015) "No New HIV Infections with Increasing Use of HIV Preexposure Prophylaxis in a Clinical Practice Setting." *Clinical Infectious Diseases* 61: 1601–1603.

Ward, J. (2000) "Queer Sexism: Rethinking Gay Men and Masculinity," in P. Nardi, ed., *Gay Masculinities*. Thousand Oaks, CA: Sage Publications.

Ward, J. (2008) "Dude-Sex: White Masculinities and 'Authentic' Heterosexuality among Dudes Who Have Sex with Dudes." *Sexualities* 11: 414–434.

Weeks, J. (1989a) "Inverts, Perverts, and Mary-Annes," in M. Duberman, M. Vicinus, and G. Chauncey, Jr., eds., *Hidden from History*. New York: New American Library, pp. 195–211.

Weeks, J. (1989b) *Sex, Politics, and Society: The Regulation of Sexuality since 1800*. New York: Longman.

Weinberg, M.S., and C.J. Williams (1974) *Male Homosexuals: Their Problems and Adaptations*. New York: Oxford University Press.

Weitzer, R. (2005). "New Directions in Research in Prostitution." *Crime, Law and Social Change* 43: 211–235.

Weitzer, R. (2009) "Sociology of Sex Work." *Annual Review of Sociology* 35: 213–234.

West, D.J. (1993) *Male Prostitution*. New York: Haworth Press.

Whitesel, J. (2014) *Fat Gay Men: Girth, Mirth, and the Politics of Stigma*. New York: New York University Press.

Williams, M.L., A.M. Bowen, S.C. Timpson, M.W. Ross, and J.S. Atkinson (2006) "HIV Prevention and Street-Based Male Sex Workers: An Evaluation of Brief Interventions." *AIDS Education and Prevention* 18: 204–215.

Williams, M.L., S. Timpson, A. Klovdal, A.M. Bowen, M.W. Ross, and K.B. Keel (2003) "HIV Risk among a Sample of Drug Using Male Sex Workers." *AIDS* 17: 1402–1404.

Wilson, P.A., P. Valera, A. Ventuneac, I. Balan, M. Rowe, and A. Carballo-Dieguez (2009) "Race-Based Sexual Stereotyping and Sexual Partnering among Men Who Use the Internet to Identify Other Men for Bareback Sex." *Journal of Sex Research* 46: 399–413.

Wolitski, R.J., C.A. Rietmeijer, G.M. Goldbaum, and R.M. Wilson (1998) "HIV Serostatus Disclosure among Gay and Bisexual Men in Four American Cities: General Patterns and Relation to Sexual Practices." *AIDS Care* 10: 599–610.

Wright, K. (2008) *Drifting toward Love: Black, Brown, Gay, and Coming of Age on the Streets of New York*. New York: Beacon Press.

Zelizer, V.A. (1994) *The Social Meaning of Money*. New York: Basic Books.

Index

Printed in the United States
by Baker & Taylor Publisher Services